Beyond the Household

Beyond the Household

Women's Place in the Early South, 1700-1835

Cynthia A. Kierner

CORNELL UNIVERSITY PRESS
Ithaca and London

Portions of Chapter 2 appeared previously as "Hospitality, Sociability, and Gender in the Southern Colonies," *Journal of Southern History* 62 (August 1996): 449–80.

Material in Chapters 2 and 4 appeared in "Genteel Balls and Republican Parades: Gender and Early Southern Civic Rituals, 1677–1826," *Virginia Magazine of History and Biography* 104 (Spring 1996): 185–210.

First published 1998 by Cornell University Press. First printing, Cornell Paperbacks, 1998.

Library of Congress Cataloging-in-Publication Data

Kierner, Cynthia A., 1958–
    Beyond the household : women's place in the early South, 1700–1835
/ Cynthia A. Kierner.
      p.   cm.
    Includes index.
    ISBN 0-8014-3453-X (hardcover : alk. paper). — ISBN 0-8014-8462-6
(pbk. : alk. paper)
    1. Women in public life—Southern States—History.   2. Women—
Southern States—History.   I. Title.
HQ1391.U5K55   1998
305.42'0975—DC21   98-22999

Printed in the United States of America

Cornell University Press strives to use environmentally responsible suppliers and materials to the fullest extent possible in the publishing of its books. Such materials include vegetable-based, low-VOC inks and acid-free papers that are recycled, totally chlorine-free, or partly composed of nonwood fibers.

Cloth printing 10 9 8 7 6 5 4 3 2 1

Paperback printing 10 9 8 7 6 5 4 3 2 1

For the guys:
Tom, Zachary, and Anders

Contents

Illustrations

Preface

Our images of white southern women are largely products of the moon-light-and-magnolia myths of the Civil War era. Despite a wealth of scholarship showing that even the most privileged plantation mistresses were neither frail nor leisured, the image of the submissive and protected lady atop her pedestal remains compelling, as does the resulting assumption that such women had no place in the world beyond their households. In this book I take issue with that assumption. The enduring image of the southern lady was neither timeless nor unrivaled even in its antebellum heyday. More important, from the colonial era through the early nineteenth century white southern women, though members of a patriarchal society, participated in the affairs of the public sphere and, in some instances, influenced the form and content of public life. The changing ways in which they did so reflected the evolution of their culture's larger social values, as well as their own changing private or domestic roles.

In attempting to handle a large subject over an extended period, I have benefited from the insights of historians in a wide range of fields of specialization. Frederick Bode, Kathleen Brown, Jane Turner Censer, Elaine Forman Crane, Daniel Dupre, and Donna Gabaccia each read all or part of the manuscript and offered valuable advice and comments. I am also grateful to Dana Alexander, Sara Bearss, Thomas E. Buckley, S.J., James C. Green, Anya Jabour, Jean Lee, and Marie Tyler-McGraw, all of whom shared bits of their own research with me at various stages.

This project has also enjoyed the material support of generous institutions and individuals en route to completion. Mellon Foundation grants from the Virginia Historical Society and the Library Company of Philadelphia funded some early research, as did a Travel-to-Collections Grant from the National Endowment for the Humanities and a Beveridge Grant from the American Historical Association. The Chrysler Museum of Art, the

Colonial Williamsburg Foundation, and the Museum of Early Southern Decorative Arts kindly waived their fees for the reproduction of artwork in their collections. In Richmond, Howson and Betsy Cole graciously opened their home to me. Chris and Jean Lee gave me a place to stay in Williamsburg. Mary Hill Cole offered southern hospitality and good companionship in Staunton and Charlottesville on several occasions. Closer to home, faculty grants from the University of North Carolina at Charlotte funded a portion of my research. A semester's leave from UNC–Charlotte and a Cotlow Fellowship from the Department of History enabled me to devote an entire year to writing at a critical stage.

Finally, I am grateful for the continuing support of Thomas Bright, my partner in excellent adventures, and for the cheerful company of those with whom he shares this book's dedication.

CYNTHIA A. KIERNER

Charlotte, North Carolina

Beyond the Household

Introduction:
Before the Pedestal

In her pioneering book *Women's Life and Work in the Southern Colonies*, Julia Cherry Spruill noted that "while homemaking was the one occupation for which [colonial] women were trained and was probably the sole business of a large majority, it did not absorb all the energies of some," who "interested themselves in affairs beyond their households." During the revolutionary era, these and other women were deeply aware of and involved in public matters, though the Revolution ultimately neither enhanced their civic status nor expanded their legal rights. Indeed, the public visibility of southern women appears to have waned during the nineteenth century; most historians of the antebellum South unambiguously describe them as powerless dependents in a patriarchal society, consigned to their rhetorical pedestals and largely excluded from extradomestic life. "The household determined the daily lives of southern women, and the network of households determined women's social context," asserts Elizabeth Fox-Genovese. "The slave South, as a social formation, imposed special constraints on the lives of all southern women," regardless of class or race.[1]

How and why did women's relation to public life apparently change so dramatically in the decades that separated the colonial and antebellum eras? In this book I attempt to answer that question by tracing the evolution of white women's access to the public sphere between 1700 and 1835, from the emergence of relatively stable provincial societies in Virginia and the Carolinas — the area on which I focus — through the seedtime of southern sectional consciousness. Publicly active women, like those Spruill encountered in the colonial period, continued to exist after the Revolution and on into the nineteenth century. But the "household" — or more specifically, the roles and characteristics ascribed to white women within the household — continually shaped their public activities. In the southern colonies, elite women, whom contemporaries regarded as the custodians of sensibility and politeness, helped to define a genteel public culture that promoted and rein-

1

2 forced the social dominance of their class. During the revolutionary era, housewives employed their domestic skills for patriotic ends, producing homespun fabric and ersatz teas that bolstered the colonial boycotts to protest offensive imperial policies. In subsequent decades, white women from elite and middling social backgrounds entered the public sphere as virtuous wives and mothers seeking to foster religion and benevolence in their communities. Southern women shaped the affairs of the public sphere in all three instances, but they did so in ways that exploited and expanded their accepted private or domestic roles.

The social theorist Jürgen Habermas defined the public sphere as "a realm of our social life in which something approaching public opinion can be formed." According to Habermas, "all citizens" could participate in the public sphere, a portion of which "comes into being in every conversation in which private individuals assemble to form a public body . . . confer[ring] in an unrestricted fashion — that is, with the guarantee of freedom of assembly and association and the freedom to express and publish their opinions — about matters of general interest."[2] Feminist theorists rightly criticize the rigid distinction Habermas drew between public and private, which privileged the former and associated it with such activities and interests as voting and formal political debates, which historically have been masculine. Habermas implicitly accepted the rhetorical construction of opposing male/public and female/private spheres, which, though dating to ancient times, was especially popular as a metaphor both to describe and to constrain the activities of women and men in newly modernizing societies such as postrevolutionary America.[3]

This book rejects this gender-biased definition of the public sphere for one that encompasses a broader range of extradomestic activities. I define the public sphere as the site of actual or figurative exchanges on extradomestic ideas or issues and envision the affairs of the public sphere as embracing not only formal political participation but also informal civic and sociable life, the world of letters, certain business and market transactions, and religious and benevolent activities. When a woman wore homespun to a ball in the 1770s, she professed an opinion on a political issue, and doing so was as much a public act as her husband's voting to support nonimportation. When women penned letters discussing current events or wrote newspaper essays, they also, to varying degrees, participated in and possibly influenced the discourse of their communities. When they ran taverns that were venues for heated debates or when they advertised in the local press, they acquired reputations and sometimes influence outside their family circles. When women raised money to feed the poor or supplied Bibles to the unconverted, their actions were visible and consequential in the world beyond their households.

White southern women consistently participated in public life, though the prevailing gender conventions of their society just as consistently imagined them in primarily domestic roles. The fact that women's roles in private life both shaped and justified their activities in the public sphere signals the difficulties in distinguishing public from private and the extent to which these seemingly opposite spheres may have been overlapping or even interdependent. For instance, a woman usually performed her duties as hostess in the domestic sphere, but these activities were at least quasi-public to the extent that they allowed her contact and conversation with people outside her family, which in turn permitted her to cultivate a public reputation for generosity, politeness, or good conversation. When a woman read or wrote about politics, manners, or religion, she might be sitting in her parlor, but she was engaged intellectually with the wider community. At the same time, women's benevolent activities, which many contemporaries regarded as private and apolitical, complemented men's politics of competitive individualism in the antebellum era. Although men rarely acknowledged the significance of their efforts, women's benevolence helped make masculine political culture viable by easing the social costs and consequences of a public policy that scorned government-sponsored relief for the community's least fortunate members.[4]

"Women," a leading feminist political theorist has suggested, "have never been completely excluded from participation in the institutions of the public world," though they have "been incorporated into public life in a manner different from men." In male-dominated societies, which surely included the United States during the period I consider here and perhaps most especially its southern section, women's inclusion in public life "is grounded, as firmly as their position in the domestic sphere, in patriarchal beliefs and practices."[5] From the colonial period through the antebellum era, white southern women indeed occupied a public position that was sex-specific and largely served the interests of the existing order. Consequently, colonial gentlewomen participated in genteel social rituals that sought to strengthen the authority of male elites over their presumed inferiors, while the religious and benevolent activities of antebellum women rarely threatened either male dominance or the putative supremacy of white men over white women and African Americans.

Focusing on the changing boundaries and relationships between the

4   private and public spheres and white women's access to the latter, this book traces the evolution of southern gender conventions from the colonial period through the Revolution and the early decades of the nineteenth century. It shows that economic development, republican political ideals, Protestant evangelicalism, and a growing sense of regional distinctiveness successively shaped and reshaped southern culture during this period and that southern gender ideals — and ideas about white women's place in particular — evolved as part of this more general cultural transformation. Crudely summarized, this book shows how class distinctions gradually were overshadowed by those based on sex in a society in which race was consistently the most salient social category.

The book is divided into six chapters, the first two of which discuss women's roles and status during the colonial era, a time when inchoate boundaries between public and private complemented a universally acknowledged social hierarchy among southerners, as in most premodern societies.[6] By 1700, the date at which my inquiry opens, white women's status in the southern colonies was in a state of flux, though the prevailing trend was away from their engaging in typically masculine public activities and toward the replication of European gender ideals. Chapter 1 describes the economic and demographic developments that gave rise to these changes, which also heightened existing class and racial distinctions among women and the occupations in which they engaged. Above all, these changes resulted in the domestication of white women's work, at least in elite and middling families, while the growth of black slavery and a corresponding decline in white servitude meant that women who did fieldwork would be overwhelmingly African. Commercialization and economic growth created new opportunities for the paid employment of nonelite women outside the household, but access to such public arenas as the courts and the market declined during the eighteenth century for most women, regardless of social rank.

The rise of a class-specific culture of gentility, however, afforded elite women access to the public sphere and new opportunities to influence public life. Contemporary moralists and social critics increasingly idealized feminine virtue and sensibility, which they believed could influence the manners and morals of men and thereby promote improvements in society. In Chapter 2, I argue that this belief in women's improving influence was essential to the construction of gentility, a cultural style designed to enhance the moral and cultural authority of colonial elites. Gentility and its sociable and civic rituals accentuated the elite's cultural preeminence while affording women, as part of a culturally distinctive governing class, unprecedented access to and influence in the world beyond their households. Gentility and the demands of polite society, in turn, encouraged improvements in the education of girls and young women in privileged families throughout the southern colonies. While education remained gender-specific and often ornamental, the ideal of genteel sociability fostered literacy and reading among elite women in the closing decades of the colonial era.

The Revolution transformed a hierarchical political culture overtly dominated by the gentry into one that endowed all propertied white men with new opportunities and rights. Chapter 3 contends that the Revolution significantly altered the political culture of American women by discrediting some established forms of public activity while cautiously encouraging others. From the enactment of the Continental Association in 1774, revolutionary leaders repudiated genteel culture, which afforded elite women public influence, as decadent and subversive of republican political values. At the same time, however, colonial boycotts and efforts to promote domestic manufactures gave women new opportunities to participate in the affairs of the public sphere and, more specifically, in political life. In the end, in part because of its pervasive and often devastating impact, the Revolution enhanced women's political consciousness.

Women's wartime contributions and their increased political awareness inspired an unprecedented debate on their public role and status in the immediate postwar era. Chapter 4 examines that debate and concludes that, despite some imaginative attempts to justify women's public activities or to endow their domestic work with political significance, most Americans ultimately decided that women had no appropriate public role. Indeed, by the 1790s, reactionaries throughout the United States increasingly identified public-minded women with the social upheaval of the French Revolution, in which feminists were prominent participants. Fearful conservatives urged women's subservience and confinement within the patriarchal family as a means to preserve order and social authority. Postrevolutionary republicans purposefully excluded women from the affairs of the polity. Doing so was tantamount to barring them from the public sphere because, by placing the preservation of liberty above all else, republicanism envisioned politics as the sole truly public activity.

Like the prevailing republican political culture, southern religion also situated women's place in the private sphere and assumed that men alone were suited to participate in public life. Unlike republicanism, however, evangelical religion associated virtue with the domestic sphere and thereby

6   enhanced the significance of both women and domestic life. Chapter 5 shows that, partly as a result of the evangelical impulse, southerners increasingly regarded the home as the seat of virtue and morality, and they expected wives and mothers to promote religious — but not political — virtue in their households. Because the ideal of virtuous domesticity emphasized the potential benefits of women's moral influence in their families, it provided a powerful impetus for improving the education of girls and young women of elite and middling social ranks. In the early decades of the nineteenth century, those improvements were designed not to enable southern women to become patriots but to prepare prospective wives and mothers for pious and complacent domestic lives.[7]

In the early decades of the nineteenth century, however, increasingly better educated white southern women expanded the boundaries of the public sphere, using the ideals of domesticity and the proselytizing impulse of Protestant evangelicalism to justify their creation of a public realm both different and separate from men's political public life. Chapter 6 shows that the first third of the nineteenth century was an intensely creative era in the history of the public activities of white southern women, who, like their northern contemporaries, established an impressive array of prayer groups, Sabbath schools, and religious and benevolent associations.

How did the experience of white southern women differ from that of their northern contemporaries? Although this book focuses on the experiences of elite and middling women, clearly race and slavery had an enormous impact on the lives of white women and on southern culture generally. On the one hand, the perceived need to preserve slavery at all costs discouraged slaveholding women and intellectuals of either sex from engaging in radical critiques of southern society, while concerted efforts among slaveholders to stifle dissent probably prevented open debates on the issues of race and gender equality.[8] On the other hand, access to bonded labor furnished slaveholding women with the leisure time they needed to read, write letters, attend prayer meetings, and do benevolent work — activities that enabled them to participate, either figuratively or literally, in the public sphere and its concerns. Perhaps equally important, the extreme ruralness of southern life, a critical but often overlooked consequence of the region's plantation-based economy, was a tremendous obstacle for most white women seeking extradomestic companionship and information, though many found ways to overcome this severe impediment to their involvement in public life.

Slavery also permeated relations between the sexes in the household, on the plantation, and in the wider community. White southerners merged sexual and racial ideologies to justify white supremacy and to maintain social control, asserting their own moral and intellectual superiority and assuming the sexual availability of women of color. The image of amoral, robust, and sexually promiscuous African American women, in turn, became a foil for an emerging ideal of white southern womanhood that stressed passivity, chastity, and above all dependence on the protection of white men and submission to their authority. Indeed, the defense of patriarchal relations in marriage became increasingly intertwined with the defense of slavery in the minds of many antebellum southerners. Domestic relations became politicized matters of public concern as apologists for slavery emphasized the supposedly natural inequality of husband and wife to explain and justify the inequalities based on race and class that pervaded southern society.[9]

If gender relations are barometers of cultural development, the South was indeed distinctive, though probably not so much so as scholars often maintain.[10] Most historians agree that a southern sectional consciousness emerged gradually, beginning with the Missouri crisis and the tariff battles of the 1820s and spreading beyond the political arena to churches, schools, and letters in reaction to the abolitionist offensive against slavery in the 1830s and after.[11] Studies of southern women and gender conventions that begin in the 1820s or 1830s and focus only on the antebellum years assume the South's distinctiveness and probably overstate it. By beginning in the colonial period, I chart the slow divergence of North and South from common European roots without losing sight of the continued similarities in gender relations in both public and private life in the two regions.

By the 1830s, the passive, dependent, and subservient southern "lady" was the dominant ideal of white womanhood in an increasingly self-conscious region, but even among elite white women the rhetoric of patriarchy and the forcible enshrinement of the lady on her pedestal did not always fit reality.[12] Indeed, despite the growing prevalence of patriarchal rhetoric, white southern women could choose from a spectrum of feminine ideals even during the antebellum decades. First, like many northerners, some southern writers and social critics continued to exhort their readers to exercise both moral and managerial influence within the family circle, insisting that women's influence in the home could yield public benefits. Second, the evangelical ideal of virtuous womanhood gave many women moral authority in their families, which some carried into the public sphere through their religious and benevolent activities. Finally, even republican political culture, which ordinarily rejected the image of women as actors in

8   the public sphere, reluctantly conceded their patriotism in times of crisis. White southern women exploited all of the strands in southern culture to gain access to the public sphere, where class, race, and especially gender shaped their agendas and activities.

If the South was an increasingly cohesive region by 1835, when this book closes, it was not so during much of the period it embraces. During the colonial period, the southern portion of British North America consisted of a coastal area and the newer backcountry settlements, two dramatically different subregions. I do not discount these important distinctions, some of which persisted into the nineteenth century.[13] Nor do I suggest that Virginia and the Carolinas are typical of the South generally, either in the colonial period or later. These disparate communities, however, came to share the gender ideals that became dominant throughout a more self-consciously distinctive region by the antebellum decades. This book charts the evolution of those ideals and white women's real and imagined roles during the colonial, revolutionary, and early republican eras.

1

Women, Work, and Sensibility

IN THE EARLY COLONIAL PERIOD, WHITE women filled a spectrum of roles that their descendants, for better or worse, would find less accessible. At one end of that spectrum were the elite women, whose wealth and connections gave them substantial public influence and personal autonomy. Of these privileged few, perhaps the most impressive was Margaret Brent, an unmarried Maryland woman, who, in addition to possessing her own extensive landholdings, in 1647 became executrix for the estate of Governor Leonard Calvert. As Calvert's agent and as a property holder in her own right, Brent often appeared in court. In 1647, she unsuccessfully requested to "have a vote" in Maryland's colonial assembly to protect her own interests and those of the late governor.[1] In the next generation, Lady Frances Berkeley, wife and later widow of Governor Sir William Berkeley of Virginia, was a significant force in colonial public life. In 1676, Lady Berkeley traveled to London to obtain troops to support her husband's government against rebel forces during Bacon's Rebellion. When William died the following year, Frances stayed in Virginia, where she remained politically active. Her house, Green Spring, was a gathering place for Sir

William's former partisans, who now joined with her in opposition to his successor as governor.[2]

At the other extreme of the spectrum of white women's experiences were those of indentured servants during the early decades of colonization. On entering servitude, an individual relinquished autonomy and became subject to the master's will. Despite English prejudices against white women's doing heavy fieldwork, females who emigrated to the colonies as servants sometimes worked alongside their male counterparts in the tobacco fields of the Chesapeake. Whether or not they worked in the fields, servants of both sexes often labored under brutal conditions. One early Virginia planter whipped his servant Elizabeth Abbott some five hundred times, leaving her "body full of sores and holes very dangerously raunkled and putrified both above her wast and uppon her hips and thighes." Women servants also suffered sexual exploitation. For many, dehumanizing labor and sexual abuse were the consequences of migrating to a labor-scarce society in which men outnumbered women by as much as four to one.[3]

By 1700, women's status in the southern colonies was in a state of flux, though the prevailing trend was toward the replication of European gender ideals and a marked expansion of women's domestic labor. Although unabashedly powerful public women such as Brent and Berkeley would have no eighteenth-century counterparts, few white women would endure servitude in a planter's fields after 1700. By contrast, African women worked primarily in the fields, where growing numbers of enslaved people of both sexes satisfied the demand for labor and thereby facilitated the domestication of white women's work.

If race determined the location of women's work, consigning most blacks to the fields and most white women to an extended domestic sphere that included dairies and vegetable gardens, class differences shaped the extent and rigor of white women's work and their access to public life. Although elite women's ability to participate in public arenas such as the courts and the market declined during the eighteenth century, commercialization and economic growth created new opportunities for the paid employment of nonelite women outside the household. Extradomestic employment gave women varying degrees of autonomy and public visibility, but in the minds of many defeminized those who engaged in it. With few exceptions, women who performed extradomestic work could not aspire to the sentimental ideal of feminine virtue that came to dominate eighteenth-century discussions of women's nature and status.

• • •

The Europeans who settled the southern colonies brought certain ideas about gender with them to America. They deemed men women's moral, physical, and intellectual superiors and accepted a double standard that demanded female chastity but gave men sexual license. Most Europeans envisioned the family as a patriarchy in which a man reigned over his dependent wife and children. By the seventeenth century, they also increasingly distinguished men's work, which more often occurred outside the household, from that of women, which was ideally domestic and valued less highly. In English common law, the doctrine of coverture, which erased a wife's legal identity and thereby prevented her from controlling property, provided the legal basis for patriarchal authority. In seventeenth-century England, gender ideologies and the common law together deprived women of public influence and economic authority, at least in theory.[4]

Demographic conditions undermined the viability of European gender ideals in much of early colonial America. In the southern colonies especially, severely skewed sex ratios appear to have altered the conventional rules of the marriage market, giving women more freedom to choose appealing spouses and men greater incentives to please prospective wives. At the same time, appallingly high mortality rates diminished parental control over young people's marriage choices because parents, especially fathers, typically died before their children attained adulthood.[5]

High mortality rates also accounted for the unconventional division of labor in many early colonial marriages, which enhanced women's public visibility and personal authority. In the absence of stable family networks that included fathers or adult sons and brothers, women took on many nondomestic responsibilities, serving as men's deputies in business or legal matters and performing tasks that men ordinarily would have entrusted to male relatives. Thus Frances Berkeley acted as her husband's political envoy, and many less exceptional wives received powers of attorney that circumvented the legal constraints they suffered under coverture, formally empowering them to conduct business as their spouses' surrogates. It was even more common for wives to represent their husbands informally without any official change in their legal status.[6]

Because men usually married at a later age than women, short life expectancies made widowhood unusually common in the early southern colonies, while demographic circumstances augmented the economic authority that widows customarily enjoyed. Lacking stable kinship networks and nearby male relations and perhaps fearing mismanagement or embezzlement at the hands of outsiders, many seventeenth-century husbands se-

12 lected their wives to administer their estates. During this period, a colonial husband also was far more likely than his English counterpart to bequeath a large portion of his property to his wife, who, under the common law rule of dower, ordinarily would receive only a life's interest in one-third of his estate.[7]

Perhaps because women were relatively scarce, widows usually remarried, and a woman who did so repeatedly could amass a large fortune in her own right by successive inheritance. Over the course of twenty years, Sarah Offley took three husbands of progressively higher social standing, and she augmented her personal wealth on the death of each. Her first husband, Adam Thorowgood, was a former servant whom she married in 1627. Thorowgood died in 1640, and within a year Sarah married Captain John Gookin, son of one of Virginia's greatest planters. Gookin died in 1643. This time Sarah waited four years to remarry, but when she did she chose Francis Yeardley, son of Sir George Yeardley, Virginia's former governor. Sarah Offley Thorowgood Gookin Yeardley acquired property from all her husbands, and she managed additional property in trust for her minor children. At a time when most Virginians lived in poverty, she owned several pieces of expensive jewelry, including a diamond necklace.[8]

The demographic instability that allowed elasticity in women's roles inside and outside marriage gradually diminished as the seventeenth century progressed. By 1700 in the Chesapeake region and somewhat later in the Carolinas, declining mortality rates created stable family structures within which white colonists could attempt to implement a gender-based division of authority and labor.[9] Now most men had male relatives to whom they could delegate business responsibilities. At the same time, the growing availability of men with legal training led them to hire attorneys instead of empowering their wives to represent them. As men lived longer, fewer women became widows, and fewer widows inherited or administered their husbands' estates. As more parents lived to see their children reach adulthood, fathers gave more property to their adult children, especially their sons, and chose their sons rather than their wives to act as their executors.[10]

Some men, of course, continued to entrust economic matters to their female kin, but those who did so most often lacked competent male relatives. William Byrd III, who had neither brothers nor adult sons, relied on his mother to ship his tobacco when military service took him away from home during the French and Indian War. In 1739, George Lucas of Barbados showed remarkable confidence in his daughter Eliza, whom he charged with overseeing several plantations in South Carolina. Lucas clearly respected his daughter's abilities, and her success in managing his properties and achieving the production of indigo there probably exceeded his highest expectations. Nevertheless, he probably chose Eliza to manage his land only because his sons were at school in England and therefore unavailable.[11]

Like their seventeenth-century counterparts, eighteenth-century women were most likely to manage plantations or businesses when their male relations were deceased, underage, or temporarily absent. Widows of tenant farmers maintained their families' leaseholds and planters' widows worked to keep their husbands' estates prosperous and intact until their minor children came of age and took up their inheritance. As a young widow, Martha Dandridge Custis oversaw the management of some 17,500 acres before she remarried, and Mary Willing Byrd, widow of William Byrd III, ran the Byrd plantation at Westover. South Carolina widows such as Elizabeth Elliott and Eliza Lucas Pinckney marketed crops and managed plantations until their sons reached adulthood.[12] The Virginian Mary Dandridge Spotswood Campbell managed the large estate of her first husband, Governor Alexander Spotswood, as well as the lesser holdings of his successor, John Campbell, who abandoned her in the 1760s. After her sons came of age, Campbell clung to her "widow's third" of the Spotswood estate, including its slaves and a plantation that she operated for more than three decades.[13]

In most families with two cohabiting spouses, however, the eighteenth century saw a narrowing of women's economic roles, a decline in their public economic activities, and a corresponding expansion of their domestic labor. In the eighteenth century, women's domestic work, especially the production of food and clothing, gradually improved the living standards of white southerners. In households of all ranks, women increasingly tended poultry, dairies, and vegetable and herb gardens, all of which contributed to the improvement and diversification of the diets of their families. Colonial Americans clearly regarded dairying and poultry-raising as women's work. A 1772 notice in the *South Carolina Gazette*, placed by an unnamed white couple seeking employment, made explicit this sex-specific division of agricultural labor. While the husband claimed to be "capable of managing a Farm, [and] understands a little of Brick-making and Gardening," the wife offered her services in "the Management of a Dairy, raising Poultry, and other Country Business."[14]

In contrast to the domestication of white women's work, the overwhelming majority of black women continued to engage in heavy agricultural labor. As early as 1643, Virginia's House of Burgesses envisioned and attempted to codify such racial distinctions in women's work, enacting legislation that classified black women, along with men of both races, as tithable. The authors of this law and of similar ones in other colonies assumed that the labor of white women, alone among adults, would not contribute to the production of a cash crop, and consequently was not taxable. By differentiating women's roles on the basis of race, white men sought to justify the exploitation of female slaves and, by excluding white women from fieldwork, to prevent sexual liaisons between them and black men. In time, demographic changes made possible this race- and gender-based segregation in the labor force. As more white men and growing numbers of blacks of both sexes were available to do fieldwork, white women's work could be circumscribed more readily within the household.[15]

White women of all social ranks took part in the production and preparation of food for their households. When the Scotswoman Janet Schaw visited eastern North Carolina in 1775, she noted that even the wives of the province's wealthiest planters engaged in cooking, dairying, and other food-related activities. Mary Harnett, wife of one of the leading men in the Cape Fear region, tended a garden full of fruits and vegetables. Schaw marveled at Harnett's industry. "She even descends to make minced pies, cheesecakes, tarts and little biskets," Schaw observed, "besides her eggs, poultry and butter." Both Eliza Lucas Pinckney and her daughter Harriott Pinckney Horry, members of one of South Carolina's most prominent families, kept recipe books in their own hands; Horry also managed a dairy and took special pride in the quality of its butter. The young daughter of Virginia gentlefolk reported that her mother made "6 mince pies, & 7 custards, 12 tarts, 1 chicking pye, and 4 pudings" for a genteel ball at her parents' home in 1771.[16]

After food, clothing was the most important item a white woman produced, regardless of her family's social rank. As one popular advice book asserted, "After her knowledge of preserving and feeding her Family, [a housewife] must also learn how . . . to cloath them outwardly and inwardly: outwardly for defence from the cold and comeliness to the person, and inwardly for cleanliness and neatness of skin, whereby it may be kept from the filth of sweat or vermine."[17] Even among elite women, sewing and knitting were universal occupations. Female members of the affluent Carter family knitted stockings, completing one every six days. They also sewed clothing for themselves and for others. Sarah Fouace Nourse of Berkeley County, in western Virginia, spent between sixty-five and seventy-seven days a year sewing, knitting, and mending clothes for her husband, children, and slaves. Aware that her family needed the clothes and linens she produced, Nourse attempted to sew even on days when she was ill, and she continued to ply her needle despite declining health.[18]

Southern households also gradually increased their production of coarse homespun woolen, cotton, and linen cloth, which, except among poor whites, was used chiefly for clothing slaves. When John Lawson visited North Carolina in 1701, he found that the women of the colony "make a great deal of Cloath of their own Cotton, Wool and Flax; some of them keeping their Families (though large) very decently apparel'd, both with Linnens and Woollens." In 1728, William Byrd II, who described the men of North Carolina and southern Virginia as "Sloathfull in every thing but getting of Children," praised the area's women for providing their families with "so much as is absolutely Necessary" for their subsistence. Using the meager cotton and wool their farms produced, these women "all Spin, weave and knit," Byrd reported, "whereby they make a good Shift to cloath the Whole Family."[19] In elite households, by contrast, cloth production was primarily a chore for slaves. Some large plantations, such as Robert Carter's Corotoman, included a separate spinning house staffed by female slaves.[20]

By the middle decades of the eighteenth century, elite southern women delegated their most onerous household chores, such as spinning and weaving, to growing corps of domestic workers. Although slave owners still employed the overwhelming majority of their hands in fieldwork, some of Virginia's leading planters employed nearly one-fifth of their work force in housewifery or domestic service by the end of the colonial era. In 1761, ten of George Washington's fifty-five working slaves — six women and four men — engaged in household work of various sorts. In 1774, Thomas Jefferson employed ten women and six men out of his ninety-nine working slaves as his domestic staff at Monticello. Even middling planter families, who commanded much smaller labor forces, increasingly assigned some female slaves to their households. David and Elizabeth LeSuerer, who had seventeen slaves to work their property in the Virginia piedmont, employed one woman and her two daughters to make cloth from the cotton, wool, and flax produced by their land and livestock.[21]

Elite families gradually expanded their domestic staffs to facilitate the formation and management of increasingly complex and comfortable households. When women could command the labor of domestic servants, the products of their own labors could be more exotic or luxurious, at least by colonial standards. Some elite women experimented with fashionable new foods to grace their tables, planting novel vegetables or preparing unusual recipes. In 1732, an English traveler observed that artichokes were uncommon in Virginia "tho the Gentry sometimes rayse a few and have very lately tryed the Brochili, Cucumbers and Cymnells, which are a small round Gourd of the Pompion kind, with Quasshes, and Cushers, and Pompion[s] are in request, Especially Cimneles, at gent[lemen's] tables." The 1742 publication in Williamsburg of an English recipe book titled *The Compleat Housewife* also suggests the growing availability of and interest in varieties of foods, at least among literate southerners. The English author of *The Compleat Housewife*, the first cookery book published in the colonies, listed some four hundred recipes for meats, puddings, pickles, pastries, cakes, creams, and cordials. An even more popular cookbook, *The Art of Cookery*, by Hannah Glasse, included an equally impressive selection of recipes and stressed the role of servants in food preparation.[22]

Working under the direction of their mistresses or hired white housekeepers, black women increasingly contributed to the productivity of white households and enhanced the style and comfort of elite domestic life. The presence of domestic servants also allowed elite women to spend more time with their children or pursuing leisure activities. Eliza Lucas, who managed four South Carolina plantations and their work forces, nevertheless spent a good part of her day reading, playing music, or visiting her neighbors. Rising at 5:00 A.M., Lucas read for two hours. Then, after breakfast at 7:00, she played music for an hour and spent another hour "recolecting something I have learned least for want of practise it should be quite lost, such as French and short hand." In the hours before dinner, Eliza tutored her sister Polly and two young slave girls, just as she would later instruct her own daughter. After dinner and another hour of music, she did needlework "till candle light"; from dusk until bedtime she read, took care of plantation business, or wrote business or personal letters.[23]

Although Lucas was an active and energetic young woman, needlework was the only domestic chore she mentioned when she summarized her daily schedule. While most plantation mistresses supervised their servants' work and engaged in a variety of household activities, the actual performance of domestic labor probably did not dominate their daily regimens. A generation later, Eliza's son Thomas reported that each morning his wife made "Grand Rounds from the Kitchen to the Larder, then to the Poultry Yard & so on by the Garret & Store Room home to the Parlour." After instructing her staff, however, she spent the remainder of her day doing needlework or reading, writing, or playing music. Slave labor provided her and other elite southern women with the leisure time necessary to cultivate the genteel accomplishments they and their families increasingly valued.[24]

Contemporary assessments of the value and significance of women's work reflected these class differences in the quality and quantity of women's domestic labor. Although elite men — and some elite women, too — sometimes paid casual lip service to the virtues of "notable" housewifery, members of poor and middling households were more likely to recognize the true economic value of women's work. William Byrd II may have exemplified the attitudes of elite men when he proudly, but somewhat vaguely, reported that his daughters were "every Day up to their Elbows in Housewifery, which will qualify them effectually for useful Wives and if they live long enough, for Notable Women." By contrast, the tutor John Harrower, an indentured servant, advised the overseer Anthony Frazier to marry because "if he was married a great many articles might be made in his house at a verry small expence which run away with a deale of money from him when he went to the store." Sarah Trebell of Williamsburg also stressed the economic value of women's work when she lamented the illness of the wife of her brother, a tenant farmer. "I greatly fear his wife will never be able to help him get or save a living," Trebell observed, because "she mends so slowly." While Trebell and Harrower envisioned wives as frugal, industrious helpmeets, Byrd expected his daughters simply to preside over orderly and well-stocked households.[25]

Elite men increasingly identified largely ornamental domestic pastimes with feminine virtue and sensibility, which they associated with white womanhood and its privileges. For instance, Robert Carter clearly enjoyed the companionship of his wife, who, as a mother, hostess, and plantation mistress, epitomized the ideal of genteel womanhood in eighteenth-century Virginia. Moreover, as the owner of several conventional advice books, Carter probably viewed women as the "weaker sex" who depended on men's protection for their security and happiness. But the master of Nomini Hall also complacently employed enslaved women in his tobacco fields and showed special concern neither for them nor for his white female tenant farmers, whom he evicted as readily as their male counterparts.[26] Race and class disqualified such women from both the privileges and the constraints of sentimental womanhood. In that sense, their quasi-public status as extradomestic workers unsexed them in the eyes of male elites.

While the dominant trend in the eighteenth century was toward the domestication of white women's work, economic growth was simultaneously creating new opportunities for nonelite women to work outside their households. Women's extradomestic employment could be conspicuous or virtually invisible; working women could be autonomous entrepreneurs, dependent wage laborers, or their husbands' subordinates or partners. All women who engaged in extradomestic work, however, participated in the market, where their varying degrees of public visibility, autonomy, and tenacity stood in marked contrast to the seclusion and dependence of an idealized domestic life.

Most women who engaged in paid employment, like the vast majority of colonial southerners, resided in rural communities. Some rural women kept taverns or shops, but most found few opportunities for extradomestic labor. Barely visible to either scholars or contemporaries, rural women most commonly found paid employment in conventionally feminine tasks that they often performed in their households. In Rowan County, North Carolina, women worked overwhelmingly in textile-related occupations, and spinning was their most common form of skilled employment. In Edgecombe County, North Carolina, women who had looms took in weaving from their neighbors, most of whom did their own spinning. In the Chesapeake region, wives and daughters of tenant farmers and landless laborers took in both weaving and spinning, in addition to making clothes for the slaves of local planters. Other rural women, such as the Virginian Easter Sutton, who sold homemade butter to neighboring planters, worked in an economy of local exchange that increasingly included the products of women's domestic labor.[27]

Some rural women found paid employment in other people's houses, especially those of wealthy planters. Mrs. Oakley, of Westmoreland County, Virginia, hired herself out as a nurse for the Carter children at Nomini Hall. George and Martha Washington engaged Mary Wilson, a white widow, to preside over the domestic staff at Mount Vernon. In rural Hanover County, Virginia, Sarah Jones earned £5 a year as a seamstress in the home of the widow Elizabeth Littlepage. Jones and Littlepage made men's trousers, jackets, and shirts, which they sold locally, while Betty Jones — possibly Sarah's sister — worked for Littlepage as a weaver.[28]

Towns and cities offered colonial women more varied opportunities for extradomestic employment. Artisans and shopkeepers congregated in the provincial capitals, in particular, to exploit the growing markets they offered. Charleston, the region's largest city, had some 1,200 inhabitants in 1700, but its population tripled by 1730 and more than doubled again to reach 8,200 by mid-century. Williamsburg had only 2,000 residents as late as 1770, but when the colonial assembly and courts convened, the town overflowed with affluent visitors.[29]

    Lacking formal training and nondomestic skills, most women sought
types of paid employment that might be viewed as more public manifestations of their private roles as housewives and mothers. Popular assumptions
about women's abilities and temperament strengthened their claims to employment in such occupations. When women took in boarders and kept taverns, inns, and coffeehouses, they marketed their skills as hostesses, cooks,
and housekeepers. When they sought positions as schoolmistresses, gov-
ernesses, and private tutors, they attempted to capitalize on their putative
child-rearing and nurturing abilities. Like their rural counterparts,
townswomen also worked as seamstresses, domestic servants, or housekeepers. Many advertised in newspapers for generally low-paying domestic
work, which was often transitory. Contemporaries regarded all these jobs as
typically feminine — work that women ordinarily performed in their own
houses, for their own families, and without financial remuneration.

    Many women drifted in and out of the paid labor force, often between
marriages, filling a succession of jobs in order to earn a living. Some advertised only once before disappearing from the public press and perhaps from
the paid labor force. Others, such as Ruth Johnson, a schoolmaster's
widow, operated a school for one year in order to pay her husband's debts
before leaving South Carolina. Ann Imer, widow of a Charleston minister,
used the advantages of her literacy and her urban residence to get by financially during her brief widowhood, when she simultaneously ran a school,
took in boarders, and cleaned lace "as neat as in London" — activities she
abandoned on remarrying.[30]

    While teachers like Johnson and Imer, by virtue of their advertisements
and potential influence over their young charges, operated on the fringes of
the public sphere, other women pursued paid employment in a more palpa-
bly public context. In the countryside and in towns and cities, women often
kept inns and taverns, enterprises that straddled the boundary between
public and private in eighteenth-century America. Although tavern keepers
and innkeepers provided their guests with food, drink, and sometimes lodging in buildings that often included their own private living quarters, taverns and inns also were important centers of public life in many colonial
communities. As stages for conversation and communal reading, inns and
taverns played a growing role in the dissemination of political information
and ideas. When patrons gathered to read newspapers and pamphlets, to
toast the king, or later to conspire against his government, businesswomen
could learn from such discussions and, like poor or middling men, be politi-

cized by them. Even women who took in boarders on a more casual basis garnered political information and insights from the worldly men who resided temporarily in their households.[31]

Some women tavern keepers and innkeepers became active revolutionaries. For more than thirty years, Jane Vobe ran the King's Arms Tavern in Williamsburg, an establishment favored by George Washington and many other members of Virginia's House of Burgesses. During the Revolution, Vobe furnished supplies to the state militia. Elizabeth Steele of Salisbury, North Carolina, was another female tavern keeper who displayed her patriotism and political consciousness during the Revolution. Steele read Tom Paine and discussed politics in her letters and probably in her tavern. She later provided supplies to the army and passed information to General Nathanael Greene when he commanded the American forces in North Carolina.[32]

Among women who engaged in extradomestic work, the activities of milliners and printers were the most conspicuously public. Whether single, married, or widowed, milliners were collectively the most autonomous and most successful businesswomen in colonial America. Longevity in business, regular newspaper notices, and contacts in the London fashion world gave them public visibility and influence in an increasingly fashion-conscious era.[33] Women printers, as publishers and booksellers, determined what books the public read and monitored its access to political news in their capacity as newspaper editors. Perhaps fearing a popular outcry against their obvious public influence, women printers cloaked themselves in conventional images of feminine debility and dependence. In 1739, Elizabeth Timothy of Charleston, the successful publisher of one of only two southern colonial papers, described herself as a "poor afflicted Widow with six small Children and another hourly expected." When Clementina Rind took over her late husband's print office in 1773, she informed Virginians that the fate of her "orphan Family" depended on her subscribers' "generous Breasts."[34]

Although women printers were unusual in their public visibility and influence, they may have typified married women workers in having labored beside their husbands in family businesses they would later control as widows. When wives were familiar with their families' economic concerns, they could support themselves in widowhood and in some cases preserve or even enhance the prospects of the next generation. Thus Elizabeth Timothy published the *South Carolina Gazette* until her son Peter came of age. When Peter died in 1782, his wife, Ann, took over the printing business, which she ran until she passed it on to her own son some years later. In eastern North Car-

Juſt IMPORTED *from* London, *and to be* SOLD *for ready Money only, at the cheapeſt Rates, by the Sub-ſcriber, at her Shop where Mr.* Ayſcough *lately lived, oppoſite to the ſouth Side of the Capitol,*

A GENTEEL Aſſortment of MERCERY, MILLINERY, JEW-ELLERY, &c. (Part of which conſiſts of the under named Ar-ticles) of the neweſt Faſhion, being choſen by herſelf, and purchaſed ſince *July* laſt, from the eminent Shops, and on the beſt Terms.

White Satins and Luſtrings, with Trimmings ſuitable, Satin Cloaks and Bonnets wove in Imitation of Lace, plain and trimmed Silk Cloaks and Hats, the greateſt Variety of Caps, Egrets, Plumes, and Fillets, *Dreſden* Ruffles, *Ranelagh* Ruffs, *Italian* Flowers, Stomachers and Knots, Toupees and Curls, Childrens Saſhes, Bonnets, Whiſks and quilted Puddings, black Silk Aprons (much wore in *London*) white and coloured Satin quilted Coats, black and white Silk Breeches Patterns, Patent Net and other Hoods, from five Shillings to twelve and Sixpence, Ditto Aprons, Patent Net in the Piece for Ruffles and Handkerchiefs, Minionet Lace, white and coloured Head and Breaſt Flowers, Cambricks, narrow Edgings for Trimmings, a great Variety of Velvet, Silver, and other Ribands, Wires, *Didſbury's* Leather, coloured, Satin, and Stuff Shoes, white Satin and Queen's Silk Ditto, black, white, and coloured Silk Hoſe for Ladies and Gentlemen, Cotton Ditto, Mens and Boys fine Hats of the neweſt Faſhion, Wig Cauls, Silk Purſes, thin Bone and Packthread Stays for Children of three Months old and upwards, Gentlemens Flannel Waiſt-coats faced with Satin, ſingle and double Nightcaps, furred Gloves, plain Ditto for Ladies and Gentlemen, Paſte, Garnet, and Bead Earrings, Gold Wires, Paſte, Mocho, and Garnet Necklaces and Roſes, Silver and Pinch-beck Shoe and Knee Buckles, Ditto and Garnet and Silver Stock Buckles, Paſte, Tortoiſhell, and Horn crooked Combs, plain and ſet Lockets, Paſte, Garnet, and Gold Brooches, Paſte Stay Hooks, Ditto and Garnet Sprigs and Pins, Silver bowed Sciſſors, Watches and Chains, Silver Tea-ſpoons, Sugar Tongs, Nutmeg Graters, and Thimbles, neat Etwees, Toothpick Caſes, Ivory and Tortoiſhell Toothpicks, Pocket Books with Inſtruments, Aſs Skin Ditto, Travelling Shaving Caſes complete, with Razors, Glaſs, &c. Jubilee Knives and Forks, Silver Cork Screws, De-canter Corks with Labels, Coral and Bibs, Silver Pap Boats, Silver Shoe Claſps for Children, Ivory Pocket Rules, Childrens Toys of all Sorts, Gold and Silver Hatbands, Tooth Bruſhes, Ivory and Box Combs, Paſte Combs from twelve and Sixpence upwards, Black Pins, Walking Sticks and Sword Canes, Riding Whips, a very great Variety, &c. &c,

Alſo ſeveral PATENT MEDICINES, particularly *Hemet* (Dentiſt to his Majeſty) his Eſſence of Pearl, and Pearl Dentrifice, for preſerving and cleaning both Teeth and Gums; an Ointment for the Itch, and all ſcor-butick Diſorders of ever ſo long Standing, without Confinement or Regi-men; likewiſe fine IVORY BLACKING CAKES, for Shoes, in univerſal Repute, Shaving Powder, with many other Articles too numerous to mention.   CATHARINE RATHELL.

⁎ As it was impoſſible to get a Houſe on the main Street, the Sub-ſcriber hopes the little Diſtance will make no Difference to her former Cuſ-tomers.

Catharine Rathell's detailed and frequent advertisements made her a public fig-ure in eighteenth-century Virginia. This notice, which appeared in Purdie and Dixon's *Virginia Gazette* on 10 October 1771, lists various millinery goods and other fashionable items she purchased for her Williamsburg shop during a re-cent trip to London. The Library of Virginia.

olina, nearly half of the women who ran taverns similarly carried on their husbands' businesses. In rural Virginia, poor widows sometimes inherited their husbands' church jobs, and the wages they earned as sextons kept them off the parish relief rolls. Other women succeeded their husbands in managing ventures as varied as ferries, jails, and shops of various sorts.[35]

Most wives who labored alongside their husbands were probably the least autonomous women workers, especially given men's increased dominance in economic and commercial matters after 1700, though newspaper advertisements suggest that some wives enjoyed equal visibility and perhaps equal influence in partnership with their spouses. Frances Webb, a former milliner, and her husband, John Pearson Webb, advertised their Williamsburg dry goods store under both their names in the 1750s. John and Sarah Crane, a Charleston couple, likewise advertised as partners in an establishment that offered their services as tailor and mantua maker, respectively. The wigmaker Edward Charlton of Williamsburg and the milliner Jane Hunter Charlton worked both separately and in partnership during their sixteen-year marriage.[36]

Other couples operated schools, where wives usually were in charge of instructing girls or younger scholars of both sexes, while their husbands tended the more advanced male students. Daniel Thomas of Charleston taught boys "Spelling, Reading, Writing, Arithmetick and Merchants Accompts," while his wife, Judith, instructed "young Ladies" in various sorts of needlework. Patrick Thomas Duke taught English, writing, and "accounts" to young men at the Williamsburg free school, while his wife tutored "children" and took in sewing. In the 1770s, one Charleston couple ran a school for "Youth of both Sexes," at which the husband taught reading, writing, and arithmetic, while the wife offered harpsichord lessons. More unusual was a Charleston boarding school for girls at which a woman taught the academic courses while her husband provided lessons in drawing and painting.[37]

Other wives were more autonomous, pursuing separate trades and placing advertisements in their own names while sharing workshops with their husbands. In 1751, Virginian Abigail Peake announced that she would begin making wigs at her husband's shop in Yorktown. Anne Lining sold millinery and made children's clothes in the workshop of her husband, a Charleston cabinetmaker. Sabastian and Maria Martin, French immigrants who settled in Charleston, shared a shop on Broad Street, where Maria worked as a hairdresser and mantua maker and Sabastian painted, varnished, and gilded decorative moldings and furniture. Thomas Griffith ran a riding school in Charleston for at least four years, during which his wife, Mary, cleaned lace, mended fans, and sold millinery.[38]

Women who had capital and skills were the most likely to pursue independent trades. Milliners, most of whom had English training, commercial contacts, and money to invest, were the elite of women workers in colonial America. Many enjoyed long and prosperous careers in the southern provincial capitals. One of the most successful was Catherine Rathell, a London widow who immigrated to Virginia and ran several shops in that colony and in Maryland between 1765 and 1775. The Charleston milliner Anne Matthewes was in business for fourteen years, from 1756 until 1770. Most enduring, however, were the enterprises of the English sisters Jane Hunter Charlton and Margaret Hunter, who arrived in Virginia in the mid-1760s and sold millinery goods in Williamsburg for more than three decades. After a brief partnership, the sisters set up rival shops in Virginia's provincial capital. Like many other milliners, Jane continued her lucrative trade after marrying. She had an estate worth nearly $7,000 when she died in 1802.[39]

A working woman who plied a trade in her own name had an independent public identity and perhaps even an autonomous economic life. But some wives sought more than nominal autonomy, defining themselves as "feme sole" traders, a status that had precedent in English custom and was recognized by statute in eighteenth-century South Carolina. By claiming feme sole status, married women could avoid the legal and economic disabilities imposed by coverture. Feme sole traders had the right to control property, to make binding contracts, and to sue and be sued, which facilitated their ability to transact business independently. Although South Carolina law did not require businesswomen to register officially as sole traders, some sought formal recognition of their status by petitioning the courts or by publicly declaring their legal and economic independence in a local newspaper.[40]

Some South Carolina women became feme sole traders to avoid the inconvenience of having to conduct business in their husbands' names. Ann Gailliard, who was married to a prominent Charleston merchant, acquired feme sole status in 1761 and opened a store of her own. The milliner Jane Thomson was the feme sole wife of another Charleston merchant. Anne Cross, a Charleston tavern keeper, was the wife of Paul Cross, a merchant, slave trader, and ship's master who was often away from South Carolina. Because her business required frequent purchases of large quantities of rum and other liquors, Anne Cross needed to deal with local merchants when her husband was at sea. Although she does not appear to have announced publicly her economic independence, she clearly conducted her business as a feme sole trader.[41]

In colonies other than South Carolina, wives could not obtain official feme sole status, though some managed to circumvent coverture, doubtless with the support of their husbands. Sarah Garland Pitt, a Williamsburg merchant and milliner, continued trading during her twenty-two-year marriage to the physician George Pitt, despite giving birth to seven children during that period. As a feme covert, Sarah technically could not trade in her own right. Either her business associates recognized her de facto status as a feme sole or her husband acted as the nominal head of her business, for which, under coverture, he was legally liable.[42]

Besides offering entrepreneurial wives the convenience of circumventing their disabilities under the common law, feme sole status offered women a means to protect their property from financially troubled or irresponsible spouses. Most South Carolina wives who sought and proclaimed their feme sole status probably did so to shield themselves and their children from their husbands' creditors. Rachel Lawrence, who began her business by securing credit from some Charleston merchants, and Susanna Colleton, who used "credit from some of her friends" to open a tavern in Jacksonburgh, both claimed to have sought their economic independence "by advice of counsel at law." The lawyers probably recommended such a step to enable them to support themselves and their families without interference from their insolvent spouses. The overwhelming majority of women who publicly announced their feme sole status in the *South Carolina Gazette* simultaneously noted that they were taking in boarders or running public houses. Both occupations capitalized on their domestic skills and allowed them to use their houses as sources of profit. Other feme sole traders followed several occupations simultaneously to make ends meet. Mary Kelsey sold liquor and dry goods, but she also claimed to be a midwife of "many Years Experience." Elizabeth Knight had a small stock of dry goods that she sold from her home, but she also took in sewing.[43]

The case of Frances Swallow illustrates how a married woman of middling circumstances could gradually become responsible for the welfare of her family and, in the process, assume a public identity distinct from that of her husband. By 1765, the wife of the merchant Newman Swallow had for some time sold millinery goods as a partner in her husband's Charleston store. Two years later, however, Newman was in financial trouble and Frances placed an advertisement in the *South Carolina Gazette* describing herself for the first time as a "Sole-Trader" who continued to do business in "her shop" at the same location her husband had occupied previously. By 1768, Newman Swallow was in debtor's prison, and though he was back in business by 1770, Frances continued to work on her own at a variety of occupations to earn money for her family. In October 1770, she opened a boarding school in her house in Charleston, where she and an apprentice continued to work as milliners. In October 1772, Newman Swallow died. A few months later, Frances, her millinery business disrupted by prerevolutionary boycotts of British goods, took over the Charleston tavern formerly operated by William Holliday, though she continued to sell small quantities of imported finery. Swallow continued her business after remarrying in 1774. By then, as a milliner, tavern keeper, feme sole, and mother of six, she was a familiar figure in Charleston's commercial community.[44]

Women who, like Frances Swallow, engaged in extradomestic work for extended periods and whose stories can be traced through their frequent advertisements were public figures to a degree unusual for women of their era, but the economic pursuits of all women who engaged in extradomestic work involved them to varying degrees in the world beyond their family circles. Women's economic activities were symptomatic of sweeping social changes. Those who produced food, clothing, and other necessities helped to improve colonial living standards, while those who worked as milliners, shopkeepers, and booksellers both promoted and exploited the commercial revolution that transformed the economy and culture of colonial British America.[45] That eighteenth-century commercial revolution coincided with a general reassessment of traditional assumptions about women's essential nature.

The eighteenth century was a transitional era in the evolution of Western gender ideals, a time when religious and secular thinkers were revising traditionally perjorative conceptions of women's nature and their appropriate social roles. For centuries, clergy and philosophers alike disparaged women as men's mental and moral inferiors. Even the Enlightenment philosophers, who by the late seventeenth century questioned much of the existing orthodoxy, continued to look on women as intellectually deficient and morally suspect. Enlightenment writers celebrated human reason as a panacea for all social ills, but they identified men with reason and women with passion, its antithesis. As a result, with few exceptions, those who considered the status of women saw their relative lack of influence as the logical and desirable consequence of their supposedly ungovernable passions and inferior powers of reason.[46]

By the early decades of the eighteenth century, however, others suggested that feminine emotion was a virtue that could yield significant social benefits. Writing partly in reaction to extreme versions of Enlightenment rationalism, sentimental novelists, Protestant evangelicals, and Scottish philosophers — all of whom accepted the dichotomy between feminine emotion and masculine reason — argued that emotion, not reason, was the true source of human virtue. Proponents of heartfelt religious experience argued that women's natural emotionalism endowed them with a greater capacity for genuine piety. Scottish moral philosophers suggested that human virtue was the fruit of an innate emotional sensibility that was strongest in women, who, in turn, could nurture the development of sensibility in others. Meanwhile, beginning in the 1740s, sentimental novelists and essayists created new fictional heroines, women of piety, chastity, and high sensibility, who epitomized and popularized this new vision of virtuous womanhood.[47]

That vision valorized domesticity and women's moral influence in their households, while idealizing the leisured gentility that elites increasingly valued. This newly sentimentalized feminine ideal, moreover, ignored the value of women's productive work, stressing instead the moral and emotional benefits of feminine companionship, which positioned women to be consumers of clothing, books, musical instruments, and other accoutrements of sensibility. The new sentimentalized feminine ideal was a marked improvement over the pejorative images of woman that predominated in earlier centuries. By praising attributes accessible to only the most privileged women, however, it accentuated distinctions of class and race among colonial southerners.

The sentimentalization of domesticity, marriage, and family life also suggested a potentially rigid dichotomy between a masculine public sphere and a feminine private one, a dichotomy reflected in the emerging gender-based division of labor in religious life. Although men dominated religion in its formal public manifestations, contemporaries now regarded piety and spirituality as peculiarly feminine attributes. Moralists and social critics envisioned women deploying their piety in the private sphere, while elite men used religious institutions and rituals to exemplify and fortify their dominance in public life.

Images of virtuous and genteel womanhood appeared in the earliest southern newspapers, which began publication in Williamsburg and Charleston in the early 1730s. In 1732, one South Carolinian complained that men too frequently considered women "meerly Objects of *Sight*. . . . How much nobler is the Contemplation of *Beauty* heightened by *Virtue*.

How faint and spiritless are the Charms of a *Coquet*, when compared with the real Loveliness of *Innocence, Piety, Good-Humour* and *Truth.*" A contemporary Virginian similarly maintained that women were virtuous as well as beautiful, characterizing that "excellent Sex" as both "great Instruments of Good, and the Prettinesses of Society."[48]

Such conceptions of beauty and virtue were narrowly class-specific. Using the language of advice manuals and etiquette books, accessible only to literate elites, one essayist defined beauty as natural loveliness "adorned with unpremeditated graces" and conceived of feminine virtue as a combination of "rational Piety, modest Hope, and chearful Resignation." Modesty and cheerfulness were qualities infrequently associated with busy housewives or hard-driving tradeswomen. Cultivating religious insight and social graces, however seemingly unstudied, required reading and reflection at a time when most southern women were neither literate nor leisured.[49]

In the early eighteenth century, class-specific gender ideals suited the needs of colonial elites, who consciously strove to secure their authority by distinguishing themselves from their imagined inferiors. The ideal of the genteel, virtuous, and accomplished woman — whose masculine counterpart was the equally genteel, authoritative, and enlightened patriarch — complemented a material culture of books, balls, and Georgian mansions that blossomed among southern elites by the century's middle decades.[50] Furthermore, this sentimental vision of white womanhood resonated profoundly among people who already defined themselves in terms of racial differences. Pejorative images of women of color must have accentuated the idealized virtues that philosophers, moralists, and clergymen now increasingly ascribed to the women who were their mistresses.[51]

While white men came to idealize women of their own race as modest and virtuous, they consistently portrayed black women as promiscuous and sexually accessible. One particularly crude essay, which appeared in the *South Carolina Gazette* in 1736, advised the bachelors and widowers of Charleston, "if they are in a Strait for Women, to wait for the next Shipping from the Coast of Guinny. Those African Ladies are of strong, robust Constitution . . . able to serve them by Night, as well as day." Moreover, when slave women were sick, the essayist claimed, they did not need tending; when they died, their funerals were not costly. "The cheapness of a Commodi-ty becomes more taking," he added, "when it fully Answers the end, or T — — l." When another Carolinian, in response, claimed that "our [white] Country-Women are full as capable for Service either night or day as any African Ladies . . . [and] have always the praise for their Activity of

Hipps and humoring a Jest to the Life in what Posture soever their Partners may fancy," clearly he referred to poor white women and not to the privileged wives and daughters of South Carolina's elite.[52]

Because contemporaries believed that they lived in an era of growing sensibility and public decorum, such sexually explicit discussions gradually disappeared from the pages of respectable publications. Although white men continued to assuage their sexual appetites by exploiting black women, they were less likely to publicize their illicit sexual liaisons.[53] Bawdy portrayals of white women, which were commonplace in the sixteenth and seventeenth centuries, also became less socially acceptable. Although male pundits continued to satirize women and their supposed foibles, sentimental essays gradually displaced the more traditional depictions of women as spendthrifts and shrews.

Perhaps most significant, a new image of wifely companionship increasingly supplanted that of the nagging spouse. If the eighteenth century, as historians suggest, saw the emergence of a new "companionate" marriage ideal,[54] that ideal was one-sided, at least in its earliest form. Reevaluating the utility of marriage from a masculine standpoint, male moralists and philosophers suggested that husbands could find happiness in the companionship of virtuous, modest, and affectionate women. This marriage ideal thus combined a new appreciation for feminine sensibility, or improving emotion, with the more traditional assumption that the sole function of a wife was to serve her husband's needs and interests.

Popular advice books idealized marriages based on affection and urged men to look on their wives as companions but not as their equals. William Kenrick, a British clergyman whose book *The Whole Duty of Woman* was reprinted in part in the *South Carolina Gazette,* believed that young people should choose their own spouses — with their parents' consent — because "without love the husband is a tyrant, and the woman is a slave." Once married, however, a woman was obliged to obey her husband. An "imperious" wife, he warned, "raiseth a storm for her own shipwreck and she that affects dominion should be made the slave of her husband." John Gregory, the Scottish author of *A Father's Legacy to His Daughters,* the most popular advice book for young women in eighteenth-century America, downplayed the notion of subordination, describing women as men's "companions and equals," but even he instructed his female readers to cultivate such qualities as modesty and cheerfulness, which were pleasing to men and therefore suited to the "natural character and place in society . . . peculiar to your sex."[55]

Colonial writers also embraced this ideal of feminine companionship and its matrimonial implications. Condemning "fashionable" satirists who doubted the value of marriage, one early contributor to the *Virginia Gazette* asserted that "a good Wife is the greatest Blessing, and the most valuable Possession" of her husband because a man of "Sense and Discretion" could expect his wife to serve his needs, both physically and emotionally. "She is a Man's best Companion in Prosperity, and his only Friend in Adversity," the author claimed, as well as the "carefullest Preserver of his Health, and the kindest Attendant on his Sickness, a faithful Advisor in Distress, a Comforter in Affliction, and a prudent Manager of all his Domestic Affairs."[56]

Some women clearly internalized the feminine ideals that this prescriptive literature promoted. Eliza Lucas Pinckney recorded her marital ideals and aspirations in a private prayer she composed a few years after her nuptials. Pledging to "make a good Wife to my D[ea]r Husband . . . [and] to make all my actions Correspond with that sincere Love and Duty I bear him," she resolved to preserve his physical health, promote his spiritual welfare, and "do him all the good in my power, and next to my God to make it my [duty] to please him." Pinckney also promised to be a "good Mother" to her children, "to root out the first appearance and endings of vice; and to instill piety, Virtue, and true religion into them." With God's help, she hoped to "govern my passions, to endeavour constantly to subdue every vice," and to avoid "haughtiness, ambition, or ostentation, or contempt of others."[57] Although her marriage clearly was happy, Pinckney never enumerated her husband's obligations to her or the emotional, intellectual, or social benefits she expected to gain as a result of her union with him.

John Moultrie of South Carolina instilled in his daughter Sarah ideals similar to those Pinckney articulated. Writing to Sarah in 1776, Moultrie reminded her that he sought "to train you in the paths of virtue, and give you the nicest sentiments of piety, virtue, modesty, chastity, and prudence, the only true principles of your sex's happiness . . . as well as their most valuable and shining ornaments." Moultrie envisioned his adult daughter as "a fit, worthy and acceptable companion of a worthy, virtuous and sensible man." Together, they would preside over "a respectable house where virtue keeps the door," and Sarah would be the "joyfull mother of a virtuous and happy family."[58] Neither Moultrie nor the public proponents of companionate marriage ever inverted this formula for conjugal happiness, suggesting that men might make themselves "acceptable" companions for their future wives.

This new marriage ideal clearly put men's needs and interests first, but by emphasizing the benefits of feminine virtue and affection it implicitly encouraged men to respect and value their wives. Likening marriage to a ship at sea, Moultrie informed his daughter that her husband would be its "pilot and chief commander," but he believed that she deserved a spouse who would be "skillful, careful and good natured otherwise the vessell will be in great distress, the passengers ill treated." Another South Carolinian argued that men who could not recognize and esteem virtuous women were not fit to become their husbands. "When a man who looks upon a wife as but an upper servant, and believes that the sole end of woman's creation was to propagate the species," this anonymous essayist observed, "his ideas qualify him more for a Mahometan paradise, than for the company and conversation of a virtuous and sensible woman." This writer concluded that "no man should marry, who has not the candour to look upon the [female] sex in the most amiable and respectable light." Conversely, moralist John Gregory urged his real and fictive daughters to remain single rather than jeopardize their happiness and virtue by taking unworthy spouses.[59] The ideal marriage therefore united a virtuous woman with a man who recognized feminine sensibility and was susceptible to its influence.

Modesty, compassion, and cheerfulness were hallmarks of sensibility, but most observers agreed that piety was its highest expression. Moralists and social critics who championed companionate marriage and sentimental womanhood identified women with the private and emotional aspects of religious life, which they considered natural concomitants of women's superior sensibility. James Fordyce, Scottish author of the widely read *Sermons to Young Women,* was typical in his insistence that because women were inherently "susceptible of all the tender affections," they inevitably possessed "certain Qualities, which seem particularly calculated, by the grace of God, . . . for the reception and culture" of piety. John Gregory likewise asserted that women were "peculiarly susceptible" to pious devotions because their "natural softness and sensibility . . . particularly fit [them] for the practice of those duties where the heart is chiefly concerned." Gregory deemed piety and the sensibility it presupposed the essence of true womanhood. "Every man who knows human nature, connects a religious taste in your sex with softness and sensibility of heart," he explained, while men considered a lack of piety "proof of that hard and masculine spirit, which of all your faults we dislike the most."[60]

Feminine piety ideally exhibited the same combination of emotion and decorum as sensibility itself. Envisioning female piety as a private virtue

"Favour is Deceptive and Beauty is Vein but a Woman that Feareth the Lord She Shall be Praised," concluded the text of this sampler stitched by nine-year-old Elizabeth Gibbs of Charleston in 1729. This piece illustrates both the increasing domestication of women's work and the growing association of women with piety and sensibility in eighteenth-century America. Courtesy of the Museum of Early Southern Decorative Arts, Winston-Salem, N.C.

best cultivated and displayed within one's family circle, authors of conduct manuals and advice books discouraged women from participating in theological debates or raucous revivals — both public and potentially empowering activities in which the laity might engage. On the one hand, most writers agreed that women's religion was "rather a matter of sentiment than reasoning" and advised them to avoid theological disputes that could entangle them "in the endless maze of opinions and systems." On the other hand, philosophers, moralists, and the better sort of people generally frowned on excessive emotionalism, or "enthusiasm," which they regarded as unseemly and potentially licentious.[61]

Some women dabbled in quasi-public activities beyond the bounds of feminine piety, as described by the moralists, without disgracing their families or themselves. Erring on the side of emotion, many "polite ladies" attended the revival George Whitefield staged in Charleston in 1740. Ann Manigault, member of a prominent Charleston family, reported hearing the great revivalist preach three times — in 1755, 1765, and 1769 — long after the majority of southern elites had taken a firm stand against the Great Awakening and its adherents.[62] By contrast, Ann Tasker Carter may have erred on the side of reason when she engaged in theological debates with Philip Fithian, the college-educated tutor who resided with her family at Nomini Hall. Fithian observed that Carter discussed Protestant theology "with great propriety," asserting the superiority of "the Religion of the established Church [of England]" and debating with her daughter Priscilla the question whether women, like men, possessed immortal souls.[63]

Devotional reading, not complex theology or titillating oratory, was the chief stimulant to decorous piety for most literate provincials. Parents, clergy, and authors of prescriptive literature encouraged girls and women to use their literacy and their reason to cultivate their supposedly innate religious emotions — and it was in this sense that feminine piety could be construed as rational. A woman could use rational means to attain pious ends, and she could do so within the confines of her household. Contemporaries deemed private reading, or so-called closet devotionals, a critical part of the religious regimen of all literate females who aspired to sensibility.[64]

Colonial southerners were reticent about spiritual matters, but the letters and other writings of two young South Carolina women, Eliza Lucas and Martha Laurens, reveal the interplay between reason and emotion in the religious outlook of elite women during this period. By contemporary standards, Lucas and Laurens, both of whom attended English schools, were studious and well educated; both were also self-consciously pious. In the 1740s, as a young woman, Lucas read devotional works, wrote out prayers in her own hand, and believed that "God is Truth it self and . . . the Christian religion is what the wisest men in all ages have assented too." Epitomizing the ideal of rational piety, she declared that disbelief defied reason and that "tho' their may be things in the Xtian sistem above reason such as the incarnation of our Saviour . . . surely they highly dishonor our religion who affirm there is any thing in it contrary to reason." A generation later, reflecting the growing influence of the culture of sensibility, Martha Laurens expressed her religious insights in a much more emotional idiom. Each day, Laurens prayed and read devotional works; she also kept an introspective journal of her religious exercises, describing her feelings toward the deity and exploring such topics as "A Self Dedication and Solemn Covenant with God." Preparing for an "Hour of Trial" among "profane company" in 1776, she asked God to show her "the effectual moments, the proper opportunities for speaking in defence of the Gospel, for glorifying the name of Jesus."[65]

Both Lucas and Laurens responded to a cultural imperative to promote piety in their hearts and in their households, while their male relations could aspire to a religious ideal that was not only less emotional but also more public than private. In the southern colonies, some Anglican gentlemen strove to follow "Rules of Civility" that were reprinted in various conduct books during the period. In contrast to prescriptive literature for young women, which stressed heartfelt religious devotion, the "Rules of Civility" simply codified the externals of Christian morality. "When you Speak of God or his Atributes, let it be Seriously & [with] Reverence," wrote a young George Washington. "Let your Recreations be Manfull not Sinfull [and] Labour to keep alive in your Breast that Little Spark of Ce[les]tial fire Called Conscience." The Earl of Chesterfield, author of the century's most popular advice book for young men, went even further, describing religion not as a devotional experience but as merely one of several facets of a gentleman's public persona. "Every man is the worse looked upon, and the less trusted, for being thought to have no religion," he warned, cynically adding that a "Free-thinker, or Moral Philosopher, and a wise Atheist (if such a thing there is) would, for his own interest, and character in this world, pretend to some religion."[66]

As ministers and deacons, vestrymen or church elders, elite men orchestrated public religious observances that were in many ways the antithesis of the introspective piety and devotion they expected of virtuous women. Church services were sociable, sometimes rowdy occasions in many southern communities. In 1686, a French visitor noted the gregarious disposition of churchgoers in Gloucester County, Virginia, where "men, women, girls and boys from the age of seven years" joined the minister in a round of smoking both before and after the service. Elsewhere, members of congregations interrupted their religious observances to take refreshments or chat with neighbors. In 1746, one South Carolina minister complained that worshipers left church during his service to drink punch, returning to their pews some time later.[67]

Church services and the buildings in which they were conducted reflected the values of the elite men who ran them. Composed primarily of a series of prayers prescribed by the legislature for weekly recitation, the Anglican liturgy exemplified the values of emotional restraint and deference to established authority. Sermons stressing metaphysics and morality, not pious sensibility, encouraged deference and demonstrated the superior learning of the parson and his gentry patrons. Inside the churches, congregants sat according to social rank; the private pews of elite families were set apart from those of other worshipers. When the people took their seats for Sunday services, elite men entered the church last, making a grand processional entrance that betokened their exalted social status.[68]

As members of families, women participated in the public life of their communities on the Sabbath day. The wives of common planters, like the wives of prominent gentlemen, took their places in church, where their presence signified membership in a world beyond their households. Their membership in that world, however, was tenuous and at best second-class. While the social status of elite women entitled them to comfortable seats in desirable locations, gender consigned even them to a secondary role on church day, as on most other public occasions.

After 1700, increasing demographic stability and economic development made viable a new ideal of womanhood that stressed domesticity and the cultivation of feminine sensibility, but this ideal was accessible only to literate and leisured members of the colonial elite. Authors of prescriptive literature called on elite women to promote virtue and piety in their households but did not urge them to enter the public sphere. Unlike their nineteenth-century counterparts, southern colonial women would not use their piety as a springboard to public activism.

The growing regard for women's sensibility, however, coupled with the emergence of genteel culture, would give elite women other opportunities to influence public life. In the last half-century of the colonial era, southern gentlewomen helped to define and legitimize a demonstrably genteel culture of sociability in which they were prominent participants. Although traditional public activities such as Sabbath observances excluded or marginalized women of all ranks, elite women made a place for themselves in the public sphere, exploiting the virtues of sentimental womanhood that their class increasingly valued.

2

Gender, Community, and Hierarchy

IN 1697, DANIEL PARKE FLED VIRGINIA TO escape his political enemies, leaving behind his wife, Jane Ludwell Parke, their two daughters, Frances and Lucy, and his illegitimate son. Eight years later, when Daniel still had not returned, Jane wrote him a remarkable letter in which she perceptively outlined her family's unhappy circumstances. As members of one of Virginia's leading families, she explained, the Parkes were "expeckted . . . [to] live equall with the best in the Country." Unfortunately, Daniel, who "lived so like A man of quoallety" himself and knew "so wel how A gentelwoman should live," refused to provide adequate support for his family in Virginia. Jane worried especially about the future of her daughters. Although she believed that their social position should merit them "offers of [marriage from] the best young gentelmen In the Countrey," Jane knew that the young women would need new clothes, as well as lessons in French and dancing, before they could assume their rightful places at the head of Virginia's provincial society.[1]

Like many other women of her generation, Jane Parke oversaw the operation of her husband's Virginia plantation during his extended absences, but she did not envision a similar life for her daughters. Although her own education had been indifferent at best, Parke hoped that they would study reading, writing, dancing, and French. Parke portrayed herself as an embattled working woman, but she expected her daughters to have the leisure to cultivate polite accomplishments, exhibit their virtues at balls and parties, and preside over genteel households.[2]

Jane Parke's daughters and especially her granddaughters, indeed, would participate in genteel and sociable activities far more than had women of earlier generations. In so doing, they helped shape the public culture of eighteenth-century America. Although elite women were less likely to participate in the public culture of the marketplace after 1700, they took part in the creation of a class-specific culture of gentility that became increasingly central to the identity of southern elites. Women's contributions to genteel culture, which featured dress balls, formal dinners, and new forms of civic pageantry, drew on their traditional participation in hospitality rituals and on newer ideals of domesticity and sensibility. The influence of elite women was essential to the construction of gentility, which enhanced the authority of their class while affording them unprecedented access to the world beyond their households.

The rise of gentility, in turn, generated modest changes in the educational opportunities and expectations of southern elites of both sexes. To prepare their offspring for their appropriate social roles, parents now sought more than utilitarian curricula, and they showed unprecedented interest in their daughters' education. The decades before the American Revolution were a time of marked improvement in the education of young gentlewomen, even if most colonists regarded the objectives of their schooling as primarily ornamental.

Domestic hospitality, like tavern keeping, straddled the boundary between public and private in eighteenth-century America. Sustenance and shelter, offered privately in a domestic environment, nonetheless affected and were affected by the public image of their donor. Viewing hospitality as a form of social competition and reciprocity, southern gentlemen were observant guests and careful hosts who scrutinized both their own hospitality and that of others.[3] The quality of food and drink that hosts offered could attest to their wealth and good taste as well as to the degree of esteem in which they held their guests. In addition, hospitality rituals dramatized the disparity of power between donor and recipient, establishing a hierarchical relationship between the donor, who displayed wealth and benevolence, and the recipient, who enjoyed the bounty of patronage at the cost of independence. Perhaps that is why southern gentlemen, who jealously guarded both their independence and their public reputations, assiduously paid their social debts.[4]

Southern women also opened their houses to guests, though they left little evidence of their attitudes toward hospitality and its social significance. For propertied widows, who enjoyed wealth in their own right, dispensing hospitality could have signified their independence as heads of households and their ambiguous status in a community that afforded them certain legal and economic rights denied to married women.[5] William Byrd II clearly believed that the hospitality of Mrs. Allen, a Surry County widow, reflected admirably on her abilities and character. "She entertain'd us elegantly," Byrd reported, "& seem'd to pattern Solomon's Housewife if one may Judge by the neatness of her House, & the good Order of her Family."[6]

Wives who offered hospitality in their husbands' absence, like those who made business decisions under the same circumstances, may have envisioned themselves as their spouses' surrogates or "deputy husbands." Emelia Hunter of Gloucester County, Virginia, assumed that husband and wife had different but complementary roles to play in offering hospitality. Welcoming guests to her home in 1755 while her spouse was away in Williamsburg, Hunter felt "Obliged to perform his part, as well as my own, of the Ceremony's of the House." Decades later, the Marquis de Chastellux visited the Virginia home of General Thomas Nelson, whose wife and mother stood in for him in his absence, receiving the Frenchman "with all the politeness, ease, and cordiality natural to this family."[7]

When husbands and wives offered hospitality jointly, contemporaries described their respective roles in terms that reflected the idealized division of labor in marriage during this period. Just as social critics and their readers increasingly supposed that women's work would be primarily domestic and often ornamental, they acknowledged women's role in food preparation and in molding the social environment in which hospitality was offered, but they generally assumed that men provided the material goods — including the houses — that guests enjoyed on such occasions. In 1728, William Byrd II described one Virginia house in which he lodged as the property of the man who resided there, noting that his host's "Castle consist[ed] of one Dirty Room," which his "Landlady" improved by providing a hearty meal in an atmosphere of great "Civility." Higher up the social ladder, Elizabeth Feilde held her husband responsible for acquiring the material goods she needed to be hospitable. "I am very sorry I have not a Glass of Wine to give you," Feilde informed a friend in 1776, "indeed we have been without any a long time, for Mr F has not the means of procuring it."[8]

For all women, regardless of their marital status, hospitality was at least partly a token of benevolence, which contemporaries increasingly idealized as a feminine attribute. Christianity taught both men and women to be benevolent, but sentimental writers described benevolence, like piety, as a natural outgrowth of feminine sensibility. In 1732, a contributor to the *South Carolina Gazette* described the "Fair Sex" as "compassionate without Weakness," and a decade later the first recipe book published in the colonies urged "Generous, Charitable, and Christian Gentlewomen" to "be Serviceable to their poor Country Neighbours." James Fordyce, the Scottish moralist, claimed that his female readers were peculiarly well suited, by their nature and situation, to perform benevolent works. John Gregory believed that the "best effect" of feminine piety was "a diffusive humanity to all in distress." Urging women to "set aside a certain portion of your income as sacred to charity," he also enjoined them to show "a tender and compassionate spirit" to those in need even "where your money is not wanted."[9]

In keeping with this ideal of feminine benevolence, women dispensed both hospitality and patronage to those outside their family circles. In spite or perhaps because of their exclusion from most formal church activities, their offerings of benevolence often had religious connotations. Traveling ministers frequently noted the particular generosity of women, who regularly offered them food and lodging. The Reverend Robert Rose of Albemarle County routinely enjoyed the hospitality of both Elizabeth Gaines, a widow, and Mrs. Glover, a married woman, when he made his customary circuit through central Virginia. Rose preached and read prayers in the houses of both women. When George Whitefield visited South Carolina, he likewise enjoyed the patronage of a Charleston "gentlewoman," who invited him to preach in her barn and "provided food sufficient for a great multitude" of listeners. Mary Harrison Gordon, wife of a Lancaster County, Virginia, merchant, regularly celebrated Shrove Tuesday — the last day before Lent — by treating local schoolchildren to pancakes and cider. More ambitious but less explicitly religious, Eliza Lucas, as a young woman in Charleston, planned to sell oaks to shipbuilders, reserving two-thirds of the proceeds "for a charity."[10]

Eighteenth-century women usually dispensed benevolence and patronage in their own households, but even these offerings were at least quasi-public in the sense that they displayed the virtues and enhanced the public reputations of their donors. Southern men likewise offered benevolence and

40   patronage in their houses, but they also sponsored sex-specific patronage rituals that occurred in public spaces and served explicitly public or civic purposes. These masculine public activities — militia musters, elections, and the treating rituals associated with these events and with the meeting of the county courts — excluded women but, by demonstrating both the power and benevolence of elite men, strengthened the reciprocal networks of patronage and dependence that encouraged popular deference.[11]

On these public occasions, the elite men who served as militia officers, justices, and political candidates demonstrated their authority by presiding over the day's business, but they also displayed their benevolence and affability by dispensing patronage in the form of extradomestic hospitality. Gentlemen mingled with their clients and dependents, whom they treated to liquor and other refreshments. For instance, when the militia of Lancaster County, Virginia, drilled in celebration of the coronation of George III in 1761, the officers "gave the men 50 or 60 gal[lon]s of punch."[12] Convivial drinking among white men of all classes reaffirmed a social bond between leaders and followers in an overtly hierarchical society. At the same time, the officers who sponsored the revelry sought to strengthen their claims to political and social leadership by showing the condescending liberality that most regarded as the mark of a true gentleman.

Yet elite authority was by no means certain even in the heyday of gentry dominance. Unlike most of their British counterparts, colonial elites derived their privileged status from wealth, not bloodlines, and fortunes could be made or lost quickly in a volatile colonial economy. Furthermore, the migration of white colonists to the interior in search of land and opportunity undermined the networks of patronage and dependence that prevailed in the older gentry-dominated communities of the east. Colonial elites appear to have recognized that their status was insecure, especially after mid-century, when evangelical insurgents, backcountry rebels, and the collapse of the tobacco market threatened their position more directly. By then, elite men and women throughout British America were consciously cultivating a genteel cultural style to accentuate distinctions in rank and thereby enhance the legitimacy of their putative social authority.[13]

Women played a crucial role in creating the genteel public culture that coexisted with traditionally masculine public rituals by the late colonial era. Though dramatically different in form and in content, both types of public culture sought to enhance the authority of the gentry. At a time when many viewed gentility and "politeness" as hallmarks of legitimate leadership, southern elites devised new social rituals that enabled them to exhibit their cultural accomplishments to one another and to their imagined inferiors. Those cultural accomplishments included an appreciation for fine meals lavishly presented, fashionable clothing, and, above all, mastery of learned patterns of manners and deportment that implied not only wealth but also access to a cosmopolitan world.[14] Because moralists and philosophers increasingly lauded women as the source of grace and moral improvement, true gentility also appears to have presupposed feminine influence and participation in a range of sociable activities.

In the southern colonies, the rise of gentility coincided with the introduction and popularization of sentimental feminine ideals that stressed women's superior virtue and piety. Joseph Addison and Richard Steele's *Spectator* essays, among the first to identify women with moral virtue, were standard reading among colonial elites, as was the sentimental fiction of Samuel Richardson, the most popular novelist of the era.[15] James Fordyce and John Gregory, authors of widely read advice books for young women, were members of a circle of writers who looked to women's innate sensibility as the basis of social regeneration. Feminine sensibility could influence the manners and morals of men, they suggested, and in so doing contribute to the public good.[16]

Just as southern essayists gradually embraced the ideals of wifely companionship and feminine piety, they also accepted the notion that feminine sensibility could improve the moral tone of public life. A 1738 contributor to the *Virginia Gazette* formed his readers that women's virtue and beauty made that "excellent Sex" both "great Instruments of Good, and the Prettinesses of Society." Other southerners celebrated women's improving influence even more extravagantly. "An Essay on Women," which appeared in the *Virginia Gazette* in 1773, argued that the "Empire which Women owe to Beauty was only given them for the general Good of all the human Species." If women "would strive to join Justness of Thought, and Uprightness of Heart, to the Graces of the Body," the essayist suggested, "the Taste we [men] have for them would unfold excellent Qualities in us." Without women, he declared, men would "be different from what we are. Our Endeavours to be agreeable to them polish and soften that rough severe Strain so natural to us . . . . In a Word, if Men did not converse with Women, [men] would be less perfect and less happy than they are."[17]

As early as the 1730s, elite women helped to fortify the public image of their class by lending their genteel and improving influence to an array of public rituals that supplemented, but did not supplant, the masculine rituals of the courthouse and muster field. In 1736 and again in 1737, "some merry-dispos'd Gentlemen" of Hanover County, Virginia, celebrated the feast of Saint Andrew with a collection of sporting and social events that alternately accentuated or transcended class and gender distinctions among the community's white inhabitants. Gender-specific activities included fiddling, "Foot-ball-play," running, jumping, and wrestling contests for the men and a beauty contest for the women, in keeping with the conventions of a culture that regarded men as physically vigorous and competitive and women as passive and ornamental. Reflecting the hierarchical status distinctions in the county, the gentlemen who organized the day's events welcomed gentlefolk of both sexes to the horse races but barred their less affluent neighbors from entering horses in the races or wagering with the gentlemen whose horses ran. The event's organizers stipulated that "no Person have the Liberty of putting in a Horse, unless he is a Subscriber towards defraying the Expence of this Entertainment." They also provided "a handsome Entertainment . . . for the Subscribers, and their Wives," whom they described as persons "of the best Sort."[18]

By the final decades of the colonial era, elites were adopting more pointedly exclusive sporting rituals, perhaps hoping to use such public displays of gentility to enhance a privileged status that may have appeared increasingly tenuous. Although ordinary southerners, white and black, continued to watch races and to gamble among themselves, in Virginia and the Carolinas prominent men established jockey clubs that held members-only races for extravagant purses, one of which they sometimes earmarked specifically for female bettors. These jockey clubs transformed the social environment of the races, as elegant balls and banquets supplanted the country fairs of earlier decades. By the 1760s, South Carolina's legislature went into recess the first week of every February, when its members attended a round of balls and races. In the words of one observer, on race day in Charleston processions of "beautiful women, gallant fellows, and elegant equipages" wended their way toward the racecourse in a stunning display of gentility and social authority. In 1774, the races in Fredericksburg, Virginia, lasted five days, and puppet shows and dances were given nightly. A spectator at the less elaborate races at Richmond Court House still found those assembled "exceeding polite in general."[19]

As the Virginia beauty contests suggest, women participated in social rituals as ornaments to enhance the power and prestige of the men who possessed them, but their presence also altered the character of the events they attended. While the beauty contests afforded white men yet another venue in which they might vie for status — in this case, by a competitive ranking of the physical charms of their female dependents — they also brought a temporary halt to drinking, gaming, and other disorderly activities in which men typically engaged. Similarly, there is some evidence that southern election etiquette was changing by the final decade of the colonial era largely as a result of women's presence at the postelection celebrations. Southern colonial elections traditionally were raucous affairs, sometimes punctuated by violent outbursts among participants. In 1768 and again in 1774, however, George Washington treated both men and women to refreshments after his election to Virginia's House of Burgesses. We have no firsthand account of the 1768 election festivities, but an observer reported that the polling proceeded with "order and regularity" in 1774, and the ball "was conducted with great harmony." Likewise, in 1772, when the voters of Tarboro, North Carolina, unanimously elected James Milner to represent them in the legislature, the election proceeded without incident, and the victorious Milner gave an "elegant" dinner and ball for the community's men and women.[20]

Elite gentility also reshaped southern civic pageantry, inspiring new forms of civic ritual that included elites of both sexes but excluded men and women of lesser social ranks. In the early colonial period, a militia parade, a procession of high officials, and a private dinner for the colony's leading men were the focal points of southern civic pageantry, which reflected the priorities of an English imperial regime that struggled to attain internal political stability and to defend itself militarily.[21] Southern elites subsequently integrated balls and dancing, and hence women, into their increasingly genteel public celebrations. By the 1720s, prominent Virginians had incorporated genteel balls into their celebration of the king's birthday and other civic occasions. Two decades later, the members of South Carolina's elite also were gathering each year for balls and dinners commemorating royal anniversaries and births. By the 1760s, even New Bern, North Carolina's new and comparatively rustic provincial capital, was the site of balls to celebrate the king's birthday or to greet newly arrived officials. In 1764, "near 100 Gentlemen and Ladies" attended "a very elegant Ball, in the Great Ball-Room in the Court house," to welcome Governor William Tryon and his wife to New Bern.[22]

Segregated by class but not by gender, these genteel civic rituals reflected and reinforced the existing social hierarchy. On royal birthdays, accession days, and other civic occasions, fashionably attired men and women proceeded in coaches to the site of the ball, displaying their finery and their refinement to spectators on the streets below. In Williamsburg, as early as 1724, one observer found that "at the *Governor's House* upon [royal] *Birth-*

Nights, and at *Balls* and *Assemblies,* I have seen as fine an Appearance, as good Diversion, and as splendid Entertainments . . . as I have seen any where else." In the 1730s, Virginia's elites celebrated the king's birthday "with firing of Guns, Illuminations [of buildings], and other Demonstrations of Loyalty: And at Night there was a handsome Appearance of Gentlemen and Ladies, at his Honour the Governour's where was a Ball, and an elegant Entertainment for them." In 1741, after reviewing the provincial troops, South Carolina's royal governor entertained the colony's elite with "an elegant Supper and Ball, at which was a very numerous and gay Appearance of Ladies."[23]

Genteel civic rituals promoted and justified the dominance of provincial elites by demonstrating their privileged access to a polite cosmopolitan world. Balls and the public processions of their participants presented in microcosm that world and its social values. Fine coaches and distinctive clothing signaled both wealth and familiarity with the latest London fashions, while dining and dancing with the royal governor demonstrated the gentry's political influence and dramatized their status as mediators between colonial communities and imperial authority. The structure of formal balls, where social rank determined both who attended and the order in which they danced, reflected the elite's regard for decorum and hierarchy. Intricate dance steps, learned largely from European masters, suggested that elites alone commanded the knowledge and talents that could enable provincials to consort with great men like the royal governor, who represented the king in British colonial America.

The rise of balls as forms of civic ritual, like their inclusion in sporting and election day events, attested to the critical place of elite women in genteel culture and society. At a time when men sought increasingly to exclude women from the economic and legal aspects of the public sphere, elite women nonetheless made themselves indispensable to the civic and social rituals that the gentry constructed to demonstrate and reinforce their putative social authority. Indeed, the rise of gentility resulted in the feminization of certain aspects of public life, which defined the political and cultural relationship between gentry and common folk. It also resulted in an even more pervasive feminine presence and influence in the quasi-public sociability rituals that gentlefolk practiced among themselves.

Class-specific and purposefully genteel, sociability rituals fostered the development of a distinctive elite culture in eighteenth-century America. Stylized manners and conspicuous consumption were hallmarks of elite so-

Sir Foplings Airs, artist unknown, 1710. Genteel dances mirrored the elaborate stylized manners of the elites who engaged in them. The satiric instructions for this country dance, performed at the English court in 1710, included an exchange of snuff between partners and then "the 1st and 2nd Man toss the right, then the left knot of their Wigs, then clap their right, then their left hand on their sides, the Women do the same, only they smooth their hair with the back of their hands, dance carelessly, turn singly, and look surprizingly at each other." Courtesy The Winterthur Library, Joseph Downs Collection of Manuscripts and Printed Ephemera.

ciability. So, too, was the participation of refined women, whose presence many believed would augment the virtue of the men who governed the community and influenced its character.[24] Sociability therefore provided self-conscious elites with evidence of their own superior wealth, sophistication, and virtue and thereby justified their claim to be society's natural governors.

Changes in domestic architecture and consumption during the eighteenth century reflected the rise of genteel sociability. By mid-century, southern elites were building bigger, more elaborate houses, many of which had a room for formal dining and also one large enough to accommodate genteel balls.[25] Inside these houses, a growing variety of specialized tableware and dining utensils, along with numerous matched dining chairs, reflected the elites' increasing desire to offer fashionable meals to large but select parties of discerning guests. In Virginia, the Custis and Ludwell mansions each contained more than 80 chairs, and Philip Ludwell owned 127 china plates and 58 wineglasses when he died in 1767.[26]

The growing numbers of southern milliners and the expanding lists of goods they carried reflected the centrality of women as both producers and consumers of the accoutrements of sociability. Only one milliner is known to have conducted business in Williamsburg before 1730, but at least eight sold goods there by the early 1770s. In Charleston, the ranks of milliners and mantua makers swelled from five to seventeen during the same period. Women also sold millinery goods in Fredericksburg, Richmond, New Bern, and several backcountry communities by the 1770s.[27] Such tradeswomen both cultivated and expoited demand for fashionable clothing among "gentlemen and ladies," touting their merchandise as "genteel," "fashionable," or "lately arrived from London." Moreover, while a typical early advertisement simply announced the availability of "all Silks, Linnens, Damasks, Calicoes . . . Womens Gowns and Petticoats, . . . Mens Night Gowns, Silk and Thread Stockings, &c.," after mid-century advertisers increasingly listed dozens of specific fabrics, trims, and laces, along with various types of gloves, stockings, shoes, caps, and other accessories.[28]

As members of a class who sought prestige and comfort in an ever-widening array of English consumer goods, elite women took fashion seriously. A fan and a suit of clothing sent by a friend in London thrilled young Harriott Pinckney, according to her mother, "the more so as they are the first to have reached this part of the world, so she has an opportunity of seting the fashion" in South Carolina. Some women exploited their personal or business contacts to order goods directly from London. Jane Allen Pringle had her husband, a Charleston merchant, send two gowns to London to be dyed, and Elizabeth Galloway Sprigg of Virginia prevailed on a friend to send her a velvet cloak, a silk dress, and a "fashionable" fan when she visited England. When Martha Washington ordered clothes for herself and her daughter, Patsy Custis, from a London milliner in 1764, the British merchants who marketed the Custis tobacco paid her accounts.[29]

Men had long been attentive to clothing and fashion, but, the rise of women's fashion signaled their assumption of a central place in the rituals of genteel sociability.[30] Dining, dancing, and polite conversation were the chief forms of elite sociability, and contemporaries believed that women's presence and influence were crucial for the proper execution of all three of these activities. Balls were by definition mixed-sex events, but feminine involvement was also essential to both the form and content of genteel dinner gatherings. Elite women introduced stylish or exotic dishes and directed the preparation of the food served to family and guests. They participated in the polite conversation around the dinner table and in their drawing rooms, where their sensibility could heighten the moral tone of the proceedings.

Men as diverse as William Byrd II and the tutor Philip Fithian identified women with the production, preparation, and management of food in their households. When Byrd lodged with Colonel George Newton and his wife, he credited Mrs. Newton with providing "a clean Supper without any Luxury" for their guests. When he stayed with Captain Embry and his wife, he reported in his journal that the captain offered him and his companions lodging, while his wife provided "a Supper Sufficient for a Batallion . . . [and] made us eat part of everything." A visitor to New Bern, North Carolina, acknowledged that Mary Moore of that town kept "a great plenty of provisions & fruits of the earth" in her household. Philip Fithian, who resided for roughly a year at Nomini Hall, the Virginia home of Robert and Ann Tasker Carter, noted that its mistress kept track of the vast quantities of meat, grain, and liquor consumed by the family and their guests, exercising stewardship over a larder consisting of "27000 Lb of Pork; & twenty Beeves, 550 Bushels of Wheat, besides corn — 4 Hogheads of Rum, & 150 Gallons of Brandy" annually.[31]

Although food preparation was traditionally numbered among women's chief domestic concerns, food and its presentation took on new significance among an increasingly fashion-conscious colonial elite. As early as 1705, Robert Beverley observed that the Virginia gentry "pretend to have their Victuals drest, and serv'd up as Nicely, as at the best Tables in *London*."[32] In the coming decades, provincial elites grew even more preoccupied with presenting extravagant and artful meals to their guests on social occasions. Elite men, who routinely traded with London merchants, ordered fashionable items to adorn their tables, and some women ordered such items on their own, suggesting that they shared the men's interest in genteel dining. Martha Dandridge Custis included "one silver nutmeg grinder" among her purchases of new clothing and household goods at the end of the mourning period following the death of her husband. Ann Carter sent to London for £30 worth of plate in the form of "fashionable" goblets, "beautiful" sauce cups, and "elegant" decanter holders.[33]

In most households, women oversaw one of the key rituals of genteel sociability, the formal presentation of food to guests. As the English author of *The Compleat Housewife* informed her readers, the preparation of food was no longer "a simple Science, or a bare Piece of Housewifery or Family Oeconomy, but in process of Time, when Luxury enter'd the World, it grew to an

48   Art." Promising to turn her literate — and thus presumably well-heeled — readers into "Accomplished Gentlewomen," she shared the fruits of her experience as a cook for "fashionable and noble Families," including not only her recipes but also "Schemes engraven on Copper-Plates for . . . Placing the Dishes of Provision on the Table according to the best Manner." Recent changes in etiquette also made the hostess, who sat at the "place of honor" at the table's head, responsible for distributing the food among her guests. Similarly, women, not men, performed the honors of the tea table, a ritual that was second only to dancing as an archetype of gentility.[34]

By providing both a showcase for genteel manners and accomplishments and a carefully regulated forum in which the sexes could meet and mingle, dancing, perhaps more than any other activity, epitomized the ideals and objectives of elite sociability. For youngsters, the commencement of dancing lessons was a rite of passage into adult society. When her young granddaughter began to learn to dance in 1768, Ann Manigault thought the event worth recording in her diary. Dancing classes also initiated young people into the world of fashion because boys and girls alike donned stylish, grown-up clothes when they began to learn to dance. Thus Henry Laurens advised a friend that he should delay sending his ten-year-old son to dancing school because "such a Measure would unavoidably create an Expence for Clothing which must be preserved when once enter'd upon & he is rather a wild Spark as yet & does not much regard his apparel."[35]

Dancing was the means by which young men and women acquired the social and physical graces they needed to enter genteel society. As one Delaware man informed his son, dancing "adds to the Accomplishment of Behavior & Carriage and Qualifies a person for Polite Company." Lord Chesterfield, whose *Letters* influenced the education and deportment of at least a generation of prospective American gentlemen, advised his own son that a gentleman "must dance well, in order to sit, stand, and walk well; and you must do all these things well in order to please" those he would encounter in genteel society. Fearing promiscuity or perhaps assuming that females were innately graceful, contemporary moralists were more ambivalent in their advice to young women. Fordyce approved only "moderate and discreet dancing," while Gregory recommended dancing as a means to cultivate "ease and grace" but warned his readers against being "so far transported with mirth, as to forget the delicacy of your sex."[36]

Such concerns notwithstanding, women were central figures in southern colonial dance culture. According to one observer, "Old Women, Young wives with children in the lap, widows, maids, and girls" all attended balls in

Family Group, Gawen Hamilton, ca. 1730. Women presided over the ceremonies of the tea table, which were important rituals of elite sociability. Although contemporaries frequently spoke of tea parties as women's affairs, people of both sexes often assembled to drink tea and enjoy polite conversation. Colonial Williamsburg Foundation.

colonial Virginia. At least three women operated dancing schools in Williamsburg at different times and another dancing mistress set up shop in Charleston in the early 1750s. Dancing mistresses and female tavern keepers, like their male counterparts, sponsored public dancing assemblies for gentry patrons. In at least one Virginia community, elite women joined with their husbands to sponsor an annual ball, drawing lots to see which woman would provide the "large rich cake" and which man would supply the "Six or Seven Pounds" for the hall and the other refreshments.[37]

In rural areas, dancing created opportunities for elite women to socialize with gentry friends and neighbors. The arrival of an itinerant dancing master was a great occasion for sociability. Francis Christian, a popular Virginia dancing master, met his pupils for two days every three weeks at alternating plantations. When Christian convened his school at Nomini Hall, women accompanied their daughters and sons, taking advantage of the opportunity to visit with Ann Carter, who, in turn, escorted her son Bob and daughter Nancy to their dancing lessons at Bushfield, the home of her friend Hannah Bushrod Washington. When Christian held his two-day session at Mount Vernon in 1770, some students and their parents stayed overnight in the Washingtons' home. Looking back on her youth in prerevolutionary Virginia, Eliza Custis recalled that her twice-weekly dancing classes were appealing opportunities to socialize with other young women.[38]

Elite women attended balls at neighboring plantations, as well as in larger towns and in the colonial capitals. From November 1773 through October 1774, Ann Carter attended at least six balls in Westmoreland County homes, some with and some without her husband, Robert. Dancing teachers in Williamsburg and Charleston sponsored balls regularly, and by the close of the colonial period, trading communities such as Alexandria and Norfolk also had dancing assemblies.[39]

Most significant, however, was the annual social season that, particularly in Williamsburg and Charleston, coincided with the meeting of the courts and legislature. In the 1730s, Henry Holt, a popular Charleston dancing master, began holding balls each April and December for members of the low country elite, who purchased tickets for these increasingly fashionable events. By 1752, two competing entrepreneurs held weekly balls in Williamsburg during the judicial and legislative sessions. When the courts and the assembly met, one visitor reported, Williamsburg was "crowded with the gentry of the country," who came to enjoy the "balls and other amusements," but when the government concluded its business, "the town is in a manner deserted." Charleston's population fluctuated less dramatically, but the number of the city's inhabitants increased seasonally there as well, in accordance with the political calendar and climatic conditions in the disease-ridden low country.[40]

In the development of their social season, as in so many other things, southern elites emulated the English country gentry, who, decades earlier, began gathering in London for an annual round of balls and other sociable activities. Some English writers believed that women were instrumental in the creation of the social season, which enabled them to escape the isolation of their country estates to engage in the pleasant rites of sociability.[41] Colonial southerners never directly attributed the development of the social season to women's influence, but revolutionary-era champions of republican simplicity certainly regarded balls and other genteel entertainments as "effeminate" and some believed that women instigated such activities.[42] Although women were not solely responsible for the proliferation of mixed-sex social gatherings, the pervasiveness of balls demonstrates the central place they occupied in genteel culture in its most public form.

The polite conversation that was part of every dinner, ball, and other sociable gathering was the third chief component of elite sociability. At balls, participants acted out stylized forms of social intercourse in fashionable minuets, and men and women conversed between dances. At formal dinners, newly fashionable oval-shaped dining tables encouraged conversation. "Tables without corners," one scholar has suggested, "made a closed circle of men and women" who shared a "commitment to the arts of civility."[43]

Because contemporaries regarded women as the chief sources of civility and moral virtue, polite and improving conversation necessarily included both sexes, though gender shaped the roles they played in it, as in other sociable activities. Women's role in genteel conversation was emblematic of their ambiguous status in the wider culture of sociability. Expected to influence subtly the moral tone and content of conversation, women were nonetheless warned against attempting to dominate the discourse on social occasions. John Gregory, who envisioned women as men's "companions and equals . . . designed to soften our hearts and polish our manners," also counseled his readers to be modest in society. "One may take a share in a conversation without uttering a syllable. The expression in the countenance shews it, and this never escapes an observing eye." Warning against the unseemliness of feminine vanity and wit, Gregory advised young women to "be ever cautious in displaying your good sense" for fear that "it will be thought you assume a superiority over the rest of the company."[44]

Gregory and other moralists regarded modesty as the cardinal feminine virtue, but they expected women to wield a gentle and improving influence over the men with whom they associated.[45] With the rise of genteel sociability, elite men spent more time with women, who, subtly or not, appear to have influenced their manners and leisure activities. In women's presence, men often substituted dancing, conversation, and sedate cardplaying for rougher masculine pastimes. When a company of guests visited William Byrd at Westover in 1741, the men left the house after dinner to play bowls, only to be interrupted by "the women," who prevailed on them to dance a quadrille. When Lucinda Lee spent three months visiting a series of prominent Virginia planter families, the men in each household spent nearly every evening dancing and hence in the company of women. William Byrd's kinswoman Jane Pratt Taylor believed that the popularity of genteel cardplaying also "engaged the men of all ages to keep company with women more than ever [any] thing did before . . . for tell [whist] came in fashion a reasonable man wou'd have thought his character forfeted for ever, had it bin known that he spent six evenings a week in the company of women." Taylor believed that mixed-sex cardplaying discouraged men's drunkenness. The whist fad, she asserted, resulted in at least "one good thing . . . & that is sobriety, for sertainly there never was so little drinking in the world as at present, for in a twelve month together you dont see such a thing as a person of fashion drunk."[46]

Fragmentary evidence suggests that gentility and men's new appreciation for feminine sensibility also altered the character of sociable occasions that traditionally had included both men and women, just as it inspired changes in election etiquette during this period. The most vivid description of a seventeenth-century southern wedding comes from the French Huguenot Durand de Dauphiné, who attended such a "great festival" in Virginia in 1686. Durand described an unruly scene in which more than one hundred guests, many of them gentry, dined at two o'clock and then "did nothing afterwards, for the rest of the day & all night, but drink, smoke, sing & dance." Most of the women and girls eventually went off to bed, but the men "caroused all night long," so that by morning none "could stand straight." A century later, when the Scotsman Robert Hunter toured Virginia, he attended a much more decorous wedding at Robert Beverley's Blandfield. At this three-day celebration with approximately one hundred guests, the main activities were dancing "cotillions, minuets, Virginia and Scotch reels, country dances, jigs, etc." and partaking of "sumptuous and elegant" meals. Each evening, guests of both sexes retired at midnight or earlier, and arrived refreshed at the "elegant breakfast, at ten, consisting of tea, coffee, chocolate, cold ham, fowls, hashed mutton, and various other dishes."[47]

Perhaps the best evidence of elite women's increased cultural influence was the criticism of their participation in sociability and its rituals. Although Baptists and other New Light evangelicals assailed genteel sociability as a source of unholy decadence and irrelevant status distinctions, conservative moralists, most of whom were at least nominally Anglican, made gender the focal point of their critique of elite culture both in Britain and in America. Indeed, as early as the 1670s, some English writers began preaching the gospel of domesticity, contending that sociability undermined feminine virtue, which they believed was best preserved and exerted in the private sphere of the household.[48]

Alarmed by women's growing public visibility and influence, some

Playing at the Game of Quadrille, artist unknown. Elite women and men played quadrille, whist, and other fashionable card games at home and on sociable occasions. Some contemporaries believed that men's conduct was improved by leisure time spent in the company of their wives and other women. Colonial Williamsburg Foundation.

eighteenth-century moralists sought to erect a barrier between women's domestic realm and the potentially corrupting public sphere into which they believed only men should venture. In 1753, in a work reprinted in part in the *South Carolina Gazette,* the conservative English clergyman William Kenrick praised women who "frequenteth not the publick haunts of men" and condemned mothers who, by engaging in extradomestic activities, supposedly valued their "pleasures dearer than thine offspring." Warning that the pursuit of knowledge of the "ways of man" could lead women to seduction and ruin, Kenrick encouraged his young readers to cultivate instead the domestic skills that might contribute to "the comfort of thy future husband." Similarly, one of Kenrick's colonial contemporaries warned that sociability bred vanity, extravagance, and immodesty in women. Blaming women's sociability for a growing list of "Offenses against Common Sense in the Ladies, particularly Wives," this South Carolinian declared that "every Attachment, when indulg'd, will ingross too much of the female Mind, and leave too little Room for domestick Cares." Another anonymous essayist especially decried the growing popularity of tea parties, which he believed encouraged dangerous political discussions among the women who attended them.[49]

Elite women, for their part, found entertainment and companionship in sociability and its rituals. When the arrival of three British naval vessels in Hampton, Virginia, resulted in "Balls both by Land and by Water in abundance," Anne Blair celebrated "the Happiness we now enjoy" because the town was "now more gay then the Metropolis" of Williamsburg. Mary Spotswood characterized Williamsburg as "extreamly dull" on one occasion because she had "been at but one ball" since her arrival in the capital. A generation earlier, Lucy Parke Byrd and her daughters sorely missed "the Plays, the Operas and the Masquerades . . . [and] their friends" when they returned to their Virginia plantation after an exciting sojourn in London.[50]

Some women valued social life for the intellectual stimulation it offered. When Alice Lee of Maryland returned home to Blenheim plantation after a season in Annapolis in 1774, she could not "divest myself of regret for leaving Town," adding tartly that "the genius of a Pope . . . must have vanished if surrounded by such perpetual Scenes of dullness as B[lenheim] exhibits." Many women must have found in sociability a welcome respite from "Domestic Business," which, at least one Virginia woman believed, "deprives thought of its Native freedom" by confining it to "one particular subject without suffering it to entertain itself with the contemplation of any thing New or improving."[51]

In 1747, a "young Lady" penned a verse, published in the *South Carolina Gazette,* praising "society" as "a Bliss design'd / To form the Manners and instruct the Mind; / By mutual Converse mutual Wants supply, / To teach us how to live and die." Writing under the pseudonym "Carolina," the poet urged her father to allow her to participate in social life, which she considered an expression of personal liberty. "Forgive, *dear Sire,* if an Offense it be," she concluded, "For *British* Fair to sue for *Liberty.*"[52] Like Alice Lee, "Carolina" recognized the advantages that sociability brought her. Perhaps the greatest of those advantages was education, which improved for elite women, as it did for their male counterparts, largely as a result of their changing public and social roles.

Like genteel balls and fine houses, education was part of the class-specific cultural ideal to which colonial elites aspired. Early improvements in men's education coincided with the emergence of stable elites throughout British colonial America.[53] Improvements in the education of elite women came later, largely as a result of new ideas about feminine sensibility and its social applications. Education prepared pupils of both sexes to be exemplars of a cultural ethos that accentuated the social gap between plebeians and elites and lent legitimacy to the authority of the latter. Young gentlemen learned to be enlightened and disinterested leaders, while young gentle-women were trained to be pleasant and improving companions for men both at home and in society. Similarities in the education of young women and men reflected their common participation in genteel social rituals, while differences in their training showed how gender determined both the extent and nature of their public roles.

Education, even for boys, was an unnecessary luxury for the rough and practical-minded southerners of the early colonial era. As late as 1687, one prominent Virginian asserted that because "Good Education of Children is almost impossible" in the colony, he intended to send his eldest son to school in England.[54] In 1693, however, some of Virginia's leading men secured a charter for the College of William and Mary, which opened in Williamsburg a few years later. In the coming decades, academies, schools, and private tutors met growing demands for the education of young gentlemen in Virginia and elsewhere. The Charleston area had at least ten schools that taught reading, writing, and arithmetic, besides at least three academies where older boys studied curricula that included "Latin, Greek, Prosody, Rhetoric, Logic, Natural Philosophy, . . . Geography, Chronology, Dialing, Survey-ing, Mensuration, Navigation, &c."[55] Although schools were less common elsewhere in the southern colonies, they appeared in some larger towns dur-ing the eighteenth century. Wealthy planters often preferred to hire private tutors, many of whom were college-educated, to teach their sons at home.[56]

Young men who learned their early lessons from private tutors or local schoolmasters increasingly left home to complete their education. Eighteenth-century Virginians sent their sons overwhelmingly to the Col-lege of William and Mary, though by mid-century they were attending other colonial institutions, most notably the College of New Jersey in Princeton.[57] South Carolina elites, who were on average wealthier than their Virginia counterparts, continued to favor the English universities, sending three times as many students to Oxford and Cambridge than to their colonial ri-vals.[58] Thirty young North Carolinians went to American colleges, though none attended an English university.[59] Students from all three colonies read law at the Inns of Court, though by the eighteenth century the advantages those institutions afforded were more social than intellectual.[60]

Although boys clearly received the more rigorous academic training, their education, like that of their sisters, was both intellectual and ornamen-tal. For generations, young men had learned, as they would continue to learn, the utilitarian skills that enabled them to manage plantations or busi-

56   nesses. The classical education they now received in schools and colleges, however, had no similarly practical applications. The willingness of even backcountry parvenus and debt-ridden Virginia planters to invest vast sums in their sons' college training shows the extent to which they valued learning as an emblem of social status. Richard Ambler of Virginia, who sent his sons to English schools, instructed them to "acquire such an Education as may set you above the common level & drudgery of life." Wealth and class privilege empowered Ambler to give his sons opportunities that could ensure the maintenance of his family's social position through the next generation. He pointedly advised them to work hard and to "adore the Divine Providence who has placed you[r] Parents above the lower Class and thereby enabled them to be at the expence of giving you such an Education (which if not now neglected by you) will preserve you in the same Class & Rank among mankind."[61]

Southern elites believed that education could mold the public demeanor and aspirations of their sons and, in turn, shape the public reputation of their families in future generations. One Virginia gentleman chastised his brother for neglecting his studies, claiming that the resulting deficiencies in his education made him appear "noways capable of the management of his own affairs & unfit for any Gentleman's conversation, & therefore a Scandalous person & a shame to his Relations." Eliza Lucas Pinckney reminded her sons that "the welfair of a whole family depends in a great measure on the progress you make in moral Virtue, Religion, and learning." Another South Carolinian asserted that "the name of a family always depends on the sons," though "its respectability, comfort, and domestic happiness, often [depends] on the daughters."[62]

Higher education prepared young men for public life by promoting masculine ideals of leadership and affording students the connections, knowledge, and experience they needed to attain them. In so doing, it also reinforced elite cultural solidarity and political authority. Between 1720 and 1776, nearly all of the 405 young men who attended the College of William and Mary were Virginians, many of whom subsequently served together on the county courts and in the House of Burgesses. When southern elites attended northern colleges, they forged bonds that crossed provincial boundaries. When they traveled to England to be educated, they acquired important business and political contacts and perhaps developed a sense of identity with other American provincials.[63]

Southern elites regarded education as more than book-learning, and they expected their sons to use their schooldays to gain worldly experience among their peers in preparation for public and sociable life. An early student orator at William and Mary stressed the advantages of situating the college in Williamsburg, the political and social hub of Virginia. In a more remote location, "far from business and action," he declared, "if we make scholars, they are in danger of proving mere scholars." Far from being suited to public leadership, he suggested, such learned men would "make a very ridiculous figure, made up of pedantry, disputatiousness, positiveness, and a great many other ill qualities which render them not so fit for action and conversation." Conversely, the proprietor of an academy in rural New Kent County, Virginia, reassured wary parents that students at his relatively remote school "would not be wholly destitute of the improvement of polite company, so necessary to the education of a Gentleman."[64]

By exposing young men to the wider world, education prepared them for politics, business, and sociability. Consequently, though some parents may have shared Eliza Pinckney's concern that her sons might succumb to dissipating "temptations," most urged young men to take advantage of their opportunities to acquire the worldly knowledge and experience that could enhance their future prospects. George Washington believed that "knowledge of books is the basis upon which other knowledge is to be built," but he did not think that "becoming a mere scholar is a desireable education for a gentleman." Richard Ambler, who enjoined his sons to attend to their books, also encouraged them to see as much of England as possible "but always be mindfull to keep good Company, such as will be able to assist you in making prudent observations."[65]

Such sentiments were conventional wisdom among gentlefolk by 1774, when the letters of the Earl of Chesterfield appeared in print and acquired widespread readership both in Britain and America. Chesterfield advised his son to learn all he could from books before being "thrown out into the great world" to begin the second and more important phase of his educational training. "Learning is acquired by reading books," he conceded, "but the much more necessary learning, the knowledge of the world, is only to be acquired by reading men, and studying all the various editions of them." To acquire worldly wisdom and a knowledge of human nature, Chesterfield believed, a man "must not stay at home, but go abroad . . . [where] you will not find it in booksellers shops and stalls, but in courts, in *hotêls*, at entertainments, balls, assemblies, [and] spectacles." He also recognized the importance of genteel manners and accomplishments — especially dancing, dressing, and polite conversation — for men who aspired to distinguish themselves among their peers and in society.[66]

Colonial parents also expected their sons to master the external manifestations of gentility, particularly dancing, which accounted for a significant part of their educational training. As early as 1716, the dancing master
William Levingstone was giving lessons to students at the College of
William and Mary. The college's board of governors valued Levingstone's
services so much that they offered him the use of "the lower Room at the
South End of the Colledge . . . until his own Danceing School in Williams-
burgh is finished." At least one later dancing master also catered specifically
to the "young gentlemen" of Williamsburg, many of whom must have been
students at the college.[67]

Because dancing played such a central role in the rituals of genteel sociability, southern elites deemed dancing lessons essential for both their
sons and daughters. George Washington regarded his stepson's lessons as
important enough to justify his leaving school in Annapolis to attend the
dancing master at Mount Vernon. Ann Manigault asked detailed questions
about the progress of her son Peter at a dancing school in London. Robert
Carter of Nomini Hall spent nearly as much money on his children's dancing lessons as he did on their academic training. Even the cantankerous
Landon Carter, who constantly criticized frivolous amusements and laziness
among young people, conceded the importance of dancing and hired a master to instruct his sons and daughters.[68]

Youngsters and their teachers took dancing classes seriously. According
to one observer, Francis Christian, the respected Virginia dancing master,
subjected his charges to "rigid" discipline. Mr. Pike, who ran a popular
Charleston dancing school, barred all visitors from his classes, maintaining
that the "coming and going of a variety of company, entirely takes off the
children's attention to their figures." When Pike and his rivals held balls,
they routinely invited participants to practice with them for a few days before the event so as to perfect their technique before they attempted to
dance in public. At least one young man confided, "The first time I danced a
Minuet in public, my Knees trembled," but six months of lessons and of
"taking all Opportunities of dancing in Public" helped him get over his
"foolish Bashfulness." Intent on cutting an impressive figure in Charleston's
polite society, Peter Manigault professed a "a great Inclination to be a good
Dancer," and after attending classes for six months, he "resolved to continue
learning a few Months longer."[69]

Dancing was the most essential ornamental accomplishment that young
gentlemen cultivated, but there is some evidence that they began to pursue
others as well in the closing decades of the colonial era. In the 1760s and

1770s, newspapers in Williamsburg and Charleston carried occasional advertisements offering French lessons and music lessons to "Ladies and Gentlemen." By 1771, Charleston also had a riding master who taught "Young Gentlemen and Ladies to ride, with the same Safety, Ease and Gentility, as is now practised in the best Riding-Schools in London."[70] Most notable was the growing popularity of fencing among elite men after 1770. Between 1770 and 1773, three fencing masters — two of whom also gave dancing lessons — advertised their services in Charleston newspapers. A Virginia master, who was also a physician, gave lessons in the "manly art of FENCING" in Williamsburg and York for an entrance fee of £1 and an additional 15 shillings each month.[71]

The education of young gentlemen thus diversified and expanded to prepare them for a growing array of public roles. Classical learning, worldliness, and personal connections gave elite men the influence and experience they needed to preside over the public affairs of their communities and to act as liaisons between their neighbors and remote political authorities. Ornamental accomplishments enabled them to participate in a genteel culture that enhanced their authority by fostering solidarity among elites and accentuating the cultural gap between them and their less cosmopolitan neighbors.

In the eighteenth century, the rise of gentility also provided the impetus for improvements in women's education. Although contemporaries did not expect young women to aspire to independence or public leadership, they increasingly regarded women as indispensable participants in the genteel social rituals that complemented and reinforced the existing social hierachy. Genteel sociability brought elite women into the public sphere to exercise significant cultural influence. Southern elites began to educate their daughters to fulfill these new social responsibilities.

Having sent their sons to college and dancing classes to acquire the manners and ideas of enlightened gentlemen, parents somewhat later sought to ensure that their daughters would be, in the words of one North Carolina father, "taught to write and read and some feminine accomplishments which may render [them] agreeable," as well as "what appertains to be a good house wife in the management of household affairs."[72] Southern elites wanted their daughters to be good mistresses, hostesses, and social companions. For young women, even more than for their brothers, the objectives of education were more ornamental than intellectual, but class privilege and the ideals of genteel culture enabled them to be far better educated than southern women of earlier generations.[73] Before the second quarter of the eighteenth century, few southerners worried about educating their daughters. Few letters written by women have survived from the early colonial period, but those that exist are poorly written, even by contemporary standards. Both the quantity and quality of women's writing increased dramatically by the century's middle decades, as did evidence of women's reading. Both changes signaled a growing concern for the education of young women, which roughly coincided with the rise of genteel sociability.[74]

Colonial Americans, like their British contemporaries, regarded intellectual women with a combination of scorn and curiosity. In the southern colonies, newspapers carried occasional stories chronicling the intellectual exploits of Italian women who "held publick Disputations" or took university degrees. Although the press did not denounce such women, it clearly regarded them as unusual, even exotic, and thus not potentially corrupting exemplars for Anglo-American ladies.[75] Colonial observers were more critical of intellectually ambitious women who were closer to home, both culturally and geographically, because such women could be more subversive of existing gender hierarchies. Margaret Wake Tryon, the learned wife of North Carolina's governor and the author of a book on fortifications, received a cool reception from some colonial southerners who viewed her conduct and aspirations as unsuitably masculine. Tryon unfairly acquired a reputation as one who dominated her husband and "took no notice of the Ladies," thereby upsetting the prescribed relationships both in marriage and in society. Among lower-class men, many of whom were illiterate, a women who even aspired to literacy might be regarded as a threat to male honor and authority. When Lucy Gaines, a Virginia housekeeper, decided to learn to read and write, her desire to improve herself outraged her lover, who "declared . . . that he wou'd suffer to lose his right hand, if he ever had or ever wou'd mention it to any[one]."[76]

Elite parents and moralists judiciously encouraged young gentlewomen to cultivate their intellects without compromising the sensibility and modesty that men now expected of them both at home and in society. James Fordyce, the Scottish moralist, recommended history, geography, astronomy, travel accounts, and natural and moral philosophy as suitable reading for young women, both as fodder for polite conversation and as sources of moral teachings. He even advised young women "whom Nature . . . has endowed with any signal strength of genius" to pursue "severe studies to every prudent length," but cautioned lest "they push their application so far as to hurt their tender health, to hinder those family duties for which the sex are chiefly intended" and thereby "relinquish their just sphere, for one much less amiable, much less beneficial." John Gregory similarly idealized feminine modesty, advising young women, "There is no impropriety in your reading history, or cultivating any art or science to which genius or accident leads you . . . [but] I think I may very probably do you an injury by artificially creating a taste, which, if nature never gave it to you, would only serve to embarrass your future conduct."[77]

Even those who advocated improvements in women's education disapproved of females who aspired to serious scholarship and public recognition for their accomplishments. "For my part, I could heartily wish to see the female world more accomplished than it is," declared Fordyce, "but I do not wish to see it abound with metaphysicians, historians, speculative philosophers, or Learned Ladies of any kind . . . lest the sex should lose in softness what they gained in force; and lest the pursuit of such elevation should interfere a little with the plain duties and humble virtues of life." Gregory advised his readers that "if you happen to have any learning, keep it a profound secret, especially from the men, who generally look with a jealous and malignant eye on a woman of great parts, and a cultivated understanding." Lord Chesterfield likewise wrote approvingly of Lady Hervey, an Englishwoman who "understands Latin perfectly well, though she wisely conceals it." Eliza Lucas Pinckney, who did not publicize her important experiments with indigo cultivation, received no public censure, though at least one of her Charleston neighbors warned that she would "read [her]self mad" and age prematurely, thereby rendering herself unmarriageable as a result of her intellectual activities.[78]

Women's education, unlike that of their brothers, was designed primarily to serve neither their own interests nor those of the general public. While young men were educated to empower themselves to exercise public leadership, their sisters learned to cultivate genteel sensibility and other qualities that would make them pleasing companions for men at home and in society. Accordingly, contemporaries championed women's education, just as they promoted the ideal of companionate marriage, for the benefits it might bring men. As one Virginia "Lady" asserted in 1773, education would discourage "Dissipation" in women and "teach us Vice from Virtue to divide," while promoting common sense, cheerfulness, and other qualities that would make women better companions and wives. "Be it your Task our Intellects to aid," she promised, "And you with tenfold interest shall be paid. . . . Be generous then, and us to Knowledge lead, / And Happiness to you will sure succeed."[79]

With domestic and sociable considerations foremost in their minds, southern elites encouraged their daughters to cultivate the desired practical, ornamental, and intellectual accomplishments without compromising the cheerful subservience that men expected of them. Henry Laurens, who advised his daughter Martha to read, also enjoined her to "be virtuous dutiful, affable, courteous, modest" and to "think of a plumb pudding and other domestic duties." John Moultrie praised his daughter Sarah for reading the Bible and instructed her to "read some other books too, for your improv[e]m[en]t, as well as for your recreation," but he also counseled her that "a steady, easy & Cheerfull obedience will at all times & in all places most certainly produce the greatest happyness." An anonymous South Carolinian cautioned his unmarried countrywomen to "endeavour to be *wise* without *affectation*," if they hoped to appeal to prospective husbands. "Let your *modesty* be accompanied with *gaiety*," he warned. "Apply yourself to *learn* what will adorn your mind, but be not *vain* in your own conceit."[80]

Because worldliness was not an objective of women's education, few girls left home to be educated, though some attempted to experience the world vicariously through their more privileged brothers. When Elizabeth Elliott sent her son Barnard to London to be educated, she asked him to give his sisters "an Account of every thing worth notice, very minutely for we long to have a full Account of that City and Country." Nancy and Polly Spotswood, whose brother John was a student at Eton, prevailed on him to tell them "a deal about" England when he returned to Virginia. Eleven-year-old Betty Pratt quickly recognized the advantages gender afforded her younger brother when he left home for school in England. "I find you have got the start of me in learning very much," she sadly observed, "for you write better already than I can expect to do as long as I live."[81]

At home or in the custody of female relations, young girls learned both domestic skills and manners appropriate to the social position of their families. Maria Taylor Byrd taught her six-year-old granddaughter to sew and tried to prevent her from playing with the "servants & Negro children . . . from whom she has learnt a dreadfull collection of words." Anne Blair taught her young niece Betsey Braxton to read and enrolled her in dancing school. Blair happily reported that Betsey was not "fond of Negroes Company nor have I heard lat[e]ly of any bad Words," though she did reprimand the girl for "not keeping the Head smooth." Lucy Carter of Sabine Hall, whose mother had died several years earlier, spent the winter of 1765 with a married sister, who probably taught her how to manage a genteel household. Maria Carter of Cleve lived for a time with a married sister in

Massachusetts, where she attended school and perhaps acquired the domestic skills she would find necessary in adulthood.[82]

Women's changing public role and growing social visibility also led some parents to take seriously their daughters' intellectual development. Some mothers, in particular, took a special interest in overseeing their daughters' education. Eliza Pinckney called the education of her daughter Harriott "one of the greatest Businesses of my life." Emelia Hunter of Virginia believed that "the fatigues attending" her nine-year-old daughter's daily lessons "are recompenc'd by her improvements and the Applause of my own Heart." Eleanor Ball Laurens attended to the education of her daughter Martha until she died in 1770 and her unmarried sister-in-law became responsible for the girl's education.[83]

Most daughters in elite families learned their lessons at home from kin or, less frequently, from hired tutors, but some attended schools to complete their education. Although schools for young women were uncommon in Virginia and North Carolina, they proliferated in and around Charleston, especially after 1760. In 1741, Mary Hext opened a boarding school that offered instruction in needlework, writing, arithmetic, dancing, and music. Between 1760 and 1776, Charleston had at least ten new boarding schools for "young ladies," and two more opened in nearby Ansonborough in the 1770s.[84] Of these schools, Elizabeth Duneau's was the most prestigious. A self-described "Gentlewoman . . . who has brought up many Ladies of Rank and Distinction, having herself kept one of the genteelest Boarding-Schools about London," Duneau taught her pupils English and French grammar, writing, arithmetic, geography, history, and "many instructing Amusements to improve the Mind." Her students also learned "all Sorts of fashionable Needle Work," and they took dancing, music, and drawing lessons from "Proper Masters."[85]

Other schools focused more thoroughly on academic subjects. Beginning in 1767, both male and female pupils at William Johnson's school in Charleston studied reading, writing, grammar, arithmetic, and geography, along with a "course of experiments in MECHANICS" and natural philosophy. In 1774, another academy opened in Charleston "for the Instruction of both Sexes." Its proprietors, an English clergyman and a university-trained French master, advertised a curriculum consisting of English, French, Latin, Greek, writing, geography, arithmetic, bookkeeping, algebra, geometry, and "different Branches of Natural Philosophy." Although the female students probably did not learn the classical languages, this course of study

Martha Ryan's cipher book, 1781. Like many eighteenth-century girls, this young North Carolinian probably received her early lessons from her mother. A knowledge of basic arithmetic and how to add pounds, shillings, and pence was essential for efficient household management. Southern Historical Collection, Library of the University of North Carolina at Chapel Hill.

was clearly the most extensive open to young women in the southern colonies or elsewhere during this period.[86]

Even among the gentry, most daughters did not attend such schools, but the rise of sociability and the demands of polite conversation encouraged these young women to read, while the expansion of the book trade made reading material more accessible. Throughout the southern colonies, moreover, women's reading gradually shifted in emphasis, from devotional tracts and practical books on domestic matters to works that would embellish their minds and prepare them to understand and perhaps contribute to edifying conversations both at home and in society.[87] As a young woman, Eliza Lucas of Charleston thus read Plutarch, Virgil, Milton, and Locke, as well as Richardson's *Pamela*. Maria Carter of Cleve read the works of Shakespeare, Milton, Pope, and Jonson, besides the fashionable *Spectator* essays and the sermons of Archbishop Tillotson. Mary Ann Elizabeth Stevens of Charleston read and transcribed passages from Shakespeare and Voltaire. Betsey Nourse of Berkeley County, in western Virginia, read Oliver Goldsmith's *Vicar of Wakefield*, a popular English novel.[88]

Family libraries were important sources of learning for elite girls and women, who usually did not leave home to be educated. Martha Laurens, who could read by the time she was three, learned Latin from her brothers' schoolbooks and later studied the medical texts in the library of her physician husband. Ann Carter, who, according to her husband, read "more than the Parson of the parish," could discuss theology and "the American Constitution" at least in part because she had access to Nomini Hall's library, which included some seven hundred titles.[89] Reliance on home libraries meant that women's reading often was influenced by the tastes and needs of the men around them, but access to books clearly broadened their intellectual horizons.

By the closing decades of the colonial period, parents were educating their daughters to be both ornamental and improving companions for men and capable domestic managers. These objectives dictated that women's education would remain inferior to men's, though it would be substantially better than in previous generations. At Nomini Hall, for instance, five of Philip Fithian's eight pupils were girls, whose education both he and his employer, Robert Carter, appeared to take seriously, but gender, more than age, determined the content of their studies. All of Fithian's students learned English grammar and arithmetic, but only the boys learned Greek and Latin. A sixteen-year-old son and two teenaged daughters took dancing lessons, but only the two young women studied music, which was in-

Many young gentlewomen studied decorative needlework as part of an increasingly varied ornamental education. Elizabeth Boush made this elaborate needlepoint picture, showing the biblical scene of the sacrifice of Isaac, while a student at Elizabeth Gardner's school in Norfolk in 1768–69. Collection of the Museum of Early Southern Decorative Arts, Winston-Salem, N.C.

tended to "raise the *sociable and happy Passions*" of those who heard it. Carter's eldest daughter, Priscilla, spent two days each week studying the pianoforte and harpsichord. While her younger siblings studied spelling books, the fifteen-year-old Priscilla read the *Spectator*, which epitomized the eighteenth-century ideal of genteel, improving literature — in other words, literature that cultivated the sensibility of its readers.[90] Gender clearly limited the formal educational opportunities of young women like Priscilla Carter, whose brothers would go on to attend the College of William and Mary.

Women recognized the advantages of learning, and some privately protested the extent to which gender inhibited their opportunities for intellectual growth. One Virginia mother wished in vain to have her "darling daughter educated in the best manner in England with her ever blessed brothers." At least one young woman thwarted her aunt's persistent efforts to "make me a notable needlewoman," recalling that her "love for reading was so much greater than for sewing that I often had a book under my work to look into as opportunity offered." Young Eliza Custis "thought it hard they would not teach me Greek & Latin because I was a girl," and later lamented that her tutor and her stepfather "laughed & said women ought not to know those things, & [that] mending, writing, Arithmetic, & Music was all I could be permitted to acquire," besides the dancing lessons requisite for all genteel young Virginians in the 1770s. Alice Lee, a contemporary of Custis who quoted Plato in her elegant letters, likewise complained that the "Lords of Creation" prevented women from learning Greek. "I must observe that I think we females ought to have an exclusive right to the Tree of Knowledge," Lee asserted in 1774, "since Mother Eve was the first that took possession thereof — which you know is all the right that the Europeans have to America."[91]

Elite women of Alice Lee's generation read more and wrote better than their colonial predecessors, but their education was designed to serve sociability and its objectives. Through sociability and its rituals, women participated in the creation of a genteel cultural consciousness that strengthened both patriarchy and elite rule, but as members of the ruling elite, they benefited from its dominance and wielded significant cultural influence. The culture of gentility brought elite women into the public sphere and thereby justified improvements in their education. It did not make them men's equals, but it afforded them educational and social opportunities that far exceeded those accessible to other women of their region and granted them a degree of power within the ruling elite.

Mama Reading, Philip Mercier, 1756. By mid-century, elite women read much more than had women of earlier generations. Literacy and education served both domestic and sociable ends, preparing women to be teachers and moral exemplars for their children and pleasant companions for men in their households and on sociable occasions. Colonial Williamsburg Foundation.

Gender, and especially assumptions about women's attributes, played a key role in the formation of a class-specific elite culture in southern colonial society. In different ways, elite women and men participated in the rituals of hospitality that illustrated networks of obligation and dependence, while the same women and men defined the culture of genteel sociability that accentuated social distances between elites and less privileged southerners. Gentility and its social requirements both expanded and constrained the social and intellectual opportunities of gentlewomen in the late colonial era. The ideal of feminine sensibility, which lauded modesty, compassion, decorum, and complacency, limited women's autonomy and self-assertion, while affording them access to the world of people and ideas beyond their households.

3

Revolution

THE REVOLUTION WAS A TURNING POINT IN
the life of Jane Spurgin, as it was for many of her contemporaries.
Wife of a slaveholding planter and justice of the peace, Spurgin lived
quietly and comfortably with her husband and eight children in Rowan
County, North Carolina. In 1776, however, William Spurgin declared himself
loyal to King George III and raised troops to defend the royal government of
his province. As a result, North Carolina's ascendant revolutionaries soon
banished him and confiscated his estate. William fled to England, but Jane
remained with her children in Rowan County, where she spent the war years
attempting to sustain her family and protect its interests from the state and
soldiers who "almost Continually harrassed" them, taking "grain, Meat, and
many other Articles without the least recompense."[1]

The Revolution effectively ended Jane Spurgin's marriage, and, equally
important, it politicized her and forced her to conceptualize her relation to
the wider political community. In three petitions to the North Carolina state
assembly between 1785 and 1791, Spurgin demonstrated a thorough
knowledge of the statutes pertaining to loyalists and their families. She also
gradually dissociated her own political conduct and allegiance from those of

her banished husband. Unlike William, Jane asserted, she had "always be-
haved herself as a good Citizen and well attached to the government" and
therefore found it "extremely hard to be deprived of the Common rights of
other Citizens." Although a skeptical legislature denied her petitions,
Spurgin's sense of her own merit and of the hardships she endured propelled her into the public sphere to articulate her perceived relationship
with North Carolina's new republican government.[2]

The Revolution significantly altered the political culture of American
women by discrediting some established modes of public activity while cautiously encouraging others. Beginning with the Stamp Act crisis of 1765–66,
boycotting British imports was the colonists' most effective weapon against
objectionable imperial policies. The proscription of imported goods and of
luxuries in general was tantamount to a rejection of the culture of gentility
in which elite women were so prominent. At the same time, however, the
imperial crisis and the war that followed brought women into the public
sphere as boycotters, essayists, and government contractors. After 1776,
moreover, women in the southern states petitioned their legislatures in unprecedented numbers.

In part because of its inescapable impact on their daily lives, the Revolution enhanced the political consciousness of women of all social ranks.
Boycotts and the wartime disruption of trade made households more dependent on domestic production, especially of homespun cloth, which became
emblematic of women's patriotism. War changed the character of women's
work, as wives ran farms and businesses while their husbands served in the
army or in government. In the southern states and elsewhere, civilians
weathered both physical violence and economic hardship. As the case of
Jane Spurgin suggests, adversity could be a catalyst for the development of
women's political consciousness.

From its inception, colonial resistance to British imperial authority had
grave consequences for women's involvement in public life. Although evangelical Christians, backcountry rebels, and urban artisans had previously
challenged the cultural pretensions of a self-consciously genteel governing
class, the politicization of consumption after 1765 led elites themselves to
reassess their fondness for anglicized gentility. In the short term, the prerevolutionary attack on gentility afforded women new avenues to public life
as boycotters and producers of domestic manufactures. In the long term,
however, it led to the redefinition of public virtue as a largely masculine
quality, as men took up arms to fight for liberty and women's continued

identification with genteel values and activities rendered them politically suspect.

Before the Revolution, insurgents in the Carolina backcountry produced the most violent opposition to gentry dominance and the culture on which it rested. The North Carolina Regulators offered a trenchant critique of the existing order, assailing the moral, cultural, and institutional bases of elite political authority. The Regulators attacked the county courts, the militia, and North Carolina's Anglican establishment, all of which bolstered the elite's political and social dominance. Questioning the supposed moral and cultural superiority of the gentry, they decried corruption and wastefulness in government, using as their prime example Governor William Tryon's £15,000 palace, the premier symbol of the genteel aspirations of North Carolina's colonial elite.[3]

Protestant evangelicalism, which somewhat influenced the Regulator movement, posed a more significant and enduring challenge to genteel culture in the southern colonies.[4] By the 1760s, the Separate Baptists, in particular, articulated a system of beliefs that was fundamentally at odds with the gentry's social values. Early southern evangelicals repudiated conventional assumptions about class, race, and gender, ignoring earthly status distinctions and downplaying the social significance of race and gender differences. Baptists and Methodists welcomed white women, slaves, and free blacks as full and individual members of their congregations, sometimes even accepting them as preachers or prayer leaders. White evangelicals' acceptance of black southerners as their spiritual equals raised profound questions about the legitimacy of slavery, an institution at least partly responsible for the gentry's wealth and power. Moreover, early evangelical women, who were neither ornamental nor genteel, stood in marked contrast to their elite counterparts, who kept silent in their churches, entering the public sphere primarily to participate in the rituals of sociability. Evangelicals never sought a formal redistribution of wealth or political power, but by stressing the centrality of faith and the spiritual equality of the faithful, they challenged the social ideals of the gentry and thus implicitly questioned the legitimacy of their power.[5]

While pious evangelicals and disgruntled westerners assailed gentility as a symptom of political and spiritual decadence and unwonted inequality, others made gender the focus of their critique of elite culture in both Britain and America. Even moderate writers who generally favored women's sociability and the educational improvements it fostered worried that social life might readily degenerate into frivolous dissipation. The usually sympathetic

John Gregory warned his female readers that "the natural vivacity, and perhaps the natural vanity of your sex, are very apt to lead you into a dissipated state of life, that deceives you, under the appearance of innocent pleasure." Gregory reserved his greatest praise for amusements that were "connected with qualities really useful, as different kinds of women's work, and all the domestic concerns of a family."[6]

Before the Revolution, most elite men and women never seriously considered renouncing gentility and its rituals, but some did worry about the moral and intellectual costs of excessive sociability. As a young woman, Eliza Lucas enjoyed playing cards, going to balls, and other social amusements, but, having internalized the prevailing stereotypes of feminine frivolity, she admitted that the "danger [that] arises from the too frequent indulging of our selves in [balls and parties] . . . tends to *effaminate* the mind." Martha Laurens worried that endless talk of "laces, dresses, ornaments, and finery . . . of this party, that set, and other amusements" kept her from her religious devotions, and Emelia Hunter echoed the concerns of conservative moralists when she worried that "a Constant Succession of Pleasures and Amusements" would interfere with her maternal duties. Landon Carter conceded the advantages of dancing but believed that frequent lessons distracted youngsters from their studies.[7]

Elite ambivalence toward sociability and conspicuous consumption was most evident after 1763, when the colonial economy became depressed after the conclusion of the French and Indian War.[8] That ambivalence acquired an added political dimension when merchants in New York, Boston, and Philadelphia organized an intercolonial boycott of British imports to protest the Stamp Act of 1765, which empowered Parliament to tax the colonists without their consent and, as a result, set off a storm of ultimately successful resistance throughout the British provinces in America. Led by the radical Sons of Liberty, the colonists later reinstated nonimportation in response to the Townshend Revenue Act of 1767. That boycott dissipated in 1770, when Parliament repealed all the offensive levies except the tax on tea. Some provincials continued to abjure the dutied tea, and the passage of the Tea Act of 1773 formally revived the colonial boycott of that commodity. Finally, in 1774, all thirteen mainland colonies adopted the Continental Association, which mandated a general ban on British imports in response to the Coercive Acts, which Parliament passed to punish the colonists for the Boston Tea Party.[9]

During the imperial crisis, nonimportation had both cultural and political significance. Economic sanctions were the colonists' most effective weapon against Parliament's offensive measures. Twice during the 1760s, colonial boycotts produced changes in British imperial policy. But renouncing imported luxuries also allowed the colonists to perceive themselves as virtuous and therefore deserving of the rights and liberties they cherished. The virtue they ascribed to themselves as a result of abjuring imported amenities became an integral part of their emerging national consciousness. At a time when many moralists and political theorists deemed luxury both morally and politically corrupting, the colonists identified luxury as the source of their economic, political, and cultural dependence. By divesting themselves of British luxuries, colonial women and men would preserve their liberties by regaining their virtue and asserting their independence.[10]

In the southern colonies, entrenched elites led the fight to preserve American liberty. In Virginia and the Carolinas, Charleston was the only community in which large numbers of artisans and mechanics took the initiative and pressed local elites to take a hard line against British imperial policies. Throughout the colonies, however, patriots — whether elite or plebeian — promoted popular resistance to parliamentary legislation. Because only mass support could ensure the success of nonimportation and nonconsumption, the implementation of economic sanctions necessarily brought previously quiescent groups into the public sphere and encouraged them to act politically. Accordingly, southern women participated in the resistance movement, despite widespread prejudices against female involvement in most aspects of political life.[11]

Continued participation in the rituals of genteel sociability may have provided the first step in the politicization of elite women, especially those residing in rural areas far removed from the protests and provincial congresses. Women who attended genteel balls and dinners witnessed or took part in political rituals and conversations in the 1760s and 1770s. In 1766, the *Virginia Gazette* reported that a "large and Genteel company of Ladies and Gentlemen" gathered at the Governor's Palace in Williamsburg to celebrate the repeal of the Stamp Act, and that the "Ladies and Gentlemen" of Norfolk "made a brilliant appearance, and seemed to vie with each other in demonstrations of loyalty and joy" on that occasion. Three years later, the "Ladies" of Williamsburg, along with the female kin of visiting legislators, showed their support for the colonial boycotts of British goods by wearing homespun gowns to a public ball at the capitol. After Parliament enacted the Coercive Acts in 1774, balls became occasions for exchanging public news, singing patriotic songs, and drinking political toasts. When Philip Fithian attended a ball in Virginia in January 1774, he reported that all the women "did not join in the Dance for there were parties in Rooms made up, . . . some toasting the Sons of america; some singing 'Liberty Songs.' " At another ball in Alexandria, men and women drank punch, wine, coffee, and chocolate but purposefully avoided tea, the "forbidden herb" that symbolized British tyranny.[12]

For nonelite women, active and acknowledged participation in the resistance movement came much more slowly. The Stamp Act crisis, which marked the beginning of widespread popular resistance to British imperial policies, afforded nonelite men access to the public sphere but offered women few new opportunities to participate in public life. In southern cities and towns, as in many northern communities, crowds of men rioted against the Stamp Act and intimidated local leaders who appeared willing to comply with the hated legislation. Nearly five hundred people gathered in Wilmington in October 1765 to hang and burn in effigy a "certain HONOURABLE GENTLEMAN" who "several Times expressed himself much in Favour of the STAMP-DUTY." That same month, a "croud of Men chiefly in disguise" forced their way into the Charleston home of Henry Laurens, whom they wrongly accused of hiding the stamped paper needed to enforce the law in South Carolina. Shouting *"Liberty & Stamp'd Paper,"* the intruders demanded to search the premises and attempted to force Laurens to take a "Bible Oath" to prove his innocence. In Charleston, Wilmington, and Williamsburg, angry mobs stormed the houses of resident stamp distributors and secured their resignations. In May 1766, Charleston's Sons of Liberty also spent two days celebrating the repeal of the Stamp Act, partly by abusing the "many people" who had not illuminated their houses to commemorate the occasion. According to Henry Laurens, "Some people suffer'd very much in both the evenings of rejoicing." More ominous still was the spectacle of slaves chanting "Liberty" in the streets of Charleston to protest their bondage and call attention to the hypocrisy of their enslavers.[13]

Although women probably watched these riots, rituals, and celebrations, they do not appear to have participated actively in them.[14] Newspaper and eyewitness accounts of the popular response to the Stamp Act crisis do not mention women's participation, though contemporaries would report their involvement in later patriotic activities. As producers and consumers, women would come to play a significant role in the revolutionary movement. Nevertheless, southern leaders, who increasingly appealed to middling men, made few attempts to arouse or to recognize women's patriotism before the early 1770s.[15]

Some southern women, elite and plebeian alike, took the initiative and publicly demonstrated their public spirit before the press and political leaders called on them to do so. Initially, patriotic women took advantage of occasions that ordinarily afforded them public visibility, rather than creating new and potentially controversial ways to participate in public life. In April 1767, shortly after the passage of the Townshend Act, the Reverend Charles Woodmason reported that "50 Young Ladies all drest in White of their own Spinning" were among those who attended his Sunday service in the backcountry community of Camden, South Carolina. When elite women donned homespun to attend formal balls, they likewise used a conventional gathering as a forum in which to display their newly awakened political consciousness.[16]

Men, nevertheless, remained reluctant to appeal directly to women to support their efforts to influence British imperial policies. In June 1769, when the men of Charleston promulgated their nonimportation and nonconsumption resolutions, they mentioned women's role only implicitly, asserting that South Carolinians should promote domestic manufactures and "use the utmost OECONOMY, in our Persons, Families, Houses and Furniture." Christopher Gadsden, leader of Charleston's Sons of Liberty, recognized the potential significance of women's contributions, yet he, too, did not appeal to them directly. Gadsden worried that "the *greatest difficulty* of all" facing patriotic South Carolinians was "to persuade our wives to give us their assistence, without which 'tis impossible to succeed." Gadsden clearly relied on husbands to "point out the necessity" of nonimportation and to ensure their wives' cooperation.[17]

Although cloth was one of the most important items the colonists imported and women's clothmaking came to be emblematic of female patriotism, early attempts to stimulate domestic cloth production neither addressed women directly nor recognized the potential political significance of their domestic labor. As early as March 1769, the *South Carolina Gazette* vaguely reported, "Many of the Inhabitants of the North and Eastern Parts of this Province have this Winter cloathed themselves in their own Manufactures," though women almost certainly were the ones who produced the homespun fabric that clothed the colony's entire population. In June, "A Planter" encouraged his "Brother Planters" to promote local production of cloth and other items, as well as to "wear our old cloaths as long as ever will hang on us," without mentioning what women could and did do to benefit the colonial cause. In 1771, the *Virginia Gazette* blandly solicited homespun from "whoever has such to sell." A South Carolinian encouraged "families" to save rags for the local paper mill, though in most households this task would have devolved on their female members.[18]

Notwithstanding this lack of explicit encouragement or recognition, southern women increased their domestic production of cloth during and after the imperial crisis. When Nicholas Cresswell visited Leesburg, Virginia, and the surrounding area in 1777, he found "Spinning wheels and flax-breaks" for making linen "at every house." Thomas Anburey, who toured Virginia in 1779, reported, "The carding and spinning of cotton is the chief employment of the female negroes . . . and almost all the families in this Province, both male and female, are cloathed with their own manufacture, the superior class as an example to their inferiors, who are compelled by necessity." Similarly, on the plantations of eastern North Carolina, each household had a loom for weaving cotton and woolen cloth "to dress [the] entire family."[19]

Although southern women may have produced more cloth than their northern counterparts, southern settlement patterns and the plantation system inhibited public recognition of women's domestic labor. In the 1760s and 1770s, northern women who lived in towns or on family farms came together for neighborhood spinning bees, which publicly demonstrated the participants' patriotism and likely enhanced their political consciousness. By contrast, most southern women did their weaving and spinning isolated in their own houses. In many areas, the distance between southern farms and plantations prevented women from traveling to spend the day working with their neighbors. Poor white women thus worked at home alone or with other female household members. Many middling women had at least one young slave girl to help with their spinning and weaving. On larger plantations, however, slaves and indentured servants furnished most of the labor expended in large-scale clothmaking operations.[20]

Unlike northern women, who publicly presented the fruits of their collective labor to local committees and officials, southern women toiled in obscurity. White women working alone at home, making products for consumption by their own households, rarely had access to a public forum in which to showcase their accomplishments. At the same time, black women who worked on plantations could not be credited with either virtue or industry at a time when some slaveholders were becoming aware of the contradiction between the reality of slavery and the ideals of liberty they professed when they opposed British imperial policies.[21]

Rather than acknowledging that women were as willing as men to de-

prive themselves of imported luxuries, the southern press invoked unflatter-
ing feminine stereotypes to shame women into compliance or, more typically, to use them as scapegoats for the widespread violations of the
associations. Men trivialized women's political contributions, suggesting
that their innate vanity eclipsed any capacity for true political consciousness. When pundits portrayed men as vain or extravagant, they invariably
cited the example of the "macaroni," a man corrupted by European fashions
and moral decadence. By contrast, they ascribed such qualities to all
women, defining vanity, extravagance, and frivolity as essential components
of their nature.[22]

Prerevolutionary Americans did not invent the image of vain and frivolous woman, nor were they the first to associate femininity with a lack of patriotism and public spirit. Eighteenth-century Britons, who defined their
national character in opposition to that of France, contrasted what they believed to be the vigorous masculinity of British culture and the liberties it
cherished with the supposed effeminacy of French absolutism and aristocratic decadence. Over the course of the eighteenth century, moreover, elite
men, both in Britain and in British America, discarded their ostentatious
apparel — modeled on that of the French court — in favor of simpler styles
in subdued colors and fabrics.[23] Although men clearly remained avid consumers of imported luxuries in general, at a time when apparel was acquiring a new political significance, women were increasingly identified as the
chief consumers of extravagant clothing and accessories.

The denunciation of women as consumers of imported finery, which acquired a new urgency during the imperial crisis, had precedents both in
Britain and in British America. In 1739, for instance, the *Virginia Gazette*
reprinted a British essay that urged women to wear indigenous rather than
foreign fabrics, informing them that "should your Sex resolve by Degrees to
redress the Grievances this Nation suffers by the Importation of what
partly composes your Dress, you will justly deserve Praise, as well as reap
the Benefit of so reasonable an Alteration." James Fordyce also observed
that British women could support their country's continuing rivalry with
France by abjuring "French gewgaws" and letting "frugality and simplicity"
govern their style of dress. In so doing, the women of Britain "would practice that species of patriotism, which is the most proper for their sex; they
would serve their country in their own way." In the 1770s, colonial writers
likewise ridiculed frivolous women who adorned themselves with "Flowers,
Egrets, Lappets, [and] Ruffles" and condemned the milliners who promoted "London Fashions" among them. In fact, milliners appear to have

78   been among the chief economic casualties of the imperial crisis in many
southern communities. Prevented from importing British goods, most of
these small businesswomen closed their shops for good during the prerevolutionary years.[24]

Unlike the general colonial boycotts, which did little to enhance
women's public image or expand their public activities, the tea boycott,
which began in earnest in 1773, was a watershed in the development and
public recognition of women's political consciousness. The tea boycott focused public attention on a single item, one that contemporaries usually associated with domesticity and women's sociability. Consequently, women
almost inevitably became prominent participants in this latest colonial attempt to thwart British designs to subvert American liberties.

The tea boycott resulted in the first appearance of women's political
writing in southern newspapers. By this time, the press was an important
forum for discussing community or public concerns, but aside from an occasional woman who wrote on manners or fashion, propertied white men mo-
nopolized authorship and constructed in their own image the readership
they equated with the general public. Conflating citizenship with authorship and readership and posing as virtuous citizens of the public sphere,
such men presented their conception of the public good as rational and disinterested. In the process, they particularized and marginalized the views of
groups and individuals who did not share their own.[25]

During the tea boycott, however, women writers and men writing under
feminine pseudonyms suggested that women, too, could discern the public
good and participate in the printed discourse that was an increasingly vital
component of the civic life of their communities.[26] Essays by real and fictive
women were in some ways equally significant in that both sought to demonstrate feminine capacity for patriotism and intelligent public discourse, as
well as to provide public-spirited exemplars for female readers. In addition,
such writings challenged the assumption that authorship — and perhaps
citizenship, too — was necessarily a masculine vocation. They did so not by
seeking to promote women's particular interests but rather by claiming that
white female members of respectable families shared the political values and
interests of the propertied white men who dominated public life.

Beginning in 1773, southern women and men posing as women wrote
and published essays and verses describing models of feminine patriotism
that their readers could emulate. That year, a verse published in the *Virginia
Gazette* portrayed a woman renouncing her beloved tea table because tea
drinking "will *fasten Slavish Chains upon my Country.*" Another female poet

described her feelings on receiving "a handsome Set of Tea China," which, despite its beauty, she rejected as a "Snare" designed by the king's evil ministers to corrupt the colonists and violate their liberties.[27]

Other real or fictive women published essays that pointedly called on their "sisters" to be patriotic, thereby demonstrating women's political consciousness. On 15 September 1774, the front page of Clementina Rind's *Virginia Gazette* included two substantial essays written by women for women — probably the greatest concentration of women's writing to date in an American periodical and certainly the greatest in any southern colonial newspaper.[28] In one of these essays, the women of Virginia addressed their "countrywomen" in the province of Pennsylvania, where merchants were reluctant to support the intercolonial boycott of duties tea. The Virginians advised the "Ladies of Pennsylvania" to assist men in their efforts to "extricate America from the evils that threaten her." Claiming a public role for women in this time of crisis, they counseled their readers to "be firm in withstanding luxuries of every kind; but above all, as the most pernicious of all, that you will (as we universally have done) banish *India tea* from your tables, and in its stead, substitute some of those aromatic herbs with which our fruitful soil abounds." These patriotic actions would enable women to claim a public role as well as a historical legacy. "Much, very much, depends on the public virtue the ladies will exert at this critical juncture," warned the Virginians, who optimistically predicted that American women "will be so far instrumental in bringing about a redress of the evils complained of, that history may be hereafter filled with their praises, and teach posterity to venerate their virtues."[29]

Alongside the address of the Virginia women, Rind reprinted a recent essay from the *South Carolina Gazette* in which "A Planter's Wife" attacked conventional images of feminine venality and weakness and strongly asserted the responsibility of women to display both individual and collective public virtue in their country's defense. Because tea was "a matter which chiefly respects our sex," the author observed, "surely, my sisters, we cannot be tame spectators." By renouncing tea and other imported luxuries, she declared, "we shall . . . disappoint our enemies (who no doubt build much on our weakness in this respect) and greatly assist our husbands, brethren, and countrymen, in this their arduous struggle." Collectively, women could ruin the East India Company and, closer to home, strengthen the patriotic resolve of the men around them. "Every mistress of a family may prohibit the use of tea and East India goods in her family, and among her children," declared the "Planter's Wife." Women's willingness to sacrifice their tea would induce men to "forego the use of [imported] *wines*, which are equally pernicious; they will not refuse to pay this compliment to our self-denial, and public virtue."[30]

Writing newspaper essays for an unknown and impersonal audience was undeniably a public activity, but the "Planter's Wife" believed that renouncing tea and other imported goods afforded even women less outspoken than herself an opportunity to influence public life. Within her own household, a woman's political virtue could inspire her husband and instruct her sons, and, she might encourage the patriotism of others by refusing to serve tea to guests. The "Planter's Wife" also expected her readers to make their patriotism "evident to the world" by declining to purchase tea in shops and by appearing plainly dressed at church and on other social occasions.[31] By doing so, women could cultivate or fortify the public virtue of their neighbors and, at the same time, contribute to the success of the boycotts that sought to bring about changes in British imperial policies.

Like most of her contemporaries, however, the "Planter's Wife" envisioned women less as individuals than as members of households or families. She enjoined mothers, wives, and daughters to support the efforts of their sons, husbands, and fathers to preserve American liberty. She encouraged mistresses to monitor consumption in their households. In short, she defined women's public duties according to their private status and thus posited a distinctly feminine vision of patriotism and public spirit. Unlike many colonial Americans, however, the "Planter's Wife" believed that women and men had an equal stake in the outcome of the impending crisis, and she asserted that women should be prepared to sacrifice as much as men "in saving this devoted land." Women "who have fathers or brethren, husbands or children, have much to fear," she predicted, "but let not a single wish escape us that they should ever give up the cause . . . . Rather let us perish with them, and be buried together in the ruins of our country; and let our enemies remember, that liberty, as well as religion, will always flourish under persecution."[32]

The tea boycott inspired women to enter the public sphere and to experiment with new environments and occasions in which to express themselves publicly. While some entered public life by writing essays on timely issues, others organized the first American women's groups explicitly devoted to political activities. In August 1774, probably in response to the observations of the "Planter's Wife," some "respectable Ladies" in Charleston organized a meeting at which women could "converse and agree upon some general Plan of Conduct with Respect to the Article of TEA." Two weeks later, writing under the pseudonym Andromache, a Charleston woman reported that she and her associates had "engaged in a Promise . . . to reject, and totally renounce the baneful Herb" and devised a plan to promote the boycott among their townswomen. This group planned to "nominate a certain Number of Ladies, of the first Character," who would divide the town among them and visit its households "to obtain the Assent of every Mistress of a Family" in Charleston. "Our Countrymen have more than once been told, that their greatest Enemies are those of their own Houses," observed Andromache, but now the women of Charleston had "an Opportunity to manifest the Fallacy of the invidious Insinuation, or forever lye under the Imputation of it . . . . We agree . . . that the Complexion of the Times is truly alarming, and calls aloud to every Inhabitant of America, whether Male or Female, to exert themselves in Defence of those Rights which God and Nature has bestowed on us."[33]

Some North Carolina women also organized publicly to show their support for the tea boycott and for the more general nonimportation agreement adopted in October 1774 by the First Continental Congress. On 25 October 1774, fifty-one women in the coastal town of Edenton signed a petition endorsing the nonimportation resolutions to safeguard "the peace and happiness of our country." More dramatically, the women of Wilmington "burnt their tea in a solemn procession," according to one observer. The *South Carolina Gazette* praised the women of Wilmington for having "declined the use of Tea," noting that "such a sacrifice by the fair Sex, should inspire ours with that firmness and public virtue, so necessary to preserve . . . our rights, as British subjects."[34]

Women's private correspondence also shows a growing awareness and understanding of political issues, which increasingly affected their daily lives. The escalation of the "present troubles" alarmed Elizabeth Feilde of York County, Virginia, the wife of an Anglican minister. Feilde distrusted Virginia's Whig leaders, who "brought a Deluge of Calamities on this unhappy Country." She worried about the prospect of war and its attendant horrors and resented the social upheaval that threatened to disrupt her previously stable and predictable world. "I hope after we have been well jolted, jumbled & shak'd together," Feilde wrote, "we may by some lucky hit be thrown into our old Places and stations, that the world will settle into its usual course, & things move in the same order & regularity as formerly." A like-minded Alice Lee criticized the inclusion of "Ignorant or designing men" on local committees and declared that "many of the measures that are adopted by at least *part* of every Committee, [are] destructive of those very

rights they profess to protect, & if generally pursued will probably intro-
duce as much violence & oppression as we can possibly apprehend from the
Mother Country."[35]

Lee, Feilde, and many of their contemporaries felt obliged to justify
their frank discussion of matters that many believed were, in Alice Lee's
words, "unfit for the female pen." Women's genuine or feigned reluctance to
discuss politics suggests that they were unaccustomed to expressing political opinions, even in their private writing. Even Eliza Pinckney, who un-
apologetically followed political developments during the imperial crisis,
rarely mentioned politics in earlier letters to friends and relatives.[36] As the
crisis deepened, however, politicized women such as Pinckney, Lee, and
Feilde reported the latest public news, expressed political opinions, and
conveyed their nascent public spirit to the rising generation. Martha Ryan,
a young North Carolina girl, decorated her cipher book with patriotic say-
ings and elaborate drawings of American flags and ships named in honor of
John Hancock and Washington. Martha learned that in 1775 "The Brave
General Montgomery in defending the rights of America, fell at Quebec."
Educated at home in wartime, she most likely learned her lessons from her
mother.[37]

Still, many Americans remained skeptical of women's capacity to act pa-
triotically. When informed that Abigail Adams had written a letter expressing her willingness to suffer the absence of her congressman husband
"rather than live under any tyrannick Government," Landon Carter
doubted its authenticity. "A fine woman this," he sniffed, "if the letter was
not made for her." In 1774, a South Carolina Whig leader ignored women's
participation in the nonimportation movement when he asked, "Who that
has the spirit of *a man,* but would rather forego the elegancies and luxuries
of life, than entail slavery on his unborn posterity to the end of time?" Conversely, English cartoonists, who acknowledged women's support for nonimportation, suggested that the presence of women, blacks, and nonelite
white men undermined the legitimacy of the colonial opposition to British
imperial policies. One 1775 cartoon, "The Alternative of Williams-Burg,"
portrays a mob — which includes at least one black man and one masculine-looking white woman — forcing respectable merchants to sign the
Continental Association. Another depicts the Edenton tea party as a gathering of mannish crones, negligent mothers, and sexually promiscuous
women.[38]

Most men envisioned women at best as passive patriots whose chief role
was to admire and reward brave and virtuous men and, conversely, to with-

Martha Ryan's cipher book, 1781. This North Carolina girl showed her familiarity with revolutionary political culture when she embellished the cover of her copybook with patriotic symbols and slogans, including Patrick Henry's "Liberty or Death." Southern Historical Collection, Library of the University of North Carolina at Chapel Hill.

hold favor from cowards and traitors. One Virginia poet idealized the woman who "scorns the Man, however pretty, / However Riches round him flow, / However wise, or great, or witty, / That's to his Country's Rights a Foe." Two years later, a Charleston newspaper praised the women of Mecklenburg County, North Carolina, for publicly declaring their refusal to socialize with men who avoided military service. The *Virginia Gazette* likewise applauded the "young ladies" of Amelia County, who "entered into a resolution not to permit the addresses of any person . . . unless he has served in the American armies to prove, by his valour, that he is deserving of their love." When the women of Rowan County, North Carolina, took a similar position, their local committee of safety commended their resolve as "worthy [of] the imitation of every young lady in America."[39]

Especially in its latest stages, the imperial crisis forged a new moral consensus that made industry, frugality, simplicity, and self-sacrifice the bases

The Alternative of Williamsburg, Philip Dawes, 1775. Virginia patriots compelled merchants to choose between accepting the Continental Association and being tarred and feathered. Well dressed and wearing wigs, respectable merchants in this British cartoon stood in marked contrast to the unsavory and seemingly licentious crowd, whose members included both white women and African Americans. The Library of Congress, Washington, D.C.

A Society of Patriotic Ladies, Philip Dawes, 1775. This British cartoon satirized the fifty-one women of Edenton, North Carolina, who prepared and signed a statement endorsing the Continental Association of 1774. Because most contemporaries regarded women as inherently apolitical, these politically minded women were portrayed as masculine-looking and lacking the modesty, maternal devotion, and other qualities ascribed to virtuous women. The Library of Congress, Washington, D.C.

of public virtue. By cultivating these attributes, all Americans, regardless of class or sex, could become patriots, at least in theory. Women could claim access to the public sphere by writing patriotic essays or participating in rituals of nonconsumption, or they could show their patriotism by supporting male defenders of American liberty. At the same time, however, the Continental Association of 1774, which banned horse racing, cockfighting, gambling, theater, and "other expensive diversions and entertainments," discredited the genteel social rituals in which elite women were so prominent.[40] Women's continued identification with such activities made them politically suspect, while their proscription curtailed women's public visibility at a time when most white men found public life increasingly accessible.

While revolutionary committees pressured local elites to cancel their balls and close their theaters, they urged white men of all ranks to show their patriotism by heeding the call to arms. As martial vigor replaced gentility as a mark of prestige and public spirit and military encounters supplanted commercial warfare, gender became an obstacle to women's acknowledged participation in public life. The citizen-soldier, who willingly sacrificed himself for his country, came to embody America's dominant patriotic ideal. It was an ideal that was accessible to most white men but one that custom and convention barred women from attaining, whatever wartime hardships they suffered.[41]

In the southern states and elsewhere, women were active participants in the War of Independence, despite their civilian status. When men went off to serve in regiments and in congresses, they left their wives and children behind to run their farms and businesses. Civilians faced economic deprivation and sometimes physical violence. In the southern states, the heaviest fighting occurred after 1778, subjecting an already weary and economically depleted region to three years of warfare, which in some ways differed from the earlier northern campaigns. Racial tensions complicated matters in southern plantation districts, where the British offered freedom to slaves who turned against their Whig enslavers. Divisions between Whigs and Tories made the southern backcountry the site of some of the war's most vicious episodes, many of them involving the civilian population.

The war in the South had three distinct phases, each of which posed new challenges for civilians. The first, which lasted from late 1775 through 1776, featured British attempts to muster support among slaves, Indians, and other dissidents. Despite the burning of Norfolk and the bombardment of Charleston, a series of patriot victories resulted in the withdrawal of

British troops from the region. The war's second phase, which lasted more than two years, was a period of relative peace, though civilians still suffered hardships born of inflation, high taxes, and the departure of men to fight in the northern states or, in the case of some Tories, to begin their years in exile. During the war's third phase, which began with the British seizure of Savannah in late 1778 and concluded with General Charles Cornwallis's surrender at Yorktown nearly three years later, the southern states became the war's main theater. During this period, southerners witnessed and participated in some of the Revolution's bloodiest battles.[42]

Southern military recruiters often equated defense of country with defense of family, and emphasized the duty of men to protect their wives and children from a rapacious enemy. Seeking men to fight in Georgia in 1779, one Carolinian asked his countrymen, "where will we find secure retreats for our wives, our children, our negroes, and our moveable property" in the event of a British invasion? Another Carolinian called on "the awful Voice of your Country — with the supplicating Voice of a Mother, Wife, Child, or Sister" to inspire his readers to heed the call to arms.[43]

But most southern women could not escape the war and its effects on their households. As early as 1776, Anne Terrel of Bedford County, Virginia, the wife of a Continental soldier, correctly predicted that the war would bring hardship to the women of her region. Terrel warned that the British were "conspiring with our slaves to cut our throats" and "instigating the savage Indians to fall on our frontiers" to murder "whole families . . . without regard to age or sex." Their lives imperiled, women would also suffer economically as a result of the stoppage of trade and the loss of their husbands' labor. Terrel believed that women should "support ourselves under the absence of our husbands as well as we can." Although they were not "well able to help [men] to fight," she believed that women could devote themselves to "another branch of American politics, which comes more immediately under our province, namely, in frugality and industry, at home particularly in manufacturing our own wearing." Terrel thus recognized women's inevitable involvement in "so glorious a cause," and she believed that women's work and perseverance were politically significant.[44]

The war's first phase gave civilians a sample of the hardships they would suffer. Elite families could flee coastal communities for their inland plantations, but less fortunate civilians remained in their homes, having nowhere to go and neither horses nor carriages to carry them to safety. Those who remained behind risked physical danger and often witnessed the destruction of their homes and other property. On New Year's Day 1776,

Mary Webley "while suckling her Child . . . had her Leg Broken by a Cannon Ball from the Liverpool Man of War" that attacked the town of Norfolk. Webley and her family lost their house and "all their Effects" when the British burned their coastal community. Sarah Hutchings, who lived outside of town, survived the attack, but she lost her house in the "general conflagration." The British also captured her husband, who commanded a regiment in the local militia.[45]

Even friendly troops posed problems for civilians in contested areas. Wherever troops encamped, they commandeered and sometimes damaged the property of civilian residents. Families in coastal communities saw their homes destroyed by British bombs or damaged by soldiers who appropriated them as barracks. Whig troops who lodged for seven months in the Norfolk County, Virginia, home of Charles and Lydia Mayle damaged the house and other property, and the widow Elizabeth Elliott attributed the destruction of a warehouse on her property to the "negligence" of the militia quartered in it. Henry Laurens found it "melancholy to see the abuse of so many good houses in [Charleston], which are now made barracks for the country militia, who strip the paper-hangings, chop wood upon parlour floors, and do a thousand such improper acts." Mary Camp of Williamsburg complained that soldiers who built a magazine on her plantation destroyed her cornfield and took her firewood.[46]

By example or necessity, the presence of troops led some women to involve themselves directly in the war effort. In coastal Virginia and probably at the sites of other early engagements, the Whig militia depended on civilians to supply them with food and quarters, and they relied on women, in particular, to nurse sick and wounded soldiers. A Virginia militia captain brought one of his men to the home of Margaret Rawlings, who tended the soldier for sixteen days before he recovered from "the Flux." Maria Carter Armistead boarded prisoners in her house in Williamsburg, where one British officer died, presumably under her care. Other women later took up nursing on a more formal basis. As early as July 1776, the newly established Continental Hospital in Williamsburg solicited "some Nurses to attend the sick." Poorly paid, overworked, and usually inexperienced, women served as nurses throughout the war in hospitals Congress created to house diseased or injured soldiers.[47]

After more than a year of intermittent fighting in scattered locations, British troops withdrew from the southern states to focus their attention on New York City and its environs. During the war's second and relatively tranquil phase, partisan raids occasionally terrorized civilians in backcountry communities. One North Carolina Whig later recalled that his widowed mother, an ardent patriot who urged her sons "to be true to the cause of American liberty," was "tied up and whipped by the Tories, her house burned, and property all destroyed" in 1777 while he was with the militia suppressing Tory insurgents elsewhere.[48] Civilians of all political persuasions sought to preserve their homes and families from the violence that erupted from time to time during this period, but the most pervasive challenges of the war's second phase were economic.

When men left home to serve in the military or in government, patriot leaders appealed to women to work on their farms and in their homes to sustain their families and to produce commodities that could aid the American cause. In the fall of 1776, the *Virginia Gazette* informed its readers that women in Chester County, Pennsylvania, were "determined to put in the crop themselves" should their "fathers, brothers, and lovers, be detained abroad in the defence of the liberties of these states," and deemed the Pennsylvanians a "very laudable example . . . highly worthy of imitation" by the women of Virginia. A year later, the proprietors of a new paper mill near Hillsborough, North Carolina, called on the women of their state to save rags, fabric scraps, and "old Handkerchief[s], no longer fit to cover their snowy Breasts," to be used as raw materials for this "necessary Manufacture."[49]

Women's work was especially crucial in areas where the disruption of trade by British naval blockades caused shortages of most manufactured items. One Virginia woman regretted that the scarcity of ink — an item normally imported from Europe — prevented her from writing more than the briefest of notes to her fiancé during their frequent separations. In eastern North Carolina, the war and the resulting scarcity of imported manufactures led families to set up looms in their houses so that women could make "cotton and woolen clothes to dress [their] entire family." One Charleston woman later recalled that she "used to darn my stockings with the ravellings of another, and we flossed out our old Silk Gowns to spin together with Cotton to knit our gloves." Sarah Nourse of Virginia spent the war years patching her family's old clothes; she received a parcel of new goods from Europe only after the British surrender. Many women must have shared her preoccupation with mending, aware that cloth would be difficult to obtain until peace made possible the resumption of the European trade.[50]

By the late 1770s, shortages worsened and inflation soared as state governments issued paper money to finance the war and called on civilians to pay increasingly higher taxes. Wartime taxes and inflation were especially onerous for soldiers' families, who often suffered economically when men left home to serve in the army. At best, such families exchanged the labor of their men for soldiers' wages paid in nearly worthless government certificates. At worst, soldiers neither received their pay nor survived their enlistment to resume their participation in the family economy.[51]

When common soldiers died of disease or in battle, they left their families bereaved, impoverished, and often dependent on public relief. Elizabeth Black, whose husband was fatally wounded during the defense of Charleston in 1776, found herself alone with five children and "no friends or relations in this State from whom she can expect the least assistance." Black turned to the South Carolina legislature for aid, and was granted funds to return to her native Pennsylvania to live among her "friends and relations." Ann Meadows of Fayetteville, North Carolina, was "reduced to real poverty" by the death of her only son, "who Inlisted in Captain Rowans Company in the year 1776 and never returned to assist her in her old age." Margaret Irvine of York County, Virginia, saw her husband join the Continental Army in January 1777 only to die of disease a few months later. Irvine's husband died "much in Debted & having but very small property not Enough to Satisfie . . . his Crediters," leaving her with four young children "& Pregnent with the fifth." Not surprisingly, even some women who supported the Revolution were "in dread" of the possible consequences of their husbands' enlistment.[52]

Even for more affluent families, a man's death or extended absence could have dire economic consequences. John Seayers, who rose to the rank of lieutenant colonel and was considered a gentleman by his Virginia neighbors, died in battle at Germantown, Pennsylvania, in 1777. Seayers supported his family comfortably until 1776, when the Revolution aroused his patriotic ardor and he went off to fight for American liberty. According to John's widow, Frances, "his death was as fatal to his family, as it was Glorious to himself." Although he "had formed a Plan for Educating his sons, in the best manner that the circumstances of the country would allow, and their Genius's would admit of," now she worried that his death would leave her "indigent" and unable to execute "his benevolent and truly Paternal designs." Frances Seayers, erstwhile wife of a Virginia gentleman, now found her own prospects and those of her three children dependent on a modest government pension.[53]

Wartime inflation posed special problems for widows and orphans who lived on fixed incomes from estates or government pensions. When Elizabeth Crowley's husband died fighting the western Indians in 1774, she successfully requested a pension of £10 "towards the Relief of her Self and her numerous Family of small Children." Six years later, the "extraordinary & unexpected Depreciation of the Money" rendered this pension "quite inadequate to that benevolent & charitable Purpose." At least one North Carolina widow worried that inflation would diminish the inheritance of her fatherless children by enabling debtors to her late husband's estate to repay what they owed in depreciated paper currency. A group of men from Brunswick County, Virginia, echoed her concern, urging their state legislators to stem the rising tide of inflation and reminding them that orphans who "had been comfortably provided for by their Deceased Parents, are now reduced to that State of Indigence & Poverty as to depend solely . . . on the charitable Assistance of their Friends and Relations."[54]

Although most white southerners suffered economic reverses during the war years, households headed by women appear to have been the most vulnerable. In 1783, authorities in Princess Anne County, Virginia, seized and sold land belonging to residents unable to pay the preceding year's taxes. Women, who by virtue of coverture accounted for only a small minority of landowners in eighteenth-century America, owned twenty-one of the fifty-seven tracts that the county confiscated. Seven other affected tracts belonged to the estates of deceased men, who ordinarily left the bulk of their property to their wives and children. Thus women — the overwhelming majority of whom must have been widows — headed nearly half of the delinquent households that lost property as a result of the county's action.[55]

Shortages, taxes, and wartime inflation became secondary considerations for most civilians, however, as the war entered its third and final phase. In December 1778, British forces landed in Savannah and reinstated Georgia's royal government with the assistance of thousands of runaway slaves. The invading army then marched into South Carolina, plundering plantations en route to Charleston, where, with the help of reinforcements from New York and Virginia, the British forced General Benjamin Lincoln to surrender both the city and its defending army in May 1780. Cornwallis then marched his troops inland, winning a major victory at Camden and moving on into North Carolina. British fortunes deteriorated in the coming months, however, as General Nathanael Greene, the new American commander, led Cornwallis's army on an arduous trek through the Carolinas before engaging them in a costly battle at Guilford Court House in March 1781. Cornwallis retreated to Wilmington before marching northward to Virginia, where he was ultimately trapped on the Yorktown peninsula. Meanwhile, Whig and Tory militias fought a series of battles in the backcountry, including two decisive Whig victories at Kings Mountain and at Cowpens.[56]

During this major British offensive, both black and white southerners were unusually mobile. Thousands of enslaved men and women deserted their masters and joined the British forces; Continental and state forces impressed others to work for the army or to be used as bounties for its soldiers. Other slaves simply ran away when their owners left them behind unattended in their haste to escape the advancing enemy. As soon as the first British troops arrived in Georgia, many of the state's white residents fled to South Carolina. When the British occupied Charleston, many of that city's residents withdrew to their plantations upriver, just as many residents of coastal North Carolina and Virginia later would move inland in anticipation of the enemy's arrival.[57]

During this campaign, however, flight from the coastal towns did not ensure safety. In 1781, the Amblers of Yorktown fled first to Richmond and then to rural Louisa County — "a spot," declared young Betsey Ambler, "that I defy the British or even the d[e]vel himself to find." On several occasions, the Amblers narrowly escaped enemy forces, who pursued Betsey's father and the other members of Virginia's state government. "War in itself, however distant, is indeed terrible," observed Betsey during their flight, "but when brought to our very doors — when those we most love are personally engaged in it, When our friends and neighbors are exposed to its ravages, when we know how assuredly that without sacrificing many dear to us [or] our own lives, our country must remain Subject to British tyrany, the reflection is indeed overwhelming."[58]

Other civilians undertook equally difficult wartime odysseys. In May 1779, when a British fleet appeared off the coast of Virginia and proceeded to attack the towns of Portsmouth and Suffolk, Frances Bland Randolph Tucker left her Williamsburg home, planning to "send for the Waggons & move every thing" to Bizarre, a family plantation in central Virginia. Tucker returned to Williamsburg after hearing that the British had departed for North Carolina, but by January 1781, she, her husband, and their newborn child fled again, this time to Matoax, a plantation near Petersburg, in anticipation of what would be the final British offensive. St. George Tucker, aide to General Thomas Nelson, returned to the coast in two months, leaving Frances to make her way back to Bizarre in Prince Edward County, some sixty miles distant. Frances Tucker spent the next six months at various family estates, venturing as far west as Roanoke.[59]

Wartime migrations made food and lodging scarce in some southern

communities. After the fall of Charleston, the exodus from North Carolina's
Cape Fear region swelled the population of New Bern, where James Iredell
reported that refugees filled the town's houses and rooms, despite wildly in-
flated rents. Iredell himself incurred "monstrous" expenses when he stayed
in New Bern in 1781 — £160 a day for food and lodging. When Jean Johnson Blair moved her family inland from Edenton to Windsor, she found the
available dwellings "very indifferent" and admitted that "we shall live very
poor for sometime as there is nothing fresh ever to be bought here." Blair
crowded twenty white relatives and several slaves into the house at Windsor. "I hardly ever knew the trouble of keeping house before," she informed
her sister Hannah in May 1781, "a large family and continual confusion and
not anything to eat but salt meat and hoe cake and no conveniences to dress
them."[60]

Whether they remained at home or sought safety elsewhere, civilians
risked dangerous encounters with soldiers who roamed the region. Eliza
Wilkinson and her sisters-in-law left Charleston when the arrival of the
British seemed imminent, hoping to take refuge at a nearby plantation upriver. Shortly after they arrived there, however, British troops stormed the
plantation house, plundered its contents, and insulted Wilkinson and her
companions. The soldiers returned the following day to carry off more
household goods, clothes, jewelry, and shoe buckles. The women later suffered the visits of Tory bandits and American soldiers before abandoning
the house for what they hoped would be safer lodgings elsewhere.[61]

Mary Willing Byrd, a widow who spent the war years with her eight
children at Westover plantation in tidewater Virginia, tried to offend neither
Whigs nor Tories but eventually received poor treatment from soldiers on
both sides. In February 1781, American troops, who suspected Byrd of
helping the British, arrived at her house before daybreak, awakened her
and her daughters, and "made prisoners of [the] whole family." Byrd complained to the governor of "the *savage* treatment" inflicted on her family by
the soldiers, who entered her house with their swords drawn, though they
apparently neither damaged the house nor injured its residents. A few
months later, when British troops quartered themselves at Westover, she
was less fortunate. When the soldiers left, forty-nine slaves and several
horses departed with them.[62]

Frustrated by an unexpectedly long war against an inexplicably re-
silient foe, the British inflicted violence and intimidation on civilians
throughout the region. During a brief attack on southeastern Virginia in the
spring of 1779, four British soldiers plundered the Nansemond County

home of a Mrs. Straghn and forced three "young Ladies" to board their ships. When Cornwallis arrived in Duplin County in eastern North Carolina in April 1781, his army seized slaves and crops and forced local women "to deliver them the Rings off their fingers and the Buckles out of their Shoes." At several houses, the soldiers "Ramsacked every Chest & Trunk, took away all the Beding etc. all the appeareal even the Baby Cloathes . . . [and] Choaked the Children in order to make them confess if their Father had not hid his money and to tell where it was." Residents of the coastal towns did not fare much better. When Mildred Smith returned to Yorktown after the British surrender, she was shocked to see that "more than half of our much loved little town is destroyed, and many of these elegant edifices that to youthful minds appeared so magnificently beautiful are levelled with the dust, others that remain are so mutilated . . . as to grieve one's very soul."[63]

The most brutal confrontations between soldiers and civilians occurred in the backcountry, where the inhabitants were deeply divided in their political loyalties. Backcountry Whigs persecuted local Tories during the war's first phase, but the Tories got their revenge when the British later invaded the area. In the war's final phase, Whig and Tory militias engaged in a bloody partisan war. Soldiers on both sides committed atrocities, though the Whigs appear to have been less bloodthirsty than their opponents, whose ruthlessness alienated even some people who previously had been hostile or indifferent to the revolutionary cause.[64]

After the British victories at Savannah and Charleston, loyalist militiamen and British regulars terrorized the backcountry's civilian population. Tory marauders turned Whig families out of their homes in winter, leaving them without food or shelter. Loyalist troops, under the command of Lieutenant Colonel Banastre Tarleton, tortured the families of Whig militiamen to obtain information, and sometimes forced them to witness the execution of their relatives and neighbors. In the backcountry, where guerrilla warfare predominated, civilians also occasionally found themselves in the middle of armed confrontations. One North Carolina woman graciously agreed to share her meager stock of food with some hungry Whig soldiers, only to have her house become the scene of a minor skirmish. The enemy approached the house and the battle ensued, a militiaman later recalled, "while the woman was frying our hominy."[65]

In the backcountry, perhaps more than anywhere else, women were among the perpetrators as well as the victims of wartime violence. According to some reports, women were prominent in the ranks of Tory robbers, riding "the best Horses and Side Saddles, and Drest in the finest and best cloaths that could be taken from the Inhabitants as the [British] army marched through the country." Some Whig women shared this taste for partisan fighting. One South Carolinian claimed that the female supporters of the Revolution in his state "talk as familiarly of sheding blood & destroying the Tories as the men do," and the women who accompanied Greene's army may have joined the soldiers in burning Tory houses near Gum Swamp, South Carolina. The legendary Nancy Hart of Wilkes County, on the Georgia frontier, shot one loyalist, wounded another, and held their three associates at bay in her home until some Whig men arrived to finish off the intruders. Another Whig woman heroically joined with her son-in-law to fight off a party of 150 Tories who attempted to destroy a cache of ammunition at Ninety-Six, South Carolina.[66]

Few women demonstrated their political consciousness so flamboyantly, but many found other ways to show their commitment to the revolutionary cause. Mary Pratt, who served as housekeeper to the South Carolina state legislature, lost her job to "another person who was more attached to the British Government" rather than accede to the reinstatement of British rule in occupied Charleston. Margaret Monroe and Sarah McIver of North Carolina and Elizabeth Sinkler of South Carolina, along with countless other civilians, ran farms and plantations that supplied their state's forces with necessary provisions. Others, such as Catherine Park, who operated a Richmond tannery, manufactured goods that were crucial to the war effort. Many women, white and black, traveled with the armies as cooks and laundresses, prostitutes and plunderers. In 1781 the South Carolina company commanded by Captain John Irwin included twenty-seven men "for duty," along with thirty-eight women, eighty-one children, and eight "old men" unfit for combat.[67]

Elite women found more decorous ways to display their patriotism and to contribute to the revolutionary cause. Some elite Virginia women, including Martha Jefferson, followed the example of their counterparts in Pennsylvania and Maryland by organizing a fund-raising campaign among the women of their state to benefit American soldiers. The Whig women of Charleston visited soldiers interred in British prison ships and pointedly spurned the advances of enemy soldiers, showing "an amazing fortitude, and the strongest attachment to the cause of their country," according to one observer. In a gesture reminiscent of the prerevolutionary wearing of homespun, these "rebel ladies" also celebrated the victories of General Nathanael Greene "by dressing in green and ornamenting their persons

with green feathers and ribbons, and thus parading the streets in triumph."
One Charleston woman braved the wrath of the city's occupiers by refusing
to illuminate the windows of her house to commemorate the reinstatement
of British rule. Taken prisoner and shipped to Philadelphia, where she died
the following year, Elizabeth Heyward Matthewes paid dearly for her
steadfast attachment to the American cause.[68]

The war years posed new challenges for women in the southern states
and drew many of them, by necessity or by design, into the public sphere of
military and political life. Women affected and were affected by the economic hardships and armed confrontations of wartime. And for many of
them the personal and economic dislocations of the war persisted long after
the defeat of Cornwallis at Yorktown in October 1781.

Between the surrender at Yorktown and the signing of the Treaty of
Paris in September 1783, southerners celebrated their great victory with
balls, parades, and other diversions that had been rare in wartime. In December 1781, Mary Burwell reported that Williamsburg was the site of
many weddings and that the town's residents, for the first time in several
years, enjoyed a play performed by students at the College of William and
Mary. In the spring of 1782, the dancing master returned to Berkeley
County, Virginia, after a two-year absence. That autumn, residents of Camden, South Carolina, attended a ball, where they expected to "stuff ourselves . . . on minced pyes and nicknacks" and other delicacies.[69]

In celebrating their victory, some southerners rehabilitated the traditionally elitist public ball, making it more compatible with republican political values. The balls of 1782 and 1783 were more socially inclusive than
their colonial predecessors. At the Camden ball, for instance, "there was so
large an assembly that they coud not find a sufficient space for every one to
dance." In 1783, "all ranks and sexes" joined the "elegant and plentiful" celebration of the peace in Fredericksburg, Virginia. The organizers of some
postwar balls determined the order of dancers by lot, not by social rank.
When the people of Richmond held a ball to commemorate the signing of
the Treaty of Paris, a shoemaker's daughter drew the honor of dancing first.
Although the wife and daughters of the governor resented their loss of
precedence, according to one observer, all the other participants agreed
"that the lot should be as valid against any claims of rank."[70]

Such celebrations belied the personal and economic dislocations of the
immediate postwar era. After Yorktown, impoverished soldiers' widows attempted to collect their husbands' back pay or to secure meager govern-

ment pensions, while those who had advanced supplies to the state tried to recover the debts owed them. Wives of banished loyalists petitioned to regain confiscated property. Most sought their husbands' repatriation, but others chose to join them in exile.

Because most men assumed that women were apolitical or that a wife had no choice but to share her husband's political opinions, most states neither banished nor imprisoned the wives of loyalists unless the women themselves committed acts of treason. Although many women followed their Tory husbands into exile, others remained in America to attempt to preserve at least a portion of their family's property. The confiscation statutes of both Virginia and North Carolina explicitly guaranteed such women a dower interest in their husbands' estates, the one-third of a man's property that the common law customarily afforded his widow. In South Carolina, resident wives of banished loyalists could secure their dower rights by petitioning the state assembly.[71]

The treatment of women under the anti-Tory statutes demonstrated the ambiguity of their relation to the public sphere and to political life. Under ordinary circumstances, state governments subjected only men to loyalty oaths and other political tests. The preservation of the dower rights of wives who did not follow their husbands into exile owed less to the notion that such women exercised independent political judgment than to the assumption that they were apolitical, blameless, and deserving of the protection of a benevolent government.[72]

Recognizing the property rights of the wife of an exiled loyalist by presuming her political innocence, however, implied that she could be a distinct political being with an allegiance of her own. Some women interpreted the state's position in this way, emphasizing their own individual merit and claiming autonomous public identity. As we have seen, Jane Spurgin rhetorically divorced herself from her discredited Tory husband when she petitioned the North Carolina assembly to retrieve part of his property and to collect debt she believed the state owed her. When Mary Rowand of Charleston sought leniency for her banished husband, she admitted that "from his Education [he] had imbibed . . . favourable principles to the British Government," but she informed the legislators that she herself was "descended from Ancestors whose Industry and Valour Contributed greatly to the prosperity of [South Carolina]." Hoping to recover her husband's property, Margaret Cotton of North Carolina claimed that although he "imprudently took part with the enemies of America, . . . she and her children have been hitherto conformable" to the laws of the state. Another petitioner

98   attributed her husband's political offenses to mental illness and maintained that she and her family were "well affected to [South Carolina]." Florence Cook of Charleston, another wife of a dispossessed Tory, described herself as a "Sincere friend to her Country" who "has always endeavourd to inculcate in [her daughter] the love of Liberty and this her Native Country."[73]

Some families of Tories spent years attempting to reverse banishments and confiscations. These problems were especially persistent in the South Carolina low country, where the most southern Tories were prosecuted.[74] In 1782, South Carolina's state government banished James Fraser, a Charleston physician who served as deputy commissary of prisoners under the British government. Mary Fraser, James's wife, was torn between the duty and affection she felt for her husband and the "filial piety" she, as an only daughter, owed to her aged and ailing mother, who remained in Charleston after the war. Mary left South Carolina to join her husband in "a foreign land, where she was made to taste, in Common with her young and unoffending Offspring, the bitter Cup of Sorrow and Affliction." Later, however, she returned to care for her mother, and in 1796, with the support of 191 women who endorsed her petition, she requested a reversal of James's sentence, "which virtually banishes your petitioner and her Nine helpless Children." James himself petitioned the legislature the following year, but there is no evidence that the government formally allowed him to return South Carolina.[75]

The family of Robert Philp also spent more than a decade recovering his confiscated estate and then seeking to exempt it from the punitive amercement South Carolina imposed on all restored loyalist property. In 1783 and 1784, his widow, Mary Philp, petitioned to regain a portion of his confiscated estate. Having attained her objective, in 1785 she unsuccessfully requested relief from the amercement. When Philp died in 1785, she left as her heir an infant granddaughter named Margaret Campbell. In 1793 and 1794, Margaret Williams, mother of Mary Philp, continued to seek relief from the amercement, petitioning on behalf of her great-granddaughter Margaret.[76]

Women's postwar petitions suggest that those who remained at home without their husbands during the war learned a great deal about their family's business and financial concerns. Unlike women who followed their husbands into exile, who showed little knowledge of extradomestic matters when they filed claims with British authorities, those who remained in America knew what property their families owned and how the law could jeopardize — or in some cases protect — their economic interests. Mar-

garet Orde, wife of Captain John Orde, a Tory, knew that her marriage settlement gave him only a life interest in her estate, which she successfully re-
claimed from confiscation. Ann Williams and her husband, Robert,
anticipated South Carolina's confiscation laws by conveying "unto Certain
Trustees for her Separate Use, the Tenements where she now resides, together with Sundry Negro Slaves." When the state confiscated the
dwelling, slaves, and furniture of Elizabeth Oats, who had a similar
arrangement with her husband, she purchased parts of the estate as they
came up for sale, correctly expecting that she could later prevail on the legislature to reverse the confiscation.[77]

The economic dislocation of the postwar decades led Whig women, too,
into the public sphere to petition their state governments. For more than a
decade after the war ended, soldiers' widows continued to seek pensions or
back pay due to their late husbands. Hoping to secure the necessary docu-
mentation of her husband's military service, Mary Dorton "travelled a great
distance on foot . . . but never could get the Cirtificate to prove who was the
Commanding Officer of the Regiment to which her . . . husband belonged
. . . by which means [she] and her children have suffered greatly for want of
the bounty intended for them" by the government. Sarah Welsh, whose husband died in service in 1780, waited eleven years to request his back pay,
"being a destress widow not knowing how to or whom aplication was to be
made . . . untill it was too late." Jeanne Tols of Newberry, South Carolina,
had depended on her husband's fellow officers to submit her claim for relief
after his death in 1781. After waiting in vain for eight years for them to do
so, Tols successfully petitioned the legislature for "Such Relief as Your Ho-
nours Shall think fit."[78]

Many more Whig women — most of whom were widows and many of
whom administered their husbands' estates — attempted to recover lost or
stolen property and to obtain payment for goods they or their husbands had
advanced on credit to the state in wartime. In the quarter-century after independence, hundreds of women in Virginia and the Carolinas presented
claims for payment of public debts contracted during the war years, and at
least 129 who failed to obtain satisfaction from public officials submitted
their grievances to their state legislatures. Some petitioners, like Mary Taggart of South Carolina, spent years seeking restitution for property — in
her case a house and outbuildings destroyed by order of the American commander to prevent their use by approaching British forces. Others, like
Lucy Armistead of Virginia, sought compensation for food and livestock
supplied to state troops.[79]

Either because of their husbands' negligent record keeping or their own lack of familiarity with government procedures, some women had difficulty collecting what the authorities owed them. In 1792 Margaret Clendening and Ann Dabney both petitioned the South Carolina legislature for payment for the use of wagons and teams their husbands had furnished to state forces in 1779. Because neither they nor their husbands filed the claim before the legally prescribed deadline, the assembly denied their petitions, though both women claimed to be impoverished. Dabney was dependent on "Relief from the County," and Clendening was "Reduced to Necessatious Circumstances by the Ravages of the warr & the Loss of her husband." Mary Boush, the wife of a naval officer, who was widowed and left with "Six Small Children" in 1779, spent the next eleven years "Struggling thro' life without being burthensome to her friends or her Country . . . without any Support but what proceeded from her own Industry," before successfully seeking a government pension in 1790. Mary Cornhill delayed eighteen years after the death of her husband before applying for a government pension, explaining that "her own personal strength" supported her family until she "bec[a]me much enfeebled by age and infirmities" and thus reduced "to the necessity of soliciting the public Bounty by Way of Pension for Life." "Feeling a zeal for the cause of her native Country and of course an unwillingness to ask for a favour," Elizabeth Jameson survived with the help of the "continued benevolence of the Society of Free Masons" until 1797, when "her external resources failed her as well as her abilities for exertion" and she was forced "to cast herself upon the humanity of her Country."[80]

For such women, the Revolution brought more hardship than opportunity, more personal loss than political consciousness, but when they petitioned the courts, legislatures, and local committees for redress of wartime grievances, these women interacted with their government in unprecedented numbers. Although the right to petition was medieval in origin and accessible to all colonists before 1776, women rarely petitioned the southern colonial assemblies. Between 1776 and 1800, however, they submitted at least 780 petitions to the legislatures of the four southernmost American states and many others to county and federal authorities.[81] Petitioning forced women to define their relation to government and thereby contributed to the development and articulation of their political consciousness. The quantity and contents of women's petitions reveal both that political awareness and the extent to which the affairs of the public sphere encroached on and influenced their private lives.

By bringing women into the public sphere as petitioners, boycotters, essayists, and government contractors, the Revolution marked a turning point in the development of their political culture and consciousness. Some prominent southerners recognized this change, acknowledging and praising women's patriotism after the war was over. In his memoirs, General William Moultrie of South Carolina lauded the "patriotic fair . . . for their heroism and virtue in those dreadful and dangerous times," adding that "their conduct during the war contributed much to the independence of America." David Ramsay, an early historian of the Revolution, also reserved special praise for the Whig women of South Carolina, who "conducted themselves with more than Spartan magnanimity . . . [and] like guardian Angels, preserved their husbands from falling in the hour of temptation, when interest and convenience had almost gotten the better of honour and patriotism."[82]

Yet even such admiring observers did not envision a continuing public role for women. In 1796, Ramsay composed a hagiographic biography of his wife, Martha, in the hope that future generations would find in her an instructive model of American womanhood. He idealized her as a wholly devoted wife and mother, one who, despite her wide reading and obvious intelligence, "acknowledged the dependent, subordinate position of her sex." According to Ramsay, his beloved wife lived in contented domesticity, aspiring to be neither knowledgeable nor influential in public matters but only to wield a gentle moral influence in her household.[83] In the postrevolutionary years, many Americans embraced this ideal of domesticity, despite its seeming incompatibility with the recent history of women's public activism.

4

Republicanism

I N 1786, MARY MOORE SUBMITTED TWO PETI-
tions to the North Carolina state legislature. In the first, which she filed
as the widow of a revolutionary soldier seeking back pay due his estate,
Moore emphasized her husband's patriotism and honorable service to the
revolutionary cause. In her second petition, Mary Moore sought restitution
for her own patriotism in wartime, when, deprived of her husband's labor, she
ran the family farm and "performed many signal Services . . . to the Cause of
the United States of America." Moore witnessed the American defeat at
Camden, where she claimed to have prevented a cache of money from falling
into enemy hands. Conscious of her own contributions to the war effort, she
asserted a political identity distinct from that of her husband and sought
recognition of her service to the public in the form of compensation.[1]

Moore's rhetoric, like the services she performed, betokened political
consciousness but not the attainment of full citizenship. Barred by coverture from controlling property and by custom from bearing arms, women
could partake fully of neither the rights nor the obligations of republican
citizenship. Unlike many of the men who petitioned the legislature, Moore
had no other formal means to address or influence her government. White

male property owners asserted their sovereignty at elections and militia musters. The petitioning ritual, by contrast, dramatized the subordination and dependence of the supplicant, who humbly requested the favor of a superior. In a political culture that ordinarily presumed women to be politically powerless and economically dependent, the petitioning ritual aptly reflected women's official status.[2]

During the revolutionary era, few women explicitly rejected the disabilities that law and custom imposed on them, but many defied feminine stereotypes of passivity and dependence, playing active roles in the resistance movement and in the war that followed. Their wartime contributions and increased political awareness prompted an unprecedented debate on women's rights and duties during the postwar years, when national periodicals featured essays advocating public roles for women alongside their more conventional offerings. The progressive spirit of the 1780s, however, soon gave way to conservative reaction. By the 1790s, reactionaries throughout America identified politically minded women with sexual licentiousness and the turmoil of the French Revolution, and many looked to the patriarchal family to restore order and social authority. Men abandoned the notion of women as political actors, promoting instead a specifically masculine ideal of citizenship. Southerners, in particular, constructed citizenship to exclude both white women and African Americans. They celebrated white citizen-soldiers and their female dependents in their Fourth of July observances, reluctantly reviving the image of the female patriot only in times of crisis.

Before the Revolution, genteel political culture had accentuated class distinctions to strengthen elite authority and popular deference. Revolutionary ideology undermined deference but promoted stability and social harmony by downplaying the political significance of inequalities of wealth and status. By making the preservation of liberty the all-encompassing social goal, revolutionary republicanism also sought to make politics, more than even before, the sole focus of public life. By idealizing the citizen-soldier and the sovereignty of propertied white men, republican political culture downplayed class distinctions, empowering and even obliging white men to participate in public life. In so doing, it accentuated gender differences, rarely acknowledging women's past patriotism or envisioning them in future public roles.

Southern elites were part of the fledgling republic of letters that cautiously reconsidered women's public and private roles in the years after the Treaty of Paris. By 1787, two Philadelphia-based periodicals, the *Columbian*

Petition of Mary Moore, 29 December 1786. During and after the Revolution, hundreds of women petitioned the southern legislatures for compensation for wartime losses and redress of other war-related grievances. Mary Moore of North Carolina claimed to have done "many signal Services" for the cause of American liberty. Courtesy of the North Carolina Division of Archives and History.

Magazine and the *American Museum*, were providing select readers in every state with a combination of original American writing and reprinted English pieces as part of a more general effort to stimulate the development of a distinctive national identity. In 1786, the editor of the *Columbian Magazine* engaged printers in Baltimore, Charleston, and Savannah to serve prospective southern readers. In 1787, the *American Museum's* subscribers included 9 Virginians, 5 North Carolinians, 1 South Carolinian, and 1 Georgian, but two years later, Mathew Carey, the magazine's editor, claimed to have a total of 140 subscribers in those four southern states, including the Charleston Society Library. Carey used his contacts with southern printers and booksellers to make his magazine available even to nonsubscribers. When another Philadelphian launched the short-lived *Lady's Magazine* — the first American publication for women — in 1792, he similarly marketed his magazine through a network of booksellers, half of whom were located south of Baltimore.[3]

These three magazines, all of which ceased publication by 1793, provided a forum for a national discourse on women's issues during the republic's formative years.[4] Colonial newspapers and imported English magazines had provided readers with occasional essays on manners, morality, and education; now these new publications offered an unprecedented number of essays, poems, and stories devoted to women's issues, many of them apparently by female authors. After the Revolution, shrewd editors may have sought to profit from women's rising literacy rates by appealing to a growing female readership, or perhaps they regarded women's status as a timely issue left unresolved by the revolutionary upheaval.[5] Whatever their editors' motives, the national magazines published the most important discussions of women's status and condition in postrevolutionary America.

To be sure, magazines carried conventional essays in support of the sexual status quo, but they also included occasional criticisms of women's legal, economic, and educational disabilities.[6] In 1788, the *Columbian Magazine* treated its readers to a lengthy "Tract on the Unreasonableness of the Laws of England, in regard to Wives" — an attack on the common law doctrine of coverture, which still governed the legal status of married women in the United States. The anonymous essayist complained that the common law gave husbands powers that exceeded those of monarchs and rendered the legal position of wives "more disadvantageous than *slavery* itself." In 1791, an anonymous contributor to the *American Museum* criticized the social conventions that consigned all women, whether married or single, to economic dependence. "Instructed in no one art by which they can obtain subsistence," this writer lamented, "[women] depend almost entirely on their husbands: and when they have the misfortune to lose them, they are too generally reduced by the last degree of wretchedness and misery, to abject poverty." The author suggested that women be trained to monopolize certain occupations, such as the "whole business of making garments." Economic independence would ease the burdens of single life and widowhood, while providing new opportunities for those who wished to marry but suffered spinsterhood as a result of penury. Another contributor urged Americans to follow the example of Dutch republicans, whose "children of both sexes are . . . initiated in some line of industrious avocation . . . [to] render them virtuous and independent citizens, a credit to themselves and an ornament to society."[7]

Other contributors bemoaned the debasement of women in the patriarchal family. In 1789, "a lady" lamented the "hard fate" of women destined for lifetimes of subservience to their male relatives. The poet envisioned woman suffering under the "slavish chains" of male dominance, subjected to a "father's stern command," a "lordly brother," or a "tyrant husband."[8] Three years later, a woman who identified herself as a "Matrimonial Republican" took issue with the wedding vow of unconditional obedience that made a wife a "slave" to her husband. "The obedience between man and wife . . . ought to be mutual for the sake of their interest . . . . And it ought to be mutual for the sake of their happiness," she contended. "Marriage ought never to be considered a contract between a superior and an inferior, but a reciprocal union of interest . . . where all differences are accommodated by conference."[9]

Because women's contemporary status derived from deeply rooted ideas about the nature of the sexes, reformers challenged the time-honored stereotypes of women as innately weak, irrational, and best represented in the public sphere by their fathers, husbands, and brothers. To assertions of women's inherent timidity and submissiveness, the female "Visitant" retorted, "As maids, as wives, and as widows, we meet with a thousand occasions in life, where fortitude and resolution are absolutely necessary." To charges that women were naturally more vain and more frivolous than men, the "American Spectator" declared that both sexes had their "passions and propensities" but that the "different modes of male and female education create a difference of opinions and manners, which is merely artificial."[10]

Other writers agreed that women's alleged deficiencies resulted from their inferior education. An anonymous "Lady" assailed "that assumption of superiority, by which men claim an implicit obedience from our sex." This

writer contended that men used the "imaginary inability" of women to justify their own assumption of despotic powers. Men claimed that their physical and intellectual superiority made them women's natural guardians, but
this "Lady" called on the "daily victims of [men's] infidelity" to judge "how
worthy they are of the boasted title of protectors." She also questioned the
supposed natural superiority of men, suggesting that their physical strength
"may be chiefly attributed to the exercise permitted and encouraged in their
youth" and deeming their intellectual prowess the product of their superior
education. "Thus," she concluded, "it is the united folly of parents which has
brought on so wide a distinction of the sexes; not the impartial wisdom of
the Creator, who must equally delight in seeing all his creatures wise and
happy." If women were better educated, she suggested, they would not need
the protection of men, "but did our education disencumber [men] from our
dependence, they could not as readily dispense with the assistance" of
women.[11]

Postrevolutionary magazines also carried items that recognized
women's capacity to act independently and to contribute to public life.
"Julia" celebrated the biblical examples of Judith and Deborah and found
in England's Queen Elizabeth a more contemporary heroine. The *Columbian
Magazine*'s frequent essays on historical topics included one describing the
"exemplary patriotism" of the Whig women of South Carolina, who suffered cheerfully and visited American soldiers aboard squalid prison ships
during the British occupation of Charleston. Another featured an excerpt
from the journals of the Continental Congress, which in 1779 awarded a
pension to Margaret Corbin, "who was wounded and disabled in the attack
on Fort-Washington, whilst she heroically filled the [artillery] post of her
husband." Although other contributors denounced "female politicians" as
unnaturally crude and ambitious, these historical vignettes preserved important exemplars of women's public activism for the postrevolutionary
generation.[12]

Other accounts suggested the unique contributions that educated
women could make to their society. The press continued the colonial practice of reporting the academic achievements of extraordinary European
women, but such reports were now more likely to praise their accomplishments. One writer lauded Maria Petuncini Ferretri of Florence, who, "desirous of rendering herself useful to mankind, and especially to many of her
own sex, who often . . . fall victims to their own delicacy, has applied herself
with such assiduity to the study of surgery, that, in the space of a year, she
has enabled herself to add [honor and advantage] to science, to her sex, and

to her country." Another admiringly recounted the triumph of a female linguist who convinced the leading scholars of Spain that admitting women to the prestigious Royal Academy "would prove advantageous and honourable to our country." Closer to home, an American "gentlewoman" received praise for using her education and her fortune to open one of the first academies for "her own sex" in Philadelphia.[13]

Some reformers contended that the education of women was of special importance in a republic such as the United States, where the survival of liberty depended on the virtue of its citizens. In 1787, the *American Museum*'s list of "Maxims for republics" included the declaration that republican women must "be instructed in the principles of liberty" because "some of the first patriots of antient times, were formed by their mothers." Similarly, Noah Webster, nationalist educator and promoter of a distinctly American version of the English language, argued that educated women could play a critical role in nurturing the next generation of republican citizens. "Their own education," Webster observed, "should therefore enable them to implant in the tender mind, such sentiments of virtue, propriety and dignity, as suited to the freedom of our governments . . . . The ladies, whose province it is to direct the inclinations of our children . . . should be possessed, not only of amiable manners, but of just sentiments and enlarged understandings."[14]

Benjamin Rush, a Philadelphia physician and patriot, was probably the most influential proponent of the civic utility of women's education in postrevolutionary America. His "Thoughts on Female Education," an address delivered in 1787, was later published as a pamphlet and then reprinted in the *Columbian Magazine* in 1790. Rush, like Webster, contended that the education of women "should be accommodated to the state of society, manners, and government of the country in which it is conducted." For American women, he advocated the adoption of an ambitious curriculum that would include reading, writing, rhetoric, and geography, as well as more advanced courses in mathematics, the classics, and natural philosophy. Rush believed that education would make women better wives and mothers by allowing them to assume a "principal share of the instruction of children" and enabling them, when necessary, to act as "stewards and guardians of their husbands' property."[15] But he also believed that republicanism gave new political significance to women's traditional domestic roles.

Rush maintained that women could be instrumental in the preservation of the civic virtue and public spirit so necessary for the survival of republics.

Educated wives could inspire their husbands to good citizenship; "the patriot — the hero — and the legislator," he asserted, "would find the sweetest
reward of their toils in the approbation and applause of their wives." In addition, Rush believed that educated American mothers could ensure the
republic's survival by inculcating the values of good citizenship in its
younger generation. He declared that American mothers "should be qualified to a certain degree, by a peculiar and suitable education, to concur in
instructing their sons in the principles of liberty and government."[16]

Rush's arguments in favor of women's education emphasized the extent
to which educated women could serve the public good by fulfilling their traditional domestic roles. He did not suggest that women could use their education to fashion new public roles for themselves, though his ideas endowed
women's domestic work with a political significance it lacked during the
colonial era. Like most other champions of women's education, Rush never
wanted women to wield formal political power, but he envisioned educated
American women exerting political influence informally in their
households.[17]

Even in its heyday, this image of politicized domesticity, now known as
republican womanhood, did not dominate the discourse on women's place
in postrevolutionary America.[18] Two rival feminine ideals also promoted improvements in women's education and sought to define their proper roles.
Like the ideal of republican womanhood, these other feminine ideals were
accessible only to white women of elite and middling social ranks. The first,
a holdover from the colonial era, was that of the genteel lady who used her
education to shine in polite society and to perpetuate a class-specific culture
of genteel sociability. The second was the ideal of the virtuous helpmeet,
whose champions envisioned both the influence and activities of educated
women as wholly circumscribed within their households.

Postrevolutionary Americans who idealized the genteel lady clung to
the colonial notion of ornamental womanhood and, like their colonial predecessors, advocated women's education chiefly to perpetuate a culture of refined sensibility. "Cultivation of the female mind is of great importance,"
contended one contributor to the *Columbian Magazine*, "not with respect to
private happiness only, but with respect to society at large. The ladies have
it in their power to reform the manners of gentlemen, and they can render
them virtuous and happy, or vicious and miserable." Another criticized the
"absurd" custom of separating the sexes for after-dinner conversation. "Is it
not ridiculous to see a company of rational, and sometimes sensible, and in

other respects polite men, discarding the most beautiful part of creation," he asked, "merely to intoxicate themselves, degrade their natures, and engage in the most vulgar and indecent discourse?"[19]

Many more writers, who probably associated genteel sociability with a discredited and effete imperial regime, emphasized the potential domestic utility of women's education without according public or political significance to their domestic roles.[20] "The cultivation of those domestic qualities, which adorn the wife and mother," declared one essayist, "should be a leading object in female education" because "with these a woman cannot fail to encrease the happiness of a good husband, and to reform the disposition of a bad one." Another writer applauded recent improvements in women's education but warned that girls' academic training should prepare them not for political debates but for domestic life. "Few men . . . wish their wives and daughters to prefer Horace and Virgil to the care of their families," he warned his readers. Insufferable to men and incomprehensible to women, classically educated girls would, he cautioned, grow into bitter and lonely old women.[21]

In the southern states and elsewhere, this apolitical domestic ideal came to dominate the discourse on women's education, especially after 1790. Although southern readers of national periodicals were familiar with the ideal of republican womanhood, which they revived during the second Anglo-American crisis preceding the War of 1812, the southern press remained aloof from the tentative questioning of women's status during the adventurous 1780s. A decade later, however, southern writers and editors were ready to join the debate on women's issues, to which they devoted growing numbers of poems and essays. Their observations, however, ignored or disparaged the progressive ideas of the preceding decade and instead reflected the deepening conservatism of Americans in the 1790s.

"In our high *republican times*," lamented the Virginian Devereux Jarratt in 1794, "there is more *levelling* than ought to be, consistent with good government."[22] The postwar accommodation between established elites and political newcomers — revealed in the democratization of voting and officeholding, the dismantling of religious establishments, and the movement westward of many state capitals — blurred class distinctions among white men, most of whom now shared access to the public sphere via the rights and obligations of republican citizenship.[23] Such changes accentuated the significance of race and gender differences. Indeed, attempting to restore order to a revolutionary world, reactionaries made both African

Americans and white women targets of a stunning backlash in the century's final decade.

Like many poor and middling whites, African Americans sought to benefit from the egalitarian spirit of the Revolution. In the 1780s, some conscience-stricken white southerners, aware that the reality of slavery belied their libertarian ideals, suggested various schemes to promote its gradual extinction. By the 1790s, however, the growing assertiveness of African Americans worried many white southerners, who watched in horror as blacks in Haiti employed the rhetoric and ideals of the American and French revolutions to overthrow their white enslavers. Fears of real and imagined slave conspiracies, coupled with African Americans' vocal support for the Haitian revolutionaries, resulted in the imposition of stricter controls on both slaves and free blacks in the southern states. The Revolution had inspired northerners to abolish slavery either immediately or in stages, but in the southern states slavery was more profitable, and the presence of a much larger black population made whites far more fearful of the consequences of emancipation.[24]

Although the position of white women was more ambiguous than that of African Americans, it too became the target of a reactionary backlash in the postrevolutionary years. In the 1790s, progressive discussions of gender issues became increasingly rare in national periodicals, while paeans to patriarchy appeared with growing frequency in both national and southern publications. Still reeling from two decades of revolutionary change at home, many Americans worried that the tumult in France would soon spread to the United States. Because feminists were prominent in the French revolutionary movement, many Americans identified feminism and women's political activism with anarchy and social upheaval. Accordingly, many looked to women's domesticity within the patriarchal family to preserve order and social authority.

In the 1790s, American periodicals rhapsodized marriage as never before, emphasizing particularly the public utility of well-ordered private lives. "Society derives its best security, from the attachments which originate in the ties of Family," declared the *Columbian Magazine* in 1790. "Fathers, mothers, and children, are the surest and best pledges of fidelity to the Commonwealth." A contributor to the *North Carolina Journal*, whose observations were reprinted approvingly in Charleston's *Columbian Herald*, explained that family life served the public good by promoting religion and morality. "Agreeable manners and good morals are highly essential in a well-ordered family," he observed. "The [biblical] injunction of *relative duties* sink into the bosoms of all, because they are tenderly concerned in their application . . . and hence is formed the affectionate parent, the dutiful child, the faithful wife and provident husband." The *Baltimore Weekly Magazine* similarly deemed marriage "agreeable to the designs of religion" and "an institution calculated to . . . increase the comforts of society." In 1800, a Richmond newspaper described *Hymen's Recruiting Serjeant* as a "patriotic treatise" because the book's sole aim was to persuade bachelors to marry.[25]

Other writers pondered the links between domestic life and public order. In 1797, the short-lived *South Carolina Weekly Museum* responded to the radical question "Why is it necessary that Marriage should be celebrated according to the particular laws of a nation?" with an unimaginatively conservative essay that praised custom and tradition, marriage and family, as the bases of social order. Another publication perpetuated the ancient ideal of the family as a little commonwealth, suggesting that "it contains every branch of government, of executive and legislative power in miniature." While according women a degree of power over children and servants — the "subjects" of family government — this writer believed that each man enjoyed sovereignty in his house, just as men alone exercised sovereignty in political life. "A man, who aims at being a statesman," he observed, "should begin with domestic politics, because, he may, at home, have a great deal of practice upon those important questions which agitate the great world."[26]

Essayists and poets also bombarded readers with portraits of unhappy marriages, all of which they attributed to wifely shortcomings. Assertive wives, in their view, acted unnaturally masculine when they sought equality with their husbands or even dominance over them. Wives, they argued, should cheerfully obey and admire their husbands, who will then "delight in [their] society, and not seek abroad for alien amusements." At least some female readers internalized the ancient but increasingly emphasized notion that marital bliss was unattainable without a wife's submission to the authority of her husband. Elizabeth Foote Washington believed that most men who were "fond of going abroad" to gamble and carouse were driven to vice by overbearing wives, and she resolved that her own husband "should court my company." To that end, she vowed "never to hold disputes" with him and always to defer to his opinions. Because Eve "was told her husband should rule over her," the pious Washington concluded, "how dare any of her daughters dispute the point."[27] Such opinions were diametrically opposed to the antipatriachal views so recently expressed in the pages of leading American periodicals.

In their zeal to promote patriarchy and social order, postrevolutionary conservatives throughout the United States also vilified men and women who chose to remain unmarried. This attack on "old maids" and "old bachelors" drew on centuries of distrust and hostility toward unmarried adults, especially single women, though these writers expressed unusually harsh criticism at a time when Western moralists were increasingly tolerant of those who remained single. For instance, in 1775, the influential John Gregory told his female readers they could enjoy "a superior degree of happiness in a married state" but warned they would be better off single than married to bad men. Gregory and other late eighteenth-century writers praised the institution of marriage without making it obligatory.[28] After 1790, criticism of unmarried adults would increasingly overshadow such sentiments in both the national and southern press. Derogatory images of "old maids" and "old bachelors" were so widespread that both were included in an exhibit of thirty-four wax figures that toured the Carolinas during this period.[29]

Many contemporaries believed that growing numbers of adults chose to remain unmarried, fueling the anxieties of those already fearful of impending social upheaval. In 1787, one Philadelphian observed that the women of his city preferred "long continued celibacy," while a significant proportion of New England's women also chose to forgo marriage so they could remain autonomous. Such women worked as teachers, shopkeepers, and mill operatives in growing northern towns and cities.[30] After the war, some observers also worried that more southern women remained single, though the rural communities in which most southerners resided offered few economic opportunities and thus little prospect of personal independence. Eliza Williams Haywood of North Carolina recognized that the single life offered autonomy and happiness only to those who were economically self-sufficient. Single women "are much happyer, . . . all things considered," Haywood surmised, "but these must be Girls of Fortune, who lead a Life of Celibacy, or they are not Respected in this World, take my word for [it]."[31]

Although visitors to the southern states immediately after the war reported a scarcity of marriageable men in many communities, the first federal census indicates that by 1790 white males outnumbered white females in every southern state and in an overwhelming majority of southern counties.[32] Nevertheless, the decision of at least some men to remain single, along with the westward migration of young men in the postwar era, may have encouraged continuing fears of skewed sex ratios and heightened resentment toward "old bachelors" in this increasingly reactionary era. Attacks on unmarried men were rare in colonial newspapers, but they were relatively common in the 1790s. Critics condemned unmarried men as unnatural, troublesome, and useless to society. "I believe that women who pretend to hate men are good for little," observed one South Carolinian, but "men who profess to hate women are absolutely good for nothing at all."[33]

According to their detractors, men who refused to marry violated the law of God and made themselves miserable by withdrawing from society. One critic contended that the bachelor "lives a useless being on earth, dies without having answered the end of his creation, in opposition to the mandate of his great Maker." Another found "nothing that appears to be desireable, or can yield any comfort or satisfaction in the life of an Old Bachelor," and urged all unmarried men to "take unto yoursel[ves] a wife . . . and embrace the ordinance that was so early initiated in the world, and become a useful member of society." Essayists described the mythical "Bachelor's Island" as "a mere desert, incapable of producing any thing but nettles, thorns, and briars," inhabited by the sort of man who delights "in bogs and morasses but hates the generous warmth of the noon day sun" and cares nothing for "social harmony."[34]

Critics regarded bachelors as at best useless and at worst dangerous. One South Carolinian suggested that a bachelor, "like an old almanac," was worthless and ineffectual. Another believed that "nature never intended to create" bachelors, who were nonetheless "formed out of all the odds and ends of what materials were left after the great work [of creation] was over." Lacking the "finer passions" of those other "creatures intended for social enjoyment," the bachelor was "popped into the world, mere lumber, without the possibility of being happy himself, or essentially contributing to the happiness of others." Others worried that bachelors and the climate in which they flourished could be "injurious to every civilized country; and . . . subversive of unguarded innocence." One Virginian described single men as selfish, artful, hypocritical, and treacherous — all qualities that Americans understood to be incompatible with republican political values.[35]

Although postrevolutionary writers could be ruthless in their condemnation of unmarried men, their attacks on "old maids" were even harsher and more frequent because single women posed the more visible threat to social order by living outside of it. Contemporaries defined men according to their professional and social status and women according to the men they married, so unmarried women, far more than their male counterparts, undermined the existing order. A single woman was dangerous because she was a potential challenge to conventional assumptions about gender relations. Although many unmarried women were economically dependent on male relations, others appeared to aspire to an autonomy that contemporaries deemed decidedly ur feminine.

Critics chastised unmarried women, like their male counterparts, for their duplicity and selfishness. Some attributed women's refusal to marry to a selfish desire to retain the freedom of their "maiden state," but warned young readers that as lonely old women they would regret their decision to remain single. Others argued that most "old maids" were veteran coquets who had teased and flirted with "all the beaus" until the men deserted them for younger, prettier companions. One North Carolinian, lamenting the "extraordinary celibacy" among women "in every part of America," claimed that most women "look for general admiration, and prefer the empty compliments of a number to the sincere professions of an individual." Female readers encountered many cautionary tales of superannuated coquets who squandered their beauty and their youth in vain flirtation, only to repent in lonely middle age.[36]

Critics described "old maids" as domineering and emotionless at a time when most Americans considered modesty and sensibility women's most valued attributes. "An old maid is one of the most cranky, ill-natured, maggotty, peevish, conceited, disagreeable, hypocritical, fretful, noisy, gibing, canting, censorious, out-of-the-way, never-to-be-pleased — good for nothing creatures!" began one often-reprinted essay, which went on to describe unmarried women as man-haters who corrupted innocent "young ladies" by poisoning their minds against marriage. The author believed that an unmarried woman, unlike a wife and mother, "enters the world, to take up room, not to make room for others," and that her "heart is of all hearts, the most detestable" because "it contains neither sympathy, feeling, or any one thing pertaining to the *tender passions*."[37]

Selfish, unproductive, and overbearing, a single woman was not a woman at all but rather, like an old bachelor, an unnatural deviation from "the laws of reason and society." "Why is an *old maid* like a book in sheets?" asked one southern wit. Because she, like an unused book, remained unpenetrated by man and thus contributed nothing to the commonwealth. By the early decades of the nineteenth century, male physicians even argued that a woman's decision to violate her sex's natural disposition to marriage and motherhood could be hazardous to her health. James Ewell, author of a popular southern medical compendium, believed that "unmarried or barren women" were particularly susceptible to "hysteric-fits" during their childbearing years. Subsequent writers developed an extensive pathology of feminine disorders, many of which they attributed to women's failure to fulfill their biological destinies by becoming wives and mothers.[38]

Postrevolutionary writers who urged women to marry and bear children also discouraged their participation in public life, thereby mounting a two-pronged offensive against the notion of women's citizenship. First, they promoted the long-standing stereotypes that portrayed women as vain, frivolous, passive, and irrational and contended that these qualities undermined their capacity for public spirit. Second, beginning in the late 1790s especially, they attacked and ridiculed women who sought formal access to the public sphere by engaging in activities that were overtly political.

During the economically depressed postwar years, male orators and essayists bemoaned the fate of the republic, reviving the images and rhetoric of the colonial boycotts, which attributed the nation's lack of civic virtue at least partly to the vanity and extravagance of its women. Moralists described formal balls and dinners as "fashionable female amusements" that generated increased demand for imported luxuries, which jeopardized the economy of the United States and the virtue of its people. In 1787, a Fourth of July speaker cautioned listeners in Petersburg, Virginia, against a "general decay of public and private virtue," which he partly attributed to "a rapid increase of luxury and dissipation [and] a strong passion for foreign frippery and foreign vices."[39]

Others censured women's allegedly "natural propensity to parade and ostentation," portraying them as unpatriotically covetous of foreign manufactures. "Your country is independent of European power," one essayist declared in 1787, "and your modes of dress should be independent of a group of coquettes, milliners, and manufacturers, who . . . endeavour to enslave the fancy of the whole world." Another writer praised "our *homespun* and our *own* fashions," urging women readers to have "the patriotism to disappoint both Gaul and Albion in their arts, to drain your every copper for their trifles and baubles." A South Carolinian portrayed fashion as "a tyrant," implying that women's regard for fashion made them agents of tyranny and thus politically suspect.[40]

Proponents of this gendered critique of extravagance believed that feminine vanity had political ramifications, but they did not accuse covetous women of purposefully plotting to sabotage the American republic. Instead, like their colonial predecessors who made women the scapegoats for the imperfect compliance with nonimportation, they portrayed women as politically apathetic or ignorant and naturally susceptible to the allures of fashion and luxury. Polemicists lampooned male vanity much less frequently; when they did so, they portrayed vain men as reprehensible but politically conscious. In the 1789 dialogue between the fictional dandies Will Toilet and Bobby Button, Toilet declared his hatred for the "levelling" principles of American republicanism. "Our boasted independence I wished to the devil," he confessed, "and sighed for a speedy re-establishment of British government and British modes." Disappointed on learning that "Washington and some others in the new Congress dressed in homespun," Toilet "thought it high time to leave a stupid savage country." His clothes, unlike those of fashionable women, were emblematic of social and political principles. Toilet could not change his style of dress without altering his politics.[41]

Criticism of politically active women was a logical corollary to the belief that they were innately apolitical and thus best suited to domestic life. The outcry against public women did not begin in earnest until the late 1790s, perhaps because few Americans expressly advocated women's formal participation in political life. Both southern newspapers and national magazines printed essays sympathetic to public women as diverse as the English feminist Mary Wollstonecraft, the radical English historian Catherine Macauley, and Charlotte Corday, the French woman who assassinated Jean-Paul Marat in 1793 in an ill-fated attempt to stop the Reign of Terror.[42] Wollstonecraft's *Vindication of the Rights of Woman* was published in the United States in 1792 and received mildly favorable reviews. American reviewers approved of Wollstonecraft's republicanism and her advocacy of women's education, but they ignored her work's most radically egalitarian implications.[43]

Americans avidly discussed Wollstonecraft's feminism only after 1798, when the publication of William Godwin's *Memoirs of Mary Wollstonecraft* revealed a scandalous private life and destroyed her previously respectable public reputation. If the Izards of South Carolina were typical, well-read southerners were aware of Wollstonecraft's book as early as 1792, but they did not read it until after the appearance of Godwin's *Memoirs*. In 1801, Alice DeLancey Izard reported to her daughter that she and her husband were reading Wollstonecraft's treatise, though they considered its author "a vulgar, impudent Hussy." Unlike Wollstonecraft, Izard believed that the "great author of Nature has stamped a different character on each sex, [and] that character ought to be cultivated in a distinct manner to make each equally useful & equally amiable." A woman could act "like a guardian Angel" by quietly inspiring men to do good, Izard believed, but she should

not participate directly in public life. Her daughter Margaret Izard Manigault agreed, adding that Wollstonecraft's radical ideas "did not succeed in
making her [life] a happy one."[44]

In the wake of Wollstonecraft's disgrace and America's increasing disil-
lusion with French republicanism, the discrediting of feminist ideas paved
the way for the proscription of public women. In the decade following 1798,
public discussions of women's political activities were rare and overwhelmingly critical. Three short-lived Charleston magazines, all published between 1805 and 1807, denounced the progressive and feminist ideals that
Americans had come to identify with anarchy, irreligion, and sexual promiscuity. The editors of *Monthly Register, and Review of the United States* condemned such "books, which, under the most treacherous and seductive
form, contain the most deadly poison to the morals of society," and pledged
to use their magazine to promote the "improvement of the public mind and
morals" by exposing the follies of deism, atheism, and other dangerous liberal philosophies. The *Charleston Spectator and Ladies Literary Portfolio* — the
first southern women's magazine — included among its first fictional offerings the tale of a "female philosopher" whose progressive ideas and lack of
modesty led to her seduction and ruin at the hands of a man who married
another soon thereafter.[45] In 1807, the *Monthly Review and Literary Miscellany
of the United States* denounced as "ridiculous" the 1792 proposals of a French
champion of women's political rights, including one "to raise an army of
thirty thousand women, [and] another, that women . . . be admitted into
every part of the administration." Clearly, the editors regarded feminism as
one of the more bizarre excesses of a now discredited revolution.[46]

The eventual rejection of gender equality and celebration of women's
distinctively subservient and apolitical domestic role typified the emerging
consensus on women's place after 1790. Despite some imaginative recent attempts to bring women into the public sphere or, more commonly, to invest
their domestic activities with greater political significance, Americans increasingly held that respectable women ought not to participate in public
life. White southerners, in particular, construed patriotism as a uniquely
masculine attribute, despite compelling evidence of women's continuing patriotism and political consciousness.

By undermining traditional ties of patronage and dependency, by rejecting privilege and emphasizing instead the rights and responsibilities of all
citizens, the Revolution separated the public and private spheres and valorized public life.[47] By the 1790s, most southerners probably believed that

women's place was in the private sphere and that their private or domestic activities had little public significance. Conversely, they equated the public sphere with the affairs of the republican polity and described patriots as men who had rights and obligations in addition to — and sometimes at odds with — those that pertained to private life. "A true patriot must be a virtuous man!" exclaimed one South Carolinian, whose "wife and children, though dearer than life, are nothing when his country demands the sacrifice."[48]

In the postrevolutionary era, however, southern women participated both directly and indirectly in political life. Elite women, unlike their colonial forebears, increasingly discussed public matters, and small but growing numbers of women of all classes interacted with their government as petitioners. Others influenced the outcomes of elections or contributed to newspaper debates on public issues. Few southern women claimed the rights and obligations of republican citizenship, but many demonstrated a new political consciousness.

Women's involvement in the Revolution led them to question the conventions that discouraged them from discussing and learning about public matters. Women like the North Carolina tavern keeper Elizabeth Steele, who read Tom Paine, followed the progress of troops and diplomacy, and lent gold and silver to the Continental Army, were unlikely to lose their interest in public affairs after the war was over. Young Nelly Blair, who learned about politics both by corresponding with her uncle James Iredell and by fleeing British invaders, later complained of men who "treat women as Ideiots," refusing to recognize them as "reasonable beings" capable of understanding serious topics. Although Eliza Wilkinson claimed that she did "not love to meddle in political matters," her painful wartime odyssey led her to criticize "the men [who] say [women] have no business with them. . . . I won't have it thought," Wilkinson declared, "that because we are the weaker sex as to *bodily* strength . . . we are capable of nothing more than minding the dairy, visiting the poultry-house, and all such domestic concerns." Wilkinson believed that women's minds "can soar aloft" and that they "can form conceptions of things of higher nature; and have as just a sense of honor, glory, and great actions, as these 'Lords of Creation' " who would suppress their "liberty of thought."[49]

A few brave women challenged the laws and customs that prevented their formal participation in public life. The Virginians Hannah Lee Corbin and Mary Willing Byrd applied the revolutionary dictum "no taxation without representation" to widows and other propertied women, who paid taxes but remained unable to vote or hold political office. "I have paid my taxes

120   and have not been Personally, or Virtually represented," Byrd complained
to Governor Thomas Nelson, alluding to the prerevolutionary debate over
the nature of representation. Postrevolutionary women lacked voting rights,
but some attended elections and engaged in electioneering, unlike their
colonial forebears. When the New Englander Elkanah Watson visited Warrenton, North Carolina, in 1786, he met one woman who was "an active
leader at the polls" in that community. "I never met with a more sensible,
spirited old lady," Watson later recalled. "She was a great politician; and . . .
she had more political influence, and exerted it with greater effect, than any
man in her county."[50]

An increasingly reactionary political climate may have deterred later
women from claiming rights and exerting influence, but it did not diminish
their knowledge of and interest in political matters. In the postrevolutionary
era, rising literacy rates and the increasing availability of both magazines
and newspapers promoted women's political awareness. Newspapers articulated abstract political values and thus perpetuated the libertarian ideals of
the Revolution among a new generation of southern readers. At least one
Charleston girl learned about liberty by transcribing a text from her local
paper. "*Liberty* is so sacred a treasure," wrote Mary Ann Elizabeth Stevens a
quarter-century after the Declaration of Independence, "it is the means of
enjoying every other blessing in civil society, and is dearer to the noble &
enlightened mind than life itself."[51]

Newspaper coverage of the acrimonious partisan debates of the postwar
decades also stimulated women's interest in political life. In the late 1780s,
Margaret Izard Manigault closely followed the contest between supporters
and opponents of the federal Constitution. Fanny Bassett Washington enjoyed reading the newspapers that came weekly to Mount Vernon, where
she was a frequent visitor. Elizabeth Preston Madison, who resided in western Virginia, eagerly awaited the arrival of the Richmond papers. "Please
write to me & send me some of your News Papers," she wrote to her
brother in 1798. "I have not seen one since you left us & dislike living in the
World & knowing so little of or about it."[52]

In the 1790s, as Americans divided into Federalists and Republicans,
elite women pursued political news and declared their allegiance to one or
the other of the contending parties. The sisters Judith Randolph and Nancy
Randolph of Virginia used the title "Citizen" to address their correspon-
dents, thus showing their support for the French Revolution and for
Thomas Jefferson's emerging Republican party. Their kinswoman Fanny
Coalter expressed her Republican partisanship in letters to her half-brother

Female political consciousness survived into the postrevolutionary decades. Peggy Castleman's sampler, worked at Mrs. Lurrir's school in Frederick County, Virginia, in 1802, includes a patriotic representation of an American eagle alongside its more conventional domestic and decorative imagery. Courtesy of the Museum of Early Southern Decorative Arts, Winston-Salem, N.C.

"Citizen John Randolph." At the opposite end of the political spectrum, Eleanor Parke Custis condemned "those barbarous *democratic murderers*" in France and "those poor misguided multitudes" who supported them in America. "I am becoming an outrageous politician, perfectly *federal*[ist]," observed this granddaughter of Martha Washington, proclaiming that she was "determined even to lend a hand to extirpate the *Demons* if their unparellel'd impudence, & thirst of conquest should make them attempt an invasion of our peaceable happy Land."[53]

Federalist women often bitterly criticized their opponents, especially as their own party suffered its irreversible decline after 1800. When Jefferson assumed the presidency in 1801, Elizabeth Gamble of Richmond complained that the "Democrats . . . have by Intrigue, & Fals[e]hoods, raised their *Idol* to a station, of which He is . . . very unworthy. God grant that His may not be the 'Reign of Terror.'" From Mount Vernon, Nelly Custis also "deplored the infatuation of our Countrymen and the triumph of democracy." but expected Americans shortly to "regret . . . their own folly . . . and we may then hope for the *Millenium* so long predicted . . . after [Jefferson's] term expires." In 1801, she and other Federalist women wore white plumes to dancing assemblies and other public functions to symbolize their opposition to the French Revolution and their allegiance to the defeated party. In 1802, Nelly did not pay her "annual visit" to the nation's capital, where there were "too great a number of Democrats . . . for any person to be comfortable, who has a natural antipathy to those animals." Anne Blair Banister likewise worried that consorting with "so many Democrats" would corrupt young Wilson Cary when he studied law in Richmond.[54]

The Federalist women of the intermarried, Charleston-based Pinckney, Izard, and Manigault families engaged in spirited political discussions spanning a quarter-century of party rivalry. Mary Stead Pinckney corresponded with Federalist women in other states, and when she accompanied her diplomat husband on a mission to France in 1796, she sent political news back to her female relations in South Carolina. An encounter with Thomas Paine, outspoken supporter of the French Revolution and author of *The Rights of Man*, was the highlight of Pinckney's sojourn in Paris. After recounting her brief exchange with the hated radical, she smugly confided to Margaret Izard Manigault that Paine "is almost continually in liquor."[55]

Pinckney's cousins Alice DeLancey Izard and her daughter Margaret Izard Manigault shared both her political interests and her Federalist partisanship. In the 1790s, Manigault denounced the Jeffersonian "reptiles" who sympathized with the French revolutionaries, and both women later criticized the Republican administrations. Like any orthodox Federalist, Izard condemned the Embargo Act of 1807 and accused Jefferson of paying "little attention to the military . . . which [is] so essential and without which no Country can preserve its proper station in the World." In 1809, she rejoiced that the "hour of Mr. Jefferson's authority is passed" and hoped that his successor, James Madison, would reverse the "train of mistakes" perpetrated during the past eight years. "We may then hope to see spirit & courage rising from their late funeral," she asserted, "& rising with accumulated lustre." Izard and her daughter ridiculed Mary Wollstonecraft and read with pleasure assorted Federalist polemics. Alice mocked the pretensions of Napoleon, while Margaret rejoiced with her sister Georgina at the prospect of the restoration of the ousted Bourbon dynasty.[56]

Elite women of both parties traded political information with each other and with their male relatives. Women whose husbands held state or national office often pumped them for the latest political news from the capital. During a rare separation from her husband, James, Dolly Madison declared herself "extremely anxious to hear (as far as you think proper) what is going forward in the Cabinet" in which he served. Mary Stanford of North Carolina and Elizabeth Lowndes of South Carolina regularly received political news from their husbands, both of whom were members of Congress.[57]

Just as some women depended on men for news from Washington or their state capitals, some men relied on women to keep them abreast of local politics during their absence. Traveling through the Peedee River counties in 1794, Alice DeLancey Izard learned that the people there opposed Alexander Hamilton's plan for funding the national debt and intended to vote against the plan's Federalist supporters. Aware that her own husband's congressional seat was in jeopardy, Izard advised him and his colleague William Lowndes Smith to pass through the Peedee region on their way home from Philadelphia to cultivate the goodwill of its disenchanted voters. Similarly, Elizabeth Preston Madison looked out for the political interests of her brother John Preston, a state legislator, to whom she relayed the details of local politics while he was away in Richmond. When court business kept Judge William Gaston away from his home in New Bern, North Carolina, in 1810, his wife, Hannah, helped organize his bid for a congressional seat, garnering electioneering advice from politically influential men throughout the district. Passing on information from one local strategist, Hannah advised William to spend "at least a day" campaigning in Johnston County so that he "might become better acquainted with the people" and thereby "do better in that County, than . . . at the last Election."[58]

While most women shared the political allegiances of the men around them, some refused to defer to men's political opinions, at least in private. John Chesnut, a South Carolina Federalist, complained that his sister-in-law Mary Cox Chesnut was "so much of a Democrat," but the two engaged in a good-natured exchange over the virtues of their respective parties. Elizabeth Gamble, a much more truculent Federalist, mocked the politics of a Republican suitor, informing him that though the Federalists of Richmond ignored the festivities marking Jefferson's inauguration, they enjoyed their annual Washington's birthnight ball, "at which . . . not more than two or three Democrats attended."[59]

Others were less mindful of partisan disputes but equally politically conscious. Although she described herself as "nothing of a Politician," Catherine Read of Charleston asserted that she did not "always think it necessary to think as my Husband does," and she criticized as shortsighted the southern men who appeared determined to involve the United States in European wars. "War," Read advised her sister, "is a species of Madness hardly to be equalled . . . contemplate the horrors of St. Domingo, ours will be a similar fate." As the United States neared the brink of war in 1812, Rachel Mordecai of North Carolina censured what she judged to be her brother's lack of patriotism. When the merchant Samuel Mordecai complained that the trade embargo hurt his business, Rachel tartly reminded him that "patriotick individuals will endeavour to bear its temporary effects without complaining" to promote the "general advantage."[60]

Like the increase in the political content of women's private writing, changes in the quality and quantity of women's petitions suggest that the Revolution profoundly enhanced their political consciousness. After the Revolution, southern women of all social ranks petitioned their legislatures far more frequently, and their petitions also accounted for a larger proportion of those the assemblies considered.[61] The rhetoric and logic of these petitions show how some postrevolutionary women cautiously attempted to define their political status, portraying themselves as members of a community who, though lacking full legal and political rights, were nonetheless entitled to just and equitable treatment by their government. Appealing to a discursive model of equity that ascribed to government moral obligations to its dependents, these petitioners called on legislators to address a growing range of issues.

When Mary Davidson, widow of General William Davidson, petitioned the North Carolina legislature for her husband's back pay, she couched her expectations of equity and justice in the formulaic language of subservience that the petitioning ritual required, especially of women supplicants. Davidson explained that as "a helpless woman with seven small Children — without one Slave, without Furniture," she "suffered extreme misery." She then declared that her husband, who had died in battle, "had a Claim on the Patriotism, the Honor and the Justice of his Fellow Citizens for Pay while he served the State," and suggested that his family now sought the "poor recompense of Pay earned at the Expence of Life." Davidson thus described herself in terms that evoked conventional images of feminine debility and dependence, but she also justified her claim to restitution by invoking the ideals of equity and justice.[62]

During and after the Revolution, women routinely used this language of equity to assert government's moral obligation to redress their war-related grievances, but they also increasingly employed this idiom to solicit government action in other matters that were not war-related. Ann Timothy, who succeeded her husband as South Carolina's public printer in 1783, emphasized both the state's obligations and her own merit when she petitioned to settle her public accounts, declaring that "her patriotism would induce her to serve the public for no other reward than the satisfaction she would enjoy in . . . having served her country," but the government's reluctance to satisfy her "just and reasonable" claims unfairly prevented her from meeting the demands of her own insistent creditors. Hope Mulford, the widow of a Richmond health officer who perished in the yellow fever epidemic of 1800, also invoked the ideal of equity when she requested a government pension as compensation for the "calamity" of widowhood "brought on . . . by a strict attention to the public Interest, & from which, most probably, much safety & tranquility has arisen to the State at large, but more particularly to the inhabitants . . . [of] the Seat of Government."[63]

Southern women invoked the ideal of equity most emphatically when they called on their government to consider their requests for divorces and separate estates, two options that had become slightly more accessible to women in the southern states and elsewhere in the postrevolutionary era. The libertarian ideals of the Revolution led some Americans to question colonial prohibitions against divorce, and most states made some modest progress toward liberalization. Among the southern states, South Carolina made no provision for divorce before Reconstruction, but other state assemblies began hearing — if only rarely granting — divorce petitions shortly after independence.[64] Similarly, though Americans did not seriously consider abolishing coverture, most states increasingly recognized that under certain circumstances wives should be empowered to maintain separate estates. Formal feme sole status, which was the peculiar privilege of a few South Carolina women in the colonial period, now became a possible remedy for wives left destitute by irresponsible and insolvent husbands.[65]

When they sought separate estates, women stressed their spouses' shortcomings and their own worthiness of the assembly's special consideration. Twenty-seven North Carolina wives petitioned for separate estates through 1800; of the fourteen whose petitions have survived, eleven asserted that their husbands abandoned them and nine described their spouses more specifically as debt-ridden and irresponsible.[66] In a political culture that valued independence, industry, and rationality, these characteristics presumably rendered such men unfit to exercise the extensive property rights the common law gave to husbands.[67] Like the wives of Tories who petitioned to recover confiscated property, these women sought to appropriate the property rights of spouses who, by virtue of their political or moral failings, could not be trusted to act responsibly.

Because their requests were unusual and seemed to undermine the existing sexual hierarchy, women who sought separate estates took special pains to portray themselves as exemplars of republican womanhood, if not claimants of republican citizenship. These petitioners attempted to counteract stereotypes of women as extravagant, idle, and irrational — and thus politically and morally defective — by describing themselves as frugal, industrious, and self-reliant. Elizabeth Carter, whose husband left her with "a parcel of Suffering children," asked for a separate estate to "Prevent her Ungrateful Husband from Cumming Back and distressing of her what little She git by her Industry." Elizabeth Whitworth asserted that she was "anxious to Support herself & family by her & their Labour" but worried that her "Gameing, Drinking," and insolvent husband would return to seize her property. Another petitioner requested a separate estate after being deserted by her drunken spendthrift of a husband, explaining that "by her honest industry" she had "accumulated some little property" since his departure. Similarly, the poor abandoned wife of a French-Canadian peddler claimed to have acquired "a Small Maintenance for me and my little Son . . . by Sore Work and frugality." Petitioning for a separate estate, this North Carolinian requested "the Privilege of enjoying the fruits of my Labour" by freeing her "from any and all claims of my dissipating husband."[68]

When women sought divorces, they described their husbands as financially irresponsible and morally debauched and appealed to the legislatures to redress the injustices they suffered. The seduction motif, so prominent in postrevolutionary fiction, was also a staple of women's divorce petitions during this period.[69] Susannah Wersley, who in 1781 married a man who "professed himself an officer of the North Carolina line," found herself abandoned within a month of their wedding. Five years later, she requested a divorce on the grounds that her spouse "was activated by a principle of convenience and deception alone in Marr[y]ing your Petitioner." Polly Wilson likewise portrayed herself as a virtuous woman who "was made to experience the most Mortifying and Cruel treatment" at the hands of her husband, who expelled her from his house so he could live "in open adultry with another woman," with whom he had several children. After eight years of "this degraded and Wretched life," Wilson appealed to "those from whom alone [she] can Expect relief," unsuccessfully requesting "a Bill of Divorcement, which she thinks Upon an investigation of the facts will be deemed Just and Reasonable."[70]

The form and content of women's petitions demonstrate both the extent and the limits of their political experience and consciousness. Perhaps most significant, the fact that women submitted so few group petitions suggests that their political consciousness was less collective than individual. Aside from a few short-lived attempts to support the colonial boycotts and a singular effort by elite Virginia women to raise funds for Continental troops, the Revolution did not foster collective action by southern women in pursuit of political ends. During the imperial crisis, nonelite white men acted in concert, and after 1776 they increasingly used group petitions, legislative instructions, and other techniques to advance their collective interests and to influence public policy.[71] By contrast, with few exceptions, women who petitioned the legislature did so as individuals seeking redress for specific personal grievances.

Of the eighteen group petitions that women did file on their own or with men in the four southern states before 1800, at least seven dealt with family or domestic issues reflecting conventional notions of woman's place and status. In 1780, in the earliest of these petitions, 51 South Carolina women — "deserted by their husbands gone over to the Enemy" — requested relief from the punitive taxes imposed on Tories, noting that a total of 203 children depended on them for shelter and sustenance. In 1782, 21 Whig women from North Carolina's Cape Fear region petitioned to prevent the expulsion of the "helpless and innocent" wives and children of Wilmington's Tories. In 1796, 191 women cosigned Mary Fraser's petition for the repatriation of her banished husband, and 3 women joined with their male neighbors in defense of a Randolph County, North Carolina, man who pulled down a house where women "were Very Loose with their Virtue & their tongues Such as Making mischief between men and their Wives." On three other occasions, widows petitioned in pairs to collect government pensions or recover wartime losses.[72]

On other occasions, women acted collectively to pursue objectives that were less readily compatible with their conventional domestic roles. In 1783, a group of Charleston widows petitioned to protest a change in market regulations that jeopardized their livelihood. Six years later, the seamstresses of Charleston unsuccessfully sought the imposition of a tariff on imported clothing to protect their business from foreign competition. In 1797, the Moravian "single women" requested and received a tax exemption for their school at Salem, North Carolina. Widows and single women also occasionally joined with men to express shared grievances. In 1794, the free "People of Colour of South Carolina" — five women and twenty men — unsuccessfully petitioned for a repeal of a racially based state poll tax. Even more boldly, in 1790, forty-nine tenant farmers who leased lands from the College of William and Mary criticized the terms of the college's leases and condemned the institution as a remnant of the imperial past that had no place in the republic. These seven women and forty-two men asked the state assembly to abolish to college, which they believed had outlived its original mandate to train ministers and convert Virginia's Indians.[73]

As these group petitions suggest, shared occupational or economic interests could foster collective political consciousness. As housewives on dispersed farms and plantations, however, most southern women were isolated in their occupations. At the same time, the exclusion of women from active participation in the republic's chief political institutions — the legislature, the courts, and the militia — not only inhibited the development of group consciousness but also deprived them of full citizenship in the eyes of most Americans. Men's rhetoric characteristically distinguished "ladies" from "citizens," and, reflecting both this rhetorical convention and the realities of their legal status, women rarely identified themselves as citizens, even in their private writing. Only five women did so when they petitioned their state assemblies.[74]

An extraordinary newspaper essay, penned by "Anne Matilda," was an exception that proved the rule of women's exclusion from republican citizenship. In 1806, this South Carolina woman spoke out against men who sought to seduce and corrupt virtuous women. In so doing, "Anne Matilda" claimed to be a "citizen of the world, free and independent," but even she described normative citizenship in overtly masculine terms. "Tho' precluded by the laws of propriety from wielding a sword, or shooting a pistol in the field," she declared, "yet I shall maintain the post of a private citizen, and chastise the insolence that [dares] to riot upon the rights of my sex." The essayist's familiarity with the rhetoric and ideals of republican political culture therefore led her to claim for herself a lesser form of citizenship that was more private than public, more passive than participatory.[75]

Like "Anne Matilda," most southern women did not defy the conventions that barred them from wielding swords and pistols, though, like her, many must have recognized that their exclusion from military service and its rituals effectively excluded them from most other aspects of political life. The civic rituals that southern men orchestrated dramatized their exclusion, celebrating the image of citizen-soldier and relegating women to the fringes of public life.

The transition from monarchy to republic transformed southern civic pageantry as republicans invented new rituals to replace those of their imperial past, to redefine the relationship between government and the people, and to instill in citizens a new sense of American national identity. Before the Revolution, though the militia often paraded on public occasions, genteel balls gradually supplanted martial displays as the favored form of civic celebration. After the Revolution, however, genteel civic rituals declined in importance and Fourth of July parades became ubiquitous. Orchestrated to celebrate and to promote civic virtue, the parades showcased arms-bearing, propertied, and ostensibly independent white men as exemplars of republican citizenship. Accessible to most white men, these republican civic rituals purposefully excluded white women and African Americans.

By the 1790s, militia parades reemerged to replace balls as the dominant civic rituals, except among Federalist men and women, who disdained the largely Jeffersonian gatherings as — in the words of the Virginian Elizabeth Gamble — disorderly and "*crowded* with every *description* of persons." Always a minority in most southern communities, Federalists did not define the civic rituals of the postrevolutionary era. After 1800, the Republican ascendancy, coupled with the rise of new external threats to the security of the republic, gradually silenced Federalist criticism of the increasingly pervasive Fourth of July celebrations.[76]

By the first decade of the new century, southerners had developed a standard format for their Independence Day rituals. The day's observances began at dawn with an artillery salute. In late morning, the local militia companies drilled, paraded, and fired more celebratory volleys. After the completion of the military exercises, a local worthy publicly read the Declaration of Independence, whereupon he or another prominent man delivered a patriotic oration to a vast gathering of listeners. By early afternoon, the crowds dispersed, and men adjourned to taverns, inns, or fields, where they dined and drank patriotic toasts, one for each state in the federal Union. After the men completed their dining and toasts, they fired another artillery salute to signal the official end of the day's observances. In some larger southern communities, fireworks displays and theatrical presentations enhanced the didactic impact of the celebrations.

Though comparatively inclusive, republican civic rituals were not egalitarian. The Fourth of July observances reflected the revolutionary expansion of the public sphere to include most white men, but they also recognized and reinforced the existing social hierarchy. All propertied white men could march in parades and attend public dinners, but only brilliantly uniformed elite volunteer companies led the procession and fired the volleys that punctuated the day's festivities. Similarly, only gentlemen formally expressed their political views by delivering patriotic toasts and speeches.[77]

In addition to upholding class distinctions, republican rituals asserted the collective authority of white men over blacks and white women. After the revolution in Haiti and Gabriel's Rebellion in Virginia, displays of white military power sought to inspire fear and deference among black southerners, a consideration that probably made southern parades more socially inclusive and more militaristic than their northern counterparts, which sometimes celebrated the occupational and associational bonds among men, as well as their military prowess. Militarized republican rituals pointedly contrasted men's vigor and public spirit with women's passive dependence, ignoring both women's participation in the Revolution and the concept of republican womanhood, which endowed their domestic work with public significance. By identifying citizenship with arms-bearing, by barring women from marching in parades and drinking toasts, and by describing them as passive and apolitical, white men claimed exclusive access to the public sphere by virtue of their supposedly unique capacity for patriotism.[78]

Independence Day orations glorified the past achievements of patriotic men and enjoined male listeners to follow the example of their virtuous forefathers. One typical oration, delivered in Richmond in 1812, described the "patriots of the revolution" as "men of undaunted courage and unbending fortitude. What better thing can we ask for our country," the speaker queried, "than that the sons of the patriots of '76 may be worthy of their sires . . . . Let us their descendants, while commemorating the 4th of July, remember our fathers; and do nothing unworthy of them." That same year, a Raleigh orator addressed particularly "the young men, exhorting them to emulate their Sires in defence of their country."[79] In 1814, an Independence Day speaker in Winchester, Virginia, used a cannon as "his Rostrum," as if to emphasize the masculine and military tone of the holiday observances. In the deeply gendered political language of the times, newspapers routinely praised such orations as "manly," "handsome," or "masterly." "Alarming to tyrants and delightful to freemen," the Declaration of Independence also was deemed a "masculine document" by its admirers.[80]

Men and women listened together to patriotic orations, but gender conditioned the purpose of their presence, as well as the meaning of the message from the speaker's platform. Orations celebrating the past achievements of male patriots could provide inspiration for male listeners, but Fourth of July speakers rarely mentioned women patriots or even acknowledged the presence of females in their audience. On the sidelines, watching the parades and military exhibitions, women were foils for the men whose patriotic vigor these events displayed and celebrated.

Yet white women's presence was essential to the didactic purpose of the Independence Day observances, which sought to inspire a new generation of citizen-soldiers.[81] The mothers, wives, and daughters of propertied white men, standing, sitting, and waving along the parade route, were supposedly those most vulnerable to both black rebels and foreign invaders and thus most dependent on the protection of the parading soldiers. Men sometimes acknowledged the symbolic significance of female spectators on civic occasions. In 1808, a "numerous concourse of ladies, at the church and on the parade ground" in Petersburg, Virginia, reportedly "infused an additional joy in the feelings of every citizen and soldier, and emphatically impressed on their minds this truth, that in the hour of danger and distress, it is on THEM, the virtuous fair reposed for their safety and protection." In 1814, the men of Petersburg carefully choreographed their militia muster to dramatize the protection of white women by their community's citizen-soldiers. After the militiamen paraded, they and the other male "Citizens" formed a protective circle "around the Ladies" who gathered to hear the oration. On other occasions, the women watched the proceedings from the windows of nearby buildings, distancing themselves from the potentially dangerous streets and from activities that were explicitly political.[82]

Independence Day toasts also celebrated the virtue and courage of male patriots, often invoking images of feminine dependence to inspire valor in

Washington's Reception by the Ladies, on passing the Bridge at Trenton, N.J., April 1789, Nathaniel Currier, 1845. Postrevolutionary civic rituals celebrated the patriotism and bravery of citizen-soldiers and relegated white women to the fringes of public life. Females participated in such rituals chiefly as passive admirers of the parading men, as on this occasion when they honored Washington for defending and protecting the women of America. The Library of Congress, Washington, D.C.

male celebrants. In 1809, the Richmond troop of cavalry made explicit this comparison between the sexes, toasting first the "heroes of '76" and the "Militia of the U[nited] States," who fought for liberty, and then the "American Fair," whose passive "smiles will reward the brave." Similarly, in 1805, the men of Caswell County, North Carolina, toasted the "American fair," that "the sons of freedom [may] find a rich reward in the smiles of beauty," and the men of Fayetteville saluted women who "never receive to their Embrace, any but the Lovers of their Country." In 1808, Charleston's Irish Volunteers asserted, "It is the duty of Soldiers to protect the [fair] sex; their smiles await the brave." In 1813, Richmond's Society of the Friends of the Revolution toasted the "daughters of Columbia," explicitly contrasting male patriotism with female panic in the face of a second Anglo-American war. "That barbarity, which has inspired one sex with terror," they declared, "has only enflamed the courage of the other."[83]

Like republicans elsewhere, southerners used female forms to represent abstract political and cultural values. Studies of republican iconography have shown that feminine representations of Liberty, Justice, and the republic betokened not only a rejection of political patriarchy but also the exclusion of women from civic life. Because republican men assumed that real women could not espouse particular political views, they could appropriate the generic image of woman to represent universal political ideals. Accordingly, a parade in Richmond in 1811 had no female participants, but it prominently featured an image of Liberty, portrayed as a goddess in classical dress. On other occasions, young women of eminent families posed as living statuary, representing not themselves but the supposedly apolitical feminine attributes — beauty, chastity, vulnerability — that the parading soldiers cherished and defended. Similarly, marathon sessions of patriotic toasts recounted the particular achievements of male patriots of all classes but often concluded with a generic salute to the "American Fair," thus implying that either collectively or individually women did nothing specific of public value.[84]

The crisis that culminated in the War of 1812, however, revealed tensions and ambiguities in the gender ideals of postrevolutionary southerners. Beginning with the Embargo Act of 1807, the Republican administrations imposed a succession of prohibitions on imports to discourage European interference with American shipping during the Anglo-French war. Reminiscent of colonial boycotts of British goods in the decade before independence, the Republican measures necessitated the revival of rhetoric condemning European luxuries and promoting domestic manufactures. In

134 this second Anglo-American crisis, as in the first, women's work was crucial to the success of the patriot cause and men, despite their reluctance to acknowledge women's political consciousness, occasionally recognized the public significance of women's domestic labor.

Like their prerevolutionary predecessors, many proponents of domestic manufactures neither addressed women directly nor acknowledged their work's significance. The proprietor of a fledgling paper manufactory in Columbia, South Carolina, suggested that the "preservation of rags" would promote "education, literature and liberty itself" without identifying women as the probable providers of this service that was "of vast importance to the general interest." In 1808, the members of Virginia's Surry Society to Encourage Domestic Manufactures proudly reported that they were "already for the most part, clad in homespun" but did not acknowledge the patriotism of the women who produced that fabric. Another Virginian, who was aware of the economic and political value of women's work, appealed to patriotic men to encourage their wives to "spin, card, weave, dye, and manufacture, in the various modes for flax, hemp, cotton and wool." By addressing only men, this anonymous farmer implicitly denied the existence of women's political consciousness. Like most of his contemporaries, he assumed that women were more susceptible to a husband's influence than to impersonal appeals to their duty to their country and the public.[85]

Other southerners, who viewed the embargo as a potential stimulus to the development of factory-based manufacturing implicitly or explicitly disparaged the public significance of women's domestic labor. One Henrico County, Virginia, man — posing as "An Associator of 1774" — claimed that if every "friend of America" wore homespun, the demand for American textiles would exceed the production of "every private spinning wheel and loom" and "many of the best weavers in England, Scotland, Ireland, France, Italy, Holland, &c. &c. would slip over to us, and manufactures of cloth . . . would soon be brought to perfection among us." Others looked to large-scale manufacturing to "stimulat[e] the poorer class of people to industry" or to feed "poor women and children, who can earn from 20 to 40 cents per day in moating cotton." South Carolinians explored the possibility of employing slave women to make "lily white cloth" in factories and workshops. The labor of poor women and European immigrants, these southerners believed, could end their dependence on foreign manufactures. At the same time, mass production of cloth in factories would have marginalized the political significance of women's domestic labor.[86]

During the era of the embargo, southern women produced great quanti-

ties of homespun, despite men's growing enthusiasm for large-scale manufactures. Women put their slaves and their daughters to work spinning,
weaving, and sewing, aware that their work benefited both their families
and their country. Knowing that the "embargo has playd mischief" with
South Carolina's cotton planters, in 1808 Anne Coalter gave up her annual
visit to her Virginia kin so that she could "remain at home to attend to spinning." Other women explicitly declared the political significance of their domestic labor. "With all due respect to what you call the resolves of Congress,
I think the resolves of our sex of full as much consequence to the nation,"
proclaimed "Dorothy Distaff" in 1810, "a hundred thousand spinning
wheels put in motion by female hands will do as much towards establishing
our independence, as a hundred thousand of the best militia men in America." By 1812, even the aristocratic Elizabeth Manigault Izard was learning
to spin because she believed that "in such hard times as these it [is] necessary for us to endeavour to make our own clothes at home."[87]

During the crisis preceding the War of 1812, women took pride in applying their domestic skills to patriotic purposes. One Virginia Methodist,
who presented her minister with a homespun coat in 1807, must have glo-
ried in his observation that homespun "was more suitable for Virginians to
wear than any other cloth and especially [for] a Methodist minister." In
1808, women in Sampson County, North Carolina, quietly asserted their
patriotism when they made homespun suits for their men to wear at that
year's Fourth of July celebration.[88]

Other patriotic women purposefully sought public recognition of their
work's political significance. Like their predecessors in prerevolutionary
Williamsburg, the "ladies" of Richmond wore homespun clothing to their
city's Fourth of July festivities in 1808. That same year, approximately fifty
"ladies" dressed in "specimens of their own ingenious and elegant handiwork" attended the Fourth of July ceremonies in Goochland County, Virginia. In Ebenezer Hill, South Carolina, 250 women "whose grateful
sensibility to the political blessings of our country was evinced . . . by their
appearance in domestic manufactory" were among the audience at their
community's Independence Day observances.[89]

In these communities and probably in many others, women publicly asserted a distinctly feminine construction of patriotism, shaped by their domestic identities, which men celebrated in both patriotic toasts and
newspaper notices. In July 1807, in the wake of the British attack on the
U.S.S. Chesapeake off the Virginia coast, one observer praised the women of
Norfolk for their "patriotism which does them much honour," noting that

they had "offered to lay aside their *needles* and make [ammunition] cartridges for the Volunteers . . . employed in the defence of their country." In 1808, perhaps in response to the display of homespun attire at recent Independence Day parades, one South Carolinian denied the need for large-scale textile manufacturing, contending that "almost every matron of a family attends to the concerns of spinning and weaving at least . . . for their own families," making the household "a manufacturing establishment within themselves." Toasting the "American Fair," the men of Edgefield, South Carolina, declared that women, "fired by a love of country . . . will clothe their fathers, brothers and sons in *homespun* to fight its battles." Once the war began, men praised women who raised funds to provide shirts and other clothing for "our brave volunteers who have relinquished the ease and comforts of their families and firesides . . . in defence of their country's rights and honor."[90]

Unlike earlier Fourth of July toasts, which typically obscured women's contributions to the Revolution, in this time of crisis some toasts explicitly linked the women patriots of the present to their revolutionary predecessors, just as appeals to men's martial spirit characteristically invoked the image of the Revolution's citizen-soldiers. The men of Orangeburg, South Carolina, saluted women who "emulate the Fair of '76 in domestic manufactures, and in sentiments and deeds of patriotism." Charleston's South Carolina Volunteers hoped that women's patriotism would be "equal to their virtues . . . [and] manifest to the world that they are worthy descendants of the matrons of '76."[91]

Women's response to the war emergency also inspired rare public tributes to republican womanhood, or the notion that women's domestic work, particularly their duties as wives and mothers, was of public value. In 1811, a patriotic Virginian worried that "since the revolution [the nation's] character has most wofully declined" and asserted that the "virtues of this country are with our women, and the only hope of the resurrection of the genius and character of the nation rests with them" in their capacity as mothers. Two years later, the *Richmond Compiler* celebrated the ideal of republican motherhood in a Fourth of July song in which present-day patriots proclaimed to their revolutionary ancestors: "We are a Band of Brothers, / By your gallant deeds inspired — / By the precepts of our Mothers / With your ardent spirit fired." In 1816, the men of Goochland County appealed to that same ideal of republican motherhood when they toasted the "American Fair," who "instruct their daughters by their own example, and point their sons to the deeds of the men of '76." The men of Camden, South Carolina, lauded the "mothers, wives and sisters of such men as Decatur . . . and a host of heroes and statesmen."[92]

An 1812 essay in the *Raleigh Register* praised "female patriotism" and provided a real-life role model for its female readers. The wife of a revolutionary veteran and mother of sixteen children, Mary Pruitt of Georgia exemplified the self-sacrificing virtue of the ideal republican woman. Her industry and frugality helped her husband, John, to become "an independent farmer, clear of debt" — in other words, the virtuous yeoman so idealized by republican ideologues in postrevolutionary America. Her patriotism also inspired her six eldest sons to serve in the state militia. When the seventh and eighth sons, "glowing with patriotic zeal," desired to enlist, John Pruitt demurred, but Mary refused to stand in their way. Likening the patriotism of Mary Pruitt to that of the women of revolutionary times, the *Register* announced, "The heroic firmness, and public virtue of the Spartan females, is again realised in our day, and country. Let those who think lightly of female patriotism, read this and blush for shame."[93]

Notwithstanding such forceful vindications of republican womanhood, southern men did not envision women's political contributions as permanent and ongoing. Although they acknowledged and praised women's patriotism during these years of crisis, with the return of peace and the resumption of trade, southern men discarded this image of politicized domesticity in favor of more conventional portrayals of women as passive dependents who had no public role.[94]

Southern Independence Day rituals aptly reflected white women's presumed relation to the political world that constituted the public sphere for postrevolutionary republicans. Those who orchestrated the celebratory parades relegated women to the role of admiring spectators, rendering them dependent on men's patriotism and public spirit and barring them from influencing or participating directly in public life. Yet southern women continued to petition their legislatures, read newspapers, and write letters full of political news and observations. Though most were unwilling or unable to reject explicitly the culture that sought to circumscribe their activities and interests, when women wore homespun to parades or published essays or poems, they publicly asserted their political consciousness.

Equally important, in the early decades of the nineteenth century, southern women would attempt to expand the public sphere to embrace activities and concerns other than those formal political ones from which they were excluded. After 1800, southern women participated in public life chiefly by forming their own religious and benevolent associations. Those institutions and the public roles women fashioned for themselves derived less from republican political ideology than from the ideals of feminine domesticity and Protestant evangelicalism.

5

Domesticity

I N 1820, THE *SOUTHERN LITERARY REGISTER*
celebrated the exemplary life of the late Mary D. Woods of the Darling-
ton District of South Carolina. Nineteenth-century magazines and newspapers occasionally published obituaries of the wives and daughters of
prominent men, whose actual or idealized lives could provide models for their
female readers. Woods's obituary, which typified the genre, praised the
twenty-nine-year-old mother of seven for her piety and thorough devotion to
home and family. The *Register* thus subtly reminded its female readers that religion and domesticity should be the chief concerns of women's lives.

"In vain may panegyric exhaust its powers to paint with justice the amiable qualities and the unobtrusive virtues of this lovely, interesting woman,"
began this laudatory account of Woods's brief life. "It is true her ambition
did not prompt her to blaze in the meridian splendor of fashion, or to attract
the gaze of the multitude, by personal embellishments," though "in the active sphere of retired life, she possessed all the necessary qualifications to
form a useful and valuable member of society." The obituary went on to describe Woods's excellence as a Christian — "she was the personification of
virtue" — wife, mother, and daughter. For most nineteenth-century south-

erners, these roles, rather than those of citizen, scholar, reformer, and so-
cialite, were synonymous with virtuous womanhood.[1]

The decades following the Revolution were critical in the development
of gender ideals in the southern states and elsewhere. During this period, as
we have seen, the region's dominant political culture idealized men's public
or civic virtue, characteristically portraying women as dependent, vulnerable, and both physically and temperamentally removed from public life.
This political culture, however, coexisted with an equally influential culture
of religious evangelicalism, which originated in the great revivals of the
eighteenth and early nineteenth centuries and gradually came to dominate
southern religious life. Both republican political ideology and evangelical
religion sought to circumscribe women's activities and influence within the
household, but women joined in the shaping of evangelical culture, which
relocated virtue in the private sphere, thus augmenting the significance of
both women and domestic life.[2]

Many early nineteenth-century southerners, like their northern contemporaries, celebrated the ideal of sexually defined "separate spheres," which
gave men exclusive access to the public world outside the home while en-
dowing women with special moral authority and influence within it.[3] Partly
as a result of the evangelical impulse, southerners increasingly regarded the
home as the seat of virtue and morality, and they looked to wives and mothers to promote religious — but not political — virtue in their domestic circles. Such champions of domesticity achieved vast improvements in the
education of elite and middling women in the postrevolutionary era.[4] Unlike
some earlier proponents of women's education, however, these southerners
defined their objectives in strictly domestic terms. Through their schools
and academies, they sought to turn young women into wives and mothers
who would instill Christian morality in their families while living cheerfully
and complacently in their often secluded households.

Yet in the South, as in the North, the glorification of feminine domesticity and the metaphorical separation of men's and women's spheres never ex-
actly matched reality. Few women sentimentalized domesticity, though
many clearly found both love and happiness in marriage and in motherhood. Although men idealized the home as the seat of domestic bliss, women
did not romanticize the site of their often demanding domestic labors.
Southern women continued to enter the public sphere, writing for publication, buying and selling goods and services, and occasionally participating
in community civic celebrations. Nevertheless, women's domestic work and
the characteristics ascribed to them in the domestic sphere, informed new

public roles they defined for themselves in the nineteenth century's early decades.

During the postrevolutionary decades, evangelicalism expanded beyond its modest colonial beginnings to become increasingly influential among both white and black southerners. In the late 1780s and early 1790s, several relatively small revivals in Virginia, North Carolina, and Kentucky brought new converts into the evangelical fold. Then, in 1799, the Great Revival began among Kentucky's frontier settlers and spread throughout the southern states during the ensuing decade. Baptists, Methodists, and Presbyterians — the chief evangelical denominations — reported unprecedented attendance at revivals and camp meetings and significant growth in church membership. In addition, the evangelicals' pious emotionalism influenced the development of the now disestablished Church of England, known in the United States as the Protestant Episcopal Church.[5]

Unlike colonial Anglicanism, which used external forms and rituals to promote outward conformity, evangelicalism employed emotional preaching fraught with stirring imagery to stimulate the cataclysmic spiritual rebirth of each individual. Rejecting the outward-looking formalism of the colonial establishment and other liturgical churches, evangelicals embraced an introspective religion of emotion and sensibility. Evangelicals of all denominations believed that sinners attained salvation through faith alone and that faith was a direct gift from God to the individual. Once converted, or reborn, the faithful became exemplars of piety, morality, and missionary fervor. Nurturing the faith in their own hearts, they also sought to spread God's word among the unconverted.[6]

Unlike some of their more radical predecessors, postrevolutionary southern evangelicals generally accepted earthly inequalities of gender, class, and race. Despite their early uneasiness about slavery, after 1800 southern Baptists and Methodists rarely criticized that institution and, along with the region's other denominations, they defended it explicitly in the coming decades. Similarly, while evangelicals continued to condemn worldly vanity and extravagance and to assert the spiritual equality of souls in the eyes of God, they accepted temporal inequalities as evidence of a divinely ordained social hierarchy. Many nineteenth-century evangelical leaders embraced the ideal of an educated ministry, which colonial radicals rejected as elitist, and Presbyterians and Baptists increasingly abandoned or modified the unruly camp meetings that initially brought them so many plebeian converts. Bowing to conventional gender hierarchies, most evangeli-

142   cal congregations also formally barred women from preaching in public and otherwise wielding religious authority.[7]

The social conservatism of the postrevolutionary evangelicals enabled them to appeal to a wider audience than their colonial predecessors had done. This less egalitarian and more decorous version of Protestant evangelicalism found new adherents particularly among southern elites, many of whom had actively opposed the spread of the colonial revivals. Colonial elites had rightly feared that the evangelicals' success would undermine the authority of both the established church and its gentry patrons, but the Revolution dismantled the southern religious establishments and challenged the elite's organic view of society. Disillusioned, perhaps, with their relative social and political decline and with the economic uncertainties of the postwar decades, many coastal elites remained in the Episcopal church but adopted the pious, introspective ideals of evangelicalism. Backcountry elites also participated in the postrevolutionary revivals. In South Carolina, a shared culture of evangelicalism united backcountry residents across class lines, and ties between coastal and backcountry Baptist leaders contributed to the statewide unification of a planter class previously riven by regional differences.[8]

Southern women were prominent supporters of the itinerant ministers who carried the evangelical message across the region. In many southern communities, the great Methodist leader Francis Asbury found that most of his listeners were white women and African Americans. In 1785, Asbury described the "inhabitants" of Yorktown, Virginia, as "careless and dissolute," with the exception of "a few serious women" who heard him preach twice in one afternoon. In Charleston, where he found the white male residents "intolerably ignorant of God," Asbury reported that only "women and Africans attend our meetings, and some few strangers also." In Jones County, North Carolina, "many women, but few men" were among those who shared his fellowship. In 1813, during his last visit to the South Carolina low country, Asbury had "about one thousand blacks, and about one hundred white members" at Georgetown, and the latter were mostly women. Asbury believed that the area's white men "kill themselves with strong drink before we can get them" to hear and heed the word of God. Anne Newport Royall, an unsympathetic observer of southern revivals, similarly found that most men in frontier areas remained aloof from them. Preachers, especially Methodists, she believed, "all draw too many women after them."[9]

Although men attended revivals and camp meetings, itinerant ministers often depended on white women for material support when they rode their southern circuits. Women sometimes invited Asbury to hold services and prayer meetings in their homes, and he often lodged with widows. When William Spencer, another Methodist itinerant, rode his circuit through eastern Virginia, he also benefited from the generosity of local women. Although he traveled in an era when females headed only a tiny fraction of the region's households, one-fifth of the houses in which Spencer lodged were headed by pious women. In other cases, wives may have persuaded their husbands to provide food and lodging to him and to other poor itinerant preachers who traversed the southern states in search of converts.[10]

Scholars and contemporaries agree that women found the evangelical message particularly appealing and that they, far more than men, self-consciously invoked and analyzed their religious ideals to guide them through their daily lives. Reflecting the evangelical predisposition toward introspection, many literate women in the southern states and elsewhere kept religious journals in which they contemplated the significance of their relationship with God and the meaning of their earthly lives. Far more than the decorous devotional reading of colonial Anglicans, devotional writing and meditation were exercises in self-actualization for southern evangelicals. By urging white southern women to unprecedented levels of introspection, evangelicalism enriched them spiritually and encouraged them to cultivate a potentially empowering sense of self. In their private writing, evangelical women probed the meaning of their faith, which sometimes justified their involvement in Sunday schools, missionary societies, and other pious activities.[11]

Many women clearly found solace in their faith and in their devotional writing. Ann Cleland Kinloch of Charleston described religious faith as "a direct promise from the word of God . . . [that] is an anchor to the soul, both sure and steadfast." Faith, she observed on the death of a loved one in 1794, "has given consolation & refuge to many a virtuous heart, at a time when the most cogent reasonings would have proved utterly unavailing." As a young wife, eighteen-year-old Anne Randolph Meade Page may have turned to religion to ease the trauma of moving to a Virginia plantation some eighty miles away from her childhood home. Martha Laurens Ramsay also looked to faith to provide a refuge from the trials of earthly life. "Pressed by care, surrounded by difficulties, and in sore perplexity from some domestic circumstances," she explained in 1805, "I come to thee, O my God, who hast commanded us to cast all our care on thee, and to draw nigh in every time of trial." At least one southerner believed that piety

144   brought hope to women who lived in a "state of subjection and pain . . . convert[ing] the veriest hovel into a palace, and adapting the spirit to its lodgment, makes it happy." A prominent Presbyterian clergyman argued that religion brought women security and influence, as well as spiritual uplift. "In proportion of the prevalence of true religion," wrote the Reverend John Holt Rice of Richmond, "the condition of wives, mothers, and daughters is comfortable and honorable."[12]

Some women, many of whom lived in rural seclusion, sought community in their churches, which sustained them both socially and spiritually. Lucy Thornton of Caroline County, Virginia, was a lonely widow before she experienced religious conversion some time around 1812. After she joined the local Baptist congregation, Thornton's letters, which previously had been bitter and complaining, became animated, prayerful, and full of church gossip. Between 1813 and 1816, she discussed and analyzed the theological disputes that ultimately divided her "little church" and worried that "when you carefully examine the doctrines it is like splitting a hair." She also filled her letters with the names of brothers and sisters who made up her Christian community. "Sister Patton last Lords day joined in the Episcopalian communion to the great grief of the Church," she informed a cousin in 1813, adding that Patton had been "called to an account by 3 of the Sisters . . . and She is to attend on a [committee] of brethren to deal with her according to Scripture."[13]

Other women looked to religious faith to foster order and harmony in their domestic lives. Some evangelical women turned to their congregations for protection from abusive husbands. Men, not women, conducted all church hearings and decided appropriate punishments, and women, like men, were subject to the discipline of church authorities. Nevertheless, at a time when courts rarely compromised white men's authority over their dependents, under certain circumstances church discipline might provide women with welcome recourse against cruel or unruly spouses.[14]

Women's prominence in the evangelical churches shaped changing ideals of feminine virtue in the postrevolutionary decades. Whereas mid-eighteenth-century moralists routinely included piety on their lists of desirable feminine attributes, later writers increasingly regarded it as the one essential mark of virtuous womanhood. "Devoid of religion, the female character is incomplete," asserted the anonymous author of the frequently reprinted "Vision of Female Excellence." Another popular piece reminded female readers that their beauty and wit were but "frail and fading" gifts, but the "divine lustre" of piety would survive aging, illness, and misfortune to "support the drooping soul." Hannah More, the celebrated and widely read English evangelical, declared herself "unwilling to believe, that there is in nature so monstrously incongruous a being, as a *female infidel.*" A contemporary southern writer observed that the "benign and generous" Christian faith endowed women with "the most valuable ornaments, invests them with the highest dignity, and affords them their best enjoyments." Another declared, "Religion in a female . . . graces her character, promotes her peace, endears her friendship, secures esteem, and adds a dignity and a worth . . . to all her deeds."[15]

The evangelical ideal of pious womanhood was more socially inclusive than that of the genteel lady, though it too presupposed literacy and sufficient leisure to cultivate religious sensibility. Unlike colonial champions of feminine sensibility, however, evangelicals criticized genteel sociability and construed feminine virtue in primarily domestic terms. Earlier moralists had cautioned female readers to avoid excessive sociability, but evangelical writers categorically condemned balls, parties, and other genteel social activities. Believing that sociability distracted women from their religious and domestic obligations, the English clergyman John Bennett asserted that "a woman's amusements should, as much as possible, be *domestic.*" While Hannah More conceded that virtuous women should endeavor to improve the morals and manners of those around them, she also lamented women's propensity to cultivate the polite accomplishments that enabled them "to dazzle for an hour, when they are candidates for eternity." True religion, More maintained, "does not direct [women] to fly from the multitude . . . but . . . [it] positively forbids them to follow a multitude to do evil."[16]

Southern evangelicals, like republican ideologues, condemned "fashionable amusements" as wasteful and corrupting. "How many hundreds, nay how many thousands of dollars are sometimes wasted in one night at the theatre, at the card table, or at a single ball!" exclaimed the *Monthly Visitant,* adding that "reason and scripture demand, that we devote our property, as well as our other talents, to the service of the Redeemer" by forming "institutions . . . to ameliorate the present condition of man, and to open to him the gates of immortality." Another southern publication stressed the physical, material, and emotional costs of excessive sociability. Although a company of partygoers could leave home clean, sober, healthy, and happy, with pockets full of money, they would inevitably become dirty, drunken, sick, sad, and penniless in the course of an evening's revelry. The *Christian Moni-*

tor likewise attacked balls, gambling, horse racing, and other so-called inno-cent amusements. "Indeed, if I take our gentry's word for it," he mused, "I must think that there is no such thing as a criminal diversion."[17]

In part to accommodate such criticism and in part because the Revolu-tion undermined the public significance of genteel social rituals, elite socia-bility became increasingly privatized in the postrevolutionary decades. Republican parades and tavern dinners replaced sumptuous public balls and banquets as the chief forms of civic celebration, and though elites con-tinued to form dancing assemblies and jockey clubs, they now seldom publi-cized their activities. Visitors to the southern states also noticed the decline of the gentry's much-vaunted hospitality. Whereas colonial elites sometimes extended extravagant hospitality to their entire neighborhoods, postrevolu-tionary southerners entertained mainly familiar guests of their own social standing. Southern elites treated unknown guests politely but more imper-sonally than in earlier decades. In 1810, a Scottish visitor praised the gentle-men of Charleston for inviting him to their "publick" amusements, but noted that only a stranger who was "properly introduced" could gain admis-sion to "private Society."[18]

Genteel balls, once the most visible token of the gentry's cultural dis-tinction, now were valued chiefly as part of an elaborate courtship ritual for young members of the elite. Defending dancing against the charge of frivolity, one Virginian asserted, "At balls, gay Cupid takes his fav'rite stand, /"And gives the blushing fair a *Hymen's* hand." Accordingly, though adults of all ages had participated in colonial balls, after the Revolution, the dancers at such events were almost always unmarried young people.[19]

Affluent parents often sent their adolescent daughters to visit relatives in nearby cities, where they could attend balls, meet marriageable young men of their own class, and learn the "common etiquette" of society. Balls, dancing assemblies, formal visits, and other rituals of urban sociability were alien to many first-time visitors. Accustomed to the less elaborate social life of the town of Fredericksburg, Laura Rootes criticized the fashionable peo-ple who gathered in Richmond as "so ceremonious and formal." When Har-riet Randolph visited Virginia's capital in the early 1820s, she complained of "the drudgery of dressing two or three times a day," but admitted that once she and her companions "become habituated to . . . the etiquette of the place, our time will pass very pleasantly indeed." The painfully shy Cornelia Randolph probably never enjoyed the society of the capital, but even she conceded that participation in the rituals of the ballroom somewhat allevi-ated her "awkward bashfulness" in society. The "easiest intercourse among the company was while dancing," she reported, keeping her family informed of her social triumphs and failures during a season in Richmond.[20]

Unlike their colonial ancestors, most women attended few balls after they married. Some clearly regretted the postnuptial curtailment of their social activities. Nelly Custis Lewis often reminisced about her days as a belle when she enjoyed "an opportunity to cultivate the *fine arts abroad*," and she advised a newly married friend not to "give up music & painting, for pickling, preserving, & *puddings* although I have done so in great measure." Rachel Mordecai Lazarus, who spent her single days as a teacher, enjoyed marriage and motherhood but wistfully regretted her isolation from "intelligent and improving society." Other women had fewer reservations about trading the attractions of sociability for the joys of domestic life. "I give up the gayeties of a town with as little reluctance as any young person," declared one Virginia matron, "but I could not be happy deprived of that little harmonious society which I have around me [at home] . . . there are few of us together, but never was there a set more bound by the ties of love and Friendship."[21]

After the Revolution, the South's dominant religious and political ideals appeared to suggest, more forcefully than ever before, that white women of any class had no place in public life. Republican political culture identified genteel sociability with a decadent imperial past and ordinarily afforded women no direct role in activities of the public sphere. Evangelicalism also condemned sociability without explicitly recognizing that piety could justifiably inspire women to public activism. By devaluing genteel sociability, moreover, these new political and religious ideals undermined an important justification for improvements in women's education. Subsequent proponents of schooling for young women therefore would stress the moral and emotional benefits of education and, above all, laud its domestic applications.

The education of girls and young women improved dramatically in the postrevolutionary decades. In the southern states, scores of academies and boarding schools opened, especially after 1800, offering new educational opportunities to unprecedented numbers of elite and middling southerners. Many of these institutions were academically rigorous, at least in comparison with their colonial predecessors. Mindful of increasing criticism of both genteel education and intellectually ambitious women, however, the schools' proprietors domesticated women's education, stressing its usefulness as preparation for marriage, motherhood, and domestic life.

By the 1790s, American and English moralists were condemning the

148   prevailing mode of genteel education as incompatible with domestic virtue. Criticizing the genteel curriculum of "accomplishments, dissipation, and intrigue," evangelical writers especially complained that young women acquired "every thing but solid knowledge — every thing but piety — every thing but virtue." Others accused genteel women of neglecting their children and their household duties to pursue an unending round of social pleasures. Some critics conceded that music, dancing, and drawing could provide modest domestic amusement for women and their families, but they condemned public displays of these accomplishments, which "exalt a woman to an unnatural and invidious eminence, . . . [and] depress her to an abject state of frivolousness, insipidity, and contempt."[22]

Genteel education, these men argued, rendered women unfit for domestic life. "Always in pursuit of company, and anxious about dress, and fashions," genteel women could not be "amiable" companions for their husbands, who would "seek repose in a mistress . . . or pine in secret; till welcome death affords relief." Women who craved balls, self-adornment, and public display, one southern evangelical asserted, "can have little relish for the exercises of religion," which were so essential to feminine virtue and the domestic tranquillity it fostered.[23]

Other conservative writers worried that efforts to augment the intellectual content of women's education would create a generation ill suited for marriage and motherhood. Some argued that learned women inevitably indulged a "passion for reading," which would compromise their "attention to domestic duties, and regard for personal decorum, without which, no woman can be either useful, happy, or respectable." Others believed that giving women "masculine" education would lead them to indulge in typically masculine crimes and vices. "One *lady writer* is for having her sex educated in the same manner with boys," lamented one of Wollstonecraft's many American critics, "and if so, who knows but in a few years, a sober citizen may be called out of his bed to give bail for his wife, who has beat the [night] watch?" Observing that "all the science of Newton, could not be exchanged in market for a pound of butter," another male enemy of female education contended that "a woman had much better know nothing about the population of China, than to be ignorant of the contents of her hen-coop, or her egg-basket."[24]

Most postrevolutionary critics of women's education blamed boarding schools for corrupting their young charges. Some believed that the camaraderie among classmates fostered the development of a competitive spirit that was "unbecoming" to young women and "not infrequently impair[ed] their health." Others believed that boarding schools and day schools alike neglected religious and moral instruction. Schools that were located in cities, moreover, often exposed their innocent pupils to pernicious temptations and vices.[25]

To prepare young women for virtuous domesticity, such critics reasoned, mothers should educate them in a wholesome domestic environment. "To love a domestic life, it is necessary to know it, and have been, from the time of one's infancy, accustomed to its sweets," one southern moralist asserted, noting that the "taste for retirement is acquired only by having been brought up at home." Academic or "public" schooling, by contrast, undermined women's taste for domesticity and consequently was inappropriate training for their future lives. "Whatever *undomesticates* a woman," warned one popular moralist, " . . . is, at once, the bane of her usefulness, her happiness and virtue."[26]

Proponents of boarding schools and female academies countered such criticisms by arguing that academic education, if properly conceived, could prepare young women to delight and excel in virtuous domesticity. Following popular British writers such as Hannah More and Maria Edgeworth, some southerners asserted that education, shorn of its more frivolous excesses, made women better wives and mothers. A mother's virtue and intelligence "commonly descends in rich inheritance to her children," claimed one Virginian, while a wife's accomplishments made her "an engaging companion to a man of understanding." Others suggested that education enabled women to manage their households more efficiently. Most agreed that schooling, by molding women's literary tastes, could promote religion and virtue in the family and, by extension, in society. By training women to seek amusement in wholesome books and activities, education also prepared them to weather the social isolation many would encounter later as housebound wives and mothers.[27]

Proprietors of boarding schools and female academies were entrepreneurs who exploited growing demands for education that could confer social status while reflecting and reinforcing the domestic ideals of the postrevolutionary era. When Mrs. Jervoise opened her boarding school in Camden, South Carolina, in 1794, its limited curriculum of music, fancy needlework, and the fundamentals of reading, writing, and arithmetic was on the verge of obsolescence.[28] Newer schools throughout the southern states soon instructed students in an array of academic subjects. Genteel accomplishments, though still taught in many schools, occupied a decidedly subordinate place in the revised curriculum, which emphasized the moral

150 and intellectual disciplines that educators and parents deemed compatible with domestic values.

The curriculum of North Carolina's Raleigh Academy, which opened in 1805, typified those offered by larger southern schools after 1800. At the Raleigh Academy, female students progressed through six increasingly demanding grades or "classes." In her first class, a student learned the fundamentals of reading, penmanship, spelling, and arithmetic, as well as the New Testament. The second class continued her instruction in spelling and arithmetic and introduced her to geography, English grammar, and the Old Testament. By the third class, students were ready to begin writing compositions, which they would continue to do in each of their remaining terms at the academy. Students in the third class also studied geography, the "Use of Globes," grammar and syntax, and "the remainder of Arithmetic." In the fourth, fifth, and sixth terms, students read poetry, ancient and modern history, logic, astronomy, and natural and moral philosophy. Although the Raleigh Academy's "Female Department" did not include Latin in its standard curriculum, students could engage a Latin tutor from the school's "Male Department" to study the classics.[29]

Like many other postrevolutionary southern schools, the Raleigh Academy offered students instruction in French, music, painting, and drawing, but its proprietors regarded these accomplishments as optional additions to the main course of study. In an 1811 advertisement, the academy's proprietors published a detailed description of its academic curriculum, adding, almost as an afterthought, that a "Female Teacher" would provide instruction in polite accomplishments to "Such of her Pupils as desire it." Students at Virginia's short-lived Richmond Academy for Female Education also could acquire genteel accomplishments, but no student could "elect the ornamental subjects without taking at least one of the academic courses." Other schools charged extra for lessons in music, drawing, and dancing, thus implying that training students in the ways of gentility was not among their basic objectives. Many new schools offered complete academic curricula for several years before hiring music, dancing, and drawing teachers. Financial considerations led many cash-poor educators to delay hiring additional teachers, but the fact that most waited longest to engage instructors in the "ornamental branches" of education indicates that they deemed those subjects less indispensable than the academic disciplines.[30]

The success of North Carolina's Salem Academy suggests that many postrevolutionary southerners expected schools to emphasize academic and practical subjects instead of ornamental accomplishments. Operated by

Moravians who dressed plainly and forbade dancing, the Salem Academy had rigorous academic standards and a pious environment that made it an attractive choice for many southern parents who could afford to educate their daughters. From the time it began accepting non-Moravian students in 1804, the Salem Academy always had a waiting list, and it was unique among southern boarding schools in occasionally placing newspaper advertisements to discourage, rather than to solicit, additional applications. When Mary Moore Stanford visited her stepdaughters at Salem in 1805, she reported that the school's "arrangements for the solid improvements of young ladies seem'd complete," though "all the personal accomplishments they will undoubtedly have to seek elsewhere." Richard and Mary Stanford, like many other southern parents, expected their daughters to learn dancing and music, but they regarded ornamental education as a "secondary accomplishment."[31]

Southern parents wanted their daughters' education to be thorough and demanding, but they also expected it to prepare them for domestic life. Consequently, the same educators who promoted ambitious academic curricula sometimes took special pains to reassure parents that learning arithmetic, history, and even Latin would make young women better daughters, wives, and mothers. James Garnett, who, with his wife, operated an academy in Essex County, Virginia, urged students to read widely, but he also denounced "learned ladies," affirmed women's calling as men's "best comforters" and "beloved friends," and declared that "to render married life even tolerably comfortable, qualities for *use*, rather than for *show*, should always be preferred." L. A. Anderson, who for nearly a decade promoted the "study of the Ancient Classics *in their original strength and beauty*" at his Cornelia Academy in Richmond, insisted that knowledge of Latin and Greek would give young women "private enjoyment, social satisfaction, and permanent usefulness thro' every period of life."[32]

Although most southerners did not encourage girls to study Latin and Greek, parents recognized the domestic utility of "English education" and sent their daughters off to school in increasing numbers. Even more than their colonial predecessors, postrevolutionary parents urged their daughters to perfect their penmanship, spelling, and grammar, aware that exchanging letters was now an important phase of courtship among the refined classes and that writing and receiving letters could ease the pain of separation from family and friends after marriage. Jacob Mordecai, who later founded the Warrenton Female Academy, pushed his daughter Rachel to improve her writing because "in Communicating to others your own [pleasure] will be

Embroidered sampler text:

Do you my fair endeavour to possess
An elegance of mind as well as dress
Be that your ornament and know to please
By graceful natures unaffectid ease

Elizabeth Barton Aged 11 years

Elizabeth Barton, eleven-year-old daughter of an Alexandria, Virginia, silversmith, stitched this sampler in 1809. Its text reminded Barton and her contemporaries that they might aspire to "elegance of mind" so long as they remained "graceful," "unaffected," and proficient in domestic skills such as needlework. Courtesy of the Museum of Early Southern Decorative Arts, Winston-Salem, N.C.

increas'd" — a sentiment that Rachel echoed as an adult and presumably passed on to her three daughters. Anne Nicholas encouraged a young acquaintance to "write with ease and felicity," noting that many women found letter writing "repleat with pleasure to themselves, and to their friends." Lucy Johnston Ambler looked on anxiously as her younger sisters struggled to improve their writing, and William Polk reminded his daughter Mary that careful writing would "ornament yourself & give felicity to your parents." Virginians Eliza King and Louisa Maxwell simply asserted that "letter writing is one of the finest accomplishments a lady can possess."[33]

Parents also stressed the importance of reading, which they believed not only made women better wives and mothers but also would enable them to endure decades of secluded domestic life. As Thomas Jefferson explained to his daughter Martha, "Music, drawing, books, invention and exercise will be so many resources to you against ennui" born of rural isolation, though he advised that reading was "useful for only filling up the chinks of more useful and healthy [domestic] occupations." Another Virginian, Hore Browse Trist, believed that his daughters should read "*improving* authors" even after they married. "For some time at least," he maintained, "they will have much leisure, which cannot be better employed. Besides the fund of amusement they will possess by *Study*, . . . it will enable them . . . to superintend the domestic education of their children in the earlier periods, [and] of their daughters completely." Peter Lyons recommended that his granddaughter Lucy Hopkins read widely in history and philosophy. If she pursued her studies diligently, he believed, she would "never be in want of company."[34] Unlike their colonial predecessors, post revolutionary parents and educators saw reading more as a way for women to amuse themselves in domestic seclusion than as a means by which they might excel in polite society. As students and later as wives, educated women appreciated the companionship of books and letters.

Letters were the lifelines that connected women to the world beyond their households, enabling them to communicate with absent friends and relatives, many of whom they saw infrequently after marrying. Letters provided them with comfort and amusement, relieving the tedium of domestic isolation. For that reason, Sarah Spotswood sent a servant each day to the local post office, only to be disappointed when "the cry is allways no letters," and Elizabeth Ruffin extended visitors "a double welcome" when they came bearing "letters from friends." One Virginia woman relied on a male friend to post her letters and retrieve her mail, protesting when his other business prevented him from performing this valued service. Another fretted about the health of her riding horse, which she needed "to go for letters." Jane Williams and her daughters wrote each other hurried missives, apologizing for "bad writeing" from "a penn Directed by the Hand of a woman who's whole life has been occupied by Domestic concerns and raising Children." Impatiently awaiting news from her daughters, Williams worried that postal officials "seem to care very little about" women's letters.[35]

Many educated women were also lifelong readers, finding in books the companionship and intellectual stimulation often lacking in their daily lives. As a young unmarried woman at her father's isolated Virginia plantation, Mary Pocahontas Campbell found that reading "makes the time pass tolerably well." Elizabeth Ruffin, who spent many days alone at her plantation home, likewise sought company in books. "Beguiled away the time enjoying Don Quixote," she reported in her diary, adding that she wished "no greater momentary amusement could it always come anew." Rebecca Tayloe Beverley, who attended school in Philadelphia, believed that her education was worth "five times the sum that I have expended in acquiring it" because "now when I can get books and drawing utensils I shall never feel lonesome" on returning to rural Virginia. Sarah Alexander indulged her "novel reading propensities" when her husband's absence left her "so lonely and sorrowful."[36]

Books remained important to many women after they married. As a young wife, Anne Cary Randolph Bankhead continued to read French and history and to practice her arithmetic, and the childless Maria Campbell claimed that "the most interesting companions I have are my books" in the absence of her husband, David. Nelly Custis Lewis, who had many children, read constantly and studied Spanish on her own despite her husband's objections. Another Virginia wife and mother found time to read as many as twelve days a month, choosing history, novels, and advice literature, as well as religious and devotional writing. The studious Rachel Mordecai Lazarus read the latest British and American novels, as well as history, botany, and travel literature. A mother of three by 1828, Lazarus regretted that as a result of her "domestick duties" her "reading hours are now very limited."[37]

Many hardworking wives and mothers found their diversions chiefly in reading and ornamental needlework, activities readily pursued in the domestic sphere and, consequently, approved by parents and moralists and emphasized in female academies. As early as 1775, one popular moralist informed his female readers that proficiency in needlework would enable them not only to sew for their families and to supervise their servants' handiwork but to "fill up, in a tolerably agreeable way, some of the many solitary hours you must necessarily pass at home." As Thomas Jefferson warned his daughter Martha, "In the country life of America there are many moments when a woman can have recourse to nothing but her needle for employment" and for relief from "dull company and dull weather." One North Carolina proponent of women's education similarly recommended needlework as "oeconomical and highly useful in a family," adding that "the needle well plied" was also "a never failing remedy for spleen and vapours."[38] For these reasons, plain and ornamental needlework, alone among the accomplishments that colonial gentlewomen cultivated, maintained its standing in the curricula of the postrevolutionary academies.

In response to those who contended that boarding schools corrupted their pupils, educators protested that their students studied, worked, and lived in a protective moral environment. After 1800, most advertisements for women's schools and academies included the proprietors' promise to pay "particular attention" to "the morals of Students." Proprietors of schools having both male and female "departments" reassured parents that "the young Ladies and Gentlemen . . . shall be kept distinctly apart." Even at day schools, male and female students, who received instruction in separate classrooms, were "in no instance . . . allowed to mix or associate whilst at school." Some educators guaranteed parents that their institution would hire no instructor "whose moral character is not reputable and above suspicion"; others claimed that they would require students to participate in regular religious observances. The founders of a Warren County, North Carolina, boarding school hoped to attract prospective pupils by informing parents that they had hired a minister and his wife to oversee the operation of the fledgling institution. "Mr. Cottrell and his Lady," they reported, "are both members of the Methodist Church, himself a Preacher of the Gospel, and . . . they come recommended to us as being eminently qualified to discharge the duties attached to their trust." The trustees of the Milton Female Academy in Caswell County, North Carolina, similarly engaged a clergyman to head their school, deferring to the wishes of most parents who "choose to place their daughters at institutions where they may enjoy the advantages of religious instruction" as well as "the best opportunities of the literary and ornamental branches of education."[39]

Parents reluctant to part with their daughters needed reassurance that doing so would endanger neither their virtue nor their health.[40] Consequently, proprietors of the increasing numbers of academies located in small towns and rural villages emphasized the moral and physical wholesomeness of their surroundings. The master of a school in Lynchburg, Virginia, de-

Mourning memorial for Samuel L. Bullen, ca. 1810. Needlework served both practical and recreational ends for housebound southern women. Mourning pictures, such as this intricate silk-and-watercolor tribute to a Georgia man who died in 1806, were a popular genre among antebellum women. Courtesy of the Museum of Early Southern Decorative Arts, Winston-Salem, N.C.

clared that his institution enjoyed "one of the most healthy, commodious, and beautiful situations of the upper country: desirably removed from the intrusion of dissipation, and sufficiently accessible to agreeable and improving society." Samuel and Ann Miller, proprietors of the New London Female Academy, described its location as "equally eligible for the salubrity of its climate, and its romantic scenery." Mary C. Garlick, who operated a boarding school for girls at her King William County, Virginia, home, similarly informed the parents of prospective students that "her situation may be called uncommonly healthy." The proprietors of a boarding school outside of Charleston stressed its safety from the fevers that periodically devastated that coastal city.[41]

To allay parental fears and to counter those who asserted that only home education could prepare young women for domesticity, some educators portrayed their institutions as extended families that would give students much the same guidance and discipline they received at home. Run by married couples who often boarded students in their homes, many southern schools resembled families in both physical appearance and organizational structure. One Williamsburg couple, whose spacious house served also as classrooms and dormitory, described their school as an extension of their nuclear family. "Having daughters of their own to educate," they explained, the proprietors simultaneously sought to "render an acceptable service to society, in forming a seminary where polite literature and the arts of personal improvement may be equally cultivated."[42]

The domestication of women's education entailed, among other things, the reconception of schools as surrogate homes. Accordingly, in many schools, husbands tended to the business of administration and academics while their wives supervised the students' domestic skills and moral environment, thereby mirroring the gender-based division of labor in most contemporary families. Jacob Mordecai ran the successful Warrenton Female Academy, while his wife, Rebecca, supervised the students' "domestic arrangement," cultivating their *"Taste* for neatness in their Persons and propriety of Manners." The role of Jacob's daughter Rachel, who also taught in the school, was comparable to that of an accomplished older sister. In fact, several of Rachel's younger sisters were among her students before they, too, joined the ranks of the academy's instructors.[43]

Some educators explicitly described their schools as surrogate homes and themselves as substitute parents. The proprietor of the Williamsburg Academy admitted that "the best scene of elementary education would, under favorable circumstances, be the parental roof," but went on to declare that "should any cause prevent the domestic communication of this necessary instruction, a just confidence may be placed in the judicious regulations" of his own institution. Sarah Falkener confidently assured parents that she would exert the "utmost caution" to preserve the health, piety, and virtue of her students, who, she insisted, "shall know no other difference by being from home than the absence of their parents." A married couple who ran a "Select Boarding School for Young Ladies" in Cannonsborough, South Carolina, promised to "improve the minds of their pupils" and to train them in "the domestic duties which finally devolve on ladies . . . which may fit them for the stations they may hereafter hold in society." The proprietors of this school vowed to use "mild and parental" discipline to "induce their pupils to apply themselves diligently to their respective studies."[44]

The Crowning of Flora, Jacob Marling, 1816. Postrevolutionary schools offered academic curricula in environments that reinforced domestic ideals and values. At this ceremony at the Raleigh Female Academy, students displayed their physical grace and moral virtue, while recitations, songs, refreshments, and flower arrangements showcased accomplishments to edify their future households. The Chrysler Museum of Art, Norfolk, Va., Gift of Edgar William and Bernice Chrysler Garbish 80.181.20.

Persuaded that an academic education could safely enhance the social status and domestic comfort of women and their families, southern parents sent their daughters off to school in increasing numbers in the nineteenth century's early decades. By 1820, in response to the growing demand for academic education, entrepreneurs established at least two schools for young women and two schools for students of both sexes in the port city of Norfolk, Virginia. Richmond, Virginia's capital and social center, was home to at least twenty-five female academies and five coeducational schools in the two decades after 1800. Even more impressive were the growing numbers of academies located in country towns and rural communities during this period. Of the sixteen schools for young women and the six coeducational academies that advertised in North Carolina newspapers between 1800 and 1820, only three of the latter were located in Raleigh, the state's principal city. The demand for women's education even extended into the South Carolina backcountry, where a female academy opened in the village of Pendleton. In the backcountry and elsewhere throughout the region, schools for girls and young women multiplied at an even greater rate after 1820, when evangelicals began to found their own schools for youngsters of both sexes.[45]

The schools girls attended varied widely in size, success, and quality. Plantation schools, similar to those run by colonial tutors, survived into the antebellum era, as did day schools operated by women who also took in sewing and boarders.[46] These small, old-fashioned schools existed alongside academies that had fifty or more students, several instructors, and an ambitious course of study. Some schools, modest and ambitious alike, disbanded shortly after they opened. The Richmond Academy for Female Education, which boasted a board of prominent trustees and a "grand design" to improve women's education, failed shortly after its founding in 1807. Other institutions such as the Raleigh Academy and Richmond's MacKenzie School for Young Ladies survived for decades to educate several generations of white female southerners.[47]

Parents' desires to educate their daughters afforded young women unprecedented opportunities to leave home for extended periods. Away from parental supervision, some girls developed new confidence in themselves and their abilities. The sisters Rebecca and Jane Beverley escaped an overbearing father, overcame their initial homesickness, and eventually took pride in seeking and winning academic prizes at the schools they attended in Pennsylvania.[48] Away from home, many young women also developed intense friendships that they could not replicate when they returned to their isolated farms or plantations. Louisa Lenoir had misgivings about ending her time at the Salem Academy because she knew that "when I go home I will have to leave friends who are very dear to me." As a student at her father's Warrenton Female Academy, Caroline Mordecai similarly described the end of the school year as a "melancholy" time when students reflected "that the hour is so near, in which we are to part . . . perhaps many of us, never to meet again."[49]

The message of young women's educational experience was ambiguous in many ways. Girls left home to prepare for domesticity, but the academy experience provided them with female role models who, despite their rhetorical adherence to the ideals of domesticity, participated in public life. Rachel Mordecai, for instance, recognized that her prominent position at the Warrenton Female Academy made her a public figure in that small

Students at female academies and boarding schools often enjoyed intense friendships, which they sorely missed when they returned home after their schooldays were over. An early nineteenth-century student at North Carolina's Salem Academy received this watercolor painting from her "dear friend Louisa" as a token of the artist's affection. Collection of Old Salem, Winston-Salem, N.C.

North Carolina town. Mordecai accepted her public role and even looked forward to scholastic ceremonies, at which she often officiated. Indeed, she saw the academy's public examinations as "a great advantage to the town, for the company collected at such times, rouse people from their state of *tor-pidity* . . . and make them remember that there are others in the world besides themselves, and that they *can* occasionally think of something else, besides tobacco, cotton, spinning, weaving, and attending to their family concerns." Perhaps the academy's students shared her sense of their recitations' public value. Yet parents who pushed their daughters to "set *steadily* to work" often criticized those who excelled for being "too fond of books . . . for being a Female your great acquirements can only be known to those immediately connected with you."[50]

Mary A. Bond, a graduating student who addressed her female classmates at the Raleigh Academy in 1819, aptly summarized the objectives of the female academies and their patrons. "Let us never forget," Bond told her listeners, "that the sole end of our connexion with this Seminary, is to fix us for the proper discharge of all the duties which may devolve upon us in future life." Once they acquired the knowledge and skills necessary for domesticity, students should return to their homes and "repay at least a part of the debt [they] owe for [their] Education" by being humble, modest, and charitable to others. Because they aspired to fill the "elevated stations" of wife and mother, Bond believed that her classmates also should "learn to obey" to ensure their future happiness. "Obedience," Bond reminded her classmates, was the central objective of women's education and the only "indisputable proof" of its inherent value.[51]

The academies thus prepared all their female students to occupy the same sex-specific "sphere" in their adult lives. The metaphor of sexually defined separate spheres existed in prescriptive literature at least as early as 1615, when the Englishman Gervase Markham began his popular manual by describing the husband as "the Father and Master of the Family . . . whose Office and imployments are ever for the most part abroad, or removed from the house," and the wife as "Mother and Mistress of the family, [who] hath her most general imployments within the house." Markham envisioned the domestic sphere as a discrete place in which women performed certain types of sex-specific labor. Subsequent writers accepted this rudimentary formulation of men's and women's spheres but additionally emphasized alleged differences in temperament and intellect that supposedly suited the sexes to their respective roles. Men, according to most accounts, had strength, courage, confidence, and judgment, while women possessed beauty, modesty, taste, and sensibility. Men's attributes enabled them to "shine abroad," whereas "female excellence [was] best displayed" at home.[52]

Because the ideal of feminine domesticity became a cardinal feature of the middle-class worldview and because its emergence coincided with the rise of bourgeois capitalism in western Europe and the northern United States, scholars who argue that southerners did not embrace bourgeois economic values believe that they similarly rejected the sexual division of labor that consigned women to a domestic sphere within which they purportedly exercised substantial influences and authority.[53] To be sure, a purely economic understanding of the ideal of separate spheres, which assumed the economic and social value of men's extradomestic work but characterized women's labor as nonproductive, was irrelevant to most white southern families, who lived on farms or plantations where wives and husbands alike worked at home and contributed to the family economy. Many nineteenth-century southerners, however, did embrace both the ideal of women's domesticity and its concomitant division of intellectual and emotional roles and attributes. Like their northern contemporaries, they portrayed women as pious, pure, nurturing, and best shielded from the potentially corrupting world outside their households.[54] Compatible with republican, evangelical, and sentimental notions of virtuous womanhood, the ideal of feminine domesticity flourished in the South, even if the region lacked a dominant middle class and an economy based on wage labor.

Like their northern counterparts, early nineteenth-century southern men enjoined women to remain in the domestic sphere and lauded those characteristics that supposedly predisposed women to domestic life. "Small is the province of a wife, / And narrow is her sphere in life," advised one often-reprinted verse. "Abroad for happiness ne'er roam, / True happiness resides at home." A male contributor to the *Richmond Enquirer* believed that men "may tread the great theatre of life" but that women should "move in the narrower scenes of sweet domestic comfort, to charm away the cares which assail us, [and] soothe the soul into peace." In 1806, a Charleston magazine reprinted a British essay that stressed the separate but complementary spheres in which men and women excelled. "Man by being endowed with more strength of body, and solidity of mind than woman, is better fitted for managing affairs in public," declared the anonymous author, "and woman possessing less strength of body, but more softness of manners, has modestly sought only the care of domestic affairs," which nonetheless endowed her with influence "nearly equal [in] importance" to that enjoyed by man.[55]

In the southern states as elsewhere, the celebration of separate spheres and feminine domesticity coincided with a renewed appreciation of the joys of married life. Unlike the postrevolutionary polemicists who stressed the public benefits of marriage, which they believed promoted social order, these writers emphasized the private and emotional advantages of a loving domestic life. One South Carolinian sentimentally applauded couples who "taste the sweets of mutual love" and whose happiness is only increased by the addition of "tender offspring" to "bind in firmer bands, those hearts which true affection joined." Another southerner declared that a loving marriage was "attended with the happiest effects" of "health and happiness." One Carolina poet, pondering the comforts of marriage, likened "domestic love" to a "celestial spark" that made life worth living even in adversity, while another informed bachelors that marriage was a "bond so sweet, / Where heart and soul unite; / Where friendship, love and union meet."[56]

Reflecting both the republican and evangelical regard for virtue, as well as the growing sentimentalism of the era, essayists and social critics also mounted an unprecedented attack on mercenary matches. Although few denied the importance of economic self-sufficiency, most regarded marriages contracted primarily for financial gain as crass, immoral, and destined for misery and unhappiness. Many southerners, especially those among the elite, continued to scrutinize the material assets of their children's prospective spouses, but they also increasingly looked on mutual affection and compatibility as the chief prerequisites for wedded happiness.[57]

Men and women alike idealized romantic love and candidly sought affection and companionship in marriage. In the 1790s, the young Virginia lawyer John Coalter addressed amorous poems to his fiancée, who in turn reassured him that marital "happyness is not confined to the Luxiruius." Nearly a generation later, William Gaston wrote love letters to his fiancée, encouraged her to write him letters that were equally revealing, and playfully informed her that a friend of his had been "cured of a distressing malady by a marriage to the woman he loved." Eliza Custis hoped to marry a man for whom her love was *"as fixed as the Decrees* of fate, & no cause but death shall take me *from him."* Rebecca Tayloe Beverley, a young Virginian whose father pressed her to marry for money, insisted that she would never be "induced to marry a man that I could not esteem and respect merely because he is wealthy," though she admitted that she probably would not marry a poor man, "for a state of dependence is next to death."[58]

Yet for most women, dependence was the inevitable result of marriage, and as a result some regarded matrimony with pronounced ambivalence. In the 1780s and 1790s, perhaps influenced by the Revolution's libertarian rhetoric, some young southerners described marriage as the last act of "female liberty," while others swore to remain unmarried "until the end of time" rather than submit to the authority of a husband they could neither esteem nor love.[59] This portrayal of marriage as the enemy of women's liberty appeared much less frequently after 1800, though as late as 1816, the female author of "The Maid's Soliloquy" characterized wedlock as a state of "bondage" that always required women's submission but only sometimes rewarded her with blissful companionship. An even more pessimistic nineteenth-century contributor to the *Richmond Enquirer* deemed most marriages tyrannical arrangements that turned a good woman into "the neglected, oppressed, insulted drudge of an unprincipled and profligate husband." At least one young Virginia woman agreed, asserting that "the sweets of independence are greatly preferable to that *charming servitude* under a lord and master." Although this twenty-year-old diarist later married happily, in 1827 she chose *"perpetual celibacy"* and "bearing . . . the curses and stings showered on the *superannuated sisterhood"* over rendering "obedience . . . and . . . homage" to another.[60]

Most young women equated marriage with neither tyranny nor enslavement, but many worried that it would disrupt other cherished personal relationships. Lucinda Lee regarded marriage as the "bane of Female Friendship," and Margaret Davenport worried that her impending marriage would jeopardize her friendships with women who "are all the world to me." Eliza Waring had hoped that her "Amiable Friend" Harriet would be "an exception to the too general rule of Ladies neglecting friendships contracted in Celibacy after their entrance to the conjugal state," but she found that this former confidante now neglected to write her and "assume[d] serious, demure & consequencial airs." By 1820, as two Randolph cousins observed, conventional wisdom held that marriage "chills the fondest affections & dissolves the firmest friendships" between women. In the rural South especially, female friendships waned because marriage carried many brides miles away from their childhood homes. Faced with an often staggering array of new domestic responsibilities, they found it difficult to correspond regularly with their absent friends and relatives.[61]

Many young wives clearly regretted their separation from familiar peo-

ple and places. Maria Rind Coalter sorely missed her family and friends in
Williamsburg when she married and moved to western Virginia. When one
Fredericksburg bride left for Georgia with her new husband, she informed
her "dearest sister" that she missed her "lively conversation," adding, "altho
I cannot enjoy it awake I am conversing with you almost every night, & I
visit in my dreams Fredericksburg and all its dear inhabitants." Nancy
Cocke confessed to her parents, "Tho' I have the tenderest of Husbands,
and one who does every thing to make me happy and who I shall be happy
with I am sure as long as I live — yet it will take me some time to be weaned
from you enough to be happy without you." Nancy's mother admitted that
she too felt "anguish & distress at our seperation" and earnestly prayed that
God would make her daughter "happy without the presence of her Parents
who have fondly lov'd her from the very moment of her existance." When
Margaret Scott married and left her Virginia home for Delaware, her
mother instructed her to find solace in religion. "The person who believes
that every thing is ordered by a blind chance is like a Ship at Sea without
Anchor or rudder," she warned, "while the believer in Providence is satisfied that every thing is ordered for our benefit [and] is thankfull in prosperity & patient & resigned in adversity."[62]

Some women took years to adjust to separation from their families, especially from their female relatives. In March 1798, at the age of seventeen,
Eliza Williams of Wilmington, North Carolina, married forty-three-year-old
John Haywood and moved with him to Raleigh, some 125 miles from her
parents' home. Within a few weeks, however, Eliza returned to Wilmington,
where she remained until August, despite her husband's pleading. Separation was agonizing for both Eliza and her mother, and the young wife again
returned to Wilmington in November. The following month, she gave birth
to her first child in her parents' house, where she stayed until the following
May. Eliza Haywood gradually became accustomed to living in Raleigh
with her husband and their growing family, but as late as 1802 she was still
making extended visits to Wilmington. When Eliza's sisters also married
and had children, they too found it difficult to travel. In 1808, when Rebecca Williams Moore and Ferebee Williams Hall planned to accompany
their mother to Raleigh to visit Eliza, the women pondered the possibility
that "perhaps it may be the last time we may be alltogether." In fact, Eliza
may not have seen her sisters again. By 1816, both Rebecca and Ferebee
were dead.[63]

Southern parents surely expected their daughters to marry, but they
also recognized that marriage was a risky proposition for most young

women, who, as wives, would be isolated in their households and legally, economically, and physically dependent on their husbands. Some parents made special efforts to protect their daughters from financially irresponsible spouses. Landon Carter, who feared his daughter Judith "might be made a beggar" by her husband and his family, stipulated that her marriage settlement be a loan instead of an outright gift because, under the terms of coverture, giving Judith property "for her life . . . would constitute A Property in her husband during that time, and might be removed for debt or otherwise." Like the southern legislators who enacted the antebellum married women's property laws, Carter was probably more interested in protecting his vast estate than in guaranteeing his daughter's economic independence.[64]

By contrast, many southern women who wrote wills explicitly sought to diminish the financial dependence of their female relatives. Elizabeth Elliott divided her household goods, as well as the "money I leave in a jugg in my Closett," among her four daughters, noting that her son "had so much more of his Fathers Estate than his Sisters . . . [and] what he has of my land is more than ten times more than his Sisters had." Sarah Baugh set aside 345 acres and twelve slaves for the "Sole Seperate use" of her daughter Tabitha, whom she believed "likely to be reduced to want the Common necessaries of life" as a result of her husband's chronic indebtedness. Elizabeth Anderson bequeathed property to her grandson's wife, directing her executors to place the modest legacy "at her own Disposal . . . that her Husband should have nothing to do with it." Ann Murray made a cash bequest to her granddaughter, similarly stipulating that the money should "in no instance be subject to the control or disposal of her husband." The milliner Jane Hunter Charlton divided her estate among three nieces, two of whom were married, and ordered that her brother-in-law William Russell "shall not have any concern whatever with any part of my estate so left" to his unmarried daughter.[65]

Parents, especially mothers, also worried about the emotional travail their daughters would suffer by contracting unfortunate matches. While husbands could find entertainment, companionship, and even sexual pleasure outside of marriage, a wife's happiness depended, as Thomas Jefferson advised his daughter Martha, "on the continuing to please a single person." Martha's mother-in-law, Anne Cary Randolph, hoped to prevent her own daughters from marrying "till they were old enough to form a proper judgment of Mankind" because she knew "that a Woman's happiness depends intirely on the Husband she is united to." Marriage, she believed, was "a step that requires more deliberation, than Girls generally take," despite the fact that those who chose unwisely would be "wretched without a remedy." Years later, Martha Jefferson Randolph postponed her own seventeen-year-old daughter's betrothal to Nicholas Trist, warning that they were "both too young to be entangled by an engagement which will decide the happiness, or wretchedness of your lives." One southern matron urged her seventeen-year-old granddaughter to break her engagement if either she or her fiancé "saw any one [they] liked better than the other" because she deemed them "both so young there is no calculating on the stability of present feelings."[66]

Of course, many women ultimately found joy and happiness in marriage and especially in motherhood. Even Eleanor Parke Custis Lewis, who spent much of her married life pining for the balls of her youth, was an ecstatic bride and a doting mother. "I have not a wish beyond domestic retirement" with "the best of Husbands," she declared shortly after her marriage. "The idea of being a Mother, of watching over & forming the mind of Our little infant," she mused, "is a source of delight which none but those in similar situations can experience." Martha Jefferson Randolph, who ran both her husband's and her father's households, complained that she had "not time to attend regularly to her children," but she missed them desperately when they were absent. Many mothers admitted that they doted on their offspring. Jane Williams of Wilmington, who had such great difficulty parting with her married daughter Eliza, later observed, "A Mothers fears and anxieties especially for Daughters never I believe end but with her life." Only their own loving and companionate marriages provided many mothers with the solace they needed to face the departure of grown offspring. "If your father and I were not very loving and industrious people, we should feel very solitary at present," Martha Laurens Ramsay informed a son at Princeton in 1810. As daughters married and sons went off to college, Martha and David Ramsay experienced "a great change" in their lives — a change, she noted, that "needs both love and labor to make it tolerable."[67]

Although women often sentimentalized motherhood and romantic love, it was men who idealized both women's domesticity and the concept of the home as a separate sphere and a seat of virtuous bliss. Like their northern contemporaries, southern men, writing in regional periodicals, publicly celebrated the home as the locus of virtue and affection, a sanctuary from a tumultuous and often corrupting world. As early as 1785, an anonymous contributor to the Charleston *Columbian Herald* recommended the recuperative powers of domestic repose for men engaged in "active life." Only at home, the author suggested, could men rest their "weary mind[s], . . . shut out the acclamations of an applauding world, . . . enjoy the prattling of their little ones, and . . . partake of the endearments of family conversation." Politically active men could thus escape the false or shallow adulation of the "giddy multitude" of the public sphere to take refuge in the private "attentions paid them at their own fire side . . . [that] were the genuine result of undissembled love."[68]

Between 1780 and 1830, northern moralists and clergymen promoted the home as an antidote to the unsettling effects of political revolution, westward migration, and capitalist economic development, suggesting that domestic virtue could offset the declining influence of community, church, and traditional forms of deference. Because profound changes in class relations, labor organization, and work culture arising from economic modernization were so pervasive, northern writers constructed their ideals of home, family, and women's domestic work in opposition to an emerging capitalist ethos. Northerners emphasized the dichotomous relationship between impersonal "work" and affective "home," invoking a modern division of labor that would have been alien to most southerners.[69]

Yet contemporary southerners were no less extravagant in their praise of domestic life. As inhabitants of a largely rural region where racial divisions complicated class relations that were more traditional than modern, southern champions of women's domesticity could not share the economic perspective of their northern counterparts, though revolution, mobility, and religious disestablishment also had undermined traditional order and stability in their region.[70] Southern men may have worked their land in close proximity to their wives and chidren, but when they sold their crops and bought supplies and when they attended court and political rallies, they too exposed themselves to the world and its temptations. When they read novels and attended church services, they also encountered a sentimentalism that valued simplicity, love, and companionship. Thus southern men could join with northerners in lauding the home as a refuge for wholesome morality and praising virtuous women as the uncorrupted custodians of domestic values.

Southern men wrote poems and essays celebrating the virtue, affection, and tranquillity of domestic life. "How sweet, remote from busy life, / To press thy children and thy wife," mused a North Carolina poet who longed to be "Secure at home!" One contributor to the *Raleigh Register* craved a "happy fire-side" where "the virtues with their train of social joys" brought "health and peace and freedom" to its grateful master. Another believed that home was "the just theatre of a woman's glory . . . [and] the just bounds of a man's felicity." A man, he asserted, "will find no rest until returned to the ark of domestic tranquility . . . . Happy the man, who, with cool, determined, indifference, can withdraw from the world's applause" to the sweet and soothing "smiles of a wife." When men idealized domestic life, the devoted wife was the key figure in their imagined vistas. "Women are our mistresses in youth, our companions in manhood, and our nurses in old age," observed one Carolinian, while another sentimentalized the good wife who soothed her world-weary husband. "Nothing," he declared, "can render the power of retirement so serene and comfortable [to men] . . . as a conviction that *woman* is not indifferent to our fate."[71]

In their private writings, southern men also idealized the domestic sphere, especially when business or politics necessitated their temporary absence from it. When the Virginian Hore Browse Trist traveled to Kentucky in 1802 to inspect his recently acquired western lands, he found himself constantly thinking of his home in Charlottesville, admitting that his "fancy warmly colours the scene of domestic imployments & domestic happiness." Similarly, when court business prevented Chief Justice John Marshall from being with his wife and family, he pined for his Virginia home. "I would give a great deal to dine with you today on a cold piece of meat with our boys beside us and to see little Mary running backwards and forwards over the floor playing the sweet little tricks she is full of," he wrote to his wife, Polly, in 1797. Nearly three decades later, the aging Marshall still believed that "home is [the] place of most comfort," and he longed to leave the "busy bustling scene" of national politics to "return to the tranquility of my family and farm." John Haywood admitted that absence from home taught him "the inestimable value of the domestic Comforts and family Enjoyments with which I am blessed." In Richmond for the legislative session and its attendant balls and dinners, Wilson Jefferson Cary claimed he would "gladly . . . give up such frivolous gaieties for a quiet evening with my family by my own fireside," assuring his wife that "my mind has dwelt constantly upon my dear family since I parted with them."[72]

Men were more likely to sentimentalize domestic life because they were more often removed from it. Southern women traveled infrequently, and their sojourns away from home usually merely transferred them to a different domestic environment. Sometimes women traveled with their children or spouses. Often they made extended visits to homes of distant kin. In both cases, women travelers could idealize and long for absent loved ones, but their continued immersion in domestic life discouraged them from penning panegyrics to domesticity comparable to those of their male contemporaries.

Yet even on rare occasions when women's travels freed them from their domestic identities and occupations, they usually did not sentimentalize their temporarily interrupted domestic lives. In the 1790s, Harriott Pinckney Horry spent nearly a year touring the United States. She kept an extensive journal but never once complained of being homesick. By 1800, elite Virginia women routinely traveled to fashionable western spas to recover from childbirth and other "female complaints." Although such women often missed the company of their children and husbands, they never waxed nostalgic for woman's "sphere" or for the supposed bliss of generic domestic life. Rachel Mordecai Lazarus likewise described her two-month tour of the northern states as "a period of enjoyment unallayed except by the pain of a temporary separation from my children."[73]

Men, not women, sentimentalized domesticity because men alone identified the domestic sphere with leisure and seclusion from the trials of life. Although many southern women found happiness in marriage and motherhood, the domestic sphere was the scene of both their greatest joys and severest trials. Above all, women associated domesticity with work, the never-ending rounds of domestic chores that shaped their lives.

Women's domestic work had not changed much since the colonial era, though the social and cultural contexts in which white women labored were altered in four important ways by the early nineteenth century. First, the celebration of domesticity increased the perceived importance of and standards for women's domestic labor. Second, the peculiarly southern need to justify slavery resulted in improvements in the food, clothing, and care of enslaved people, which in turn increased the responsibilities of their mistresses.[74] Third, nineteenth-century women probably had more people to care for and to oversee than their colonial predecessors because they married younger — and therefore produced more offspring — and because the region's slave population grew substantially during this period.[75] Finally, after the Revolution, the decline of sociability heightened the domestic isolation of white women, especially in rural areas. Overall, white women of all classes probably worked harder than their ancestors, and elite women had fewer social respites from their domestic labors.

By the early decades of the nineteenth century, authors of essays and advice books, fathers, husbands, and women themselves often discussed domestic work and acknowledged its significance. Authors of a growing list of cookery books emphasized domestic economy, suggesting, in the words of one popular author, that "many families have owed their prosperity full as

much to the conduct and propriety of female management, as to the knowledge and activity of the father." Among southerners, the gospel of domestic
economy perhaps was preached most vigorously in Virginia, where, according to Jefferson, the decline of the tobacco economy made it "next to impossible for [a planter] to avoid ruin." Like other financially straitened Virginia
men, Jefferson believed that "a wife imbued with principles of prudence,
may go far towards arresting or lessening the evils" of her husband's "im-
provident management." In *A Sermon to Young Women*, a prominent Richmond minister similarly advised his readers that "industry and habits of
economy constitute an important part of the good works with which women
are to be adorned."[76]

Although southern women always worked in their households, discussions of domestic chores now occupied a larger portion of their correspondence and some wives explicitly recognized their own contributions to the
family economy. "I have wrought an entire reformation on . . . my household," explained a recently married Martha Jefferson Randolph, "and I believe there is as little wasted as possible." Another Virginian informed her
husband that "if good management consists in making a little go a great way
and having that little appear to as great an advantage as one is capable of
doing, I may be said to be a good [manager]."[77]

Like elite and middle-class northerners, some southerners also set
higher standards for women's domestic work, encouraging cleanliness as a
reflection of moral virtue and a promoter of physical health. "Virtue never
dwells long with filth and nastiness," asserted one contributor to the *Raleigh
Register*; "nor do I believe there was ever a person scrupulously attentive to
cleanliness, who was a consummate villain." Bishop James Madison advised his daughter Susan to "let neatness, order, and judgment be seen" in
both her person and her house. Another southerner claimed that cleanliness
was "the most sovereign preservative against all diseases, endemical as well
as constitutional," while filth "never fails to disgust and sometimes to
injure."[78]

Slaveholding women supervised corps of domestic servants who
scrubbed, laundered, sewed, and cooked, but even elite women performed
some domestic labor, as they had done since the colonial era. Ann Cleland
Kinloch, a slave-owning Charleston woman whose urban residence enabled
her to enjoy far more leisure than the average plantation mistress, made
breakfast every day and knitted or mended stockings on most evenings.[79]
Plantation mistresses were much busier, overseeing the slaughter of livestock, the preserving of meat, and the weaving of cloth, while they them-

172 selves sewed, mended, and knitted almost daily. During the first half of 1797, Frances Baylor Hill knitted an average of six days each month and sewed an average of seventeen, making and mending new stockings and clothing for both white and black members of her plantation household. In the 1820s, Lucy Johnston Ambler, the wife of a slaveholding planter, did all her family's sewing. Young wives made curtains, quilts, and counterpanes for their homes. Mistresses and their daughters alike knitted stockings for their families and the enslaved people who served them.[80]

Women also raised poultry and engaged in dairying and gardening like their colonial ancestors. Although most used what they produced in their own kitchens, others sold some of their butter and eggs or traded them with a local storekeeper. In 1819, the *Raleigh Register* praised a Virginia woman who supplied a Shepherdstown storekeeper with 1,668 eggs from her hens over an eight-day period. "This is an example worthy of imitation," the *Register* asserted. "This industrious matron has . . . in one week, by the single article of eggs alone, cleared the amount of fourteen dollars, seventy odd cents." In 1822, Lucy Johnston Ambler marketed more than sixty pounds of butter, besides producing both butter and turkeys for her family's use. Peggy Nicholas hired a boatman to sell her butter farther from home, hoping to get a higher price. Nancy Cocke, like many planters' wives, raised hens, turkeys, chicken, geese, and pigs. Some women were friendly rivals in stock-raising. One Virginia woman, who had both pigs and fowl, challenged a friend "to arm yourself with all the resolution you are Mistress of" and attend to her poultry, "or at the end of the year when we come to compare notes the victory will be mine."[81]

Urban housewives were less likely than their rural counterparts to raise pigs and turkeys, but they too usually kept a cow and tended a garden on their house lots. Margaret Davenport Coalter's house in the town of Staunton, Virginia, had both a dairy and a "Garden-spot." When the Englishwoman Anne Ritson visited Norfolk at the turn of the century, she found that the city's women kept both cows and gardens that often produced enough milk and vegetables to feed their families along with a surplus to send to market. Ritson also reported that the women of Norfolk saved fat and ashes to make soap and candles "for common use," a practice that would become less common among city dwellers, though not among rural families, in the coming decades.[82]

In the early decades of the nineteenth century, cloth was still the most important commodity that rural women and their slaves manufactured. Although the resumption of trade and the restoration of peace in 1816 dimin-

Nondescripts, attracted by a neighbouring barbecue, near the Oaks, Virginia, Benjamin Latrobe, 1796. Despite the increasing sentimentalization of domestic life, women's productive labor in and around the household continued to be essential in many southern families. This poor white woman and her children sought to earn money by selling peaches to people enjoying a barbecue in their neighborhood. The Papers of Benjamin Henry Latrobe, Maryland Historical Society, Baltimore.

ished the perceived political significance of women's spinning and weaving, domestic clothmaking remained an essential part of the southern agricultural economy. Many families raised a few sheep for wool and grew or purchased small quantities of cotton for home consumption. According to the 1840 federal census, approximately 1,400 free households in Louisa County, in central Virginia, produced a total of 21,289 pounds of wool and 19,129 pounds of cotton — significant amounts, though not enough to make either product commercially viable. Some 2,450 free households in Mecklenburg County, North Carolina, located at the northern edge of the South's cotton-producing region, collectively accounted for 22,876 pounds of wool, along with 1,595,327 pounds of cotton, most of which was sent to market. In both communities, women, their daughters, and their slaves spun wool and sometimes cotton, and though some hired outsiders to weave their fibers, many completed the clothmaking process in their own houses.[83]

In 1821, Peggy Nicholas oversaw the making of some 250 yards of cloth in the neighborhood surrounding her plantation in northern Virginia. The mistress of approximately thirty slaves, she employed a combination of free and slave labor to clothe her bondpeople. Nicholas had to buy the raw cotton, which could not have been grown in her part of Virginia. Her slaves probably spun the fibers into thread, and then two hired white women, working in their own homes, wove the thread into fabric. When Nicholas received the finished cloth, she herself cut out the garments' pieces, which were then marked by a slave woman named Harriet. Four slave women appear to have sewn the clothing, which included breeches, shirts, and other articles of clothing for adults and children of both sexes.[84]

Altogether, these routine and seasonal domestic chores were hard work, even for white women who could delegate the most onerous tasks to their slaves. Women's work was essential to maintaining the solvency and comfort of a household, but men and youngsters who were not in charge of households probably underestimated the demands of women's domestic labor. Many husbands must have shared the dismay of the recently widowed Henry Izard, who candidly admitted that he was "as ignorant as a schoolboy about the most common articles of necessity for my house," having always depended on his wife, Emma, for "all the little indoor accommodations of my life." Left in charge of her grandfather's house briefly in 1820, a young Cornelia Randolph found that "more laborious work both to mind & body I never did before & hope never to do after." Directed by her mother to close the house for the winter, Cornelia was "*terrified* out of my senses by the servants who seemed to think they must make their provision for the winter before we all left . . . & then such a numberless variety of directions to be recolected & given, which mama had left, & such a countless number that I had to give, all out of my own head." Cornelia confided to her sister that "the above mentioned hard work made me really sick for some days after."[85]

Full-time housewives, of course, combined routine and seasonal housework with their equally demanding maternal obligations. Unlike the northern middle class, who increasingly limited the size of their families, most white southerners probably did not attempt to curtail their fertility in the postrevolutionary decades. Most white southern women married young and became pregnant roughly every second year thereafter. Although infant mortality rates remained high, large families were common. For example, among North Carolina's antebellum planters, families had an average of seven surviving children. Birth rates appear to have been equally high in contemporary yeoman households.[86]

Mothers were responsible for their children's physical and moral well-being, as well as for their early intellectual development. Indeed, the senti-mentalization of women and domesticity led to a new emphasis on the du-ties of motherhood in the postrevolutionary decades. By the 1790s, for instance, British and American writers were increasingly urging women to breast-feed their infants, though the use of both black and white wetnurses may have been common among elite southerners during the colonial era.[87] Now advice books and newspaper essays warned women that breast-feeding was both medically desirable and morally requisite. Breast-feeding, they argued, gave the infant sustenance while strengthening the moral and emotional bond between a mother and her child. Mothers who refused to breast-feed their infants, such writers insisted, selfishly put their own com-fort and pleasure ahead of this sacred maternal duty. One popular medical guide advised physicians and midwives to persuade women to nurse their infants by telling them that "those mothers who suckle their children are the longest livers, and not so liable to cancer." Inspired by maternal tenderness, social pressure, or fear of cancer, even most elite women appear to have breast-fed their own infants by the antebellum era.[88]

Postrevolutionary prescriptive literature also increasingly stressed a mother's duty to provide her children with early educational and religious training, time-consuming tasks that only educated women with servants to attend to their other domestic work could hope to perform adequately. Ann Cleland Kinloch relied on her slaves to clean her house and to cook dinner daily, thus enabling her to spend a portion of most days overseeing the lessons of her motherless granddaughter, who resided in her Charleston home. Eliza Burgwin Clitherall spent two hours each morning teaching reading, writing, and catechism to her two daughters, Eliza and Emily. "Having excellent servants, & a good sempstress," she later recalled, "I had abundance of time to devote to my precious children without neglecting my family domestic duties."[89]

Slaveholding women often complained of the indolence, dishonesty, or recalcitrance of their slaves, but they also occasionally admitted the value of their domestic labor. In the 1790s, Virginian Mary Dandridge Spotswood Campbell, who owned more than fifty slaves, considered selling all "but such as my house Servants," whom she presumably considered indispens-able. Eliza Haywood relied on her "own Black People" to prepare dinners for large companies of often unexpected guests. Judith Randolph, mistress of Bizarre plantation, depended on her slaves John and Amelia to cook and clean, respectively. In 1804, when illness prevented both from working, Randolph noted that her house was in disarray as a result of their absence.

In their wills, some women also recognized and rewarded exemplary domestic service. Susanna Harrison Hoxton instructed her son to take her old cook Peg into his household, where her husband resided. Hoxton hoped that Peg would have a happy old age, "indulged and treated kindly, & not . . . made to work, as she has been a good & Faithful Servant."[90]

Most white women appear to have acquiesced quietly in the demands of their domestic work, complaining only when unexpected circumstances complicated their already heavy work loads. In 1803, Eliza Haywood of Raleigh, who recently had given birth to her fourth child in as many years, complained that her husband obliged her to have as many as thirty men to dinner each night the state legislature was in session. Between caring for her children and entertaining such large numbers of guests, Haywood was "almost worn out and Broke down, with Fatigue and want of rest," and she complained to her mother that when the federal court convened she expected to "have the same Trouble over again." Similarly, when some acquaintances wheedled an invitation to Poplar Forest plantation, its mistress privately complained that her guests were "utterly odious to me, the very last people in the county with whom I *will* be familiar, and yet I am forced to 'make a dinner' for their dainty palates, with all the *labour and turmoil* which a young housekeeper must have on such occasions, and deck my face with smiles of welcome, while in my heart I would sooner see them on their way to Jericho, or in Sailor's phrase, to the S.E. corner of h — l."[91]

Illness in the family also increased women's work. Although southerners who could afford to consult physicians increasingly did so, women continued to dispense home remedies and to nurse family members between doctors' visits. Many women, such as Martha Jefferson Randolph, must have made themselves ill tending houses full of sick children who required "unwearied attention to their diet." When Anne Nicholas nursed an ailing son and sister simultaneously in 1804, she complained to her sister-in-law that she had never "experienced such a time of fatigue in my life." When Eliza Haywood nursed her husband through a difficult illness, she was "up Night and Day, except an hour or so [when] I might get behind him in bed and sleep." Haywood was "continually up and on my Feet handing Medicine and Teas and other Things" to her husband, John, who regained his health gradually. Their ordeal sparked Eliza's religious conversion. Another woman spent six sleepless weeks nursing her ailing husband and daughter, "devoutly thankful for [God's] supporting hand which appears to sustain me under all my affliction."[92]

Women most frequently complained not of the number or difficulty of their duties but of the domestic isolation in which they labored. When one young Williamsburg woman visited the plantation home of her married sister, she found rural domesticity lonely and monotonous. "We rise about seven o clock and as soon as we are dresst go to work or read and about eight breakfast comes in [and] as soon as it is over Sister Byrd goes about her family affairs," explained Lucy Armistead. The family dined at three, then took a short walk, and "at night we work while Mr Byrd reads to us" before retiring at nine. "This is the manner in which we spend our time," Armistead reported to her mother, "when we are intirely alone." Hetty Carr, the widowed mistress of Carrsbrook plantation, found evenings especially difficult. "You can have no Idea how lonesome our Nights are," she wistfully reported to her eldest son, who had left home to study in Baltimore.[93]

Many rural women were alone often. When Anne Nicholas moved to her husband's plantation at Bremo Recess, she found herself "absolutely as far removed from every thing like intercourse from my species, as if I was in a solitary tomb." After months of rural isolation, Nicholas claimed to "be afraid at going in the world again," fearing that she had "forgotten the commonest interchange of civilities; and shall be regarded as a wild unpolished rustic untamed from the dreary woods of Fluvanna." Eleanor Parke Custis Lewis, who as a youngster enjoyed a rich and varied social life, spent her adulthood in rural retirement. Passing entire seasons housebound and without guests, Lewis lamented her own isolation as well as that of her eldest daughter, who followed her husband to Louisiana and "a life of domestic toil far away from every one of congenial tastes and habits."[94]

Rural women complained of boredom and loneliness, despite their often hectic domestic schedules. Although Jefferson's Monticello was livelier than the homes of less celebrated planters, Martha Jefferson Randolph bemoaned the monotony of life at her father's house and looked forward to the arrival of "some body to put a few ideas in our heads." Another Virginia mother longed for her son's "Sociable and improving chat" on his return from college.[95]

Isolated rural women especially craved the companionship of female friends and relatives. Describing herself as "a poor unprotected, desolate being, cut off from society," Judith Randolph of Bizarre wrote pathetic letters to her female kin, begging them to relieve her misery by coming to see her or inviting her to visit. Less despondent women also lamented their remoteness from female companions. Lucy Thornton, a widowed plantation mistress who visited her kin in Fredericksburg as often as possible, wrote long and frequent letters to her female cousins in which she described her home as a "poor lon[ely] dwelling, where no friendly voice enters." Ann Cleve Armistead commiserated with her sister, a lonely Virginia plantation mistress, declaring, "I wish you could have one of our sisters with you, as I am sure you must want a female companion."[96]

Although middling farm women, many of whom were illiterate, wrote few surviving letters describing their rural seclusion, scattered evidence suggests that they too shared the dearth of female companionship lamented by their more prosperous neighbors. If the Norfolk, Virginia, area was typical, only the most disreputable white women attended the public markets, which could have been occasions for casual sociability. Nor did less affluent southerners engage in more formal rounds of social visits. A newcomer to one rural Virginia county found her neighbors "not very desirous of company" because "their Land is poor and they are obliged to be great economists to live." In addition, southern farm women rarely came together to perform communal work, such as the sewing, spinning, and quilting bees enjoyed by their northern contemporaries. When the South Carolinian Alice DeLancey Izard visited rural Pennsylvania, she found such a gathering of working women novel enough to describe in detail in a letter to her daughter Margaret. "A Bee consists of a number of people assembled to do any particular piece of work," she explained, and on this occasion she witnessed "a female party of decently dressed, well-looking Women of all ages, who were sporting a quantity of Wool belonging to the Master of the House." Concluding that these gatherings provided "a pleasant way of getting business done, which requires a number of hands for a short time," this visiting southerner was clearly impressed by the Pennsylvania women's combination of work and sociability.[97]

Just as the ruralness of southern society inhibited the development of communal patterns of work among white women, it also impeded their access to the world beyond their households. Domesticity was the idealized destiny of most white southern women, and that ideal may have dictated the physical and intellectual boundaries of most women's lives. Many, however, maintained contact with distant family and friends through letters, and read books and newspapers to stimulate their intellectual and moral sensibilities and to learn about current events and issues. Some would circumvent the cultural and logistical obstacles their environment posed to carve for themselves a distinctive place in public life.

In the early decades of the nineteenth century, both southerners and northerners used the metaphor of separate spheres to describe the respective roles of men and women, identifying men with the public sphere and women with private domestic life. Southerners and northerners alike drew on the republican and evangelical traditions, both of which envisioned women as wholly domestic beings. While republicans were at best ambivalent toward women and their capacity to influence men, Protestant evangelicals celebrated women's superior piety and virtue, lauded the influence of wives and mothers, and idealized domesticity and the values it represented. Southern women, like their northern counterparts, would use those values to shape and legitimize their incursions into public life.

6

Women's Spheres

MARY NICHOLAS WAS A VIRGINIA WOMAN who, according to her obituary, met all the criteria for virtuous womanhood. "She loved virtue, both because it was the cement of society, and the pure emanation from heaven," intoned an admiring *Richmond Enquirer* on her death in 1820. "Her parental rule was firm yet endearing; and while her precepts pointed out the path of virtue, her example led the way." Although Nicholas did not wholly reject "worldly considerations," she was "equally far from suffering them to engross her whole thoughts . . . ever preferring solid utility to false glitter." Wife, mother, gracious neighbor, and virtuous Christian, Mary Nicholas appeared to be a paragon of southern womanhood.[1]

Nicholas's obituary overlooked her significant public achievements. In fact, she was one of three founding members of the Richmond Female Humane Association, chartered in 1811 to promote "the general purposes of charity and benevolence, the relief and comfort of distressed females, and . . . the maintenance and instruction of destitute white female children residing in the city of Richmond and its suburbs."[2] Like many other southern women, especially those who lived in towns and cities, Nicholas took her

Christian religion to heart, using its precepts both to inspire and to justify participation in her community's public life. Because her public activities derived from an appropriately feminine benevolent impulse, they did not disqualify her as a model for female readers, but in a society that idealized quiet domesticity, most purveyors of prescriptive literature sought neither to recognize nor to encourage women's public activism.

By 1830, southern essayists and etiquette writers promoted a spectrum of feminine ideals, though none explicitly sanctioned women's public activities. Some southern writers, such as the Virginian Mary Randolph, idealized the competent housewife, who wielded both moral and managerial influence in the family circle. Others, such as the popular advice book author Virginia Randolph Cary, emphasized women's moral, legal, and religious duty to submit to male authority.[3] The continued coexistence of these two seemingly conflicting ideals suggests that southern gender conventions, like women's lives, were not monolithic. The fact that both Randolph and Cary were public figures who did not acknowledge women's public roles suggests that prescriptive literature often did not reflect the reality of women's lives.

Religion was the key loophole through which most white women, southern and northern, entered public life. Rural isolation and the suppression of ideas and activities that appeared to undermine the institution of slavery surely deprived southerners of some of the organizational opportunities that were becoming accessible to women elsewhere, but in the first third of the nineteenth century, white southern women, like their northern contemporaries, entered the public sphere to hold prayer meetings, teach Sunday school, and found assorted religious and benevolent associations.[4] Although church institutions ordinarily afforded women no formal authority, pious women exerted their moral influence both in their homes and in society.[5]

In the antebellum decades, republican and paternalistic ideals of male dominance coexisted with an ideal of maternal virtue, and, with the approval of evangelical moralists, many women promoted Christian values and doctrines among their children, slaves, and spouses.[6] In the 1820s and 1830s, pious writers continued to call on southern women to promote religion and morality in their households, emphasizing mothers' particular responsibility for the moral and spiritual well-being of their offspring. "To the mother belong most appropriately the duty and privilege of . . . bring[ing] up her children for God," asserted the Presbyterian *Charleston Observer* in

1828. Three years later, the Baptist *Christian Index* offered detailed advice to mothers on the religious instruction of their children, reminding them that they alone were responsible for molding the characters of their sons and daughters. The *Charleston Gospel Messenger,* an Episcopal publication, likewise maintained that children's "minds are in the hands of their mothers," who were responsible for leading "their infant affections to God, . . . supporting them amidst the temptations of life, and assist[ing] them in working out their salvation." Even secular newspapers, such as the *Raleigh Register,* occasionally reminded female readers that they were "admirably fitted for training their offspring in the nurture and admonition of the Lord."[7]

Some evangelicals charged women with the moral reformation of their entire households. "The domestic influence of women is great," asserted one southern Presbyterian, noting that "it is most salutary, when they diffuse through their dwellings the light that shines from on high." Mothers should be "ministers of the gospel to their children and their servants," observed another moralist, who also believed a wife could influence her husband "to good or evil." In 1832, a Baptist writer lauded the "peculiar" influence that "married ladies" derived from "their connexion and intercourse with their husbands and their children." He encouraged women to use "gentleness of manners, sweetness of disposition, and a well cultivated mind" to influence subtly the conduct of their spouses, though admitting that they exercised an even greater impact on the conduct of their children, who "in the early period of life, are almost always under the care and direction of their mother." A "pious, intelligent, and faithful mother," he concluded, "is the greatest earthly blessing that a merciful Providence can bestow on a child," and if a Christian mother performs her sacred duty, "her offspring will rise up and call her blessed."[8]

Some antebellum writers invoked the ideal of separate spheres when they described women's moral authority within their households. "Female influence is great *in the family circle,*" insisted one Baptist writer, and "in countries blessed by civilization and Christianity, the wife and mother is a kind of presiding spirit in the sanctuary of domestic life." Not only were children subject to the moral "authority" of their mothers, but "in all ordinary circumstances, [the wife] must exert an influence over the husband." Woman's "dominion is the fireside and the family circle," this southern Baptist concluded. "The order, the moral habits, the piety and the happiness of families, are more emphatically under the control of females than they are of the other sex."[9]

Scattered evidence suggests that pious women took their domestic

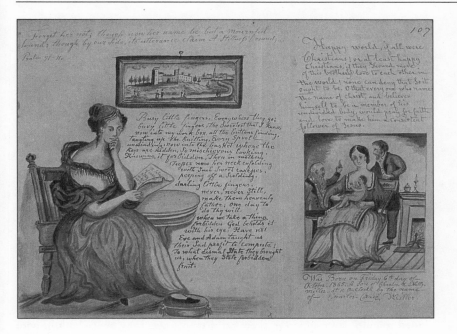

Lewis Miller's drawing book, ca. 1865. Reflecting prevailing gender ideals, these drawings celebrate feminine piety, mothers' moral influence, and domesticity. On the left, a pensive woman prays: "Darling little fingers, never still, make them, heavenly father, one day to do thy will." On the right, a mother cradles her infant and exclaims, "Happy world, if all were Christians!" Virginia Historical Society, Richmond.

moral obligations seriously. Ann Randolph Meade Page provided religious instruction to both her daughters and her slaves, and she distributed religious tracts to guests at her Virginia home. Mary Moore Stanford of North Carolina urged her husband to "strive daily" for religious faith and encouraged both her mother and her sister to attend the camp meetings that she herself frequented. Some wives persuaded their husbands to embrace religion. Armand DeRosset, a North Carolina Episcopalian, attributed his own conversion to the efforts of his wife, Catherine. "To think of the life we might have led," he mused, "but for your example of forbearance." Sarah Hillhouse Gilbert warned her fiancé, Adam Alexander, that they "need not look for happiness to any thing but religion." When, after three years of marriage, Alexander experienced a religious conversion, he informed his wife that he had "learned the truth which you have often told me that it is not *here* that I may place my trust . . . at the feet of Jesus Would I gladly ac-

184   knowledge that in him alone is to be found an *all-sufficient* good — in him is the fullness of joy."[10]

Scattered statistical evidence also suggests that more women than men initiated the process of religious conversion in their households. Of eleven men baptized at a revival near Spring Hill, South Carolina, in 1832, at least six were married to women who had been baptized previously, and the remaining five received the sacrament simultaneously with their spouses. One study of a Georgia Baptist congregation reveals that young women were more than twice as likely as young men to embrace religion. That only 8 percent of all male converts were under eighteen years of age — compared to 21 percent of their female counterparts — suggests that men more frequently joined the church as adults, perhaps as a result of the influence of wives who already were converted.[11]

Mothers assiduously promoted religion among their offspring. In the 1790s, Martha Laurens Ramsay "placed her children around her, and read alternately with them verses in the Bible and Watt's Psalms and Hymns, or sentences in other religious books." A generation later, Eliza Clitherall spent roughly an hour each day catechizing her daughters.[12] Some mothers continued to cultivate religion in their children even as they neared adulthood. When Eliza Haywood's sons left home to attend college in Chapel Hill, she reminded them to read their Bibles and to "remember your Creator & to pray daily and nightly to him." Anna Maria Garretson urged her stepson Jonah — also a college student — to consider a career in the ministry. "It is a field in which the finest powers of the human mind may be displayed," she observed, "could I perceive in *you* my son that purity of sentiment which is so essential to the Christian character nothing would afford me more pleasure than to see you devoting yourself to the study of theology." One elderly North Carolina woman, afflicted with her "final illness," prevailed on her adult son and daughter-in-law to hold daily prayer services for their children and servants, "leaving it optional to any Company, whether or not to join the family Altar."[13]

Notwithstanding the conventional rhetoric of separate spheres, religious commitment led many women to venture beyond the domestic sphere into public life. Like their northern counterparts, southern women played a crucial role in the emerging Sunday school movement. That movement started slowly in the southern states, which contained less than 7 percent of the nation's Sunday schools and 7 percent of its Sunday school teachers in 1830. If South Carolina was typical, however, women and girls predominated as both teachers and students in the region's early Sunday schools. In 1828, the

South Carolina Sunday School Union reported that females accounted for roughly 58 percent of the teachers and 56 percent of the pupils in its nine church-affiliated schools, most of which were located in and around Charleston. Two years later, the Union reported that ninety-eight women and seventy-five men taught in its twelve constituent schools, in which 591 girls and 492 boys attended classes. Another early southern Sunday school, founded in 1819 in Trail Creek, Georgia, exhibited a similar sex distribution among both students and teachers. Eleven men and thirteen women were among the school's founding teachers and patrons, but four more women joined the group shortly thereafter. The school began operation with twenty-six female and seventeen male students, and in subsequent months girls outnumbered boys among the newcomers who enrolled there.[14]

Church-affiliated Sunday schools varied in size as well as in the types of students they instructed. By the 1820s, larger southern cities such as Norfolk, Petersburg, Richmond, Raleigh, and Charleston had Sunday schools in which "poor and destitute" white children obtained religious instruction and "the first rudiments of learning." Local ministers established and oversaw these urban charity schools, where young "gentlemen and ladies" taught the classes as volunteers. Charleston's Mission School, for instance, had one man and three women to instruct twenty-five needy students. Other urban church-affiliated schools boasted as many as forty teachers and two hundred scholars of varied social backgrounds. In some towns and smaller cities, a local minister and his wife conducted Sabbath classes for boys and girls or men's Sunday school societies established schools staffed by predominantly female volunteers.[15]

Many rural Sunday schools were wholly the products of women's individual or collective efforts. In rural Virginia, Anna Maria Garretson taught Scriptures, catechism, and sacred music to at least a dozen students, for whom she ordered books from Baltimore. Eliza Johnston Drysdale founded the first Sunday school in Edgefield, South Carolina. In 1820, some "ladies" in Salisbury, North Carolina, founded a Sunday school worthy of notice by the Charleston-based *Southern Evangelical Intelligencer.* Around the same time, Eliza Clitherall, who operated an eastern North Carolina boarding school, joined with her sister-in-law and another woman to establish a Sunday school in their neighborhood. The women initially held classes in Clitherall's regular classroom, but their pupils grew so numerous that they soon moved the school to the local meetinghouse. In the 1850s, Martha Hancock Wheat taught a "large and interesting sabbath school consisting of Men & Ladies in addition to many children" in a schoolhouse her husband built especially for that purpose on the grounds of their plantation in Bedford County, Virginia.[16]

Southern religious publications praised and encouraged women's initiative in founding and operating Sunday schools. Observing the significance of a mother's religious influence in her family, one Episcopalian concluded that pious women also "may be extensively useful in exerting their influence in the aid and support of Sunday Schools" in their communities. A Baptist publication heralded a recently established North Carolina Sunday school, praising the efforts of its female founders, "to whose benevolent disinterested exertions it must look for perpetuity and usefulness." Another Baptist writer urged female readers to follow the example of a North Carolina woman who quietly braved "a deep rooted prejudice" to open a Sunday school in a neighborhood where "little regard is paid to the institution of the Sabbath, and where that holy day is devoted to visiting, and amusement, and indolence, and pleasure." Despite her neighbors' initial opposition, the school succeeded, eventually attracting some forty students. "May the seed thus sown be followed with a plentiful harvest," prayed this South Carolina Baptist, "and may many others be stimulated by this example to seek, and find opportunity for doing good."[17]

Drawing on women's supposedly inherent maternal qualities and often held in their own households, Sunday schools enabled literate, largely elite and middling, women to exert religious and moral authority without compromising their social respectability. Many, such as "Eliza," who wrote a series of letters to the *Southern Intelligencer* praising women's religious and benevolent works, clearly appreciated the sense of fulfillment that Sunday schools generated in those who labored in them. Teaching gave women the satisfaction of seeing students "improving in knowledge," as well as the more important opportunity to facilitate the saving of their souls. "A few hours spent with [children] in a Sabbath School, may be the means of leading them to a knowledge of Christ," "Eliza" reminded her readers, noting that the "souls of children are as precious here as in India, and the young lady who guides one of these little ones to God in her own neighborhood will cause the same joy in heaven, as the female missionary, who does the same in a heathen land."[18]

Sunday schools gave women the satisfaction of serving both God and their community, while affording them access to the public sphere, albeit an access often monitored by male clergy and co-workers. Still, in striking contrast to the republican Fourth of July rituals that largely excluded women, in 1833 some southern evangelicals proposed a new form of Independence

Day observance that included Christians of both sexes. In an effort to promote the spread of Sunday schools throughout the South, evangelical leaders urged both male and female teachers to spend the Fourth of July going from door to door in pairs to recruit new pupils. "Detachments of teachers may also be sent on exploring tours into neighborhoods where no schools are in existence," suggested one proponent of this alternative Independence Day celebration, which featured small "tours" of pious men and women rather than large parades of virile citizen-soldiers.[19]

Such elaborately orchestrated demonstrations of public piety may not have been typical, but Protestant evangelicalism afforded women other opportunities to influence and participate in public life. Men dominated both the formal rituals and institutional governance of family-centered southern churches, but pious women often were prominent participants in the less regimented prayer groups, revivals, and protracted meetings of the antebellum era.[20] In part because they facilitated the development of women's public identity and influence, such activities were often controversial. Many critics associated camp meetings, in particular, with social disorder and sexual license.[21]

In the spontaneous and emotional atmosphere of camp meetings and revivals, pious women bravely and sometimes reluctantly attested to their religious commitment in public and attempted to inspire a similar faith in others. Women acted as lay exhorters, dancing, crying, and praying aloud at prayer meetings and revivals. In 1831, at a six-day Baptist revival in Santee, South Carolina, an "elderly lady, the daughter of an eminent servant of Christ, . . . was the first who advanced" to pray, and her "example was soon followed by others." Four years later, at a revival in Macon, Georgia, pious women "went up and down the streets in stores and homes exhorting men and women to accept Jesus as Lord and Savior." One Virginia Methodist, the wife of a slaveholding planter, struggled for years to defy long-standing prohibitions against women's public speaking, finally heeding what she believed to be God's will that she pray aloud at a protracted meeting. Years later, the same woman proudly recorded in her diary that she had spoken three times in one day at a recent Methodist revival.[22]

In the eyes of many elite and middling southerners, camp meetings and women's public prayer, which challenged the conventional allocation of power between the sexes, also breached accepted standards of propriety. Women's attendance at sermons and prayer meetings was more decorous and less controversial, but even these seemingly innocent activities could lead them to engage in more unconventional ventures. In Charleston, one *"female prayer meeting"* began as a weekly gathering of pious women for prayers and introspection. Soon, however, the meetings inspired their participants to "converse with some one of our irreligious acquaintance every week upon the subject of experimental religion," informing them that they are "upon the borders of hell and . . . warn[ing] them of their danger." The women would relate these conversations to their associates when they reconvened, making their impious relatives and friends "the objects of prayer in our meetings." A vigorous proselytizing effort thus grew out of a prayer meeting begun by a few pious women.[23]

Some southern men clearly worried that even these relatively cautious forms of religious activism potentially undermined female subservience and domesticity. When the Reverend John Dunn traveled from Tappahannock to Richmond in 1825, he complained that the women he encountered "were not satisfied with two Sermons a day" and prevailed on "young preachers to lecture for them at 10 o Clock at night." Dunn recognized that these women used their religious observances as opportunities to socialize outside their homes, and he worried that their "fondness for running after celebrated Preachers with itching ears impedes the growth of practical piety." Even more pointedly, in 1828, John Randolph of Roanoke criticized the many women who, "to the neglect of their domestic duties and . . . to the injury of their reputations, are running mad after popular preachers . . . forming themselves into clubs of one sort or another," which he believed "only serve to gratify the love of selfishness and notoriety."[24]

Although most churches officially consigned women to silent subservience, religious faith inspired some women to promote Christian belief and morality in their communities and their households. Conventional ideas about women's superior piety and virtue usually deflected criticism of their public religious activities, though some southerners may have shared Randolph's misgivings about such undertakings, which proliferated after 1800. In the early decades of the nineteenth century, southern women, like their northern counterparts, embraced an assortment of religious and benevolent causes and joined together to improve their neighbors' moral and material circumstances.

Scholars have identified three types of antebellum women's associations: those engaged in benevolent work, those pursuing evangelical agendas, and those that embraced egalitarian and feminist, or "ultraist," objectives. Southern women formed both benevolent and evangelical groups that undertook an impressive array of public projects, but they

never organized in support of feminism or abolitionism, the two chief programs of northern ultraists.[25] Ever conscious of the need to preserve slavery
and the patriarchal society it engendered, articulate southerners condemned
and ridiculed the northern egalitarians. As evangelical reform became increasingly associated with the perfectionist ideals of northern abolitionists,
they also grew wary of the many independent evangelical reform groups
and institutions established by the women of their region.

The earliest southern women's associations, formed by elite urban
women in the century's first decade, were benevolent societies that provided
food, shelter, and alms for the poor. Later organizations founded by evangelical women pursued more plainly religious agendas, though the work of
evangelical groups also overlapped with that of the older benevolent associations. By the 1810s, evangelical women were establishing Bible and tract
societies to promote religious instruction among the unconverted. In the
next decade, they also established organizations to support the work of
evangelical missionaries. Finally, by 1830, evangelical women were involved
in the temperance movement. Yet for them, temperance reform did not become a springboard to more radical abolitionist and feminist activities, as it
did for a significant minority of northern women.

Although religious zeal inspired and justified most of women's organizational activities, their earliest associations drew on ideals of feminine benevolence that complemented evangelical religion but developed independently
of it. Eighteenth-century moralists who sentimentalized woman's essential
nature included benevolence among her defining attributes. "To the honour
of the sex I must confess, that this virtue [of benevolence] is seldom want-
ing in any, except to those women void of that natural softness and sensibility, so firmly rooted in the female breast," proclaimed an anonymous
contributor to the *Lady's Magazine*, "but, thank heaven, these are few in
number, when compared to the rest."[26]

Although moralists and etiquette writers did not instruct women to establish charitable organizations, they did encourage them to practice benevolence individually or on an ad hoc basis. The clergyman John Bennett
urged women to set aside a "pittance" at the beginning of each week to devote to charitable purposes. "It is amazing what charities even a *small* fortune will enable people to perform," he claimed, noting that a "few
retrenchments from dress, vanity, or pleasure, poured into the Christian
flock, will make it rich indeed." Bennett also urged young women who
found that time "hangs heavy on their hands" to make "garments for the
naked" and "cordials for the sick," and at least one popular cookbook pro-

vided recipes that helped women to "assist the poor of their neighbourhood at a very trivial expense." Virginia's Bishop James Madison believed that the mistresses of households should "always reserve something for the hand of charity" and that they should never close their doors to the "voice of suffering humanity." Evangelical writers similarly lauded "that tenderness, compassion, and benevolence, which the Almighty has impressed on the female heart," urging woman to deploy these gifts "for the benefit of her fellow creatures."[27]

In obituaries, southerners recognized and praised the benevolent acts of individual women. "To the poor of her neighborhood," the late Mary Ellen Pollard was "the unceasing friend, giving alms with the charity that is unboastful of the good it renders," observed the *Richmond Enquirer* in 1818. Two years later, the *Enquirer* similarly celebrated the many charitable deeds of Elizabeth Pope Moody, whose eyes "never failed to beam with sympathy whenever an object of charity was present."[28]

Although neither Moody nor Pollard appears to have participated in organized benevolence, southern women of their generation pioneered a range of collective enterprises devoted to charitable purposes. In the South, as in the North, elite women established the first benevolent associations in urban areas, where poverty among whites was most visible and where women were less isolated from one another. By 1813, elite women in Virginia's chief cities — Fredericksburg, Norfolk, Richmond, Petersburg, and Alexandria — as well as in Charleston, New Bern, and Fayetteville, had established benevolent societies. These organizations raised money and founded schools, workshops, and orphanages to ameliorate the plight of poor whites in their communities.[29]

Founded in 1813 and incorporated the following year, the Charleston Ladies' Benevolent Society may have been representative of the early organizational efforts of the urban women of the region. Established to "relieve the distresses of the poor, and administer comfort to the sick," the society funded its efforts by collecting annual dues and soliciting outside donations. Overseen by female elected officers and an all-woman board of managers, its members met quarterly at Charleston's orphan asylum. As a nondenominational group, the Ladies' Benevolent Society often cooperated with local churches, which in turn lent moral and sometimes financial support to its efforts. Beginning in 1824, its members also resolved to work with local government to provide aid and comfort to victims of recurrent yellow fever epidemics.[30]

Charleston's benevolent women, some of whom visited the "wretched

Hovels" of the poor and the sick, to whom they dispensed food, clothing, and firewood, were acutely conscious of class distinctions and of their own privileged social status. When Mary S. Grimké, one of the society's early officers, died in 1825, its members praised her as a woman who had been "discriminating in her intercourse with the class of people with whom she had to deal, [and] firm & decided in her dealings with them." Motivated by a combination of noblesse oblige and Christian charity, Charleston's benevolent women sought to promote the physical and moral well-being of those who were sick or otherwise unable to subsist by their own efforts.[31]

Class distinctions and gender commonality combined to make destitute women and girls the main beneficiaries of women's benevolence. Recognizing "the peculiar hard situation of females without fortune," who had few opportunities to earn a living and often fell victim to sexual predators, early associations of elite women sought to shield them from urban vices and "encourage industry among the female poor" by providing waged labor for indigent women. In 1813, at the height of the movement to encourage domestic manufactures, the benevolent women of Charleston promoted the employment of poor women in clothmaking, teaching them how to spin raw cotton donated by local planters. More typically, women's associations established schools for poor girls and homes for female orphans. By 1819, Charleston's Ladies' Benevolent Society, which claimed some 350 subscribers, operated two charity schools that served a total of fifty students. In the early 1820s, the orphanages in Richmond and Petersburg each housed approximately fifteen inmates and their schools took in additional girls as "day scholars." Students in such charity schools learned "reading, writing, arithmetic, and . . . sewing in the best manner" because their patrons assumed that they would rely on their needles for "support in future life." Aware that even competent seamstresses had scant possibilities for gainful employment, some benevolent women established needlework shops in which they furnished poor women with cloth, thread, and other materials and paid them what they deemed a *"full* and *just* price for making every article."[32]

These early women's benevolent associations appear to have been relatively autonomous. Benevolent women, most of whom were married to influential men, successfully applied to their legislatures for corporate charters that enabled them to circumvent coverture, empowering them collectively "to take and hold property . . . or to make conveyances of the same for the benefit of the Association." The women of the Richmond Female Humane Society bought sixteen shares of bank stock shortly after the society's inception; stock dividends, along with annual dues and donations, provided most of the subsequent funding for their charitable enterprises. Similarly, after receiving their charter in 1814, the members of the Charleston Ladies' Benevolent Society established a "Permanent Accumulating Fund" of $858, which they invested in state bank stock, and decided that "on each succeeding year there shall be added to it out of the annual receipts, a sum not exceeding 20 per Centum . . . for the security of the charity." A decade later, the assets of the Ladies' Benevolent Society included $8,328 in stocks and public certificates, along with an additional $875 in private notes. Charleston's benevolent women owned 117 shares of stocks in four banks, as well as five interest-bearing securities issued by the federal government.[33]

Benevolence brought women together to act publicly and, in the process, encouraged them to develop their business and political talents. Women elected female presidents and boards to set policy and stewards or treasurers to keep track of their finances. They chose women solicitors to lead fund-raising efforts and committees to visit the recipients of their largesse. Benevolent women wrote constitutions and held elections, some of which were hotly contested.[34] They invested money, raised funds, and forecast future expenditures and proceeds. These early women's associations sometimes turned to men for donations and perhaps for financial advice, but they controlled most of the money they raised, as well as the projects they sponsored.

At a time when America's dominant gender ideals theoretically relegated women to the domestic sphere, aspects of those same ideals tacitly encouraged benevolent women to exercise their collective public spirit. Christian charity and morality informed women's early benevolent activities, and though those efforts were not explicitly religious, prominent evangelical leaders applauded the founding of women's benevolent associations in the southern states and elsewhere. Conversely, these associations praised and often supported the good works of churchwomen and their ministers. In 1818, for instance, some members of the Charleston Ladies' Benevolent Society were among the founders of their city's Female Domestic Mission Society. In the 1820s, the Ladies' Benevolent Society donated money to the Female Bible Society of Charleston and commended the city's Sunday schools and other evangelical reform activities. While charity could ease the pain of illness, poverty, and dependence, these benevolent women believed that "religious instruction properly conveyed" would exercise "a beneficial influence . . . over [the] future conduct" of its recipients.[35] Consequently, they supported the efforts of newer and more plainly religious women's groups, of which some of them also became members.

In most major eastern cities, the establishment of women's charitable associations antedated the rise of evangelicalism, but by the 1820s evangelical women in these and other urban communities were forming their own associations, which combined benevolence with a more specifically religious agenda. In such communities as Charleston, Richmond, Norfolk, and Petersburg, evangelical women's groups existed alongside the older benevolent associations. Pious women raised money to help the poor, establish domestic and foreign missions, and support church building projects. They also taught in Sunday schools. Like their northern counterparts, some southern evangelical women practiced more direct forms of reform-minded benevolence. They visited the poor and the sick in their homes, distributing Bibles and religious tracts along with food, clothing, and other material comforts.[36]

Perhaps most important, the spread of evangelicalism catalyzed the development of women's associations in many smaller cities and country towns throughout the region. Evangelicals of several denominations came together to found the first women's societies in the North Carolina communities of Raleigh and Hillsborough before 1815. By 1817, the evangelical women of Camden, South Carolina, had established what may have been the first women's association in their state's upcountry region.[37]

Because the men who published both secular and religious periodicals often ignored women's public activities, we know little about many of these associations. Among evangelical organizations in smaller southern cities, however, Fayetteville's Universal Female Benevolent Society may have been typical. Although they described themselves as a "benevolent society," these women explicitly pursued pious reform objectives. Founded to "raise funds, and appropriate them to such charities as . . . will best promote the cause of religion," the society engaged in a wide range of public activities. Led by a fifteen-woman board and their elected "Directress," the society's members relieved "the wants of the poor who are aged, infirm, or sick," distributed Bibles and devotional tracts, and supported both foreign and local missionaries.[38]

The activities of other associations were less varied, if equally ambitious. In 1817, evangelical women in Iredell County, North Carolina, founded the Female Benevolent Society of Society Hill and organized a school "to give instruction to poor and destitute children, in the principles and morality of religion." They also established a "spacious Female Academy," which within two years had some fifty students, three of whom the society sponsored. According to the Baptist *Southern Evangelical Intelligencer,* this "benevolent" society and the schools it supported "originated in a weekly prayer-meeting of a few pious ladies." These women raised more than $2,000 to promote their projects, and their schools were "superintended by a committee of twelve Ladies."[39]

Other evangelical women participated in Bible and tract societies. These bodies built no schools or orphanages and left behind little tangible evidence of their existence, but groups devoted to the circulation of pious literature were probably the most widespread form of women's organization in the antebellum South. Such organizations gave evangelical women a respectable and effective means of proselytizing, especially in rural areas. "When other methods for benefiting souls are beyond our control, we can distribute *tracts,*" one South Carolinian declared in 1822, "and so long as this method remains we have no excuse to plead for being idle all the day, while multitudes are perishing for that knowledge which *religious tracts* contain."[40]

By 1820, evangelical women in larger southern communities had established associations to promote the dissemination of Scriptures and devotional literature, but so had several groups of women in some rural areas. At least one resident of Cabarrus County, North Carolina, credited the local women's tract societies with stimulating a religious revival. Because of their efforts, this anonymous observer claimed, "it appears that more zeal is manifested for the cause of religion here, than has been for many years past."[41]

Women's Bible and tract societies varied in both size and tactics. In rural communities, such as Cabarrus, small groups of pious women probably dispensed their literature personally among community and family members. Members of the Hillsborough Female Tract Society in central North Carolina persuaded a Chapel Hill minister to distribute their tracts when he traveled through the surrounding countryside. The women of the much larger Raleigh Female Tract Society, by contrast, used their personal contacts to reach readers throughout North Carolina, as well as in neighboring states and in the western territories. During her tenure as the society's president, Eliza Williams Haywood enlisted her mother as a member, though she resided in the distant coastal port of Wilmington. Haywood sent tracts for her mother to circulate in the Wilmington area. In 1818, the Raleigh Female Tract Society disposed of roughly three hundred tracts in Raleigh, Norfolk, the "lower parts" of North Carolina, and the Alabama territory. The society's resources and networks expanded quickly, and by the

1820s its officers kept more than two thousand pamphlets on hand for distribution. Members also solicited donations from communities across the state and encouraged "Christian Females" in other North Carolina towns to "form similar Societies either as auxiliary to [the Raleigh organization] or as independent Societies."[42]

Like similar groups in northern cities, some southern Bible and tract societies used home visitations to proselytize the unregenerate. In 1816, evangelical women in Charleston established the Female Bible Society "to aid in the distribution of Holy Scriptures" among the unconverted. Members of the society visited the homes of the poor and the sick, as well as those of sinners, Sabbath-breakers, and Roman Catholics. Within three years, the society distributed 857 Bibles, largely through the efforts of a special committee, whose members went "to the habitations of poverty and wretchedness, [to] search out objects of our charity, and supply those with the precious word of God." Subsequent home visitations verified that the society's clients actually read the Bibles they received. The pious women of Charleston self-consciously strove to be "abundantly useful" in promoting "the glory of God and the salvation of our fellow man." Their piety propelled them into the public sphere to hold meetings, raise money, and buy Bibles, and brought them into contact with people far removed from their own domestic and social circles.[43]

Most evangelical women were not so daring, and some of their organizations were not so autonomous. Unlike the tract and Bible societies in Charleston and Raleigh, the Female Bible Society of Richmond, founded in 1818, was merely a women's auxiliary of the Bible Society of Virginia, a men's organization. Whereas the Charleston and Raleigh groups normally raised, managed, and disbursed their organizations' funds, the Richmond women gave the men's organization all or most of the money they collected. The men of the Bible Society profusely and publicly thanked the women for their "zealous and liberal contributions" but afforded them no say in allocating the funds they donated.[44]

Women compromised their autonomy in varying degrees when they organized themselves as auxiliaries, or subsidiaries, of men's groups or when their associations were church-affiliated. Many evangelical benevolent, Bible, and tract societies were interdenominational, but by the 1820s most white Protestant churches in major cities and towns also boasted an array of women's charity, missionary, and educational organizations. Unlike the more ecumenical Bible and benevolence societies, church-affiliated organizations, though organized and operated by women, were at least nominally dependent on the support of male ministers. For instance, in 1818, the Baptist women of Charleston founded the Female Domestic Missionary Society, which maintained missions and chapels in and around the city and recruited young clergymen to run them. Like the Charleston Female Bible Society, the Domestic Missionary Society sought to disseminate pious literature among the poor, the sick, and the unconverted. Unlike the members of the Bible Society, however, these women, having raised money to purchase Bibles and moral tracts, then gave the books to a male missionary to distribute. Other church-affiliated women's groups, such as the South Carolina Auxiliary Education Society and the Female Association for Educating Pious Young Men for the Gospel Ministry, raised money to sponsor the training of male clergy, presumably entrusting the funds they raised to ministerial advisers who knew more than they about evaluating potential candidates and educating the successful applicants. Moreover, though they were church-affiliated public organizations that often raised substantial sums, these women's groups usually had no formal voice in church affairs at either the state or local level. When North Carolina's state Baptist convention met in 1831, for example, only two women's associations were represented — and each sent a male delegate because women were not eligible to participate in the convention.[45]

In forming such church-affiliated associations, Baptist and other evangelical women may have compromised their autonomy in order to spread the Gospel to people who were otherwise beyond their reach for social or logistical reasons. The women of Charleston's Female Bible Society may have strained the limits of respectability when they visited the homes of the poor and the sick, but they prudently did not attempt to visit free blacks, slaves, or the unruly seamen who frequented the city's port. Yet these were precisely the groups that the Baptist Female Domestic Missionary Society targeted for conversion, just as its Episcopalian counterpart sponsored a male missionary who catechized the "coloured persons" of Charleston. Respectable white women could visit neither the wharves nor the dwellings of African Americans with whom they were unacquainted, though they could engage men to preach in such places, so long as they "studiously avoided saying any thing which would make [slaves] discontented with their situation."[46]

By sponsoring domestic missionaries, pious women also contributed to the growing efforts to provide religious instruction to slaves in the antebellum era. Sincere evangelicals believed themselves obliged to convert the region's bondpeople, while proslavery ideologues, consciously seeking to rehabilitate slavery both to assuage their own consciences and to neutralize the institution's critics, cited the conversion of blacks as evidence of both the good treatment of slaves and the morality of their masters.[47] Women's support for domestic missions promoted religion, while strengthening the emerging ideology of paternalism that white southerners increasingly invoked to justify slavery. Since support for slavery was nearly universal among southern whites and since many evangelical women were themselves slaveholders, those who promoted such efforts must have regarded both ends as laudable.

Preoccupied by their mission to Christianize first the Indians of their region and later African Americans, southern evangelicals sent comparatively few missionaries abroad in the antebellum era. In 1814, only five out of fifty foreign missionary societies established by Baptist women were located in southern communities, though Baptist women in the South gradually increased their patronage of foreign missions, founding at least twenty-three additional missionary societies before 1830. Such church-affiliated organizations allowed pious women to participate in the ambitious evangelical effort to spread God's word across the world, though relatively few were sufficiently daring to undertake missionary work themselves. Southern women lagged far behind their northern counterparts in their direct involvement in foreign missions. Not until 1846 did a female southerner travel abroad as a missionary, and only sixteen did so before 1860.[48]

Evangelical and benevolent women alike took pride in the public activities and achievements of their associations. Members of Charleston's Female Bible Society happily told tales of repentant sinners and deathbed conversions. "We . . . have seen and known the benefits resulting from our exertions," observed one member of the society's home visitation committee, "if we were the humble instruments of saving but one soul, would it not be worth all the exertions which we have made and can make?" Charleston's Congregational and Presbyterian women, who raised money to educate prospective ministers, took satisfaction in the knowledge that "our Society has done good, great good," in helping to spread the "everlasting Gospel." In 1820, the board of managers of the Charleston Ladies' Benevolent Society attributed recent improvements in the condition of the city's poor and sick to the efforts of its members, and four years later proudly declared that they had "attended and relieved the want and misery of 2,916 *Destitute sick poor* . . . from the Infant in the Cradle, to the old Man of an *hundred* and *five*" during the eleven years of their organization's existence.[49]

Individual women also indicated that they derived immense satisfaction from their public activities. Rebecca Goodwin found "sincere and heartfelt delight" in her work with the Raleigh Female Tract Society and in her "dear friends and sisters," who shared her own "Zeal for that cause in which we are all engaged." Sarah Polk, a member of Raleigh's Female Benevolent Society, admitted that she devoted "a good deal" of her time to helping the poor, adding that "it's a pleasant task when we see them profit by our exertions."[50]

"Eliza," who penned a series of essays encouraging women's pious and benevolent works, described the sense of cautious empowerment that women could gain as a result of such activities. "Our desire has long been to do good, but the sphere in which we moved, excluded in our apprehension the possibility of gratifying it," she noted at the outset of her first essay, which appeared in May 1822. "Eliza," however, then went on to argue that women could combine pious public activism with their more conventional domestic roles. "No matter how limited our sphere for activity," she asserted, "we possess a certain share of influence, and it is in our power to do something for the cause of Zion." In her subsequent essays, "Eliza" described how she and her associates founded a prayer meeting, taught Sunday school, did needlework to raise money for Christian missions, and distributed tracts and Bibles. Although she carefully paid lip service to the conventional ideal of feminine subservience — criticizing women who prayed aloud and describing her tract society as doing "good in [a] silent and inoffensive manner" — "Eliza" also derived a sense of achievement from her assorted public activities. "Our [prayer] meetings are truly interesting," she reported. "Our Sabbath School increases, and its teachers are truly engaged and much encouraged." "Eliza" and her associates enjoyed their labors together, and they believed it to be a great *"privilege,* to be in any way whatever a co-worker with God."[51]

Perhaps because most women, like "Eliza," obscured the potential radicalism of their public activities, most men either ignored those activities or accepted them as the natural and even desirable consequences of women's innate compassion and piety. The Reverend John Holt Rice argued that women's benevolent activities did not entail their "travelling out of [their] proper sphere" because he believed it "peculiarly proper that women should, while they partake of the blessings of the gospel, be instrumental in communicating them to others." Other evangelical men supported the work of women's Bible and tract societies by praising their efforts or by purchasing or distributing the literature they promoted. Although such groups "may be little esteemed by worldly men," one South Carolina minister observed, they

are "precious in the sight of the Lord." Pious and unconverted men alike tacitly condoned women's public activities when they made donations and bequests to women's organizations and patronized the craft fairs that members
held as fund-raising ventures. William Polk of Raleigh thought it reasonable
for his wife, Sarah, to devote herself to charity work while he was off poli-
ticking or managing his plantations. Doubtless other southern men agreed,
for few categorically opposed women's organizational ventures.[52]

Although southern men often employed the rhetoric of separate spheres
to describe gender relations, most did not protest women's efforts to create
their own place and purpose within the supposedly masculine public
sphere, so long as their activities did not challenge existing social hierarchies. Fragmentary evidence suggests that scattered early efforts of evangelical women to undermine masculine authority by attempting to eradicate
gambling and drinking led men to monitor women's public activities more
carefully. Subsequently, the most aggressive reform efforts that southern
women undertook targeted marginal and relatively powerless social groups:
women, children, the poor and the sick, and African Americans. Even the
most zealous evangelical women interfered with the behavior of propertied
white men only to the extent of soliciting their financial support and encouraging them to pray and read the Bible.[53]

In the antebellum era, temperance reform was the most radical of southern women's public undertakings and, not coincidentally, the arena in which
they enjoyed the least autonomy. Inspired by evangelical Protestantism,
southern temperance advocates believed that drunkenness was a sin that
endangered the church, the family, and society in general. They also recognized that women, who were both the companions of men and the main victims of their intemperance, had good reasons to support the temperance
movement and could contribute mightily to it. One temperance man predicted that if women would "courageously take the work in hand, in every
town, . . . in a few years [intemperance] would have no place among us."
But because contemporaries perceived drinking as a token of virility and
drunkenness as primarily a masculine vice, temperance advocates explicitly
and aggressively challenged men's autonomy when they attempted to mod-
ify their conduct. Early reformers preached voluntary sobriety, but they
often invoked the authority of the church in support of the temperance pro-
gram.[54] Even evangelical men were unwilling to give women free rein to
criticize their fathers and husbands and to use the power of the church to
curtail white men's sovereignty in their homes and in society.

Consequently, southern women who participated in the temperance movement did so largely as nominal members of mixed-sex organizations. In 1822, "a number of the inhabitants of Guilford County" founded North Carolina's earliest temperance society, and evangelical men in Virginia and South Carolina founded their states' first such organizations four years later. Under evangelical leadership, the temperance movement grew to include some 250 local organizations with more than 50,000 members in Virginia alone by the mid-1830s.[55] Men dominated these organizations, many of which were directly affiliated with their church congregations.

Although evangelical men also dominated early temperance activities in the northern states, northern women gradually established their own autonomous temperance organizations. In 1831, one temperance publication reported that the United States boasted twenty-four "ladies'" temperance societies, all but one of which were based in northern communities.[56] The temperance activities of northern women would be increasingly separate from those of men during the ensuing decades, while the South's antiliquor associations remained mixed-sex and male-dominated.

From the beginning, southern evangelical men actively solicited women's membership in their temperance societies, probably in part to deter them from forming their own separate organizations. When men gathered to found a local temperance society, they often adopted a constitution that recognized women's potential contributions to the movement and openly encouraged their membership. For instance, the "gentlemen" who founded Virginia's Prince William County Temperance Society in 1829 believed that "the origin and extent of the intemperate use of ardent spirits in the country have resulted primarily from the uses made of it in private families." Assuming that women wielded substantial influence over their households, they invited "the Female part of the community" to join their organization. The constitutions of temperance societies never instructed wives to defy their drunken husbands, though they vaguely directed women members to use "all the means in [their] power" to discourage intemperance. The constitutions did, however, oblige women members to teach the rising generation the virtues of temperance. Women who were "mothers of families," asserted the temperance men of Edgefield, South Carolina, must "agree to impress upon the minds of their children the baneful effects produced by an improper use of intoxicating liquors."[57]

In exchange for their cooperation and support, temperance men offered women little more than titular membership in their associations. Indeed, as the authors of the temperance constitutions made clear, men did not even expect female members to attend the societies' meetings. Most constitutions appear to have included a standard clause defining the limited organizational duties of women members. "Female members," the constitutions typically stipulated, "are not to be bound to attend the meetings of the Society." Instead, they should merely "feel themselves under obligations to countenance and support the objects of the associations by their attendance when convenient." Although some women certainly attended meetings, raised money, and participated in abstinence pledge campaigns, few reform-minded southern men encouraged women to work publicly to fight intemperance.[58]

Even women's relatively restricted involvement in the temperance movement, however, may have worried those southerners who were increasingly apprehensive of all reform activities. By the 1830s, many white southerners rightly worried that the perfectionist impulse that gave rise to temperance and other reform movements could easily lead, as it did in the North, to an organized attempt to regenerate society through the abolition of slavery. Southern critics of the temperance movement, including growing numbers of evangelicals, explicitly likened the fanaticism of teetotalers to that of abolitionists, an analogy that would become increasingly commonplace as the northern antislavery movement gathered strength in the coming years.[59] Critics attacked the entire temperance movement, not specifically its female members, but the ominous comparison of temperance with abolition evoked the specter of social upheaval in the minds of many white southerners, who associated abolition with race war and the subversion of patriarchal authority both within and beyond their households.[60]

Not coincidentally, the southern temperance movement peaked in the early 1830s and then declined simultaneously with the rise of the American Anti-Slavery Association, which in 1835 enraged white southerners by using the mails to flood their region with abolitionist literature. Indeed, in 1834, the year before the abolitionists' postal campaign, one North Carolina Baptist reported that the temperance movement "exerts a wonderful influence . . . in many parts of this State," but two years later, in the wake of the abolitionist offensive, the same clergyman observed that the "Temperance cause is on the retrograde" even in areas where it had been strongest. The temperance movement revived somewhat in the 1840s and 1850s, led by new secular organizations such as the Washingtonians and the Sons of Temperance. These organizations had women's auxiliaries, known respectively as the Martha Washingtonians and Daughters of Temperance.[61]

In several ways, these new temperance groups potentially were less disruptive of the status quo than their evangelical predecessors. For one thing, although the churches cautiously supported their efforts, these secular temperance groups claimed no religious authority. Equally important, neither organization attempted to reform the conduct of propertied white men and thereby challenge their sovereignty. Concentrated in cities, the members of these organizations were mainly working-class themselves, and they labored primarily among their social equals. Indeed, if New York's Martha Washingtonians were typical, the members of that organization focused much of their efforts on working-class women, rather than men, urging wives and mothers to renounce intoxicating beverages and to promote sobriety in their families.[62]

Many white southerners could accept and even applaud these objectives, which did not appear to jeopardize the existing social order. That social order derived from a paternalistic social ethic that justified the omnipotence of white adult propertied men. In many cases explicitly disavowing the metaphor of separate spheres, southern social theorists increasingly stressed the sovereignty of white men in their homes and on their plantations, as well as in public life. Deeming slavery a positive good because it civilized and disciplined an allegedly inferior people, proslavery theorists asserted the sovereignty of white men over African Americans. Portraying white women as weak and vulnerable to defilement at the hands of black men, in particular, they insisted on white women's submission to male authority and averred the duty of all white men to protect the purity and virtue of their women.[63]

The increasing prevalence of paternalistic and even patriarchal ideals did not extinguish women's public activities, which continued through the antebellum era. In some cases, however, men scrutinized the conduct of women's organizations, especially those with reformist objectives. Southern men also sought to co-opt women's independent concerns by taking over their public projects or forming rival men's groups that solicited women as auxiliary members. In 1858, for example, men in Petersburg assumed legal control of an orphan asylum that Methodist women had established a decade earlier. In the same city, the Sons of Temperance and the Union Agricultural Society offered women auxiliary membership in organizations that men established and governed.[64]

Some southern women, however, continued to form their own relatively autonomous benevolent associations. In the 1830s, the benevolent women of Charleston founded the Fuel Society to provide inexpensive firewood to female-headed households, distributing as much as $1,500 worth of wood annually. In 1849, women in Macon, Georgia, established the Charitable Association to "relieve the necessities of the Poor" in their city. Like many of

its predecessors, this group conducted home visits and in 1856 alone donated nearly $550 to more than fifty needy families. Governed by a board of
seventeen women officers and managers, the Charitable Association received favorable notices in the local Baptist press, which continued to regard public benevolence as a legitimate activity for godly women.[65]

Organized benevolence and to a lesser extent religious activism, unlike
republican political rituals and the potentially subversive temperance movement, gave white women respectable outlets for relatively autonomous public activism at a time when few acknowledged their desire or capacity to
contribute to public life. At home, such women may have deferred to their
husbands and fathers, but their public activism belied a strength of character that contrasted markedly with the emerging ideal of passive, dependent,
unworldly womanhood so cherished by proslavery ideologues.[66]

Although virtually all articulate southerners idealized women as domestic beings, by the 1820s some were beginning to redefine domesticity in the
context of a growing regional consciousness. Women participated in this
process, complicit in the creation of southern gender ideals, just as they
would abet their region's efforts to justify and preserve the institution of
slavery. Two Virginia sisters, Mary Randolph and Virginia Randolph Cary,
were among the earliest promoters of explicitly southern feminine ideals.
The ideals they championed differed markedly, but the writings of both
women were influential and widely read for decades.

Born into the top tier of Virginia's social elite, the Randolph sisters, like
increasing numbers of educated women, began writing to earn money when
hard times beset their families. The eldest of eleven children of Anne Cary
and Thomas Mann Randolph, Mary ran an exclusive Richmond boardinghouse for more than a decade to compensate for the political and financial
reverses of her unfortunate husband. In 1819, Mary and David Meade
Randolph moved to Washington, where she composed *The Virginia House-
Wife*, which was published five years later.[67] Virginia, the youngest child in a
family that included both Thomas Jefferson's son-in-law and Bizarre's unhappy Judith Randolph, began writing for publication after the 1823 death
of her husband, Wilson Jefferson Cary, who, like many Virginia planters,
was deeply indebted. Cary's first book, *Letters on the Female Character*, appeared in 1828. She later produced a child-rearing manual, scattered poems
and stories, and one didactic novel.[68]

Mary Randolph, whose cookbook drew on her years of experience as
one of Richmond's most celebrated hostesses, charged women with the

204   "government of a family," by which she meant the household. In the preface
to the first edition of *The Virginia House-Wife,* Randolph tacitly rejected the
ancient notion of the family as a little commonwealth governed by its domestic king. While she conceded that the "government of a family, bears a
Lilliputian resemblance to the government of a nation," she maintained that
"the mistress of the family" was primarily responsible for the "grand ar-
canum" of household management. Randolph taught her readers how to
manage money, emphasizing that the "contents of the Treasury must be
known, and great care taken to keep the expenditures from being equal to
the receipts." She urged them to marshal their time and their servants effectively, rising early to plan the day's work. "If the mistress of a family, will
every morning examine minutely the different departments of her household," she observed, "she must detect errors in their infant state, when they
can be corrected with ease," and thus circumvent "disorder, with all her attendant evils."[69]

Subsequent editions of *The Virginia House-Wife* included a longer introduction in which Randolph stressed the advantages of women's domestic influence, urging "every woman of good sense and tolerable memory" to
cultivate the "art" of household management. Like Catharine Beecher and
other northern champions of women's authority within their "sphere," Randolph believed that the "prosperity and happiness of a family depend
greatly on . . . order and regularity," which could be established only
through the efforts of a competent "mistress." Like Beecher, Randolph also
believed that women's domestic influence could benefit the world beyond
their households. The husband of a competent housewife, she asserted, "will
feel pride and exultation in the possession of a companion, who gives his
home charms that gratify every wish of his soul, and render the haunts of
dissipation hateful to him." Sons raised in such a household "will become
moral men, of steady habits." Daughters, educated by and "formed on the
model of an exemplary mother, will use the same means for securing the
happiness" of the next generation.[70]

Randolph described domesticity in terms that could empower and val-
orize its practitioners. Far from envisioning women as helpless ciphers, she
believed that wives shared responsibility for family governance and that a
woman's competence in the domestic sphere brought material and moral
benefits. As the author of a cookbook, Randolph could not be expected to
contend that women's competence should extend beyond their households,
but, like revolutionary proponents of republican womanhood, she suggested
that feminine influence in the home could improve the quality of public life.

Mary Randolph Randolph, Charles Balthazar Julien Févret de Saint-Mémin, 1817. The author of *The Virginia House-Wife* urged her readers to wield authority in the domestic sphere and advised them that "method is the soul of management." As the author of a popular cookbook and longtime proprietor of a fashionable boardinghouse, Randolph was a public figure in early nineteenth-century Virginia. Virginia Historical Society, Richmond.

Randolph presented a southern — specifically, a Virginian — model for southern readers. Although her occasional explanations of uniquely southern foods and terms suggest that she anticipated an audience beyond her region, her emphasis on the management of large household staffs, her recipes for curing hams and bacon and making soap and candles, and her designation of the doughnut as a "Yankee Cake" appealed to the women of the rural South who were the majority of her readers.[71] Randolph's descriptions of housewives cooking, pickling, preserving, and allocating tasks to domestic workers — whether slaves, servants, or daughters — reflected the reality of women's lives. Far from portraying her ideal "Virginia ladies" as either weak or frivolous, she praised them as "proverbially good managers" who were both competent and authoritative household governors.[72]

Mary Randolph's vision of southern womanhood probably drew on her own atypical experience as a city woman who ran both a household and a business, whose talents as a hostess won her a public reputation and "very numerous acquaintance."[73] Most of Randolph's readers lived in very different circumstances, though many probably identified with her model of domestic management. Nineteenth-century southern women, like their eighteenth-century predecessors, were responsible for running their households as well as for supervising the operation of farms and plantations in their husbands' absence.[74] Women, especially widows, took in boarders or ran schools to make ends meet and carefully managed their household finances. Some couples made financial decisions jointly. Sarah Alexander carefully managed the resources of her Georgia household and advised her husband against overspending because "the amount of expenses you will have to meet *next spring* is very uncertain." Eliza Clitherall and her husband, James, also shared family decision making. Eliza later recalled that James "wou'd never agree to, or form any plan without consulting me" because he believed that "in Married life, both shou'd be in heart, Mind, and Management *one*."[75]

The popularity and longevity of *The Virginia House-Wife* suggest that patriarchy was not the only model of gender relations accessible to white southerners, even as they developed their distinctive regional identity. Randolph's book, with its preface and introduction, went through nineteen editions before 1860. It remained popular in the postbellum era.[76] The first self-consciously southern cookbook, *The Virginia House-Wife* was also the only homegrown cookbook available to southerners before the 1847 publication of *The South Carolina Housewife,* by Sara Rutledge.

Mary Randolph instructed generations of southern wives, though her vision of women's strength within their sphere coexisted with another increasingly prevalent model of southern gender relations, which emphasized feminine passivity and weakness. Ironically, Randolph's youngest sister, Virginia Randolph Cary, was one of the earliest and most influential proponents of this patriarchal model. An admiring cousin described Cary as a "secluded being" whose "thoughts and pursuits are of course virtuous."[77] As a widow in rural Fluvanna County, Virginia Randolph Cary composed her *Letters on the Female Character,* the first advice book written by a southern woman for the women of her region. Like her sister Mary, Cary portrayed women as wholly domestic. Yet, rather than portraying southern women as authoritative in the domestic sphere, Cary's *Letters* redefined feminine virtue — and by extension southern womanhood — to conform to patriarchal ideals and values.

Cary argued that women should be subservient to men both at home and in society. Invoking the "laws of nature," she described women as inherently weak and dependent on male protection. Citing Scripture, she characterized women as deeply flawed daughters of the fallen Eve and declared that because she "was *formed for man,*" woman "must continue in contented subordination to his authority." Submissive women, she informed her readers, would receive God's blessing, but a woman who "breaks down the barrier erected by Omnipotence around her . . . [is] liable to the full penalty of God's violated law" and "left to the uncovenanted mercies of her Maker." Better a woman be "pitied as a submissive wife to a strict husband, than applauded as having usurped the government [of a family] from the hands of an incompetent [man]," she maintained, because "both reason and religion prompt us to choose that which is approved by God, rather than that which is deemed expedient by man."[78]

Cary was demonstrably pious, but, like many conservative clergy and theologians, she regarded religion as the chief justification for women's rightful subordination rather than as a potential avenue to empowerment and self-actualization. Like most contemporary moralists, Cary believed that "of all the moral monsters which abound on earth, women without religion are the most disgusting and mischievous." Significantly, she saw women's piety primarily as a source of feminine modesty and quiet consolation for the "sometimes keen and frequent" trials of domestic life.[79]

Cary recognized that gender relationships were power relationships. Sentimentalizing neither women nor their lot in life, she argued that feminine subordination was divinely ordained and warned against the ruinous consequences of women's desire to "grasp at more than their allotted por-

Virginia Randolph Cary, Charles Crowell Ingram. An impoverished widowhood led Cary to earn her living by writing advice books, in which she admonished young women to submit cheerfully to male authority. Cary was an early proponent of the patriarchal ideology that became increasingly influential among antebellum southerners. Virginia Historical Society, Richmond.

tion of power." According to Cary, a woman's attempt to "take her station as the *equal* of man" inevitably resulted in "misrule and disorganization." Moreover, when a woman usurped authority, she forfeited the protection of both God and man, and consequently she "soon finds her coveted privileges irksome to her." Such a woman, Cary warned, "soon discovers that she has laid down a small burden, to take up a great one, and regrets that she was ever tempted to rise above herself." Cary advised her readers that "power has its penalties." Men who govern, she intimated, "have troubles not easily discernable to those who are governed."[80]

Cary cautioned that women's unwonted ambitions had dire public and private consequences. When women rejected their subordination, she asserted, "not only individual, but national misery will be the result." Citing the example of revolutionary France, where "it was said that [women] had attained their true and legitimate station of equality," Cary declared that women's autonomy resulted in the neglect of their children, the dishonor of their husbands, and the conversion of homes into "places of abomination, where the spirit of God could never come, to rectify the disorders of nature." Cary believed that if the women of France had "retained their appropriate sphere of duty," they somehow might have "prevented the desolation of their country." American women, happily, showed no such dangerous tendencies. In the United States, and in the South especially, Cary predicted, the influence of religion, perpetuated largely by dutiful women, would help ensure the survival of public "virtue and happiness."[81]

Recognizing that knowledge was a potential source of power, Cary criticized the most ambitious improvements in women's education. In France, she reminded readers, the women of the salons were "learned in all things . . . [and] vied with men in literature, philosophy, [and] science," but none of these feminine achievements promoted virtue or happiness. Writing in 1828, Cary noted that in recent decades American women, too, "have been admitted to a liberal participation of intellectual privileges," and she regarded this development with marked ambivalence. She conceded that the "partial illumination" of women's minds could help mothers teach their children and make a wife "truly a help meet" for her husband. Yet she also worried that education was "liable to abuse" by "aspiring females [who] are not content to retain any vestige of subordination to the anointed lords of creation." Cary thus concluded that she hoped "to see women highly cultivated in mind and morals, and yet content to remain within the retirement of the family circle."[82]

For Cary, as for Mary Randolph and countless other Americans, the family circle was the "sphere" that circumscribed women's proper activities, at least in theory. But while Randolph portrayed woman as the mistress of her domain, Cary characterized housework as merely a duty a wife owed to her husband. In *Letters on the Female Character* and in her *Christian Parent's Assistant,* published the following year, Cary recognized and even emphasized women's important moral influence on their offspring, if not their husbands. Yet even as she charged the "Mothers of America" with ensuring the "continuance of our national prosperity" by "educating subjects for the Redeemer's kingdom," Cary relentlessly reminded women of their essential weakness. Pious women, she suggested, could promote religion by "example and *precept*" because, after all, there were "few persons in the world, of so little importance as not to have some influence over their fellow creatures." To keep women "humble" and to preserve the submission of women in their households, Cary also urged mothers to invoke divine authority — rather than their own — when disciplining errant children and servants. She also reminded women that their essential weakness prevented them from "arresting hardened offenders against their God."[83]

Gender, not race, was Cary's primary interest, but she recognized slavery as a source of southern distinctiveness that posed peculiar problems for the white women of her region. In particular, she believed that slavery undermined the submissiveness of white women by encouraging in them a "habit of despotism." Like her Virginia forebears, Cary regarded slavery as a "fearful evil" that demoralized both blacks and whites, but she did not appear to appreciate the genuine suffering of those in bondage. Like growing numbers of southern apologists, Cary advocated more humane treatment for slaves, but she appeared to do so less to alleviate black hardship than to discourage "habits of tyranny" among white women and their progeny.[84] For Cary, the subjugation of women was the inevitable result of divine and natural law and blacks' subservience to whites — and to white men especially — was a secondary consideration.

Later proponents of patriarchy, both male and female, would regard slavery as a positive good, and its defense would be their chief objective. They constructed a social ideal that endowed white men with sovereignty in both the public and private spheres and, like Cary, cited Scripture to justify the subordination of their black and white dependents.[85] In the decades that followed the publication of Randolph's and Cary's books, the passive, dependent, and subordinate southern "lady" became an important symbol, the prevailing ideal of white womanhood in an increasingly self-conscious region. Yet despite the growing prevalence of patriarchal rhetoric, a spectrum of feminine ideals remained accessible to white southerners, and the lives of even the most respectable women did not always conform to the ideal of submissive dependence promoted by Cary and her many successors.

Conclusion:
Patriarchy and Its Limits

In 1852, Louisa Susannah McCord of South Carolina used the rhetoric of separate spheres to describe a uniquely southern ideal of American womanhood. Like many of her northern contemporaries, McCord celebrated white women's seclusion in the home, arguing that the noblest vocations of virtuous women were those of wife and mother. Yet while northerners usually portrayed the domestic sphere as women's empire as well as their workplace, McCord emphasized their subordination and dependence even within the household. A sophisticated political economist and a loyal member of the slave-owning elite, McCord wrote and published essays to defend her class and culture from the growing ranks of their northern critics. Like other articulate southerners of her generation, she regarded slavery as a positive good. Like them, too, she believed that slavery could best be preserved by allegedly benevolent white men endowed with unlimited authority — not only in the public sphere and on their plantations but also in their households.[1]

Vociferously antifeminist, McCord nonetheless continued a long tradition of white southern women's involvement in the affairs of the public sphere. In the colonial period, elite women shaped public culture on civic and sociable occasions, while women who worked in certain occupations became visible and sometimes influential public figures in their communities. As boycotters, essayists, and increasingly politicized individuals, southern women participated in the prerevolutionary resistance movement and contributed to the political culture of revolutionary America. As we have seen, republican ideology, sentimental views of womanhood, and evangelical Protestantism together defined southern gender ideals in the postrevolutionary decades. Although those ideals were in no sense egalitarian, they emphasized women's improving influence in the domestic sphere, rather than their abject subordination to male authority. Southerners, like northerners, employed the rhetoric of separate spheres to celebrate feminine domesticity and women's unique virtue and piety. By linking femininity to moral virtue, they also inadvertently justified women's forays into certain aspects of public life.

From the colonial period through the antebellum era, white southern women were members of a patriarchal society, or one characterized by the "manifestation and institutionalization of male dominance over women and children in the family and the extension of male dominance over women in society in general."[2] Within the confines of patriarchy and without challenging it explicitly, white women, particularly those of the elite and middling social ranks, participated in the affairs of the public sphere and, in some instances, influenced the form and content of public life. The changing ways in which they did so reflected the evolution of their culture's larger social values. The public activities of colonial gentlewomen therefore reinforced the existing hierarchy in their rigidly stratified society, while white women in the revolutionary era acted in support of their communities' emerging political values. In the early nineteenth century, white southern women exploited widely held assumptions about their own superior piety and virtue to justify their religious and benevolent activities. By showing compassion for the poor and concern for the impious, those activities, in turn, buttressed the humanitarian credentials of an increasingly self-conscious planter elite and thereby legitimized its continuing dominance.[3]

During the colonial era, elite women exploited the ideals of gentility to make public culture that heightened both their own public influence and the authority of their class. In colonial communities, the ties of patronage that bound gentry to common folk and creditor to debtor were reproduced and formalized in the more explicitly public hierarchies of the courts, the church, and the provincial governments. The traditional public rituals surrounding court sessions, elections, and militia musters enabled great men to mingle with their imagined inferiors, but an increasingly genteel cultural style fortified the authority of the elites by exhibiting their unique access to the ideas and fashions of a polite cosmopolitan world. Elite women were prominent at the balls, dinners, and civic rituals associated with genteel sociability. In fact, contemporaries regarded women's innate sensibility and virtue as essential to the attainment of the genteel cultural ideals to which elites aspired by the eighteenth century's middle decades.

The Revolution was a watershed in the history of women's relationship to the public sphere, signaling both the high point and the subsequent decline of feminine participation in public activities that were explicitly political. Balls and processions commemorating the king's birthday and other patriotic occasions had given elite women access to civic rituals and to political information during the colonial era, but the prerevolutionary resistance movement and later the war itself brought unprecedented numbers of women of all ranks into the public sphere as boycotters and producers of domestic manufactures, as army nurses and laundresses, as polemicists in local newspapers, and as petitioners seeking redress of grievances from their governments. These activities and the hardships with which they were often associated enhanced women's political consciousness, though revolutionary republicanism drew new and rigid boundaries between the public and private spheres, relegating women to the latter and ascribing to men alone the rights and obligations of republican citizenship.

A political culture that afforded civic status and economic rights to all propertied white men, while excluding white women and African Americans, almost inevitably reconstructed the public sphere in gender-specific terms. Republicanism, which defined political virtue as the selfless pursuit of the public good, made personal independence, based on property ownership and arms-bearing, the chief qualifications for full membership in the polity, thus making these traditionally masculine attributes prerequisites for such access to the public sphere as citizenship afforded. Even liberalism, which lauded the pursuit of individual improvement and self-interest, idealized masculine independence, enjoining men to compete publicly in the marketplace and in politics, while envisioning women as the homebound guardians of morality and family life.[4]

American leaders in the southern states and elsewhere gradually devised new civic rituals that reflected these ideals, replacing the genteel balls of the colonial period with more socially inclusive celebrations that featured parading militiamen. By explicitly excluding women from active participation, these new civic rituals obscured the legacy of the Revolution for white women, who, though portrayed as weak and apolitical, remained politically conscious. Indeed, during the protracted crisis leading to the War of 1812, some southern women tacitly demanded at least temporary access to the political arena, donning homespun to assert their patriotism and distinguish themselves as contributors to the security of the republic. Only in such dire emergencies, however, did men grudgingly acknowledge women's patriotism or the possibility that they might appropriately participate in political life.

Women were more instrumental in the development of the culture of Protestant evangelicalism, which coexisted with the political culture of the postrevolutionary era. By locating virtue in the private sphere, evangelicals enhanced the significance of both women and domestic life. Partly as a result of the growing influence of Protestant evangelicalism, white southerners came to regard the home as the seat of virtue and morality, and southern men increasingly may have looked to women, as guardians of the private sphere, to promote virtue in their households. Unlike some of their northern contemporaries, who came to demand equal access to the public sphere, white southern women never explicitly rejected the domestic ideal that their region's clergy and moralists avidly promoted, but many did exploit the ideal of pious, moral, and nurturing womanhood to inspire and to justify their varied incursions into public life.

The ideal of pious, moral, and nurturing womanhood both legitimized and limited the public activities of white southern women. In the early decades of the nineteenth century, benevolent and evangelical women constructed a public culture that men for the most part neither condemned nor sanctioned. Women's public culture was distinct from that of men in that it was less expansive and more closely focused on religious and benevolent projects. In addition, women's public culture was less autonomous than men's insofar as it embraced mixed-sex organizations, which were generally male-dominated, along with more autonomous women's associations.

While many northern women were increasingly engaging in domestic, social, and reform activities apart from their husbands, the public sphere of southern women continued to overlap with that of their male contemporaries. Urban northerners of both sexes drew at least a rhetorical distinction between religion and benevolence, which they regarded as women's work, and politics, which they believed to be the domain of men. In southern communities, by contrast, men and women alike undertook religious and benevolent activities and sometimes came together in mixed-sex associations. Like their northern counterparts, southern women who participated in the affairs of the public sphere found their lives enriched both socially and intellectually. Relatively few, however, enjoyed the autonomy of sexual separatism, which fostered the development of a feminist critique of patriarchy among a small but significant minority of northern women in the antebellum era.[5]

The marginal place of women in the early southern temperance movement suggests that females attained access to the public sphere only to the extent that their activities were consistent with white male dominance. Southern men carefully circumscribed women's temperance activities, encouraging them to join mixed-sex groups and thereby preventing the formation of separate women's associations. They understood that women's independent attempts to change men's habits and behavior by promoting a temperance agenda would have subverted the patriarchal ideal. Similarly, the absence of egalitarian reforms in general and of feminism in particular in the Old South indicates that the guardians of patriarchy tolerated reformers of either sex only when their efforts maintained or strengthened the existing social order. As white southern men grew more sensitive to northern attacks on slavery and southern political interests, they monitored women's public activities, assiduously opposing or diluting those that undermined the class, race, and gender systems that in theory endowed them with near-absolute authority.

After 1830, the rhetoric of separate spheres, which southerners shared with their northern contemporaries, increasingly coexisted with a more explicitly patriarchal rhetoric that signaled the emergence of an avowedly proslavery ideology. As antebellum southerners found themselves increasingly pressed to defend slavery and the social order it engendered, they articulated an ideology that drew parallels between marriage and slavery to justify existing social hierarchies as natural, and in addition deemed slavery a positive good because it civilized and Christianized a supposedly inferior people. Characterizing African Americans as lustful barbarians in turn accentuated the vulnerability of white women, who, they argued, were dependent on the protection of white men and consequently obliged to submit to their authority. The rural isolation of most southern women made this ideal of feminine dependence and submission more readily attainable. Privileged by both race and class, most white women did not overtly challenge this proslavery patriarchal ideology. While some white women were passively complicit, others, like Louisa McCord, actively embraced and promoted patriarchy and the race and gender hierarchies it presupposed.[6]

The rhetorical triumph of patriarchy, however, did not result in the monolithic suppression of competing feminine ideals among antebellum southerners. Like northern proponents of the ideology of separate spheres, some white southerners continued to laud publicly the economic contributions that women could make to their families as well as the moral influence they might wield in their households. Publishers reprinted Mary Randolph's *Virginia House-Wife* frequently during the antebellum decades. Other southerners continued to praise the ideal of virtuous and authoritative housewifery that Randolph promoted.

The southern agricultural press, which catered primarily to the yeoman farmers of the region, also recognized the economic value of women's work and encouraged wives to assume the role of junior partner in the family enterprise. Like their northern counterparts, southern agricultural writers disdained the ornamental "lady" and the class privilege she represented and instead idealized the competent farmwife, who, as her husband's helpmate, would engage in productive labor that improved the living standard of her family and often added to its income. By the 1840s and 1850s, agricultural fairs publicly recognized and celebrated the domestic expertise and economic achievements of southern farm women, many of whom entered the public sphere to market the sometimes substantial fruits of their domestic labors.[7]

The continued recognition of women's domestic influence also was evident in less specialized antebellum publications. For instance, in 1837, a contributor to the Charleston-based *Southern Watchman and General Intelligencer* described the division of labor and authority in marriage in terms that would have been familiar to most of his northern contemporaries. "It is the husband's duty to bring into the house, and it is the duty of the wife to see that nothing wrongly goes out of it," he observed, explaining that "the theatre of [woman's] exploits [is] the bosom of her family, where she may do as much towards making a fortune as [her husband] possibly can do in the counting room or the workshop." Writing on the eve of the Civil War, Daniel R. Hundley, an Alabama native and eventual secessionist, more explicitly emphasized the moral authority that southern women wielded within the family circle. Decrying "all political twaddle and senseless disputes about the 'Rights of Woman,' " Hundley maintained that "woman's one sole Inalienable Right, is to be a Teacher . . . . And it is in this school [of the family] that woman finds her proper sphere and mission." According to Hundley, woman's status as the teacher and moral exemplar of her family "is her God-given privilege and honor, which the tyranny of man can never deprive her of," adding that "in this her proper sphere woman wields a power."[8]

Decades earlier, similar ideas about women's moral superiority enabled many to go beyond their "proper sphere" to participate in the world beyond their households. Although southern men may have been increasingly vigilant of women's public activities, their patriarchal rhetoric did not obliterate the reality of women's public lives. Established benevolence associations, such as the Charleston Ladies' Benevolent Society and Richmond's Female Humane Society, continued their activities uninterrupted through the Civil War and beyond. In the decades preceding the Civil War, southern women — sometimes acting on their own and sometimes joining with men — founded new benevolent, religious, and even temperance groups in both urban and rural communities.[9]

Some southern women even challenged their exclusion from conventional politics, which, as we have seen, was deeply rooted in the gendered ideology of citizenship that prevailed in postrevolutionary America. Just as the participation of women in colonial civic rituals acknowledged and even celebrated gender differences, especially in the form of women's peculiar sensibility, feminine involvement in the partisan politics of the antebellum era complemented rather than replicated men's public political roles. Reform-minded southern women mobilized in support of Henry Clay and other Whig candidates in the 1840s, but they did so as representatives of a peculiarly feminine culture of morality and benevolence, which Whig men believed could purify both politics and society. By the 1850s, Whigs and Democrats alike appealed for women's political support, which they envisioned as a corrective to a partisan culture that was increasingly amoral and contentious. Looking to women to sanitize and legitimize partisan politics, men accepted and even promoted their involvement, though they expected women's political activism to support existing political agendas and the social orders they fostered. Antebellum women thus remained politically conscious, debating issues, raising money for partisan causes, and even addressing partisan gatherings, but they did so nearly always as supporters of men's political programs and never as advocates of gender or racial equality.[10]

Like their eighteenth-century predecessors, nineteenth-century southern women clearly participated in the world beyond their households. Between 1700 and 1835, the boundaries between the public and private spheres solidified, but they remained nonetheless permeable for women who, though relegated in theory to the latter, still sought to participate in and even to influence public life. Changes in religious and political ideals, along with related improvements in women's education, identified white women with the household and with the moral, spiritual, and personal qualities that supposedly made them ideally suited for virtuous domestic life. Those same qualities informed their activities in the public sphere, which, despite their potentially radical implications, complemented and supported their communities' fundamental social hierarchies and values.

Notes

The following abbreviations are used in the notes:

AHR	*American Historical Review*
CW	Colonial Williamsburg Foundation
CWM	Swem Library, College of William and Mary, Williamsburg, Virginia
DU	Perkins Library, Duke University, Durham, North Carolina
GASR	General Assembly Sessions Records
GHQ	*Georgia Historical Quarterly*
JAH	*Journal of American History*
JER	*Journal of the Early Republic*
JSH	*Journal of Southern History*
LP	Legislative Petitions
MHS	Maryland Historical Society, Baltimore
NCDAH	North Carolina Division of Archives and History, Raleigh
NCHR	*North Carolina Historical Review*
SC Arch	South Carolina Archives, Columbia
SCHM	*South Carolina Historical Magazine*
SCHS	South Carolina Historical Society, Charleston
SHC, UNC-CH	Southern Historical Collection, University of North Carolina–Chapel Hill
USC	South Caroliniana Library, University of South Carolina, Columbia
UVa	Alderman Library, University of Virginia, Charlottesville
VHS	Virginia Historical Society, Richmond
VMHB	*Virginia Magazine of History and Biography*
VSLA	Virginia State Library and Archives, Richmond
WMQ	*William and Mary Quarterly*

Introduction

¹ Julia Cherry Spruill, *Women's Life and Work in the Southern Colonies* (Chapel Hill, N.C., 1938), p. 232, and chaps. 11–14 generally; Elizabeth Fox-Genovese, *Within the Plantation Household: Black and White Women of the Old South* (Chapel Hill, N.C., 1988), pp. 98–99.

On the Revolution, see Linda K. Kerber, *Women of the Republic: Intellect and Ideology in Revolutionary America* (Chapel Hill, N.C., 1980); Elaine F. Crane, "Dependence in the Era of Independence: The Role of Women in a Republican Society," in Jack P. Greene, ed., *The American Revolution: Its Character and Limits* (New York, 1987), pp. 251–70; Joan Hoff Wilson, "The Illusion of Change: Women and the American Revolution," in Alfred F. Young, ed., *The American Revolution: Explorations in the History of American Radicalism* (De Kalb, Ill., 1976), pp. 386–431. Mary Beth Norton, *Liberty's Daughters: The Revolutionary Experience of American Women, 1750–1800* (Boston, 1980), offers a more optimistic, but less persuasive, interpretation of the Revolution's impact on women's roles and status.

² Jürgen Habermas, "The Public Sphere: An Encyclopedia Article (1964)," *New German Critique* 5 (1974): 49–55.

³ For Habermas's critics, see Carole Pateman, *The Disorder of Women* (London, 1989), pp. 118–40; and Nancy Fraser, *Unruly Practices* (Minneapolis, 1989), pp. 113–43. On the origins and uses of the notion of separate spheres, see Linda K. Kerber, "Separate Spheres, Female Worlds, Woman's Place: The Rhetoric of Women's History," *JAH* 75 (1988): 9–24.

⁴ See Mary P. Ryan, *Women in Public: Between Banners and Ballots, 1825–1880* (Baltimore, 1990), esp. pp. 3–18, as well as the incisive discussions in Dena Goodman, "Public Sphere and Private Life: Toward a Synthesis of Current Historiographical Approaches to the Old Regime," *History and Theory* 31 (1991): 1–20, and Paula Baker, "The Domestication of Politics: Women and American Political Society, 1780–1920," *AHR* 89 (1984): 620–47.

⁵ Pateman, *Disorder of Women*, pp. 4, 132.

⁶ Rhys Isaac, *The Transformation of Virginia, 1740–1790* (Chapel Hill, N.C., 1982), esp. pp. 131–35; Gordon S. Wood, *The Radicalism of the American Revolution* (New York, 1992), pp. 57–77, 88–89.

⁷ On the ideal of "republican motherhood" and its impact on the quality of women's education, particularly in the 1780s, see Kerber, *Women of the Republic*, chaps. 7–8.

⁸ Clement Eaton, *Freedom of Thought in the Old South* (Durham, N.C., 1940), chaps. 5 and 12; W. J. Cash, *The Mind of the South* (New York, 1941), pp. 87–89; Fox-Genovese, *Within the Plantation Household*, pp. 334–39. On the efforts of southern intellectuals to win acceptance and recognition by their vigorous defense of slavery, see Drew Gilpin Faust, *A Sacred Circle: The Dilemma of the Intellectual in the Old South, 1840–1860* (Baltimore, 1977), pp. 115–16.

[9] John D'Emilio and Estelle B. Freedman, *Intimate Matters: A History of Sexuality in America* (New York, 1988), pp. 86–87, 93–96; Stephanie McCurry, "The Two Faces of Republicanism: Gender and Proslavery Politics in Antebellum South Carolina," *JAH* 78 (1992): 1246–57.

[10] The most forceful case for southern distinctiveness as it pertains to gender is Fox-Genovese, *Within the Plantation Household*, chap. 1. But see also Jean E. Friedman, *The Enclosed Garden: Women and Community in the Evangelical South, 1830–1900* (Chapel Hill, N.C., 1985), pp. 6–20; McCurry, "Two Faces of Republicanism," pp. 1245–64; Catherine Clinton, *The Plantation Mistress: Women's World in the Old South* (New York, 1982), pp. 8–15.

[11] See, for instance, William J. Cooper, Jr., *The South and the Politics of Slavery* (Baton Rouge, La., 1978), esp. chap. 3; Robert F. Durden, *The Self-Inflicted Wound: Southern Politics in the Nineteenth Century* (Lexington, Ky., 1985), pp. 13–25, 34–44; John McCardell, *The Idea of a Southern Nation: Southern Nationalists and Southern Sectionalism, 1830–1860* (New York, 1979), pp. 4–7, 44–50, 177–200; Charles S. Sydnor, *The Development of Southern Sectionalism, 1819–1848* (Baton Rouge, La., 1948), pp. 151–56, 222–48, 297–304. At least one scholar has discerned the roots of southern distinctiveness in the politics of the revolutionary era and especially in the fiscal debates of the 1790s. See John Richard Alden, *The First South* (Baton Rouge, La., 1961).

[12] On the ideal of the southern lady, which envisioned white women as delicate and powerless repositories of beauty and virtue, see Anne Firor Scott, *The Southern Lady: From Pedestal to Politics, 1830–1930* (Chicago, 1970), chap. 1.

[13] Thad W. Tate, "Defining the Colonial South," in Winthrop D. Jordan and Sheila L. Skemp, eds., *Race and Family in the Colonial South* (Jackson, Miss., 1987), pp. 14–17; Richard R. Beeman, *The Evolution of the Southern Backcountry: A Case Study of Lunenburg County, Virginia, 1746–1832* (Philadelphia, 1984), esp. chaps. 8–9; Rachel N. Klein, *Unification of a Slave State: The Rise of the Planter Class in the South Carolina Backcountry, 1760–1808* (Chapel Hill, N.C., 1990), esp. pp. 303–5; Sydnor, *Development of Southern Sectionalism*, pp. 30–31, 62–66, 82–86, 163–76, 276–79.

1. Woman, Work, and Sensibility

[1] Julia Cherry Spruill, *Women's Life and Work in the Southern Colonies* (Chapel Hill, N.C., 1938), pp. 236–41; "Brent, Margaret," in Edward T. James et al., eds., *Notable American Women, 1607–1950: A Biographical Dictionary*, 3 vols. (Cambridge, Mass., 1971), 1:236–37; Mary Beth Norton, *Founding Mothers and Fathers: Gendered Power and the Forming of American Society* (New York, 1996), pp. 281–87.

[2] Suzanne Lebsock, *"A Share of Honour": Virginia Women, 1600–1945* (Richmond, Va., 1984), pp. 26–27; "Berkeley, Lady Frances," in James et al., eds., *Notable American Women*, 1:135–36; Terri L. Snyder, " 'Rich Widows Are the Best Commodity This Country Affords': Gender Relations and the Rehabilitation of Patriarchy in Virginia, 1660–1700" (Ph.D. diss., University of Iowa, 1992), pp. 70–76.

³ Edmund S. Morgan, *American Slavery, American Freedom: The Ordeal of Colonial Virginia* (New York, 1975), pp. 126–27, 162–63, 408–9; Norton, *Founding Mothers and Fathers,* pp. 120–25; Kathleen Mary Brown, "Gender and the Genesis of a Race and Class System in Virginia, 1630–1750" (Ph.D. diss., University of Wisconsin–Madison, 1990), chap. 2; Brown, *Good Wives, Nasty Wenches, and Anxious Patriarchs: Gender, Race, and Power in Colonial Virginia* (Chapel Hill, N.C., 1996), pp. 24–27, 85–87.

⁴ Lawrence Stone, *The Family, Sex and Marriage in England, 1500–1800* (New York, 1977), pp. 195–202, 356–58, 501–7; Roger Thompson, *Women in Tudor and Stuart England and America: A Comparative Study* (London, 1974), pp. 8–11, 162–63; Susan Dwyer Amussen, *An Ordered Society: Gender and Class in Early Modern England* (London, 1988), esp. pp. 35–47, 95–104.

⁵ Lois Green Carr and Lorena S. Walsh, "The Planter's Wife: The Experience of White Women in Seventeenth-Century Maryland," *WMQ,* 3d ser., 34 (1977): 542–63; Darrett B. Rutman and Anita H. Rutman, " 'Now-Wives and Sons-in-Law': Parental Death in a Seventeenth-Century Virginia County," in Thad W. Tate and David L. Ammerman, eds., *The Chesapeake in the Seventeenth Century: Essays on Anglo-American Society and Politics* (Chapel Hill, N.C., 1979), pp. 153–82; Morgan, *American Slavery, American Freedom,* pp. 168–69.

⁶ Carr and Walsh, "Planter's Wife"; Lorena S. Walsh, "The Experience and Status of White Women in the Chesapeake," in Walter J. Fraser et al., eds., *The Web of Southern Social Relations: Women, Family, and Education* (Athens, Ga., 1985), pp. 1–15; Joan R. Gundersen and Gwen Victor Gampel, "Married Women's Legal Status in Eighteenth-Century New York and Virginia," *WMQ,* 3d ser., 39 (1982): 114–34; Cara Anzilotti, "Autonomy and the Female Planter in Colonial South Carolina," *JSH* 63 (1997): 239–41. This phenomenon was not peculiar to the southern colonies. See Laurel Thatcher Ulrich, *Good Wives: Image and Reality in the Lives of Women in Northern New England, 1650–1750* (New York, 1980), chap. 2; and Cynthia A. Kierner, *Traders and Gentlefolk: The Livingstons of New York, 1675–1790* (Ithaca, N.Y., 1992), pp. 41–42, 50–51, 148–49.

⁷ Darrett B. Rutman and Anita H. Rutman, *A Place in Time: Middlesex County, Virginia, 1650–1750* (New York, 1984), pp. 103–13; Linda E. Speth, " 'More than Her Thirds': Wives and Widows in Colonial Virginia," in Linda E. Speth and Alison Duncan Hirsh, *Women, Family, and Community in Colonial America: Two Perspectives* (New York, 1983), pp. 6, 17–20; Lorena S. Walsh, " 'Till Death Us Do Part': Marriage and Family in Seventeenth-Century Maryland," in Tate and Ammerman, eds., *Chesapeake in the Seventeenth Century,* pp. 136–37; Morgan, *American Slavery, American Freedom,* pp. 164–70.

⁸ Morgan, *American Slavery, American Freedom,* pp. 166–67, 170.

⁹ On the demography of early Virginia, see ibid., pp. 162–66, 180–84, 395–410; Daniel Blake Smith, "Mortality and Family in the Colonial Chesapeake," *Journal of Interdisciplinary History* 8 (1977–78): 403–27; Allan Kulikoff, *Tobacco and Slaves: The*

Development of Southern Cultures in the Chesapeake, 1680–1800 (Chapel Hill, N.C., 1986), pp. 32–33, 55, 60–63, 69–71, 167–73; James Horn, "Servant Emigration to the Chesapeake in the Seventeenth Century," in Tate and Ammerman, eds., *Chesapeake in the Seventeenth Century*, p. 62; John J. McCusker and Russell R. Menard, *The Economy of British America, 1607–1789* (Chapel Hill, N.C., 1985), pp. 134–35, 141–43, 228.

Data for the Carolinas are less readily available, but see James M. Gallman, "Mortality among White Males: Colonial North Carolina," *Social Science History* 4 (1980): 295–316; Peter H. Wood, *Black Majority: Negroes in Colonial South Carolina from 1670 through the Stono Rebellion* (Chapel Hill, N.C., 1974), pp. 142–66; Peter A. Coclanis, *The Shadow of a Dream: Economic Life and Death in the South Carolina Low Country, 1670–1920* (New York, 1989), pp. 64–67.

¹⁰ Lebsock, *"Share of Honour,"* pp. 47–48; Speth, " 'More Than Her Thirds,' " pp. 17–20; Kulikoff, *Tobacco and Slaves*, pp. 188–93; Snyder, " 'Rich Widows are the Best Commodity this Country Affords,' " pp. 55–62, 143–89; Marylynn Salmon, *Women and the Law of Property in Early America* (Chapel Hill, N.C., 1986), pp. 147–60, 168–75; Lois Green Carr, "Inheritance in the Colonial Chesapeake," in Ronald Hoffman and Peter J. Albert, eds., *Women in the Age of the American Revolution* (Charlottesville, Va., 1989), pp. 163–66, 171–81; Gundersen and Gampel, "Married Women's Legal Status," pp. 133–34.

¹¹ Maria Taylor Byrd to William Byrd III, 24 Dec. 1757, 18 July 1760, Byrd Family Papers, VHS; Elise Pinckney, ed., *The Letterbook of Eliza Lucas Pinckney, 1739–1762* (Chapel Hill, N.C., 1972), pp. xvi–xx, 5n; Eliza Lucas to Mrs. Boddicott, 2 May [1740], and Eliza Lucas to George Lucas, 14 June 1741, both in Pinckney, ed., *Letterbook of Eliza Lucas Pinckney*; Eliza Lucas Pinckney to Charles Cotesworth Pinckney, 10 Sept. 1785, Charles Cotesworth Pinckney Papers, Charleston Library Society.

¹² Joseph E. Fields, comp., *"Worthy Partner": The Papers of Martha Washington* (Westport, Conn., 1994), pp. 3–61; Mary Willing Byrd to Samuel Inglis, 27 Jan. 1774, Byrd Family Papers, VHS; Elizabeth Elliott to Barnard Elliott, 30 Sept. 1762, Baker-Grimké Papers, SCHS; Eliza Lucas Pinckney to [Mr. Morly], 14 Mar. 1760, in Pinckney, ed., *Letterbook of Eliza Lucas Pinckney*, pp. 143–44; Anzilotti, "Autonomy and the Female Planter." On Mary Willing Byrd, see also François Jean, Marquis de Chastellux, *Travels in North America in the Years 1780, 1781, and 1782*, ed. Howard C. Rice, Jr., 2 vols. (Chapel Hill, N.C., 1963), 2:432. For some female leaseholders, who presumably were widows, see list of rents owed to Robert Carter, 1770, Carter Family Papers, VHS.

¹³ John Campbell to Mary Dandridge Spotswood Campbell, 13 May [1766?], [ca. 1767]; Petition of Mary Dandridge Spotswood Campbell to Earl of Dunmore, [ca. 1772]; Mary Dandridge Spotswood Campbell to [John Spotswood], [ca. 1790], 29 Nov., 23 Dec. 1794, all in Spotswood Family Papers, VHS.

¹⁴ Spruill, *Women's Life and Work in the Southern Colonies*, pp. 65–70; Lois Green

Carr and Lorena S. Walsh, "Economic Diversification and Labor Organization in the Chesapeake, 1650–1820," in Stephen Innes, ed., *Work and Labor in Early America* (Chapel Hill, N.C., 1988), pp. 145–46; Ulrich, *Good Wives,* chap. 1; Joan P. Jensen, *Loosening the Bonds: Mid-Atlantic Farm Women, 1750–1850* (New Haven, 1986), chap. 3; Catherine Clinton, *Plantation Mistress: Women's World in the Old South* (New York, 1982), pp. 18–29; *South Carolina Gazette,* 11 June 1772.

[15] Brown, *Good Wives, Nasty Wenches, and Anxious Patriarchs,* pp. 107–36. On the development of slave codes generally, see John Hope Franklin, *From Slavery to Freedom: A History of Negro Americans,* 2d ed. (New York, 1956), pp. 70–73, 77–82.

[16] Evangeline Walker Andrews and Charles McLean Andrews, eds., *Journal of a Lady of Quality: Being the Narrative of a Journey from Scotland to the West Indies, North Carolina, and Portugal, in the Years 1774 to 1776* (New Haven, Conn., 1921), pp. 160–61, 178–79; *Recipe Book of Eliza Lucas Pinckney, 1756* (Charleston, S.C., 1936); Recipes of Harriott Pinckney Horry, n.d., and Eliza Lucas Pinckney to [Daniel Horry], 9 Mar. 1768, both in Pinckney Family Papers, SCHS; "Diary of a Little Colonial Girl," *VMHB* 11 (1903–4): 212.

[17] G[ervase] Markham, *The English House-Wife, contain[in]g The inward and outward Vertues which ought to be in a Compleat Woman,* 8th ed. (London, 1675). On the popularity of this book in colonial America, see Mary Tolford Wilson, "Amelia Simmons Fills a Need: *American Cookery, 1796,*" *WMQ,* 3d ser., 14 (1957): 17–18.

[18] Judith Carter Banks to Landon Carter, June 1765, Carter Family Papers, Alderman Library, UVa; Jack P. Greene, ed., *The Diary of Colonel Landon Carter of Sabine Hall, 1752–1778,* 2 vols. (Charlottesville, Va., 1965), 2:1067; Hunter Dickinson Farish, ed., *Journal and Letters of Philip Vickers Fithian, 1773–1774: A Plantation Tutor of the Old Dominion* (Williamsburg, Va., 1943), p. 51; Sarah Fouace Nourse Diary, 1781–83, Nourse Family Papers, Alderman Library, UVa.

[19] John Lawson, *A New Voyage to Carolina,* ed. Hugh Talmadge Lefler (Chapel Hill, N.C., 1967), p. 90; William Byrd II, *Histories of the Dividing Line betwixt Virginia and North Carolina,* ed. William K. Boyd (Raleigh, N.C., 1929), pp. 66, 68, 304, 306.

[20] Carole Shammas, "Black Women's Work and the Evolution of Plantation Society in Virginia," *Labor History* 26 (1985): 13–14; Andrew Burnaby, *Travels through the Middle Settlements in North America, in the Years 1759 and 1760; with Observations on the State of the Colonies,* 3d ed. (London, 1798), p. 17; "Inventory of all the Property of Robert Carter," *VMHB* 6 (1898–99): 264–66.

[21] Shammas, "Black Women's Work," p. 18; Joan R. Gundersen, "The Double Bonds of Race and Sex: Black and White Women in a Colonial Virginia Parish," *JSH* 52 (1986): 369.

[22] Gregory A. Stiverson and Patrick H. Butler III, eds., "Virginia in 1732: The Travel Journal of William Hugh Grove," *VMHB* 85 (1977): 34; E[liza] S[mith] *The Compleat Housewife: or, Accompish'd Gentlewoman's Companion,* 4th ed. (London, 1730); [Hannah] Glasse, *The Art of Cookery Made Plain and Easy* (1747; rev. ed., Alexandria,

Va., 1805), p. 1; Jane Carson, "Colonial Virginia Cookery," Colonial Williamsburg
Research Report, 1968.

²³ Eliza Lucas to [Mary Bartlett], [1742], in Pinckney, ed., *Letterbook of Eliza Lucas Pinckney*, pp. 34–35.

²⁴ Thomas Pinckney to Harriott Pinckney Horry, 22 Feb. 1779, quoted in Mary Beth Norton, *Liberty's Daughters: The Revolutionary Experience of American Women, 1750–1800* (Boston, 1980), p. 26.

²⁵ William Byrd II to John Lord Boyle, 2 Feb. 1727, in "Virginia Council Journals, 1726–1753," *VMHB* 32 (1924): 30; Sarah Trebell to John [?], 12 May 1766, Misc. Mss., Trebell, CW; Edward Miles Riley, ed., *The Journal of John Harrower: An Indentured Servant in the Colony of Virginia, 1773–1776* (Williamsburg, Va., 1963), p. 138; Norton, *Liberty's Daughters*, pp. 4–5, 36–39.

²⁶ Robert Carter to Mrs. McClanahan, 21 Nov. 1778; Carter to Mary Johnson, 11 Mar. 1779; Carter to Elizabeth Garvey, 15 Oct. 1787, all in Robert Carter Letterbooks, DU.

²⁷ Johanna Miller Lewis, "Women Artisans in Backcountry North Carolina, 1753–1790," *NCHR* 68 (1991): 215, 222–28; Alan D. Watson, "Society and Economy in Colonial Edgecombe County," *NCHR* 50 (1973): 234–35; Carr and Walsh, "Economic Diversification and Labor Organization," pp. 145–46, 173–75; Robert Carter to Easter Sutton, 16 Oct. 1781, Robert Carter Letterbooks, DU.

²⁸ Farish, ed., *Journal and Letters of Philip Vickers Fithian*, pp. 131, 133; Donald Jackson et al., eds., *The Diaries of George Washington*, 6 vols. (Charlottesville, Va., 1976–79), 2:115; Elizabeth Lewis Littlepage account book, 1767–68, Holliday Family Papers, VHS.

²⁹ Coclanis, *Shadow of a Dream*, p. 114; McCusker and Menard, *Economy of British America*, pp. 131–32; Burnaby, *Travels through the Middle Settlements*, p. 6; Lord Adam Gordon, "Journal of an Officer who Travelled in America and the West Indies in 1764 and 1765," in Newton D. Mereness, ed., *Travels in the American Colonies* (New York, 1916), p. 397.

³⁰ *South Carolina Gazette*, 12 Jan., 7 Mar., 7 Sept. 1767, 15 Feb. 1768, 26 Jan., 31 Aug. 1769, 29 Mar. 1770.

³¹ Alan D. Watson, "Ordinaries in Eastern North Carolina." *NCHR* 45 (1968): 71; Spruill, *Women's Life and Work in the Southern Colonies*, pp. 295–302; David W. Conroy, *In Public Houses: Drink and the Revolution of Authority in Colonial Massachusetts* (Chapel Hill, N.C., 1995), pp. 177–79, 236–40, 276–87, 302–9; Daniel B. Thorp, "Taverns and Tavern Culture on the Southern Colonial Frontier: Rowan County, North Carolina, 1753–1776," *JSH* 62 (1996): 661–62, 674–75; Joy Day Buel and Richard Buel, Jr., *The Way of Duty: A Woman and Her Family in Revolutionary America* (New York, 1984), pp. 65, 68–71.

³² John C. Fitzpatrick, *George Washington: Colonial Traveller, 1732–1775* (Indianapolis, 1927), pp. 109, 172, 173, 180, 210, 254, 292, 324, 355; Spruill, *Women's Life*

and Work in the Southern Colonies, p. 299; Petition of Jane Vo[b]e, 24 Nov. 1784, LP, Williamsburg, VSLA; William S. Powell, ed., *Dictionary of North Carolina Biography,* 6 vols. (Chapel Hill, N.C., 1979–96), 5:432; Johanna Miller Lewis, *Artisans in the North Carolina Backcountry* (Lexington, Ky., 1995), pp. 107–9; Elizabeth Steele to Ephraim Steele, 15 May, 30 July, 17 Oct. 1778, 29 Apr., 13 July, 29 Oct. 1780, John Steele Papers, NCDAH.

33 On southern colonial milliners, see Eleanor Kelley Cabell, "Women Merchants and Milliners in Eighteenth-Century Williamsburg," Colonial Williamsburg Research Report, 1988; Spruill, *Women's Life and Work in the Southern Colonies,* pp. 280–85.

34 *South Carolina Gazette,* 11 Jan. 1739; *Virginia Gazette* (Rind), 2 Sept. 1773.

35 Leona M. Hudak, *Early American Women Printers and Publishers, 1639–1820* (Metuchen, N.J., 1978), pp. 131–63, 471–95; "Timothy, Ann" and "Timothy, Elizabeth" in James et al., eds., *Notable American Women,* 3:465–66; Will of Ann Timothy, 5 May 1790, Charleston County Will Book, 1786–93, typescript, p. 24; Watson, "Ordinaries in Eastern North Carolina," p. 71; Speth, " 'More Than Her Thirds,' " pp. 31–32; Spruill, *Women's Life and Work in the Southern Colonies,* pp. 288–89, 302–5.

36 *Virginia Gazette,* 10 July 1752; Cabell, "Women Merchants and Milliners," pp. 39–43, 95–114; *Virginia Gazette* (Dixon and Hunter), 13 May 1775; *South Carolina Gazette and Country Journal,* 1 Mar. 1768.

37 *Virginia Gazette* (Rind), 20 Nov. 1770; *South Carolina Gazette,* 19 Dec. 1740, 13 Feb. 1775.

38 *Virginia Gazette,* 11 Apr. 1751; *South Carolina Gazette,* 12 Nov. 1753 supp., 11 Apr. 1771, 6 Aug. 1772, 27 Feb. 1775.

39 Cabell, "Women Merchants and Milliners," pp. 50–65, 95–114; *South Carolina Gazette,* 24 June 1756, 30 May 1770.

40 Salmon, *Women and the Law of Property,* pp. 44–48.

41 *South Carolina Gazette and Country Journal,* 11 Sept. 1770, 7 Sept. 1773; *South Carolina Gazette,* 30 May, 17 Sept. 1771, 12 Apr. 1773; Robert M. Weir, *Colonial South Carolina: A History* (Millwood, N.Y., 1983), pp. 232–33; Spruill, *Women's Life and Work in the Southern Colonies,* pp. 290–91; Receipts given to Anne Little Norcliffe Cross, 1768–69, Paul Cross Papers, USC.

42 Cabell, "Women Merchants and Milliners," pp. 147–53.

43 *South Carolina Gazette,* 6 Feb., 23 Oct. 1762, 10 Dec. 1763, 7 Jan. 1764, 11 July 1768, 27 July 1769, 24 Jan. 1774. See also the discussion in James William Hagy, *This Happy Land: The Jews of Colonial and Antebellum Charleston* (Tuscaloosa, Ala., 1993), pp. 224–25, 230.

44 *South Carolina Gazette,* 29 June, 19 Oct. 1765, 17 June 1766, 11 Jan. 1770, 8 Oct. 1772; *South Carolina Gazette and Country Journal,* 15 Dec. 1767, 18 Oct. 1770, 9 Aug., 11 May 1773; Spruill, *Women's Life and Work in the Southern Colonies,* p. 291.

45 On the commercial revolution and its cultural impact, see McCusker and

Menard, *Economy of British America,* esp. chaps. 3 and 13, and the excellent essays in Cary Carson, Ronald Hoffman, and Peter J. Albert, eds., *Of Consuming Interests: The Style of Life in the Eighteenth Century* (Charlottesville, Va., 1994).

⁴⁶ Stone, *Family, Sex and Marriage,* pp. 196–99; Linda K. Kerber, *Women of the Republic: Intellect and Ideology in Revolutionary America* (Chapel Hill, N.C., 1980), chap. 1.

⁴⁷ Ruth H. Bloch, "The Gendered Meanings of Virtue in Revolutionary America," *Signs* 13 (1987): 37–53; G. J. Barker-Benfield, *The Culture of Sensibility: Sex and Society in Eighteenth-Century Britain* (Chicago, 1992), pp. 248–66; John Dwyer, *Virtuous Discourse: Sensibility and Community in Late Eighteenth-Century Scotland* (Edinburgh, 1987), pp. 117–29.

⁴⁸ *South Carolina Gazette,* 4 Mar. 1732; *Virginia Gazette,* 14 Apr. 1738.

⁴⁹ *South Carolina Gazette,* 4 Mar. 1732. On literacy rates, see Kenneth A. Lockridge, *Literacy in Colonial New England: An Inquiry into the Social Context of Literacy in the Early Modern West* (New York, 1974), esp. pp. 77, 92, 97; Mary Beth Norton, "Communication," *WMQ,* 3d ser., 48 (1991): 639–45; Kerber, *Women of the Republic,* pp. 164–65, 191–93.

⁵⁰ Richard L. Bushman, "High-Style and Vernacular Cultures," in Jack P. Greene and J. R. Pole, eds., *Colonial British America: Essays in the New History of the Early Modern Era* (Baltimore, 1984), pp. 345–83, and Bushman, *The Refinement of America: Persons, Houses, Cities* (New York, 1992), chaps. 2–3; Rhys Isaac, *The Transformation of Virginia, 1740–1790* (Chapel Hill, N.C., 1982), esp. pp. 34–42, 74–79, 131–35; Kulikoff, *Tobacco and Slaves,* pp. 263–80. See also the more general discussion in Gordon S. Wood, *The Radicalism of the American Revolution* (New York, 1992), pp. 24–77.

⁵¹ Brown, *Good Wives, Nasty Wenches, and Anxious Patriarchs,* pp. 55–60, 108–28; Winthrop D. Jordan, *White over Black: American Attitudes toward the Negro, 1550–1812* (Chapel Hill, N.C., 1968), pp. 33–40, 146–51; Deborah Gray White, *Ar'n't I a Woman?: Female Slaves in the Plantation South* (New York, 1985), pp. 29–33; Michael Zuckerman, "Identity in British America: Unease in Eden," in Nicholas Canny and Anthony Pagden, eds., *Colonial Identity in the Atlantic World, 1500–1800* (Princeton, N.J., 1987), pp. 146–50.

⁵² Quoted in Jordan, *White over Black,* pp. 146–47. The image of the sexless mammy was a product of nineteenth-century attempts to defend slavery by humanizing that increasingly controversial institution (White, *Ar'n't I a Woman?,* p. 29).

⁵³ Joel Williamson, *New People: Miscegenation and Mulattoes in the United States* (New York, 1980), pp. 5–20; Clinton, *Plantation Mistress,* pp. 202–12; Bertram Wyatt-Brown, *Southern Honor: Ethics and Behavior in the Old South* (New York, 1982), pp. 294–98, 307–11.

⁵⁴ Stone, *Family, Sex and Marriage,* esp. pp. 282–87, 325–36; Daniel Blake Smith, *Inside the Great House: Planter Family Life in Eighteenth-Century Chesapeake Society* (Ithaca, N.Y., 1980), pp. 135–61; Dwyer, *Virtuous Discourse,* pp. 104–5, 109–10.

⁵⁵ [William Kenrick], *The Whole Duty of Woman, By a Lady, Written at the Desire of a Noble Lord* (London, 1753), pp. 70–76; John Gregory, *A Father's Legacy to His Daughters* (1765; Philadelphia, 1775), pp. 6–7.

⁵⁶ *Virginia Gazette,* 29 Apr. 1737.

⁵⁷ Private prayer of Eliza Lucas Pinckney, [ca. 1750], Harriott Horry Ravenel Family Papers, SCHS.

⁵⁸ John Moultrie to Sarah Moultrie, [ca. 1776], John Moultrie Papers, SCHS.

⁵⁹ Ibid.; *South Carolina Gazette,* 17 May 1773; Gregory, *Father's Legacy to His Daughters,* pp. 104–6.

⁶⁰ James Fordyce, *Sermons to Young Women, in Two Volumes,* 6th ed. (London, 1766), pp. 187–88; Gregory, *Father's Legacy to His Daughters,* pp. 9–10, 22–23.

⁶¹ Fordyce, *Sermons to Young Women,* pp. 187–88, 215–23, 228; Gregory, *Father's Legacy to His Daughters,* pp. 13–15.

⁶² George Whitefield, *Journals of George Whitefield* (Grand Rapids, Mich., n.d.), pp. 251–52, 288, 293; Mabel L. Webber, ed., "Extracts from the Journal of Mrs. Ann Manigault, 1754–1781," *SCHM* 20 (1919): 59, 208; 21 (1920): 16. On elite opposition to the evangelical revivals, see Isaac, *Transformation of Virginia,* esp. pp. 163–73; Rachel N. Klein, *Unification of a Slave State: The Rise of the Planter Class in the South Carolina Backcountry, 1760–1808* (Chapel Hill, N.C., 1990), pp. 42–45.

⁶³ Farish, ed., *Journal and Letters of Philip Vickers Fithian,* pp. 61, 83.

⁶⁴ Kevin J. Hayes, *A Colonial Woman's Bookshelf* (Knoxville, Tenn., 1996), pp. 1–3, 39–45.

⁶⁵ Eliza Lucas to [Mary Bartlett], [Mar. 1742], and Eliza Lucas to George Lucas, [1742], both in Pinckney, ed., *Letterbook of Eliza Lucas Pinckney;* Prayers of Eliza Lucas Pinckney, 1742, [ca. 1750], Harriott Horry Ravenel Family Papers, SCHS; David Ramsay, *Memoirs of the Life of Martha Laurens Ramsay* (Philadelphia, 1811), pp. 75–137. On the extreme emotional restraint of colonial elites, see Jan Lewis, *The Pursuit of Happiness: Family and Values in Jefferson's Virginia* (Cambridge, 1983), pp. 22–37.

⁶⁶ Philip Dormer Stanhope, Earl of Chesterfield, *Letters written by the Late Right Honourable Philip Dormer Stanhope, Earl of Chesterfield, to his Son, Philip Stanhope, Esq.,* 2 vols. (Dublin, 1774), pp. 541–42; Charles Moore, ed., *George Washington's Rules of Civility and Decent Behaviour in Company and Conversation* (Boston, 1926), p. 21.

⁶⁷ Gilbert Chinard, ed., *A Huguenot Exile in Virginia, or Voyages of a Frenchman exiled for his Religion with a description of Virginia & Maryland* (New York, 1934), p. 118; Charles Boschi to the Society for the Propagation of the Gospel, 7 Apr. 1746, *SCHM* 50 (1949): 190; Charles Woodmason, *The Carolina Backcountry on the Eve of the Revolution,* ed. Richard J. Hooker (Chapel Hill, N.C., 1953), p. 89; Josiah Quincy, Jr., "Journal of Josiah Quincy, Junior, 1773," ed. Mark Anthony De Wolfe Howe, Massachusetts Historical Society *Proceedings* 49 (1915–16): 444.

⁶⁸ Farish, ed., *Journal and Letters of Philip Vickers Fithian,* pp. 29, 100, 137, 167; Isaac, *Transformation of Virginia,* pp. 58–65, 326–28; Dell Upton, *Holy Things and Pro-*

fane: Anglican Parish Churches in Colonial Virginia (Cambridge, Mass., 1986), pp. 158–64, 169–83, 205, 219–26.

2. Gender, Community, and Hierarchy

[1] Jane Ludwell Parke to Daniel Parke II, 12 July 1705, Custis Family Papers, VHS; Helen Hill Miller, *Colonel Parke of Virginia: "The Greatest Hector in Town"* (Chapel Hill, N.C., 1989), chaps. 13–14.

[2] Jane Ludwell Parke to Daniel Parke II, 12 July 1705, Custis Family Papers, VHS.

[3] See, for instance, Louis B. Wright and Marion Tinling, eds., *The Secret Diary of William Byrd of Westover, 1709–1712* (Richmond, Va., 1941), p. 74; William Byrd II, *Histories of the Dividing Line betwixt Virginia and North Carolina*, ed. William K. Boyd (Raleigh, N.C., 1929), esp. pp. 53, 91; Jack P. Greene, ed., *The Diary of Landon Carter of Sabine Hall*, 2 vols. (Charlottesville, Va., 1965), 1:346, 533.

[4] On hospitality as an extension of patriarchy and as a form of social competition, see Michael Zuckerman, "William Byrd's Family," *Perspectives in American History* 21 (1979): 299–310; Daniel Blake Smith, *Inside the Great House: Planter Family Life in Eighteenth-Century Chesapeake Society* (Ithaca, N.Y., 1980), pp. 194–230; Rhys Isaac, *The Transformation of Virginia, 1740–1790* (Chapel Hill, N.C., 1982), pp. 70–88, 121–34; Jan Lewis, *The Pursuit of Happiness: Family and Values in Jefferson's Virginia* (Cambridge, 1983), pp. 21–23; Kathleen M. Brown, *Good Wives, Nasty Wenches, and Anxious Patriarchs: Gender, Race, and Power in Colonial Virginia* (Chapel Hill, N.C., 1996), pp. 267–72.

[5] On the ambiguous public status of widows, see Mary Beth Norton, *Founding Mothers and Fathers: Gendered Power and the Forming of American Society* (New York, 1996), pp. 139–49, 164–65.

[6] Byrd, *Histories of the Dividing Line*, p. 33.

[7] Emelia Hunter to Elizabeth Galloway Sprigg, 2 July 1755, Mercer Family Papers, VHS; François Jean, Marquis de Chastellux, *Travels in North America in the Years 1780, 1781, and 1782*, ed. Howard C. Rice, Jr., 2 vols. (Chapel Hill, N.C., 1963), 2:383. For the concept of the "deputy husband," see Laurel Thatcher Ulrich, *Good Wives: Image and Reality in the Lives of Women in Northern New England, 1650–1750* (New York, 1980), chap. 2.

[8] Byrd, *Histories of the Dividing Line*, pp. 313, 315; Elizabeth Feilde to Maria Carter Armistead, 13 June 1776, Armistead-Cocke Papers, CWM.

[9] *South Carolina Gazzette*, 4 Mar. 1732; E[liza] S[mith], *The Compleat Housewife: or, Accompish'd Gentlewoman's Companion*, 4th ed. (London, 1730), pp. 9–10; James Fordyce, *Sermons to Young Women, in Two Volumes*, 6th ed. (London, 1766), pp. 209–12; John Gregory, *A Father's Legacy to His Daughters* (1765; Philadelphia, 1775), pp. 20–21.

[10] Eliza Lucas to [Mary Bartlett], [1742], in Elise Pinckney, ed., *The Letterbook of Eliza Lucas Pinckney, 1739–1762* (Chapel Hill, N.C., 1972), p. 38; Ralph E. Fall, ed.,

230   *The Diary of Robert Rose: A View of Virginia by a Scottish Colonial Parson, 1746–1751*
(Verona, Va., 1977), pp. 28, 49, 53–54, 55, 60, 63, 76, 86, 90, 93, 96; George Whitefield, *Journals of George Whitefield* (Grand Rapids, Mich., n.d.), pp. 288, 293; James
Gordon, "Journal of Colonel James Gordon," *WMQ*, 1st ser., 11 (1902–3):101, 196,
227.

[11] On southern colonial court day, election, and militia rituals, see Charles S.
Sydnor, *Gentlemen Freeholders* (Chapel Hill, N.C., 1952), pp. 64, 84; Isaac, *Transformation of Virginia*, pp. 88–94, 104–10, 121–31; A. G. Roeber, "Authority, Law, and
Custom: The Rituals of Court Day in Tidewater Virginia, 1720 to 1750," *WMQ*, 3d
ser., 37 (1980): 34, 37, 47–48; John W. Shy, "A New Look at the Colonial Militia,"
WMQ, 3d ser., 20 (1963): 177–82; William L. Shea, *The Virginia Militia in the Seventeenth Century* (Baton Rouge, La., 1983), pp. 74–76, 138–39; Edmund S. Morgan, *Inventing the People: The Rise of Popular Sovereignty in England and America* (New York,
1988), pp. 170–73. Although Morgan suggests (pp. 190–95) that women played active roles in Anglo-American elections, he cites no evidence from prerevolutionary
southern communities.

[12] Gordon, "Journal of James Gordon," pp. 218–19.

[13] Jack P. Greene, "Search for Identity: An Interpretation of the Meaning of Se-
lected Patterns of Social Response in Eighteenth-Century America," *Journal of Social
History* 3 (1970): 205–17; T. H. Breen, *Tobacco Culture: The Mentality of the Great Tidewater Planters on the Eve of Revolution* (Princeton, N.J., 1985), esp. pp. 91–95, 186–210;
Isaac, *Transformation of Virginia*, pp. 163–73; Donald G. Mathews, *Religion in the Old
South* (Chicago, 1977), chap. 1; Rachel N. Klein, *Unification of a Slave State: The Rise of
the Planter Class in the South Carolina Backcountry, 1760–1808* (Chapel Hill, N.C.,
1990), chap. 2; A. Roger Ekirch, *"Poor Carolina": Politics and Society in Colonial North
Carolina, 1729–1776* (Chapel Hill, N.C., 1981), chap. 6. On the rise of gentility, see
generally, Richard L. Bushman, "American High-Style and Vernacular Cultures," in
Jack P. Greene and J. R. Pole, eds., *Colonial British America: Essays in the New History
of the Early Modern Era* (Baltimore, 1984), pp. 345–83, and Bushman, *The Refinement
of America: Persons, Houses, Cities* (New York, 1992), chaps. 1–5.

[14] Lawrence E. Klein, *Shaftesbury and the Culture of Politeness: Moral Discourse and
Cultural Politics in Early Eighteenth-Century England* (Cambridge, 1994), pp. 3–14;
Bushman, *Refinement of America*, chaps. 2–3; Cary Carson, "The Consumer Revolution in Colonial British America: Why Demand?" in Cary Carson, Ronald Hoffman,
and Peter J. Albert, eds., *Of Consuming Interests: The Style of Life in the Eighteenth Century* (Charlottesville, Va., 1994), pp. 521–22.

[15] John Dwyer, *Virtuous Discourse: Sensibility and Community in Late Eighteenth-
Century Scotland* (Edinburgh, 1987), pp. 117–19, 124–29; Rosemarie Zagarri,
"Morals, Manners, and the Republican Mother," *American Quarterly* 44 (1992):
193–203.

[16] Fordyce, *Sermons to Young Women*, pp. 11–27; Gregory, *Father's Legacy to His
Daughters*, pp. 6–10, 125–26.

[17] *Virginia Gazette,* 14 Apr. 1738; *Virginia Gazette* (Purdie and Dixon), 4 Mar. 1773.

[18] *Virginia Gazette,* 26 Nov. 1736, 7 Oct. 1737. For a similar elite-sponsored fair in Williamsburg, see ibid., 7 Dec. 1739. On the significance of class and gender on the gambling culture of colonial southerners, see T. H. Breen, "Horses and Gentlemen: The Cultural Significance of Gambling among the Gentry of Virginia," *WMQ,* 3d ser., 34 (1977): 239–57, and Linda L. Sturtz, "The Ladies and the Lottery," *VMHB* 104 (1996): 165–86.

[19] Nancy L. Struna, "The Formalizing of Sport and the Formation of an Elite: The Chesapeake Gentry, 1650–1720s," *Journal of Sport History* 13 (1986): 232, and Struna, "Sport and the Awareness of Leisure," in Carson, Hoffman, and Albert, eds., *Of Consuming Interests,* pp. 423–26; Henry Laurens to John Moultrie, 28 Jan. 1768, in George C. Rogers, Jr., et al., eds., *The Papers of Henry Laurens,* 14 vols. to date (Columbia, S.C., 1968–), 5:572; George C. Rogers, Jr., *Charleston in the Age of the Pinckneys* (Norman, Okla., 1969), pp. 113–14; Hunter Dickinson, Farish, ed., *Journal and Letters of Philip Vickers Fithian, 1773–1774: A Plantation Tutor of the Old Dominion* (Williamsburg, Va., 1943), pp. 24–25; Edward Miles Riley, ed., *The Journal of John Harrower: An Indentured Servant in the Colony of Virginia, 1773–1776* (Williamsburg, Va., 1963), pp. 40, 65; *Virginia Gazette* (Purdie and Dixon), 17 Mar. 1768, 22 Feb. 1770, 15 Aug. 1771, 11 Aug. 1774; *South Carolina Gazette and Country Journal,* 5 Mar. 1771; Josiah Quincy, Jr., "Journal of Josiah Quincy, Junior, 1773," ed. Mark Anthony De Wolfe Howe, Massachusetts Historical Society *Proceedings* 49 (1915–16): 466–67; B. W. C. Connor, "Cockfighting: An Early Entertainment in North Carolina," *NCHR* 42 (1965): 309.

[20] Donald Jackson et al., eds., *The Diaries of George Washington,* 6 vols. (Charlottesville, Va., 1976–79), 2:113–14; Nicholas Cresswell, *The Journal of Nicholas Cresswell, 1774–1777* (Port Washington, N.Y., 1968), p. 28; *Virginia Gazette* (Purdie and Dixon), 15 Oct. 1772.

[21] Jane Carson, *Colonial Virginians at Play* (1965; Williamsburg, 1989), pp. 87–88; William J. Hinke, ed. and trans., "Report of the Journey of Francis Louis Michel from Berne, Switzerland, to Virginia, October 2, 1701–December 1, 1702," *VMHB* 24 (1916): 125–29, 133–34; *South Carolina Gazette,* 2 Mar. 1734, 6 Mar. 1736.

[22] Hugh Jones, *Present State of Virginia* (London, 1724), p. 31; *South Carolina Gazette,* 7 Nov. 1740; Eliza Lucas Pinckney to George Lucas, 11 Nov. 1742, in Pinckney, ed., *Letterbook of Eliza Lucas Pinckney,* p. 57; *North Carolina Magazine; or Universal Intelligencer,* 28 Dec. 1764; John Whiting to Ezra Stiles, 8 Apr. 1767, Frederick Nash Papers, NCDAH; *Virginia Gazette* (Purdie and Dixon), 10 Jan. 1771. See also Cynthia A. Kierner, "Genteel Balls and Republican Parades: Gender and Early Southern Civic Rituals, 1677–1826," *VMHB* 104 (1996): 186–91.

[23] Jones, *Present State of Virginia,* p. 31; *Virginia Gazette,* 5 Nov. 1736; *South Carolina Gazette,* 7 Nov. 1740.

[24] Dwyer, *Virtuous Discourse,* pp. 53–54.

²⁵ Hugh Morrison, *Early American Architecture: From the First Colonial Settlements to the National Period* (New York, 1952), chaps. 11–12, and pp. 401–5, 415–25; Thomas Tileston Waterman, *The Mansions of Virginia, 1706–1776* (Chapel Hill, N.C., 1946); Isaac, *Transformation of Virginia*, pp. 36–42; Peter A. Coclanis, *The Shadow of a Dream: Economic Life and Death in the South Carolina Low Country, 1670–1920* (New York, 1989), pp. 5–11; Robert M. Weir, *Colonial South Carolina: A History* (Millwood, N.Y., 1983), pp. 244–45; Thomas J. Tobias, ed., "Charlestown in 1764," *SCHM* 67 (1966): 69; Quincy, "Journal of Josiah Quincy," pp. 444–45. Although North Carolina houses were less elaborate, they nonetheless reflected status differences as early as the 1730s. See John Brickell, *The Natural History of North Carolina*, as excerpted in Hugh Talmadge Lefler, ed., *North Carolina History: Told by Participants* (Chapel Hill, N.C., 1934), p. 63, and Catherine Bishir, *North Carolina Architecture* (Chapel Hill, N.C., 1990), chap. 1.

²⁶ Carson, "Consumer Revolution," pp. 591–604; Lois Green Carr and Lorena S. Walsh, "The Standard of Living in the Colonial Chesapeake," *WMQ*, 3d ser., 45 (1988): 138–40; Inventory of the Estate of Daniel Parke Custis, [1757], Custis Family Papers, VHS; "Appraisement of the Estate of Philip Ludwell Esqr Dec[ease]d," *VMHB* 21 (1913): 395–416.

²⁷ Eleanor Kelley Cabell, "Women Merchants and Milliners in Eighteenth-Century Williamsburg," Colonial Williamsburg Research Report, 1988; *Virginia Gazette* (Purdie), 13 Apr. 1766; *Virginia Gazette* (Rind), 19 Feb. 1767; *Virginia Gazette* (Purdie and Dixon), 24 Jan., 12 Sept. 1771, 14 May, 29 Oct., 5 Nov. 1772 supp.; *North Carolina Gazette*, 9 Jan. 1778; Johanna Miller Lewis, *Artisans in the North Carolina Backcountry* (Lexington, Ky., 1995), pp. 105–6.

In the 1730s, Elizabeth Cooper, Mrs. McClellan, Ann Wilson, Mrs. Jones, and Katherine Wells advertised as milliners or mantua makers in the *South Carolina Gazette*. The following women did so in the 1770s: Johanna Black, Elizabeth Blaikie, Katherine Bower, Hannah Coleman, Elizabeth Harvey, Sarah Henry, Mary King, Maria Martin, Anne Matthewes, Sarah Minors, Ann Nicholls, Elizabeth Prosser, Justina St. Leger, Frances Swallow, Jane Thomson, Mary Turpin, and Anne Waller.

²⁸ On advertisers' notices, see Richard L. Bushman, "Shopping and Advertising in Colonial America," in Carson, Hoffman, and Albert, eds., *Of Consuming Interests*, pp. 247–48; Carr and Walsh, "Standard of Living," pp. 139; *South Carolina Gazette*, 15 Dec. 1737, 12 Jan. 1759, 16 Feb. 1765, 28 Jan. 1773; *South Carolina Gazette and Country Journal*, 17 June 1766; *Virginia Gazette* (Purdie and Dixon), 13 Apr., 10 Oct. 1766, 10 Oct. 1771; *Virginia Gazette* (Rind), 20 Sept. 1770.

²⁹ Eliza Lucas Pinckney to [Mrs. King], 19 July 1760," in Pinckney, ed., *Letterbook of Eliza Lucas Pinckney*, p. 155; Robert Pringle to Jane Allen Pringle, 30 Aug. 1740, in Mary Pringle Fenhagen, ed., "Letters and Will of Robert Pringle (1702–1776)," *SCHM* 50 (1949): 93; Emelia Hunter to Elizabeth Galloway Sprigg, [ca. 1752], 9 Oct. 1752, Mercer Family Papers, VHS; Martha Dandridge Custis

Washington to Mrs. Shelbury, Aug. 1764, in Joseph E. Fields, comp., *"Worthy Partner": The Papers of Martha Washington* (Westport, Conn., 1994), p. 148.

[30] On men and fashion, see Karin Calvert, "The Function of Fashion in Eighteenth-Century America," in Carson, Hoffman, and Albert, eds., *Of Consuming Interests*, pp. 255–69.

[31] Byrd, *Histories of the Dividing Line*, pp. 37, 313, 315; John Whiting to Ezra Stiles, 28 June 1759, Frederick Nash Papers, NCDAH; Farish, ed., *Journal and Letters of Philip Vickers Fithian*, pp. 45, 63, 75.

[32] Robert Beverley, *The History and Present State of Virginia*, ed. Louis B. Wright (Chapel Hill, N.C., 1947), p. 291.

[33] Invoice to Mr [Robert] Cary & Company, 1758, Custis Family Papers, VHS; Farish, ed., *Journal and Letters of Philip Vickers Fithian*, p. 189. For evidence of men's interest in acquiring such fashionable consumer goods, see Breen, *Tobacco Culture*, esp. pp. 35–37, 105–7.

[34] S[mith], *Compleat Housewife*, pp. 5, 7–8; Carson, "Consumer Revolution," p. 591; Rodris Roth, "Tea-Drinking in Eighteenth-Century America," in Robert Blair St. George, ed., *Material Life in America, 1600–1860* (Boston, 1988), pp. 445–46.

[35] Mabel L. Webber, ed., "Extracts from the Journal of Mrs. Ann Manigault, 1754–1781," *SCHM* 21 (1920): 12; Henry Laurens to Lachlin McIntosh, 9 Feb. 1768, in Rogers et al., eds., *Papers of Henry Laurens*, 5:589; Jean Blair to Mary Braxton, 14 Oct. 1769, Blair, Banister, Braxton, Horner, and Whiting Papers, CWM.

[36] Nicholas Ridgely to Charles Ridgely, 12 Jan. 1754, quoted in John C. Gardner, "Contradances and Cotillions: Dancing in Eighteenth-Century Delaware," *Delaware History* 22 (1986): 40; Philip Dormer Stanhope, Earl of Chesterfield, *Letters written by the Late Right Honourable Philip Dormer Stanhope, Earl of Chesterfield, to his Son, Philip Stanhope, Esq.*, 2 vols. (Dublin, 1774), 2:81; Fordyce, *Sermons to Young Women*, p. 108; Gregory, *Father's Legacy to His Daughters*, pp. 47–48, 57–58. See also the discussions in Isaac, *Transformation of Virginia*, pp. 80–87; Dell Upton, *Holy Things and Profane: Anglican Parish Churches in Colonial Virginia* (Cambridge, Mass., 1986), p. 219; and Calvert, "Function of Fashion," pp. 272–73. American publishers printed eighteen versions of Chesterfield's letters before 1800 (Bushman, *Refinement of America*, pp. 36–37).

[37] Cresswell, *Journal of Nicholas Cresswell*, pp. 52–53; *Virginia Gazette*, 25 Feb., 22 Apr. 1737, 24 Mar. 1738; *Virginia Gazette* (Dixon and Hunter), 2 Sept. 1775; *South Carolina Gazette*, 18 Nov. 1751.

The four dancing mistresses were Barbara Needham Tempest de Graffenriedt, Mary Stagg, Sarah Hallam, and Sarah Campbell. For information on all but Campbell, see Julia Cherry Spruill, *Women's Life and Work in the Southern Colonies* (Chapel Hill, N.C., 1938), pp. 95, 204, 259–60, 262; Louis B. Wright, *The Cultural Life of the American Colonies, 1607–1763* (New York, 1957), p. 180; Maude A. Woodfin and Marion Tinling, eds., *Another Secret Diary of William Byrd of Westover, 1739–1741, with Letters and Literary Exercises, 1696–1726* (Richmond, Va., 1942), p. 86n; William Byrd II to Sir John Randolph, 21 Jan. 1736, William Byrd Papers, VHS.

[38] Farish, ed., *Journal and Letters of Philip Vickers Fithian,* pp. 32–34, 111, 123–25; Jackson et al., eds., *Diaries of George Washington,* 2:235–36, 254, 269; Greene, ed., *Diary of Landon Carter,* 2:807; William Dana Hoyt, Jr., ed., "Self-Portrait: Eliza Custis, 1809," *VMHB* 53 (1945): 98. On women's visiting, see also Fall, ed., *Diary of Robert Rose,* passim, and Lorena S. Walsh, "Community Networks in the Early Chesapeake," in Lois Green Carr, Philip D. Morgan, and Jean B. Russo, eds., *Colonial Chesapeake Society* (Chapel Hill, N.C., 1988), pp. 225–26.

[39] Farish, ed., *Journal and Letters of Philip Vickers Fithian,* pp. 33–35, 42, 56–58, 151, 154, 171; Gay Montague Moore, *Seaport in Virginia: George Washington's Alexandria* (Richmond, Va., 1949), p. 29; *Virginia Gazette,* 7 Mar., 11 Apr. 1751.

[40] *South Carolina Gazette,* 29 Nov. 1735, 10 Apr. 1736, 15 Jan. 1737; *Virginia Gazette,* 27 Feb., 5 Mar. 1752; Quincy, "Journal of Josiah Quincy," pp. 441–42; Andrew Burnaby, *Travels through the Middle Settlements in North America, in the Years 1759 and 1760; with Observations on the State of the Colonies,* 3d ed. (London, 1798), p. 6; Lord Adam Gordon, "Journal of an Officer who Travelled in America and the West Indies in 1764 and 1765," in Newton D. Mereness, ed., *Travels in the American Colonies* (New York, 1916), p. 397; Henry Laurens to John Moultrie, 28 Jan. 1768, in Rogers et al., eds., *Papers of Henry Laurens,* 5:572.

Other genteel entertainments, such as the musical evenings sponsored by Charleston's St. Cecelia Society, also occurred mainly during these periods when elites from the surrounding countryside converged in the colonial capitals. See South Carolina Gazette, 21 Sept. 1765, 22 June 1767; Weir, Colonial South Carolina, pp. 238–39.

[41] Felicity Heal, *Hospitality in Early Modern England* (Oxford, 1990), p. 152.

[42] See, for instance, "On Fashionable Female Amusements," *Lady's Magazine* 2 (1793): 125; "An oration delivered at Petersburgh, Virginia . . . ," *American Museum* 2 (1787): 420–21; "Address to the Ladies of America," *American Museum* 2 (1787): 481.

[43] Carson, "Consumer Revolution," p. 591; Calvert, "Function of Fashion," p. 272. For evidence from a somewhat later era of how dancing promoted conversation and thus alleviated shyness among some young people, see Louis B. Wright and Marion Tinling, eds., *Quebec to Carolina in 1785–1786: Being the Travel Diary and Observations of Robert Hunter, Jr., a Young Merchant of London* (San Marino, Calif., 1943), p. 206.

On the centrality of conversation in the English culture of "politeness," see Klein, *Shaftesbury and the Culture of Politeness,* pp. 4–5, 97–99, though Klein implies that women were not involved in these exchanges.

[44] Gregory, *Father's Legacy to His Daughters,* pp. 6–7, 28–31.

[45] Mary Beth Norton, *Liberty's Daughters: The Revolutionary Experience of American Women, 1750–1800* (Boston, 1980), pp. 112–13.

[46] Woodfin and Tinling, eds., *Another Secret Diary of William Byrd of Westover,* p.

149; [Lucinda Lee Orr], *Journal of a Young Lady of Virginia, 1782,* ed. Emily V. Mason (Baltimore, 1871); Jane Pratt Taylor to William Byrd II, 8 June 1741, in Marion Tinling, ed., *The Correspondence of the Three William Byrds of Westover, 1684–1776,* 2 vols. (Charlottesville, Va., 1977), 2:589. Taylor lived in London, but whist was also popular in the southern colonies. See Carson, *Colonial Virginians at Play,* pp. 22–27.

⁴⁷ Durand de Dauphiné, *A Huguenot Exile in Virginia, or Voyages of a Frenchman exiled for his Religion with a description of Virginia & Maryland,* ed. Gilbert Chinard (New York, 1934), pp. 138–39; Wright and Tinling, eds., *Quebec to Carolina,* pp. 206–9.

⁴⁸ G. J. Barker-Benfield, *The Culture of Sensibility: Sex and Society in Eighteenth-Century Britain* (Chicago, 1992), pp. 191–205. On the evangelical critique of genteel culture generally, see Isaac, *Transformation of Virginia,* esp. pp. 163–73; Mathews, *Religion in the Old South,* chap. 1.

⁴⁹ [William Kenrick], *The Whole Duty of Women, by a Lady, Written at the Desire of a Noble Lord* (London, 1753), pp. 5–6; *South Carolina Gazette,* 27 June 1748, 14 May 1753, 3 May 1754.

See also the discussion in Dwyer, *Virtuous Discourse,* pp. 96, 104–13, which shows that Scottish admirers of women's sensibility increasingly viewed the domestic sphere as the seat of moral virtue and gradually redefined sociability to consist only of "moral cultivation within the protected haven of the affectionate family." This formulation, and women's place in it, resembles the ideal of the republican family in postrevolutionary America. See Kerber, *Women of the Republic,* chap. 9, and Jan Lewis, "The Republican Wife: Virtue and Seduction in the Early Republic," *WMQ,* 3d ser., 44 (1987): 689–721.

⁵⁰ A[nne] Blair to [Mary Blair Braxton], 1768, Blair, Banister, Braxton, Horner, Whiting Papers, CWM; Mary Spotswood to [Mary Dandridge Spotswood Campbell], ca. 1768, Spotswood Family Papers, VHS; William Byrd II to John Lord Boyle, 2 Feb. 1727, in "Virginia Council Journals, 1726–1753," *VMHB* 32 (1924): 29–30.

⁵¹ Mary Jones to Frances Bland, 10 May 1769, Tucker-Coleman Papers, CWM; Alice Lee to Richard Potts, 20 Dec. 1774, Potts Family Papers, MHS.

⁵² *South Carolina Gazette,* 3 Aug. 1747.

⁵³ For an overview of this process and its timing in the southern colonies and elsewhere, see John M. Murrin, "Political Development," in Greene and Pole, eds., *Colonial British America,* pp. 408–56.

⁵⁴ William Fitzhugh to Nicholas Hayward, 30 Jan. 1687, in Richard Beale Davis, ed., *William Fitzhugh and His Chesapeake World, 1676–1701: The Fitzhugh Letters and Other Documents* (Chapel Hill, N.C., 1963), pp. 203–4.

⁵⁵ *South Carolina Gazette,* 27 Apr. 1738, 19 Dec. 1740, 29 Aug. 1743, 3 Nov. 1746, 8 Feb. 1748, 19 Feb. 1754, 12 Jan. 1760, 29 June 1769, 13 Feb. 1775; Weir, *Colonial South Carolina,* p. 240.

⁵⁶ Jones, *Present State of Virginia,* pp. 70, 94; Louis B. Wright, *The First Gentlemen of Virginia: Intellectual Qualities of the Early Colonial Ruling Class* (San Marino, Calif.,

1940), p. 101; *Virginia Gazette* (Rind), 1 Mar. 1770; *Virginia Gazette* (Purdie and Dixon), 11 Apr. 1771, 12 May 1774.

North Carolina's earliest schools opened in the towns of New Bern, Wilmington, and Charlotte in the final decade of the colonial era. See Ekirch, *"Poor Carolina,"* pp. 42–43; Alonzo Thomas Dill, *Governor Tryon and His Palace* (Chapel Hill, N.C., 1955), pp. 67–68, 165–66, 213–16; R. D. W. Connor, "Genesis of Higher Education in North Carolina," *NCHR* 28 (1951): 1–3.

[57] Between 1720 and 1776, some four hundred Virginians enrolled in the College of William and Mary. During this period, college attendance among Virginians was as follows: Oxford/Cambridge, 26; College of New Jersey, 23; College of Philadelphia, 6; Harvard College, 1; King's College (New York), 1. See *The History of the College of William and Mary: From Its Foundation, 1660, to 1874* (Richmond, Va., 1874), pp. 83–95; Willard Connely, "Colonial Americans in Oxford and Cambridge," *American Oxonian* 30 (1942): 75–77; James McLachlin et al., *Princetonians: A Biographical Dictionary,* 5 vols. (Princeton, N. J., 1976–91), 1:xx, 2:xxiii, 3:43, 62, 68, 99, 102; John Langdon Sibley and Clifford K. Shipton, *Sibley's Harvard Graduates: Biographical Sketches of Those Who Attended Harvard College* (Boston, 1873–), 13:245; "List of Southern Graduates of the University of Pennsylvania from 1757–1783," *WMQ,* 1st ser., 6 (1897): 217–18; "Virginia Graduates at Columbia College, New York, Previous to 1783," *WMQ,* 1st ser., 16 (1897): 219.

[58] Twenty-one South Carolinians attended English universities; four studied at the College of New Jersey and three went to Harvard, though the latter were all sons of New Englanders who had migrated southward (Connely, "Colonial Americans in Oxford and Cambridge," 75–77; Sibley and Shipton, *Sibley's Harvard Graduates,* 8:69, 265, 9:319, and McLachlin et al., *Princetonians,* 1:xx, 2:xxiii).

[59] Twenty North Carolinians attended the College of New Jersey, seven went to Harvard, and one each attended Yale, William and Mary, and the College of Philadelphia (*History of the College of William and Mary,* pp. 83–88; Sibley and Shipton, *Sibley's Harvard Graduates,* 12:3, 13:648, 14:25, 191, 307, 16:484, 17:59; Franklin Bowditch Dexter, *Biographical Sketches of the Graduates of Yale College, with Annals of the College History,* 6 vols. [New York, 1885–1912], 2:783; McLachlin et al., *Princetonians,* 1:xx, 2:xxiii, 3:3, 25, 128).

[60] J. G. de Roulhac Hamilton, "Southern Members of the Inns of Court," *NCHR* 10 (1933): 279–80. On the declining educational value of membership in the Inns of Court, see Paul Hamlin, *Legal Education in Colonial New York* (New York, 1939), p. 17.

[61] Richard Ambler to Edward and John Ambler, 1 Aug. 1748, Elizabeth Bourbon Ambler Papers, UVa.

[62] "Letter of Colonel Nathaniel Burwell," *WMQ,* 1st ser., 7 (1898): 43–44; Eliza Lucas Pinckney to Charles Pinckney, 15 Apr. 1761, in Pinckney, ed., *Letterbook of Eliza Lucas Pinckney,* pp. 167–68; David Ramsay, *History of South Carolina, from Its First Settlement in 1670 to the Year 1808,* 2 vols. (1808; Newberry, S.C., 1858), 2:229.

[63] *History of the College of William and Mary,* pp. 83–95; Hinke, ed. and trans., "Re-

port of the Journey of Francis Louis Michel," p. 26; Kenneth A. Lockridge, *The Diary, and Life, of William Byrd II of Virginia, 1674–1746* (New York, 1987), pp. 18–26, 103; Peter Manigault to Ann Ashby Manigault, 28 Aug. 1750, Manigault Family Papers, SCHS.

[64] Quoted in Wright, *First Gentlemen of Virginia*, p. 109; *Virginia Gazette* (Rind), 1 Mar. 1770.

[65] Eliza Lucas Pinckney to Charles Pinckney, 7 Feb. 1761, in Pinckney, ed., *Letterbook of Eliza Lucas Pinckney*, p. 159; Washington quoted in Farish, ed., *Journal and Letters of Philip Vickers Fithian*, p. xvii; Richard Ambler to Edward and John Ambler, 20 May 1749, and Richard Ambler to Edward Ambler, 31 Oct. 1751, both in Elizabeth Bourbon Ambler Papers, UVa.

[66] Chesterfield, *Letters*, 2:124, 133, 181, 221–22, 236.

[67] Minutes of the Meeting of the Governors and Visitors of the College of Wm. & Mary, 26 Mar. 1716, Lee Family Papers, VHS; *Virginia Gazette*, 25 Nov. 1737.

[68] Jackson et al., eds., *Diaries of George Washington*, 2:269; Peter Manigault to Ann Ashby Manigault, 1 Nov. 1750, 9 May 1753, Manigault Family Papers, SCHS; Greene, ed., *Diary of Landon Carter*, 2:372–73, 807; Receipts of William Fearson, 31 Mar. 1770, 10 May 1771, 5 May 1773, Carter Family Papers, VHS; Account of Robert Carter with Archibald McCall, 20 June 1775, ibid.; Farish, ed., *Journal and Letters of Philip Vickers Fithian*, pp. xxx, 6.

[69] Farish, ed., *Journal and Letters of Philip Vickers Fithian*, pp. 33–34; *South Carolina Gazette*, 13, 27 Mar. 1762, 1 Dec. 1766, 29 Mar. 1773; Peter Manigault to Ann Ashby Manigault, 1 Nov. 1750, 9 May 1753, Manigault Family Papers, SCHS.

[70] On Thomas Griffith's riding school, see *South Carolina Gazette*, 11 Apr., 22 Aug. 1771, 27 Feb. 1775. On flute and violin lessons for "gentlemen," see *South Carolina Gazette and Country Journal*, 1 Mar. 1768, *Virginia Gazette* (Purdie and Dixon), 16 May 1771. On French lessons, see *Virginia Gazette* (Purdie and Dixon), 25 Feb. 1773; *South Carolina Gazette*, 30 July 1763, 21 Jan., 21 July, 10 Dec. 1773. In the late 1740s Mark Anthony Besseleu of Charleston operated the region's earliest French school for "Gentlemen and Ladies" (*South Carolina Gazette*, 29 Sept. 1746, 27 July, 23 Nov. 1747). While French and music are not, strictly speaking, merely ornamental, scholars treat them as such in discussions of women's education. See, for instance, Norton, *Liberty's Daughters*, p. 256; Suzanne Lebsock, *"A Share of Honour": Virginia Women, 1600–1945* (Richmond, Va., 1987), p. 40.

[71] *South Carolina Gazette and Country Journal*, 17 Apr. 1770 supp.; *South Carolina Gazette*, 27 Sept. 1773; *Virginia Gazette* (Pinkney), 30 Mar. 1775. Fencing later flourished among revolutionary soldiers, partly as a result of the influence of their French allies. See Charles S. Royster, *A Revolutionary People at War: The Continental Army and the American Character, 1775–1783* (Chapel Hill, N.C., 1979), pp. 208–11.

[72] Will of John Baptista Ashe, 1734, quoted in Hugh T. Lefler and William S. Powell, *Colonial North Carolina: A History* (New York, 1973), p. 210.

[73] By beginning her study in 1750 and attributing all improvements in women's

238

education to revolutionary ideology, Mary Beth Norton misses the significant changes that began earlier. See Norton, *Liberty's Daughters,* pp. 98, 120–24, 257–60.

⁷⁴ Kevin J. Hayes, *A Colonial Woman's Bookshelf* (Knoxville, Tenn., 1996), pp. 3–27. On growing attention to the quality of penmanship and letter writing, in particular, see Smith, *Inside the Great House,* pp. 63–65; Bushman, *Refinement of America,* pp. 90–92; Farish, ed., *Journal and Letters of Philip Vickers Fithian,* p. 35; Charles Carter to Maria Carter, 25 Jan. 1764, Armistead-Cocke Papers, CWM; James Iredell to Nelly Blair, 12 Sept. 1780, Charles E. Johnson Collection, NCDAH.

⁷⁵ *South Carolina Gazette,* 24 Mar. 1733; *Virginia Gazette,* 14 Jan. 1737, 10 Jan. 1752.

⁷⁶ A[nne Blair] to [Mary Braxton], 21 Aug. 1769, Blair, Banister, Braxton, Horner, and Whiting Papers, CWM; Riley, ed., *Journal of John Harrower,* pp. 139.

For a more charitable view of Margaret Wake Tryon, see John Ross Delafield, ed., "Reminiscenses [*sic*], Written by Janet Livingston, Widow of General Richard Montgomery . . . ," Dutchess County Historical Society *Yearbook* 15 (1930): 71.

⁷⁷ *South Carolina Gazette,* 24 June 1732; Fordyce, *Sermons to Young Women,* pp. 126–32; Gregory, *Father's Legacy to His Daughters,* pp. 53–54.

⁷⁸ Fordyce, *Sermons to Young Women,* pp. 93–94; Gregory, *Father's Legacy to His Daughters,* p. 31; Chesterfield, *Letters,* 2:43; Eliza Lucas to [Mary Bartlett], [ca. March–April 1742], in Pinckney, ed., *Letterbook of Eliza Lucas Pinckney,* p. 33. On ambivalence toward women's public participation in intellectual life in contemporary England, see Sylvia Harcstark Myers, *The Bluestocking Circle: Women, Friendship, and the Life of the Mind in Eighteenth-Century England* (Oxford, 1990).

⁷⁹ *Virginia Gazette* (Purdie and Dixon), 11 Feb. 1773.

⁸⁰ Henry Laurens to Martha Laurens, 18 Aug. 1771, 18 May 1774, in David Ramsay, *Memoirs of the Life of Martha Laurens Ramsay* (Philadelphia, 1811), pp. 63–64; John Moultrie, Sr., to Sarah Moultrie, 5 Sept. 1770, John Moultrie Papers, SCHS; *South Carolina Gazette,* 27 Aug. 1772.

⁸¹ Elizabeth Elliott to Barnard Elliott, 30 Sept. 1762, Baker-Grimké Papers, SCHS; John Spotswood to Anne and Mary Spotswood, 3 Apr. 1760, Spotswood Family Papers, VHS; Betty Pratt to Keith William Pratt, 10 Aug. 1732, in "Jones Papers," *VMHB* 26 (1918): 288.

⁸² Maria Taylor Byrd to William Byrd III, [ca. Feb. 1760], 15 Aug. 1760, in Tinling, ed., *Correspondence of the Three William Byrds of Westover,* 2:682, 701, 701; A[nne Blair] to [Mary Braxton], 21 Aug. 1769, Blair, Banister, Braxton, Horner, and Whiting Papers, CWM; Elizabeth Wormeley Carter Berkeley to Landon Carter, 1 May 1765, Carter Family Papers, UVa; Charles Carter to Maria Carter, 25 Jan. 1764, Armistead-Cocke Papers, CWM; Evangeline Walker Andrews and Charles McLean Andrews, eds., *Journal of a Lady of Quality: Being the Narrative of a Journey from Scotland to the West Indies, North Carolina and Portugal* (New Haven, Conn., 1921), pp. 154–55.

83 Eliza Lucas Pinckney to [Mr. Keate], Feb. 1762, in Pinckney, ed., *Letterbook of Eliza Lucas Pinckney,* pp. 180–81; Emelia Hunter to Elizabeth Galloway Sprigg, 13 May 1766, Mercer Family Papers, VHS; Ramsay, *Memoirs of the Life of Martha Laurens Ramsay,* pp. 13–14.

84 *South Carolina Gazette,* 6 Aug. 1741, 31 Oct. 1743, 20 Sept. 1760, 5 Sept. 1761, 17 Apr. 1762, 1 Jan., 16 Apr. 1763, 26 Jan. 1769, 17 May 1770, 24 Dec. 1772, 19 July 1773, 28 Feb., 19 Sept. 1774, 13 Feb. 1775.

Only two schools that accepted female pupils — one in Williamsburg, the other in Norfolk — advertised in the *Virginia Gazette.* See *Virginia Gazette,* 17 Nov. 1752; *Virginia Gazette* (Purdie), 21 Mar. 1766; and Spruill, *Women's Life and Work in the Southern Colonies,* pp. 197–201.

85 *South Carolina Gazette,* 15 May 1770.

86 Ibid., 29 June 1767, 28 Feb. 1774.

87 Cynthia Z. Stiverson and Gregory A. Stiverson, "The Colonial Retail Book Trade: Availability and Affordability of Reading Material in Mid-Eighteenth-Century Virginia," in William L. Joyce et al., eds., *Printing and Society in Early America* (Worcester, Mass., 1983), pp. 132–73; Hayes, *Colonial Woman's Bookshelf;* Julia Cherry Spruill, "The Southern Lady's Library, 1700–1776," *South Atlantic Quarterly* 34 (1935): 23–41; Helen R. Watson, "The Books They Left: Some 'Liberies' in Edgecombe County, 1733–1783," *NCHR* 48 (1971): 245–57.

88 Eliza Lucas to [Elizabeth] Pinckney, [1741]; Eliza Lucas to [Mary Bartlett], [ca. March–April 1742]; and Eliza Lucas to Mrs. H, [1742], all in Pinckney, ed., *Letterbook of Eliza Lucas Pinckney;* Maria Carter copybook, 1763, Armistead-Cocke Papers, CWM; Mary Ann Elizabeth Stevens Cogdell commonplace book, ca. 1775, Library Company of Philadelphia; Sarah Fouace Nourse Diary, 1781–83, p. 12, Nourse Family Papers, UVa.

89 Ramsay, *Memoirs of the Life of Martha Laurens Ramsay,* pp. 12–13; Farish, ed., *Journal and Letters of Philip Vickers Fithian,* pp. 61, 71, 122, 221–29.

90 Farish, ed., *Journal and Letters of Philip Vickers Fithian,* pp. 6, 20–22, 26, 28, 90. On music, see also *North Carolina Gazette,* 13 Jan. 1775.

91 Elizabeth Hill Carter Byrd to William Byrd III, 17 May 1758, in Tinling, ed., *Correspondence of the Three William Byrds of Westover,* 2:654; Elizabeth Lichtenstein Johnston, *Recollections of a Georgia Loyalist* (New York, 1901), pp. 43–44; Alice Lee to Richard Potts, 20 Dec. 1774, Potts Family Papers, MHS; William Dana Hoyt, Jr., ed., "Self-Portrait: Eliza Custis, 1809," *VMHB* 53 (1945): 97–98.

3. Revolution

1 Lorenzo Sabine, *Biographical Sketches of Loyalists of the American Revolution,* 2 vols. (1864; Port Washington, N.Y., 1966), 2:325; Carole Watterson Troxler, *The Loyalist Experience in North Carolina* (Raleigh, N.C., 1976), p. 55; Petition of Jane Spurgin, 10 Nov. 1788, GASR, Nov.–Dec. 1788, box 2, NCDAH.

² Petitions of Jane Spurgin, 3 Dec. 1785, November–December 1785, box 1; 10 Nov. 1788, November–December 1788, box 2; 25 Nov. 1791, December 1791–January 1792, box 2, all in GASR, NCDAH.

³ Marvin L. Michael Kay, "The North Carolina Regulation: A Class Conflict," in Alfred F. Young, ed., *The American Revolution: Explorations in the History of American Radicalism* (De Kalb, Ill., 1976), pp. 84–102; James P. Whittenburg, "Planters, Merchants, and Lawyers: Social Change and the Origins of the North Carolina Regulation," *WMQ*, 3d ser., 34 (1977): 215–38; A. Roger Ekirch, *"Poor Carolina": Politics and Society in Colonial North Carolina, 1729–1776* (Chapel Hill, N.C., 1981), chap. 6; Alonzo Thomas Dill, *Governor Tryon and His Palace* (Chapel Hill, N.C., 1955), pp. 110–29; Herman Husband, *An Impartial Relation of the First Rise and Cause of the Recent Differences . . .*, in William S. Powell et al., eds., *The Regulation in North Carolina: A Documentary History, 1759–1776* (Raleigh, N.C., 1971), pp. 223–26, 231–33.

⁴ On the influence of evangelicalism among the Regulators, see Mark Hadden Jones, "Herman Husband: Millenarian, Carolina Regulator, and Whiskey Rebel" (Ph.D. diss., Northern Illinois University, 1983), pp. 160–64; James Penn Whittenburg, "Backcountry Revolutionaries: Social Context and Constitutional Theories of the North Carolina Regulators" (Ph.D. diss., University of Georgia, 1974), pp. 40–49, 274–81; Rachel N. Klein, *Unification of a Slave State: The Rise of the Planter Class in the South Carolina Backcountry, 1760–1808* (Chapel Hill, N.C., 1990), p. 66. On backcountry evangelicalism, see also Richard R. Beeman, "The Political Response to Social Conflict in the Southern Backcountry: A Comparative View of Virginia and the Carolinas during the Revolution," in Ronald Hoffman et al., eds., *An Uncivil War: The Southern Backcountry during the American Revolution* (Charlottesville, Va., 1985), pp. 224–26.

⁵ Rhys Isaac, *The Transformation of Virginia, 1740–1790* (Chapel Hill, N.C., 1982), esp. pp. 163–73; Mechal Sobel, *The World They Made Together: Black and White Values in Eighteenth-Century Virginia* (Princeton, N.J., 1987), chap. 14; Sylvia R. Frey, " 'The Year of Jubilee Is Come': Black Christianity in the Plantation South in Post-Revolutionary America," in Ronald Hoffman and Peter J. Albert, eds., *Religion in a Revolutionary Age* (Charlottesville, Va., 1993), pp. 88–96; Donald G. Mathews, *Religion in the Old South* (Chicago, 1977), pp. 66–71; John B. Boles, *Black Southerners, 1619–1869* (Lexington, Ky., 1983), pp. 155–60; William Lumpkin, "The Role of Women in 18th Century Virginia Baptist Life," *Baptist History and Heritage* 8 (1973): 160–67.

⁶ John Gregory, *A Father's Legacy to His Daughters* (1765; Philadelphia, 1775), pp. 28, 47–61.

⁷ Eliza Lucas to Mrs. H, [1742], in Elise Pinckney, ed., *The Letterbook of Eliza Lucas Pinckney, 1739–1762* (Chapel Hill, N.C., 1972), p. 48, emphasis added; David Ramsay, *Memoirs of the Life of Martha Laurens Ramsay* (Philadelphia, 1811), pp. 94–95, 109; Emelia Hunter to Elizabeth Galloway Sprigg, 13 May 1766, Mercer

Family Papers, VHS; Jack P. Greene, ed., *The Diary of Landon Carter of Sabine Hall, 1752–1778,* 2 vols. (Charlottesville, Va., 1965), 1:372–73, 2:807.

[8] T. H. Breen, *Tobacco Culture: The Mentality of the Great Tidewater Planters on the Eve of Revolution* (Princeton, N.J., 1985), chaps. 3–4; Marc Egnal, "The Economic Development of the Thirteen Continental Colonies, 1720 to 1775," *WMQ,* 3d ser., 32 (1975): 192–93, 221–22.

[9] Pauline Maier, *From Resistance to Revolution: Colonial Radicals and the Development of American Opposition to Britain* (New York, 1972), pp. 74–75, 114–38, 278–81.

[10] T. H. Breen, " 'Baubles of Britain': The American and Consumer Revolutions of the Eighteenth Century," *Past and Present* 119 (1988): 87–104; Gordon S. Wood, *The Creation of the American Republic, 1776–1787* (Chapel Hill, N.C., 1969), pp. 107–16; Drew R. McCoy, *The Elusive Republic: Political Economy in Jeffersonian America* (Chapel Hill, N.C., 1980), pp. 21–32; Ann Fairfax Withington, *Toward a More Perfect Union: Virtue and the Formation of American Republics* (New York, 1991), chap. 1.

[11] Maier, *From Resistance to Revolution,* pp. 297–300; Edmund S. Morgan, *American Slavery, American Freedom: The Ordeal of Colonial Virginia* (New York, 1975), pp. 375–87; Jeffrey J. Crow, "Liberty Men and Loyalists: Disorder and Disaffection in the North Carolina Backcountry," in Hoffman et al., eds., *Uncivil War,* pp. 127–33; Robert M. Weir, *Colonial South Carolina: A History* (Millwood, N.Y., 1983), pp. 283–84, 331–33; Richard Walsh, *Charleston's Sons of Liberty: A Study of the Artisans, 1763–1789* (Columbia, S.C., 1959), chap. 2.

On the prevailing assumption that women were — and should be — apolitical, see Linda K. Kerber, *Women of the Republic: Intellect and Ideology in Revolutionary America* (Chapel Hill, N.C., 1980), pp. 15–32, 74–80; Mary Beth Norton, *Liberty's Daughters: The Revolutionary Experience of American Women, 1750–1800* (Boston, 1980), pp. 35–39, 170–71.

[12] *Virginia Gazette* (Purdie and Dixon), 6, 20 June 1766, 14 Dec. 1769; Donald Jackson et al., eds., *The Diaries of George Washington,* 6 vols. (Charlottesville, Va., 1976–79), 2:190, 201; Hunter Dickinson Farish, ed., *The Journal and Letters of Philip Vickers Fithian: A Plantation Tutor of the Old Dominion, 1773–1774* (Williamsburg, Va., 1943), pp. 57, 191; Nicholas Cresswell, *The Journal of Nicholas Cresswell, 1774–1777* (Port Washington, N.Y., 1968), p. 53.

[13] *North Carolina Gazette,* 20 Nov. 1765; Henry Laurens to Joseph Brown, 28 Oct. 1765, in George C. Rogers, Jr., et al., eds., *The Papers of Henry Laurens,* 14 vols. to date (Columbia, S.C., 1968–), 5:29–31; Laurens to John Lewis Gervais, 12 May 1766, ibid., pp. 128–29; Edmund S. Morgan and Helen M. Morgan, *The Stamp Act Crisis: Prologue to Revolution* (Chapel Hill, N.C., 1953), pp. 200–202; Peter H. Wood., " 'Taking Care of Business' in Revolutionary South Carolina: Republicanism and the Slave Society," in Jeffrey J. Crow and Larry E. Tise., eds., *The Southern Experience in the American Revolution* (Chapel Hill, N.C., 1978), pp. 277–78.

14 Mary Beth Norton argues that women participated in crowd activities, but all her evidence comes from Massachusetts (*Liberty's Daughters*, p. 157).

15 For two seemingly lone exceptions, see *North Carolina Magazine; or, Universal Intelligencer*, 20–27 July 1764; *Virginia Gazette* (Purdie and Dixon), 24 Dec. 1767.

16 Charles Woodmason, *The Carolina Backcountry on the Eve of the Revolution*, ed. Richard J. Hooker (Chapel Hill, N.C., 1953), pp. 20–21; *Virginia Gazette* (Purdie and Dixon), 14 Dec. 1769; *Virginia Gazette* (Rind), 14 Dec. 1769; "Williamsburg: The Old Colonial Capital," *WMQ*, 1st ser., 16 (1907–8): 36.

17 *South Carolina Gazette*, 29 June 1769; Christopher Gadsden, "To the Planters, Merchants, and Freeholders of the Province of South Carolina . . . ," 22 June 1769, in Richard Walsh, ed., *The Writings of Christopher Gadsden* (Columbia, S.C., 1966), pp. 83–84.

18 *South Carolina Gazette*, 2 Mar., 1 June, 10 Aug. 1769, *Virginia Gazette* (Purdie and Dixon), 16 May 1771. A later advertisement described saving rags as the "more peculiar Province" of women (*North Carolina Gazette*, 14 Nov. 1777).

19 Cresswell, *Journal of Nicholas Cresswell*, p. 192; Thomas Anburey, *Travels through the Interior Parts of America*, 2 vols. (Boston, 1923), 2:246–47; John S. Ezell, ed., *The New Democracy in America: Travels of Francisco de Miranda in the United States, 1783–1784*, trans. Judson P. Wood (Norman, Okla., 1963), p. 8. See also Carole Shammas, *The Pre-Industrial Consumer in England and America* (Oxford, 1990), pp. 61–62, 202, and Shammas, "Black Women's Work and the Evolution of Plantation Society in Virginia," *Labor History* 26 (1985): 24.

20 Norton, *Liberty's Daughters*, pp. 166–68; Laurel Thatcher Ulrich, " 'Daughters of Liberty': Religious Women in Revolutionary New England," in Ronald Hoffman and Peter J. Albert, eds., *Women in the Age of the American Revolution* (Charlottesville, Va., 1989), pp. 214–18; Elaine Forman Crane, "Religion and Rebellion: Women of Faith and the American War for Independence," in Hoffman and Albert, eds., *Religion in a Revolutionary Age*, pp. 81–83; Shammas, "Black Women's Work," pp. 13–14; Edward Miles Riley, ed., *The Journal of John Harrower: An Indentured Servant in the Colony of Virginia, 1773–1776* (Williamsburg, Va., 1963), p. 121, 132–33; Greene, ed., *Diary of Landon Carter*, 2: 1101, 1114; "Home Manufactures in Virginia in 1791," *WMQ*, 2d ser., 2 (1922): 139–48; *Virginia Gazette* (Rind), 7 Sept. 1769; *Virginia Gazette* (Pinkney), 13 June 1777.

21 Robert Middlekauff, *The Glorious Cause: The American Revolution, 1763–1789* (New York, 1982), pp. 184–85; David Brion Davis, *The Problem of Slavery in the Age of Revolution, 1770–1823* (Ithaca, N.Y., 1975), pp. 44–49, 164–84, 196–212. See also *Virginia Gazette* (Pinkney), 16 June 1775, on the women of Bristol, Pennsylvania, who furnished a local regiment with a "suit of colours and drums" at their own expense.

22 Maier, *From Resistance to Revolution*, pp. 118–32; Breen, *Tobacco Culture*, pp. 194–95; Richard L. Bushman, *The Refinement of America: Persons, Houses, Cities* (New York, 1992), pp. 187–203. Bushman underestimates the extent to which gender

shaped this discourse. Linda Kerber dates the development of "an imaginery sumptuary system that applied only to women" to the postwar era (*Women of the Republic*, p. 45).

[23] Karin Calvert, "The Function of Fashion in Eighteenth-Century America," in Cary Carson, Ronald Hoffman, and Peter J. Albert, eds., *Of Consuming Interests: The Style of Life in Eighteenth-Century America* (Charlottesville, Va., 1994), p. 275; Linda Colley, *Britons: Forging the Nation, 1707–1837* (New Haven, Conn., 1992), pp. 187–88, 252–53. For earlier assignations of vanity as a peculiarly feminine vice, see Katherine Usher Henderson and Barbara F. McManus, eds., *Half Humankind: Contexts and Texts of the Controversy about Women in England, 1540–1640* (Urbana, Ill., 1985), pp. 47–48, 59–62.

[24] *Virginia Gazette*, 23 Mar. 1739; James Fordyce, *Sermons to Young Women, in Two Volumes*, 6th ed. (London, 1766), p. 41; *Virginia Gazette* (Purdie and Dixon), 4 June 1772; [Charleston] *Columbian Herald*, 4 Jan., 26 July 1785.

On the fates of some leading milliners, see *South Carolina Gazette*, 30 May, 21 June, 18 Oct. 1770, 11 May 1773; *Virginia Gazette* (Purdie and Dixon), 4 Mar. 1775; *Virginia Gazette* (Pinkney), 20 Apr. 1775. Of all the prerevolutionary southern milliners, only Jane Hunter Charlton and Margaret Hunter appear to have resumed their businesses after the Revolution. See Eleanor Kelley Cabell, "Women Merchants and Milliners in Eighteenth Century Williamsburg," Colonial Williamsburg Research Report, 1988, pp. 95–114.

[25] Michael Warner, *The Letters of the Republic: Publication and the Public Sphere in Eighteenth-Century America* (Cambridge, Mass., 1990), pp. 11–17, 42–43, 48–49.

[26] Ibid., pp. 32–33, 64; Bernard Bailyn, *The Ideological Origins of the American Revolution* (Cambridge, Mass., 1967), pp. 1–8.

[27] *Virginia Gazette* (Purdie and Dixon), 20 Jan. 1773, 16 June 1774.

[28] Rind, who published the *Gazette* for thirteen months after the death of her husband in August 1773, died ten days after the publication of this issue (Leona M. Hudak, *Early American Women Printers and Publishers, 1639–1820* [Metuchen, N.J., 1978], pp. 300–308).

[29] *Virginia Gazette* (Rind), 15 Sept. 1774. On the tea boycott in Pennsylvania, see Thomas M. Doerflinger, *A Vigorous Spirit of Enterprise: Merchants and Economic Development in Revolutionary Philadelphia* (Chapel Hill, N.C., 1986), pp. 192–94; Richard Alan Ryerson, *The Revolution Is Now Begun: The Radical Committees of Philadelphia* (Philadelphia, 1978), pp. 33–63.

[30] *Virginia Gazette* (Rind), 15 Sept. 1774. In a separate essay, "The Husband of a Planter's Wife" agreed that women's renunciation of tea might inspire men to give up imported wine.

[31] Ibid.

[32] Ibid. On the inability of even the most progressive eighteenth-century thinkers to see women as autonomous individuals, see Kerber, *Women of the Republic*, pp. 27–32.

33 *South Carolina Gazette and Country Journal*, 2, 16 Aug. 1774. Andromache was the faithful wife of Hector, the Trojan prince Achilles defeated in the *Iliad*.

34 Inez Parker Cumming, "The Edenton Ladies' Tea-Party," *Georgia Review* 8 (1954): 289–91; Samuel Ashe, *History of North Carolina* (Greensboro, N.C., 1925), pp. 427–29; Evangeline Walker Andrews and Charles McLean Andrews, eds., *Journal of a Lady of Quality: Being the Narrative of a Journey from Scotland to the West Indies, North Carolina and Portugal, in the Years 1774 to 1776* (New Haven, Conn., 1921), p. 155; *South Carolina Gazette*, 3 Apr. 1775.

35 E[lizabeth] Feilde to Maria Carter Armistead, 7 Feb., 3, 13 June 1776, Armistead-Cocke Papers, CWM; Alice Lee to Richard Potts, 11 Feb. 1775, Potts Family Papers, MHS.

36 Eliza Lucas Pinckney to Harriott Pinckney Horry, [ca. 1765], and Eliza Lucas Pinckney to [?], 2 Aug. 1775, in Pinckney Family Papers, SCHS; Alice Lee to Richard Potts, 11 Feb. 1775, Potts Family Papers, MHS. On women's real or pretended reluctance to discuss politics, see Kerber, *Women of the Republic*, pp. 73–80; Norton, *Liberty's Daughters*, pp. 170–71.

37 Martha Ryan cipher book, 1781, SHC, UNC-CH.

38 Greene, ed., *Diary of Landon Carter*, 2:860; "To the Inhabitants of the Province of South Carolina . . . ," 4 July 1774, in Peter Force, comp., *American Archives*, 4th ser., 6 vols. (Washington, D.C., 1837–53), 1:511, emphasis added.

39 *Virginia Gazette* (Purdie and Dixon), 2 June 1774; *South Carolina and American General Gazette*, 21 Sept. 1776; *Virginia Gazette* (Purdie), 4 July 1777; Proceedings of the Safety Committee for Rowan County, 8 May 1776, in William L. Saunders et al., eds., *The Colonial and State Records of North Carolina*, 30 vols. (Raleigh, Goldsboro, and Charlotte, N.C., 1886–1914), 10:594.

40 Withington, *Toward a More Perfect Union*, chap. 1; Elizabeth Cometti, "Morals and the American Revolution," *South Atlantic Quarterly* 46 (1947): 62–72.

41 Charles S. Royster, *A Revolutionary People at War: The Continental Army and the American Character* (Chapel Hill, N.C., 1979), pp. 38–43, 349–68.

42 John E. Selby, *The Revolution in Virginia, 1775–1783* (Williamsburg, Va., 1988), chaps. 4, 14–15; John S. Pancake, *This Destructive War: The British Campaign in the Carolinas, 1780–1782* (University, Ala., 1985); Sylvia R. Frey, *Water from the Rock: Black Resistance in a Revolutionary Age* (Princeton, N.J., 1991), chaps. 2–5; James H. O'Donnell III, *Southern Indians in the American Revolution* (Knoxville, Tenn., 1973), pp. 34–53.

43 *State Gazette of South Carolina*, 20 Jan., 24 Mar. 1779.

44 *Virginia Gazette* (Dixon and Hunter), 21 Sept. 1776.

45 Petition of Mary Webley, 1776, LP, Norfolk City, VSLA; Petition of Sarah Hutchings, 1786, LP, Norfolk County, VSLA. On the retreat of elite families from Charleston during the siege of that city, see Harriott Pinckney Horry to [?], [1776], Pinckney Family Papers, SCHS.

46 Petitions of Lydia Mayle, 1777, and Elizabeth Elliott, 1777, LP, Norfolk

County, VSLA; Petition of Mary Camp, 23 Oct. 1779, LP, Williamsburg City, VSLA; Henry Laurens to Martha Laurens, 29 Feb. 1776, in Ramsay, *Memoirs of the Life of Martha Laurens Ramsay,* pp. 67–68.

[47] Petition of Margaret Rawlings, 1 Dec. 1777, LP, Misc., VSLA; Petition of Margaret Douglass, 1777, LP, Orange County, VSLA; E[lizabeth] Feilde to Maria Carter Armistead, 7 Feb. 1776, Armistead-Cocke Papers, CWM; Kerber, *Women of the Republic,* pp. 55–61; Holly A. Mayer, *Belonging to the Army: Camp Followers and Community during the American Revolution* (Columbia, S.C., 1996), pp. 221–23.

[48] Petition of William Gipson, 1832, in John C. Dann., ed., *The Revolution Remembered: Eyewitness Accounts of the War of Independence* (Chicago, 1980), pp. 187, 189.

[49] *Virginia Gazette* (Purdie), 6 Sept. 1776; *North Carolina Gazette,* 14 Nov. 1777.

[50] Frances Bland Randolph Tucker to St. George Tucker, [July 1777], Tucker-Coleman Papers, CWM; Ezell, ed., *New Democracy in America,* p. 8; Louisa Susannah Wells, *The Journal of a Voyage from Charlestown to London* (New York, 1968), p. 2; Sarah Fouace Nourse Diary, 1781–83, esp. pp. 29, 41, Nourse Family Papers, UVa.

[51] Royster, *Revolutionary People at War,* pp. 295–308. On the southern wartime economy in general, see Selby, *Revolution in Virginia,* pp. 175–83, 229–33; Jerome J. Nadelhaft, *The Disorders of War: The Revolution in South Carolina* (Orono, Me., 1981), pp. 49–50; Walsh, *Charleston's Sons of Liberty,* pp. 77–81.

[52] Petition of Elizabeth Black, 9 Oct. 1776, in William Edwin Hemphill et al., eds., *The State Records of South Carolina: Journals of the General Assembly of the House of Representatives, 1776–1780* (Columbia, S.C., 1970), pp. 134–35; Petition of Ann Meadows, 12 Dec. 1789, GASR, November–December 1789, NCDAH; Petition of Martha Irvine, 10 Nov. 1777, LP, York County, VSLA; Sarah Fouace Nourse Diary, 1781–83, pp. 10–11, Nourse Family Papers, UVa.

[53] Petition of Frances Seayers, 1779, LP, Misc., VSLA.

[54] Petition of Elizabeth Crowley, 23 Nov. 1780, LP, Henry County, VSLA; Petition of Martha McGee Bell, 1 Jan. 1781, GASR, January–February 1781, box 1, NCDAH; Petition of Sundry Inhabitants of the County of Brunswick, 11 Nov. 1780, LP, Brunswick County, VSLA.

[55] *Virginia Gazette and American Advertiser,* 10 May 1783.

[56] Middlekauff, *Glorious Cause,* chaps. 18–19; Pancake, *This Destructive War.*

[57] Frey, *Water from the Rock,* pp. 85–89, 113–19, 156–63; Norton, *Liberty's Daughters,* pp. 209–12; Dill, *Governor Tryon and His Palace,* pp. 204–5.

[58] Elizabeth Ambler to Mildred Smith, [1781] (two letters), Elizabeth Jacquelin Ambler Papers, CW.

[59] Frances Bland Randolph Tucker to St. George Tucker, 17, 19 May 1779, 2 Mar., 9 June, 7, 14 July, 7 Sept. 1781, Tucker-Coleman Papers, CWM; Selby, *Revolution in Virginia,* pp. 204–8, 221–23.

[60] Dill, *Governor Tryon and His Palace,* pp. 204–5; Jean Johnson Blair to Hannah Johnson Iredell, 10, 19, 24 May 1781, and Jean Johnson Blair to James Iredell, 11, 15 May 1781, all in Charles Johnson Collection, NCDAH.

[61] Caroline Gilman, ed., *Letters of Eliza Wilkinson, during the Invasion and Possession of Charleston, S.C. by the British in the Revolutionary War* (1839; New York, 1969), pp. 27–67.

[62] "The Affair of Westover," in Julian P. Boyd et al., eds., *The Papers of Thomas Jefferson*, 27 vols. to date (Princeton, N.J.: Princeton University Press, 1950–), 5:671–705.

[63] *Virginia Gazette* (Dixon and Nicolson), 15 May 1779; William Dickson to Robert Dickson, 30 Nov. 1784, William Dickson Papers, NCDAH; Mildred Smith to Elizabeth Ambler, [1782], Elizabeth Jacquelin Ambler Papers, CW.

[64] Pancake, *This Destructive War,* chap. 5; Klein, *Unification of a Slave State,* pp. 95–104; Nadelhaft, *Disorders of War,* pp. 55–68; Crow, "Liberty Men and Loyalists," pp. 139–45; Ekirch, "Whig Authority and Public Order in the North Carolina Backcountry, 1776–1783," pp. 107–16, and Robert M. Weir, " 'The Violent Spirit,' the Reestablishment of Order, and the Continuity of Leadership in Post-Revolutionary South Carolina," pp. 72–77, both in Hoffman, et al., eds., *Uncivil War.*

[65] Petition of John Taylor, 1832, in Dann, ed., *Revolution Remembered,* pp. 208–9.

[66] William Dickson to Robert Dickson, 30 Nov. 1784, William Dickson Papers, NCDAH; Aedanus Burke to Arthur Middleton, 25 Jan. 1782, quoted in Nadelhaft, *Disorders of War,* p. 75; Middlekauff, *Glorious Cause,* p. 539; "Hart, Nancy," in Edward T. James et al., eds., *Notable American Women, 1607–1950: A Biographical Dictionary,* 3 vols. (Cambridge, Mass., 1971), 2:150–51; Petition of Josiah Culbertson, 1832, in Dann, ed., *Revolution Remembered,* pp. 175–76.

[67] Petition of Mary Pratt, 29 Jan. 1783, in Theodora J. Thompson and Rosa S. Lumpkin, eds., *The State Records of South Carolina: Journals of the House of Representatives, 1783–1784* (Columbia, S.C., 1977), p. 61; Petition of Margaret Monroe and Sarah McIver, 26 Dec. 1786, GASR, November 1786–January 1787, box 1, NCDAH; Catherine Park to Thomas Jefferson, 30 Mar. 1781, in Boyd et al., eds., *Papers of Thomas Jefferson,* 5:296; Mayer, *Belonging to the Army,* pp. 133–45; Norton, *Liberty's Daughters,* pp. 175–77, 196, 212–13; Middlekauff, *Glorious Cause,* pp. 476–77, 539; Frey, *Water from the Rock,* pp. 121–22, 169; John Irwin, "A List of my Company, Male and Female, Old and Young," [1781], in R. W. Gibbes, ed., *Documentary History of the American Revolution,* 3 vols. (New York, 1857), 2:145.

[68] "Female Heroism," *Columbian Magazine* 4 (1790): 139; Charles E. Claghorn, *Women Patriots of the American Revolution: A Biographical Dictionary* (Metuchen, N.J., 1991), p. 101; Martha Jefferson to Mrs. James Madison, 8 Aug. 1780, Martha Jefferson Paper, NCDAH; Kerber, *Women of the Republic,* pp. 43n, 99–103; Norton, *Liberty's Daughters,* pp. 177–88.

[69] Mary Blair Braxton Burwell to Betsey Whiting, 30 Dec. 1781, Blair, Banister, Braxton, Horner, and Whiting Papers, CWM; Sarah Fouace Nourse Diary, 1781–83, pp. 31–44, Nourse Family Papers, UVa.; Mary Clay to Anne Clay, 10 Nov. [1782], Mary Clay Letter, SHC, UNC-CH. After the British evacuation, Charleston

also experienced a "rage for matrimony." See Catherine Read to Elizabeth Ludlow Read, [1784?], Read Family Papers, USC.

[70] Johann David Schoepf, *Travels in the Confederation, 1783–1784*, trans. and ed. Alfred J. Morrison (New York, 1968), pp. 63–64; Mary Clay to Anne Clay, 10 Nov. [1782], Mary Clay Letter, SHC, UNC-CH; *Virginia Gazette and American Advertiser*, 17 May 1783.

[71] Kerber, *Women of the Republic*, pp. 125–26. On the common law right of dower, see Marylynn Salmon, *Women and the Law of Property in Early America* (Chapel Hill, N.C., 1986), pp. 141–47, 160–72.

[72] Linda K. Kerber, "The Paradox of Women's Citizenship in the Early Republic: The Case of Martin vs. Massachusetts, 1805," *AHR* 97 (1992): 358–62, 371; Kerber, *Women of the Republic*, pp. 119–27; Joan R. Gundersen, "Independence, Citizenship, and the American Revolution," *Signs* 13 (1987): 68–71.

[73] Petitions of Florence Cook, 23 Jan. 1783; Elizabeth Mitchell, 10 Feb. 1783; and Mary Rowand, 13 Feb. 1783, all in Thompson and Lumpkin, eds., *State Records of South Carolina, 1783–1784*, pp. 22, 113–14, 134; Petitions of Margaret Cotton, 15 Aug. 1778, August 1778, box 1; Jane Spurgin, 10 Nov. 1788, November–December 1788, box 2, and 25 Nov. 1791, December 1791–January 1792, box 2, all in GASR, NCDAH.

[74] Robert Stansbury Lambert, *South Carolina Loyalists in the American Revolution* (Columbia, S.C., 1987), pp. 286–302.

[75] Petition of Mary Fraser, 30 Nov. 1796, LP, 1796, SC Arch. In a similar though much earlier case, the Whig women of Wilmington protested the banishment of Tory women and their children (Petition of Anne Hooper, Sarah Nash, Mary Nash, and others, [1782], in Saunders et al., eds., *Colonial and State Records of North Carolina*, 16:467–69).

[76] Petitions of Mary Philp, 22 Jan. 1783, 11 Feb. 1784, in Thompson and Lumpkin, eds., *State Records of South Carolina, 1783–1784*, pp. 13, 15, 438, 553; Petition of Margaret Williams, 12 Dec. 1793, in Michael E. Stevens, ed., *The State Records of South Carolina: Journals of the House of Representatives, 1792–1794* (Columbia, S.C., 1988), p. 386; Petition of Margaret Williams, 1794, LP, 1794, SC Arch.; Will of Mary Philp, 26 Feb. 1785, Charleston County Will Book (typescript), 21: 672–74, SC Arch.

[77] Petition of Ann Williams, 12 Feb. 1783, in Thompson and Lumpkin, eds., *State Records of South Carolina, 1783–1784*, p. 127; Petition of Elizabeth Oats, 19 Feb. 1785, in Mark Emerson and Rosa S. Lumpkin, eds., *The State Records of South Carolina: Journals of the House of Representatives, 1785–1786* (Columbia, S.C., 1979), p. 110; Petition of Margaret Orde, 9 Feb. 1787, in Michael E. Stevens and Christine M. Allen, eds., *The State Records of South Carolina: Journals of the House of Representatives, 1787–1788* (Columbia, S.C., 1981), p. 78.

On the petitions that women exiles filed in Britain, see Mary Beth Norton,

248

"Eighteenth-Century American Women in Peace and War: The Case of the Loyalists," *WMQ* 3d ser., 33 (1976): 389–92.

[78] Petition of Mary Dorton, 17 Nov. 1788, LP, James City County, VSLA; Petition of Sarah Welsh, 8 Nov. 1791, LP, Misc., VSLA; Petition of Jeanne Tols, 6 Feb. 1789, in Michael E. Stevens and Christine M. Allen, eds., *The State: Journals of the House of Representatives, Records of South Carolina 1789–1790* (Columbia, S.C., 1984), pp. 112–13.

[79] Petition of Mary Taggart, 5 Dec. 1793, in Stevens, ed., *State Records of South Carolina, 1792–1794*, p. 311; Petition of Mary Taggart, 21 Nov. 1794, LP, 1794, SC Arch; Petition of Lucy Armistead, 1794, LP, Misc., VSLA.

[80] Petitions of Ann Dabney, 11 Dec. 1792, and Margaret Clendening, 11 Dec. 1792, in Stevens, ed., *State Records of South Carolina, 1792–1794*, p. 141; Petitions of Mary Boush, 1790, 19 Nov. 1796, LP, Norfolk City, VSLA; Petition of Mary Cornhill, 25 Nov. 1795, LP, Misc., VSLA; Petition of Elizabeth Jameson, 18 Dec. 1797, LP, Dinwiddie County, VSLA.

[81] Cynthia A. Kierner, ed., *Southern Women in Revolution, 1776–1800: Personal and Political Narratives* (Columbia, S.C., 1998), pp. xxi, 49. Southern women filed fewer than fifty petitions between 1750 and 1775. For a brief overview of women's petitioning at the national level, see George C. Chalou, "Women in the American Revolution: Vignettes or Profiles," in Mabel C. Deutrich and Virginia C. Purdy, eds., *Clio Was a Woman: Studies in the History of American Women* (Washington, D.C., 1980), pp. 73–90.

[82] William Moultrie, *Memoirs of the American Revolution*, 2 vols. (New York, 1902), 2: 357; David Ramsay, *The History of the Revolution in South Carolina*, 2 vols. (Trenton, N.J., 1785), 2:123–24.

[83] Ramsay, *Memoirs of the Life of Martha Laurens Ramsay*, pp. 49–50.

4. Republicanism

[1] Petitions of Mary Moore, 23, 29 Dec. 1786, GASR, November 1786–January 1787, box 2, NCDAH.

[2] Linda K. Kerber, *Women of the Republic: Intellect and Ideology in Revolutionary America* (Chapel Hill, N.C., 1980), pp. 85–99; Joan R. Gundersen, "Independence, Citizenship, and the American Revolution," *Signs* 13 (1987): 59–77.

[3] Frank Luther Mott, *A History of American Magazines, 1741–1850* (Cambridge, Mass., 1938), pp. 30–31, 94–104; [Charleston] *Columbian Herald*, 21 Sept. 1786; *American Museum* 2 (1787): 3–11, 5 (1789): 13–16; *Lady's Magazine* 1 (1792): v, 2 (1792): iii; James Gilreath, "Mason Weems, Mathew Carey and the Southern Book Trade," *Publishing History* 10 (1981): 27–50. New Bern's printer-bookseller sold the *American Museum* and the *Lady's Magazine* (*North Carolina Gazette*, 17 Oct. 1794). Timothy Brundige of Dumphries, Va. — an associate of Mathew Carey — sold the *American Museum* (Invoice of Books belonging to Mathew Carey now on hand at the Store of Timothy Brundige . . . , 2 Jan. 1796, Mathew Carey Papers, American An-

tiquarian Society). For a useful overview of nationalist literary and cultural development in the 1780s, see Kenneth Silverman, *A Cultural History of the American Revolution*
(New York, 1987). See also Dena Goodman, *The Republic of Letters: A Cultural History
of the French Revolution* (Ithaca, N.Y., 1994), pp. 165–75, for a contemporary attempt
to enlist periodical literature in the development and dissemination of a national
public culture.

⁴ The Post Office Act of 1792, which made no provision for the transportation
of magazines by mail, dealt a fatal blow to these early national publications. See
Mott, *History of American Magazines*, pp. 98, 103; *Columbian Magazine* 9 (1792): 362;
American Museum 12 (1792): 302.

⁵ On women's literacy, see Mary Beth Norton, "Communication," *WMQ*, 3d ser.,
48 (1991): 639–45; Kerber, *Women of the Republic*, pp. 164–65, 191–93; Kevin J.
Hayes, *A Colonial Woman's Bookshelf* (Knoxville, Tenn., 1996), chap. 1.

⁶ Carroll Smith-Rosenberg, "Dis-Covering the Subject of the 'Great Constitutional Discussion,' 1786–1789," *JAH* 79 (1992): 856–60, surveys the misogynous offerings and assesses their political significance.

⁷ "A Tract on the Unreasonableness of the Laws of England . . . ," *Columbian
Magazine* 2 (1788): 22–24, 189; "The propriety of meliorating the condition of
women in civilized societies, considered," *American Museum* 9 (1791): 248–49; "A
hint," *American Museum* 7 (1790): 208.

⁸ "Woman's hard fate," *American Museum* 6 (1789): 417–18. In response, a "gentleman" describe man as woman's "guardian-god" who gave her love, protection,
and sustenance in return for his sovereignty.

⁹ "On Matrimonial Obedience," *Lady's Magazine* 1 (1792): 64–67.

¹⁰ "The Visitant, No. XI," *American Museum* 6 (1789): 148–49; "The American
Spectator, No. X," ibid. 7 (1790): 93–94.

¹¹ "On the Supposed Superiority of the Masculine Understanding," *Columbian
Magazine* 7 (1791): 9–11.

¹² "Female Heroism," ibid. 4 (1790): 139; "Female Heroism Rewarded," ibid. 7
(1791): 120; "The Retailer, No. XVI," ibid. 4 (1790): 148–49.

¹³ "Singular Account of a Female Surgeon," ibid. 7 (1791): 238; "Account of a
. . . Defence of the Genius of Women," ibid., 323–24; "An Essay on Education," ibid.
3 (1789): 299–300.

¹⁴ "Maxims for republics," *American Museum* 2 (1787): 81; Noah Webster, "On
the Education of Youth in America," ibid. 12 (1792): 281–83. On Webster's cultural
nationalism, see David Simpson, *The Politics of American English* (New York, 1986),
chap. 2.

¹⁵ Benjamin Rush, "Thoughts on Female Education," *Columbian Magazine* 4
(1790): 209–10. The text of Rush's address also appears in Frederick Rudolph, ed.,
Essays on Education in the Early Republic (Cambridge, Mass., 1965), pp. 25–40.

¹⁶ Rush, "Thoughts on Female Education," p. 209.

¹⁷ Rush's views are in contrast to the more radical position of Judith Sargent

250   Murray of Massachusetts, who argued that education could enable women to work outside the home and thus ensure their independence. Murray's essays, however, did not reach a national audience. See Kerber, *Women of the Republic,* pp. 204–10; and Mary Beth Norton, *Liberty's Daughters: The Revolutionary Experience of American Women, 1750–1800* (Boston, 1980), pp. 247, 252–55.

18 The pathbreaking discussion of "republican motherhood" is Kerber, *Women of the Republic,* chap. 9, but see also Jan Lewis, "The Republican Wife: Virtue and Seduction in the Early Republic," *WMQ,* 3d ser., 44 (1987): 689–721.

19 "The Influence of the Female Sex on the Enjoyments of Social Life," *Columbian Magazine* 4 (1790): 154; "On the Happy Influence of the Female Sex in Society," ibid. 6 (1791): 152–54. The ideal of the genteel lady survived in conservative circles into the nineteenth century. For instance, Alice DeLancey Izard reminded her daughter that "well educated Ladies" were "the reformers of the World . . . [to whom] society has always been indebted for grace and elegance" (Alice DeLancey Izard to Margaret Izard Manigault, 31 Mar. 1811, Manigault Family Papers, USC).

20 Although affluent Americans continued to live genteelly, most at least paid lip service to the evils of corrupting luxuries and the virtues of republican simplicity. See Drew R. McCoy, *The Elusive Republic: Political Economy in Jeffersonian America* (Chapel Hill, N.C., 1980), pp. 94–104, 171–74, 187–88; Richard L. Bushman, *The Refinement of America: Persons, Houses, Cities* (New York, 1992), pp. 193–203. For criticisms of ornamental education before 1800, see Rush, "Thoughts on Female Education," pp. 289–90; Webster, "On the Education of Youth in America," pp. 282–83; "On Education," [Charleston] *Columbian Herald,* 19 Aug. 1785.

21 "Marriage Ceremonies of different Countries compared," *Columbian Magazine* 1 (1787): 497; "On Female Authorship," *Lady's Magazine* 2 (1793): 69.

22 Devereux Jarratt, *The Life of the Reverend Devereux Jarratt . . . written by himself* (Baltimore, 1806), pp. 14–15. See also Thomas Anburey, *Travels through the Interior Parts of America,* 2 vols. (Boston, 1923), 2:215.

23 On political reform during and after the Revolution, see John E. Selby, *The Revolution in Virginia, 1775–1783* (Williamsburg, Va., 1988), chaps. 3, 6, 12; Delbert Harold Gilpatrick, *Jeffersonian Democracy in North Carolina* (New York, 1931), pp. 23–30; Jerome J. Nadelhaft, *The Disorders of War: The Revolution in South Carolina* (Orono, Me., 1981), chaps. 6–7; Rachel N. Klein, *Unification of a Slave State: The Rise of the Planter Class in the South Carolina Backcountry, 1760–1808* (Chapel Hill, N.C., 1990), pp. 118–48, 257–66.

24 Sylvia R. Frey, *Water from the Rock: Black Resistance in a Revolutionary Age* (Princeton, N.J., 1991), pp. 226–42, 285–96, and Frey, " 'The Year of Jubilee Is Come': Black Christianity in the Plantation South in Post-Revolutionary America," in Ronald Hoffman and Peter Albert, eds., *Religion in a Revolutionary Age* (Charlottesville, Va., 1993), pp. 102–9; Willie Lee Rose, "The Impact of the American Revolution on the Black Population," in William W. Freehling, ed., *Slavery and Free-*

dom (New York, 1982), pp. 7–15; Douglas R. Egerton, *Gabriel's Rebellion: The Virginia Slave Conspiracies of 1800 and 1802* (Chapel Hill, N.C., 1993), pp. 5–17, 45–48; Robert McColley, *Slavery and Jeffersonian Virginia* (Urbana, Ill., 1964), pp. 141–62; David Brion Davis, *The Problem of Slavery in the Age of Revolution, 1770–1823* (Ithaca, N.Y., 1975), pp. 169–84, 196–212.

Southern antislavery sentiment should not be exaggerated. See Frederika Teute Schmidt and Barbara Ripel Wilhelm, "Early Proslavery Petitions in Virginia," *WMQ*, 3d ser., 30 (1973): 133–46. On fears of race war, even among whites who pondered the gradual abolition of slavery, see Thomas Jefferson, *Notes on the State of Virginia*, in Merrill D. Peterson, ed., *The Portable Thomas Jefferson* (New York, 1975), p. 186.

25 "On Matrimony," *Columbian Magazine* 4 (1790): 179; [Charleston] *Columbian Herald*, 30 July 1793; "Fashionable Miscellany," *Baltimore Weekly Magazine* 1 (1800): 91–92; [Richmond] *Virginia Argus*, 30 Dec. 1800. See also "In Praise of Marriage," *Wilmington Centinel and General Advertiser*, 2 July 1788.

26 *South Carolina Weekly Museum* 2 (1797): 289–92; "Domestic Politics," *Literary Magazine and American Register* 2 (1804): 93–94.

27 "The Matrimonial Creed," *Wilmington Centinel and General Advertiser*, 20 Aug. 1788; *American Museum* 6 (1789): 314, *Lady's Magazine* 1 (1792): 37–38; [Charleston] *Columbian Herald*, 22 Aug. 1793; "Rules and Maxims for Promoting Matrimonial Happiness," *Columbian Magazine* 4 (1790): 24; *South Carolina Weekly Magazine* 2 (1797): 116–17; "Hints for young married women," *American Museum* 6 (1789): 198–99; "The Ladies Friend, No. II; On Conjugal Affection," *Lady's Magazine* 1 (1792): 177; "On Temper — Respecting the Married State," *Lady's Magazine* 2 (1792): 33–34; "The Honeymoon," *North Carolina Gazette*, 21 Oct. 1793; "The Provoked Husband," [Charleston] *Columbian Herald*, 27 June 1794; "How to Keep a Husband True," [Charleston] *Columbian Herald*, 1 Aug. 1796; Diary of Elizabeth Washington Foote, 1784–89, in Elizabeth Evans, ed., *Weathering the Storm: Women of the American Revolution* (New York, 1975), pp. 344–45, 350–51.

28 Roger Thompson, *Women in Stuart England and America: A Comparative Study* (London, 1974), pp. 114–15; Lee Virginia Chambers-Schiller, *Liberty, a Better Husband: Single Women in America, the Generations of 1780–1840* (New Haven, 1984), pp. 11–27; John Gregory, *A Father's Legacy to His Daughters* (1765; Philadelphia, 1775), pp. 104–6; John Bennett, *Letters to a Young Lady, on a Variety of Useful and Interesting Subjects . . . to which is Prefixed Strictures on Female Education*, 2 vols. (Philadelphia, 1793), 2:73–75.

Focusing on the emergence of more favorable attitudes toward spinsterhood in New England, Chambers-Schiller overlooks the profoundly disparaging literature of the 1790s. For a rare public defense of unmarried women during this largely reactionary decade, see *Lady's Magazine* 1 (1792): 60–62.

29 *Wilmington Gazette*, 19 Apr. 1799.

30 "Marriage Ceremonies of different Countries compared," *Columbian Magazine* 1 (1787): 491; Chambers-Schiller, *Liberty, a Better Husband*, pp. 31–32.

[31] Eliza Williams Haywood to Jane Williams, 18 Mar. 1802, Ernest Haywood Collection, SHC, UNC-CH; Bertram Wyatt-Brown, *Southern Honor: Ethics and Behavior in the Old South* (New York, 1982), pp. 229–30, 238–39.

In Charles County, Maryland, the number of households headed by single women increased from 3.7% in 1773, to 12.5% in 1782, to 16% in 1790. Many of these women owned substantial amounts of property, however, and thus presumably chose to remain unmarried (Jean B. Lee, *The Price of Nationhood: The American Revolution in Charles County* [New York, 1994], pp. 207–8, 350 n. 40). One scholar speculates that in the antebellum decades "about a fifth to a quarter of all adult white southern women were unmarried for life" (Michael O'Brien, ed., *An Evening When Alone: Four Journals of Single Women in the South, 1827–67* [Charlottesville, Va., 1993], pp. 1–2).

[32] John S. Ezell, ed., *The New Democracy in America: Travels of Francisco de Miranda in the United States, 1783–1784*, trans. Judson P. Wood (Norman, Okla., 1963), p. 24; François Jean, Marquis de Chastellux, *Travels in North America in the Years 1780, 1781 and 1782*, 2 vols., ed. Howard C. Rice, Jr. (Chapel Hill, N.C., 1963), 2:414–15; David Ramsay, *History of South Carolina, from Its First Settlement in 1670 to the Year 1808*, 2 vols. (1808; Newberry, S.C., 1858), 1:258; *Returns of the Whole Number of Persons within the Several Districts of the United States . . .* (Philadelphia, 1791), pp. 49–55. In 1790, white females outnumbered white males in 23 of 161 southern counties.

[33] [Charleston] *Columbian Herald*, 17 Aug. 1793. For two rare early discussions, see *South Carolina Gazette*, 22 May 1749; *Virginia Gazette* (Purdie and Dixon), 15 Jan. 1767. The former criticizes bachelors for their "Contempt of the Laws both of God and Nature," while the latter merely praises marriage and describes a man who happily abandons bachelorhood. Criticism of bachelors, though not of unmarried women, abated in later decades. See Wyatt-Brown, *Southern Honor*, pp. 239–40.

[34] "Geographical description of Bachelor's island," *American Museum*, 8 (1790): 187; "Geographical description of Bachelor's Island," *Virginia Herald and Fredericksburg Advertiser*, 16 June 1795; "A Few Words to the people called Old Bachelors," [Charleston] *Columbian Herald*, 17 Dec. 1793.

[35] "Description of an Old Bachelor," *Georgetown Gazette*, 21 Sept. 1815; "Geographical description of Bachelor's Island," *Virginia Herald and Fredericksburg Advertiser*, 16 June 1795; *Camden Gazette*, 14 July 1817. On the sexual subtext of republican political culture, especially the pervasiveness of the seduction metaphor, see Lewis, "Republican Wife," pp. 701–4, 716–20.

[36] "The Old Maid," *Columbian Magazine* 2 (1788): 111; "A Song; by Celia, in her Forty-Fifth Year," ibid. 8 (1792): 379; "Original Letter from Eusebia, lately married, to Flirtilla," ibid. 7 (1791): 153–54; "A Scrap for the Ladies," *Wilmington Centinel and General Advertiser*, 9 July 1788.

[37] "Character of an Old Maid," *American Museum* 3 (1788): 146–47, and [Charleston] *State Gazette of South Carolina*, 19 Apr. 1790.

[38] "On Matrimony," *Columbian Magazine* 4 (1790): 179; *Camden Gazette*, 14 July 1817; James Ewell, *The Planter's and Mariner's Medical Companion* (1807; Baltimore, 1813), p. 149; Carroll Smith-Rosenberg, "From Puberty to Menopause: The Cycle of Femininity in Nineteenth-Century America," in Mary Hartman and Lois W. Banner, eds., *Clio's Consciousness Raised* (New York, 1974), pp. 25, 30, 34.

[39] "On Fashionable Female Amusements," *Lady's Magazine* 2 (1793): 125; "An oration delivered at Petersburgh, Virginia," *American Museum* 2 (1787): 420–21; *Raleigh Register,* 11 June 1804.

[40] "Address to the Ladies of America," *American Museum* 2 (1787): 481; William Livingston, "Homespun," ibid. 10 (1791): 17–18; "On Dress, To the ladies," ibid., appendix 1, p. 30; [Charleston] *Columbian Herald,* 4 Jan., 26 July 1785. See also Smith-Rosenberg, "Dis-Covering the Subject of the 'Great Constitutional Discussion,' " pp. 859–60.

[41] "A Dialogue in the Purgatory of Macaronis, between Will Toilet and Sir Bobby Button," *Columbian Magazine* 3 (1789): 408–10.

[42] See, for instance, [Richmond] *Virginia Gazette, or the American Advertiser,* 28 Aug. 1784; [New Bern] *North Carolina Gazette,* 1 Nov. 1793; [Charleston] *Columbian Herald,* 16 Nov. 1793; *Lady's Magazine* 1 (1792): 189–98.

[43] Patricia Jewell McAlexander, "The Creation of the American Eve: The Cultural Dialogue on the Nature and Role of Women in Late Eighteenth-Century America," *Early American Literature* 9 (1975): 255–57, 261–64.

[44] Margaret Izard Manigault to Gabriel Manigault, 20 Nov. 1792; Alice DeLancey Izard to Margaret Izard Manigault, 29 May 1801; Margaret Izard Manigault to Alice DeLancey Izard, 17 June 1801, all in Manigault Family Papers, USC.

[45] *Monthly Register, and Review of the United States* 1 (1805): 1–2; "The Female Philosophers," *Charleston Spectator and Ladies Literary Portfolio* 1 (1806): 148–50.

[46] "Valour, Ascendancy and Political Talents of Women: Speech of a French Republican Female, 1792," *Monthly Review and Literary Miscellany of the United States* 6 (1807): 167–71.

[47] Gordon S. Wood, *The Radicalism of the American Revolution* (New York, 1992), pp. 174–89.

[48] "Patriotism," *South Carolina Weekly Museum* 2 (1797): 502–3.

[49] Elizabeth Steele to Ephraim Steele, 15 May, 30 July, 17 Oct. 1778, 29 Apr., 13 July, 29 Oct. 1780, John Steele Papers, NCDAH; Alan D. Watson, "Women in Colonial North Carolina: Overlooked and Underestimated," *NCHR* 58 (1981): 15; Helen Blair to William Blair, 20 Aug. 1784, quoted in Mary Beth Norton, " 'What an Alarming Crisis Is This': Southern Women and the American Revolution," in Jeffrey J. Crow and Larry E. Tise, eds., *The Southern Experience in the American Revolution* (Chapel Hill, N.C., 1978), p. 220; Caroline Gilman, ed., *Letters of Eliza Wilkinson, during the Invasion and Possession of Charleston, S.C., by the British in the Revolutionary War* (1839; New York, 1969), pp. 60–61.

For general overviews of the Revolution's impact on the political consciousness of women throughout America, see Kerber, *Women of the Republic,* esp. chap. 3, and Norton, *Liberty's Daughters,* chaps. 6–9.

⁵⁰ Richard Henry Lee to Hannah Lee Corbin, 17 Mar. 1778, in James Curtis Ballagh, ed., *The Letters of Richard Henry Lee,* 2 vols. (New York, 1911–14), 1:392–93; Louise Belote Dawe and Sandra Gioia Treadway, "Hannah Lee Corbin: The Forgotten Lee," *Virginia Cavalcade* 29 (1979): 70–77; Mary Willing Byrd to [Thomas Nelson], [10 Aug. 1781], in Julian P. Boyd et al., eds., *The Papers of Thomas Jefferson,* 27 vols. to date (Princeton, N.J., 1950–), 5:703–4; Edmund S. Morgan, *Inventing the People: The Rise of Popular Sovereignty in England and America* (New York, 1988), pp. 193, 197.

⁵¹ Mary Ann Elizabeth Stevens Cogdell Commonplace Book, ca. 1800, Library Company of Philadelphia. On the proliferation of southern newspapers during this period, see Clarence S. Brigham, *History and Bibliography of American Newspapers, 1690–1820,* 2 vols. (Worcester, Mass., 1947), 1:111–34, 2:758–82, 1023–53, 1103–68.

⁵² Martha Dandridge Custis Washington to Fanny Bassett Washington, 25 Feb. 1788, in Joseph E. Fields, comp., *"Worthy Partner": The Papers of Martha Washington* (Westport, Conn., 1994), p. 205; Margaret Izard Manigault to Gabriel Manigault, 12 Nov. 1787, and Gabriel Manigault to Margaret Izard Manigault, 22 May 1788, Manigault Family Papers, SCHS; Elizabeth Preston Madison to John Preston, 9 Dec. 1798, 8 Jan. 1799, Preston Family Papers, VHS.

⁵³ Ann Cary Randolph to St. George Tucker, 29 Oct. 1797, and Judith Randolph to St. George Tucker, 5 Nov. 1797, Tucker-Coleman Papers, CWM; Ann Frances Bland Tucker Coalter to John Randolph, 30 Dec. 1798, Grinnan Family Papers, VHS; Eleanor Parke Custis to Elizabeth Bordley, 23 Nov. [1797], 14 May 1798, in Patricia Brady, ed., *George Washington's Beautiful Nelly: The Letters of Eleanor Parke Custis Lewis to Elizabeth Bordley Gibson, 1794–1851* (Columbia, S.C., 1991), pp. 41, 52.

⁵⁴ Elizabeth Washington Gamble to Thomas Bayly, 11–12 Mar. 1801, Elizabeth Washington Gamble Wirt Letter, VHS; Eleanor Parke Custis Lewis to Mary Stead Pinckney, 9 May 1801, 3 Jan. 1802, Pinckney Family Papers, SCHS; Anne Blair Banister to Elizabeth Whiting, 25 Oct. 1803, Blair, Banister, Braxton, Horner, and Whiting Papers, CWM.

⁵⁵ Mary Stead Pinckney to Mrs. Morris, 8 May 1796, and Eleanor Parke Custis Lewis to Mary Stead Pinckney, 9 May 1801 and 3 Jan. 1802, Pinckney Family Papers, SCHS; Mary Stead Pinckney to Elizabeth Izard, 18 Nov. 1796; Mary Stead Pinckney to Margaret Izard Manigault, 13 Dec. 1796; and Mary Stead Pinckney to Alice DeLancey Izard, 11 Dec. 1796, all in Charles F. McCombs, ed., *Letter-book of Mary Stead Pinckney: November 14th, 1796 to August 29th, 1797* (New York, 1946), pp. 17–19, 24, 32.

⁵⁶ Margaret Izard Manigault to Gabriel Manigault, 20 Nov. 1792; Alice De-

Lancey Izard to Ralph Izard, 9 Nov. 1794; Alice DeLancey Izard to Margaret Izard Manigault, 29 May 1801, 19 Aug. and 9 Dec. 1810; Margaret Izard Manigault to Alice DeLancey Izard, 17 June 1801; Alice DeLancey Izard to Henry Izard, 3 Dec. 1807, 23 Jan. and 5 Mar. 1809; Margaret Izard Manigault to Georgina Izard Smith, 12 June 1814, all in Manigault Family Papers, USC.

[57] Dolly Madison to James Madison, 1 Nov. 1805, in *Memoirs and Letters of Dolly Madison . . . edited by her Grand-Niece* (Boston, 1887), pp. 60–61; Mary Stanford to Richard Stanford, 25 Mar. 1806, 8 Mar. 1808, Richard Stanford Papers, NCDAH; William Lowndes to Elizabeth Pinckney Lowndes, 2 Jan. 1811, 9 Oct. 1814, William Lowndes Papers, SHC, UNC-CH.

[58] Alice DeLancey Izard to Ralph Izard, 4 Dec. 1794, Ralph Izard Papers, USC; Elizabeth Preston Madison to John Preston, 8 Dec. 1794, 11 Nov. 1796, Preston Family Papers, VHS; Hannah McClure Gaston to William Gaston, 2 July 1810, William Gaston Papers, SHC, UNC-CH.

[59] John Chesnut to Mary Cox Chesnut, 24 Feb., 21 May 1799, Cox-Chesnut Papers, USC; Elizabeth Washington Gamble to Thomas Bayly, 11–12 Mar. 1801, Elizabeth Washington Gamble Wirt Letter, VHS.

Republicans criticized the Federalist balls for their similarity to royal birthnight celebrations. See Rufus Wilmot Griswold, *The Republican Court; or, American Society in the Days of Washington* (New York, 1867), pp. 217, 415–16; Barry Schwartz, *George Washington: The Making of an American Symbol* (Ithaca, N.Y., 1990), pp. 77–84; Louise Burnham Dunbar, *A Study of "Monarchical" Tendencies in the United States from 1776 to 1801* (Urbana, Ill., 1923), pp. 116–19.

[60] Rachel Mordecai to Samuel Mordecai, 18 Apr. 1812, Mordecai Family Papers, SHC, UNC-CH; Catherine Read to Eizabeth Read Ludlow, [1798], Read Family Papers, USC.

[61] Cynthia A. Kierner, ed., *Southern Women in Revolution, 1776–1800: Personal and Political Narratives* (Columbia, S.C., 1998), pp. 49–56.

[62] Petition of Mary Davidson, [Dec. 1793], GASR, Dec. 1793–Jan. 1794, box 1, NCDAH. On General William Davidson, see William S. Powell, ed., *Dictionary of North Carolina Biography*, 6 vols. (Chapel Hill, N.C., 1979–96), 2:27–28.

[63] Petitions of Ann Timothy, 21 Jan. 1788, 16 Jan. 1790, 3 Dec. 1791, in Michael E. Stevens and Christine M. Allen, eds., *The State Records of South Carolina: Journals of the House of Representatives, 1787–1788* (Columbia S.C., 1981), p. 334; Stevens and Allen, eds., *The State Records of South Carolina: Journals of the House of Representatives, 1789–1790* (Columbia, S.C., 1984), pp. 336–37; Stevens and Allen, eds., *The State Records of South Carolina: Journals of the House of Representatives, 1791* (Columbia, S.C., 1985), pp. 310–11; Petition of Hope Mulford, 13 Dec. 1800, LP, Richmond City, VSLA.

[64] The North Carolina legislature heard its first divorce petition in 1779; by 1800, four wives, three husbands, and six couples had petitioned for divorce, though

256 only one of these petitions was granted. Virginia's legislature heard its first divorce petition in 1786; the legislature empowered the courts to grant only three of the petitions that twelve husbands, seven wives, and two couples submitted by 1800.

In the nineteenth century, the courts, rather than the legislatures, received most southern divorce petitions. The quantity of petitions submitted to both the legislatures and the courts increased after 1800. See Jane Turner Censer, " 'Smiling through Her Tears': Ante-Bellum Southern Women and Divorce," *American Journal of Legal History* 25 (1981): 24–47; Suzanne Lebsock, *The Free Women of Petersburg: Status and Culture in a Southern Town, 1784–1860* (New York, 1984), pp. 68–72; Guion Griffis Johnson, *Ante-Bellum North Carolina: A Social History* (Chapel Hill, N.C., 1937), pp. 217–19; Glenda Riley, "Legislative Divorce in Virginia, 1803–1850," *JER* 11 (1991): 55–61.

⁶⁵ Marylynn Salmon, *Women and the Law of Property in Early America* (Chapel Hill, N.C., 1986), pp. 190–93; Lebsock, *Free Women of Petersburg,* chap. 3. As Lebsock shows, separate estates were increasingly popular after 1820, but by then they were more commonly granted to preserve the property of indebted planter families than to address the needs of poor abandoned wives.

⁶⁶ Kierner, ed., *Southern Women in Revolution,* chap. 5.

⁶⁷ On the rhetorical fear of debt and the dishonor attributed to debtors, see T. H. Breen, *Tobacco Culture: The Mentality of the Great Tidewater Planters on the Eve of Revolution* (Princeton, N.J., 1985), pp. 91–95, 186–210; Jan Lewis, *The Pursuit of Happiness: Family and Values in Jefferson's Virginia* (Cambridge, 1983), pp. 109–10. A Carolina poet penned a "Hymn to Industry," attributing the independence of the United States to the industry of its people ([Charleston] *Columbian Herald,* 21 Feb. 1794).

In Virginia and South Carolina, women petitioned the court of chancery for separate estates, as they had done in South Carolina during the colonial era.

⁶⁸ Petition of Elizabeth Carter, [December 1798], GASR, November–December 1798, box 3, NCDAH; Petitions of Elizabeth Whitworth, [1800], and Penelope Hosea, 30 Oct. 1800, both in GASR, November–December 1800, box 3, NCDAH; Petition of Catharine Dick, December 1799, GASR, November–December 1799, box 3, NCDAH.

⁶⁹ Lewis, "Republican Wife," pp. 716–20; Cathy N. Davidson, *Revolution and the Word: The Rise of the Novel in America* (New York, 1986), esp. pp. 45–47, 101–12, 129–50.

⁷⁰ Petition of Susannah Wersley, 20 Nov. 1786, LP, Hanover County, VSLA; Petition of Polly Wilson, 6 Dec. 1800, LP, Misc., VSLA.

⁷¹ On instructions, see Gordon S. Wood, *The Creation of the American Republic, 1776–1787* (Chapel Hill, N.C., 1969), pp. 189–91, 370–72; Morgan, *Inventing the People,* p. 213. North Carolina's state constitution expressly encouraged this practice.

⁷² Petition of 51 women and 301 children, 4 Feb. 1780, in William Edwin Hemphill et al., eds., *The State Records of South Carolina: Journals of the General Assembly of the House of Representatives, 1776–1780* (Columbia, S.C., 1970), pp. 274–75; Petition of Anne Hooper et al., [1782], in William L. Saunders et al., eds., *The Colonial and*

State Records of North Carolina, 30 vols. (Raleigh, Goldsboro, and Charlotte, 1886–1914), 16:467–69; Petition of Mary Fraser et al., 11 Nov. 1796, LP, 1796, SC Arch; Petition of Elizabeth Richards et al., 13 Dec. 1796, GASR, November– December 1796, NCDAH; Petition of Jane Dixon and Sarah Millyard, 1776, LP, Norfolk City, VSLA; Petition of Mary Figg and Jane Buck, 1777, LP, Misc., VSLA; Petition of Delia Barnes and Mary Tripp, 8 June 1784, LP, Princess Anne County, VSLA. An eighth petition, submitted by the "Ladies of Augusta" to the Georgia legislature in 1783, appears to have solicited the return of a banished man to his family. This document has not survived, but it is mentioned in Allen D. Candler, ed., *The Revolutionary Records of the State of Georgia*, vol. 3: *Journal of the House of Assembly, from August 17, 1781, to February 26, 1784* (Atlanta, Ga., 1908), p. 367.

I have defined a group petition as one filed by two or more signatories not related by blood or marriage.

[73] Petition of the widows of Charleston, Aug. 1783, LP, 1783, SC Arch; Petition of Sundry Seamstresses of the City of Charleston, 26 Jan. 1789, in Stevens and Allen, eds., *State Records of South Carolina, 1789–1790*, p. 69; Petition of the Single Women at Salem in Stokes County, [December 1797], GASR, November–December 1797, box 2, NCDAH; Petition of the people of Colour of South Carolina, 1794, LP, 1794, SC Arch; Petition of the Tenants of the lands [belonging] to the College of Wm. & Mary . . . , 5 Nov. 1790, LP, Williamsburg City, VSLA.

[74] Petition of Florence Cooke, 23 Jan. 1783, LP, 1783, SC Arch; Petition of Jane Spurgin, 28 Nov. 1791, GASR, December 1791–January 1792, box 2, NCDAH; Petition of Elizabeth Beard, 16 Nov. 1796, LP, 1796, SC Arch; Petition of Elizabeth Ronaldson, 13 Jan. 1783, in Candler, ed., *Revolutionary Records of the State of Georgia*, 3:216, 465. For the rhetorical distinction between "ladies" and "citizens," see, for instance, *Richmond Enquirer*, 9 July 1811, 11 Jan. 1814, 11 July 1817; *Raleigh Register*, 4 Aug. 1801.

Linda Kerber has emphasized the extent to which the urban character of the French Revolution and the tradition of women's guilds in France encouraged collective action among women. These preconditions for women's collective action were absent in America, especially in the southern colonies. See Kerber, " 'I Have Don . . . Much to Carrey on the Warr': Women and the Shaping of Republican Ideology after the American Revolution," in Harriet B. Applewhite and Darline G. Levy, eds., *Women and Politics in the Age of Democratic Revolution* (Ann Arbor, Mich., 1990), p. 229.

[75] [Columbia] *South Carolina Gazette and Columbian Advertiser*, 5 July 1806.

[76] Elizabeth Washington Gamble to Thomas Bayly, 11–12 Mar. 1801, Wirt Family Papers, VHS; *Norfolk Gazette and Publick Ledger*, 5 July 1805, 6 July 1812; *Alexandria Daily Advertiser*, 5 July 1808; *Alexandria Daily Gazette*, 4 July 1811. See also Fletcher M. Green, "Listen to the Eagle Scream: One Hundred Years of the Fourth of July in North Carolina (1776–1876)," *NCHR* 31 (1954): 302–4; David Waldstreicher, *In the Midst of Perpetual Fetes: The Making of American Nationalism, 1776–1820* (Chapel Hill, N.C., 1997), chaps. 2–4.

[77] For detailed descriptions of representative southern Fourth of July parades, see *Virginia Argus*, 6 July 1810; *Richmond Enquirer*, 11 Jan. 1814; *Camden* (S.C.) *Gazette*, 17 June 1819. On the uniforms of regular and elite volunteer companies, see Kenneth Roberts and Anna A. Roberts, eds., *Moreau de St. Mery's American Journey, 1793–1798* (Garden City, N.Y., 1947), pp. 57–58; John Hope Franklin, *The Militant South, 1800–1861* (Cambridge, Mass., 1956), pp. 176, 188–89; Harriet A. Jacobs, *Incidents in the Life of a Slave Girl, Written by Herself*, ed. Jean Fagen Yellin (Cambridge, Mass., 1987), p. 63; Michael Stauffer, "Volunteer or Uniformed Companies in the Antebellum Militia: A Checklist of Identified Companies, 1790–1859," *SCHM* 88 (1987): 108–16.

Committees of local gentlemen composed the toasts and chose prominent men to deliver them publicly. Most of the men who delivered toasts or speeches used titles — such as "Esq.," "Dr.," or Col." — that denoted high social status. See, for instance, the lists of men who gave toasts in Smithfield, N.C., and Goochland County, Va., in 1804 and 1809, respectively (*Raleigh Register*, 16 July 1804; *Richmond Enquirer*, 7 July 1809).

[78] On the role of race in the development of the military institutions of white southerners during this period, see Franklin, *Militant South*, pp. 66–73; Egerton, *Gabriel's Rebellion*, pp. 74–78. For northern comparisons, see Susan G. Davis, *Parades and Power: Street Theater in Nineteenth-Century Philadelphia* (Philadelphia, 1986), chap. 3; Mary P. Ryan, *Women in Public: Between Banners and Ballot, 1825–1880* (Baltimore, 1990), pp. 22–31; Sean Wilentz, *Chants Democratic: New York City and the Rise of the American Working Class, 1788–1850* (New York, 1984), pp. 36–46; Waldstreicher, *In the Midst of Perpetual Fetes*, pp. 231–45, 302–28.

[79] *Richmond Enquirer*, 3 July 1812; *Raleigh Register*, 10 July 1812.

[80] [Winchester, Va.] *Republican Constellation*, 6 July 1814; *Virginia Argus*, 7 July 1804; *Raleigh Register*, 10 July 1812; *Richmond Enquirer*, 14 July 1818.

[81] For explicit acknowledgment of these didactic objectives, see *Virginia Argus*, 5 July 1808, 14 July 1809, 6 July 1810; *Richmond Compiler*, 5 July 1813.

[82] *Richmond Enquirer*, 8 July 1808, 11 Jan. 1814, 29 Oct. 1824; *Richmond Compiler*, 6 July 1814.

[83] *Richmond Enquirer*, 7 July 1809, 6 July 1813; *Raleigh Register*, 29 July 1805; *Charleston City Gazette*, 7 July 1808.

[84] Lynn Hunt, *Politics, Culture, and Class in the French Revolution* (Berkeley, Calif., 1984), pp. 64–73; Joan B. Landes, *Women and the Public Sphere in the Age of the French Revolution* (Ithaca, N.Y., 1986), pp. 159–66; Ryan, *Women in Public*, pp. 24–29; *Richmond Enquirer*, 9 July 1811, 26 Oct. 1824; Robert D. Ward, *An Account of General La Fayette's Visit to Virginia, in the Years 1824–'25 . . .* (Richmond, Va., 1881), p. 38.

[85] [Columbia] *South Carolina Gazette and Columbian Advertiser*, 15 Nov. 1806; *Richmond Enquirer*, 26 Feb., 16 June 1808.

[86] *Virginia Argus*, 20 June 1808; *Richmond Enquirer*, 17 June 1808, 3 Feb. 1814; *Raleigh Register*, 10 Apr. 1810; *Charleston City Gazette*, 21 Feb., 4, 28 July 1808.

[87] Anne Carmichael Coalter to Frances Coalter, 5 Mar. 1808, and Frances Coalter to John Coalter, 11 Apr. 1809, Brown, Coalter, Tucker Papers, CWM; Harriott Lucas Huger to Mary E. Huger, 13 May 1811, Huger Family Papers, USC; Ann Cocke to Ann Barraud, 20 Oct. 1811, John Hartwell Cocke Papers, UVa; Jane Cary Randolph to Mary Randolph Harrison, 11 Nov. 1813, Harrison Family Papers, VHS; Ellen Wayles Randolph to Thomas Jefferson, 26 Feb. 1808, in Edward M. Betts and James Adam Bear, eds., *The Family Letters of Thomas Jefferson* (Columbia, Mo., 1966), p. 330; Elizabeth Manigault Izard to Alice DeLancey Izard, 19 July 1812, Cheves-Middleton Papers, SCHS; *Raleigh Register,* 29 Mar. 1810.

[88] John Early Diary, 15 Aug. 1807, SHC, UNC-CH; *Charleston City Gazette,* 11 Aug. 1808.

[89] *Richmond Enquirer,* 8 July 1808, 12 July 1808; *Charleston City Gazette,* 19 July 1808.

[90] *Wilmington Gazette,* 21 July 1807; *Charleston City Gazette,* 15 July, 9 Aug. 1808; *Richmond Enquirer,* 7 July, 13 Oct. 1812; *Raleigh Register,* 11 Nov. 1814; *Alexandria Daily Adviser,* 6 July 1808.

[91] *Charleston City Gazette,* 15 July 1808, 5 July 1810.

[92] *Richmond Compiler,* 5 July 1813; *Richmond Enquirer,* 5 Jan. 1811, 13 July 1816; *Camden* (S.C.) *Gazette,* 11 July 1816.

[93] *Raleigh Register,* 9 Oct. 1812. On the idealization of the virtuous yeoman, see McCoy, *Elusive Republic,* pp. 13–16, 49–70, 77–85.

[94] A seemingly unique exception was an 1818 Fredericksburg, Virginia, toast that praised the "fair patriots who persist in our infant Manufactures" (*Richmond Enquirer,* 14 July 1818).

5. Domesticity

[1] *Southern Literary Register* 1 (1820): 256.

[2] See the important discussions in Ruth H. Bloch, "American Feminine Ideals in Transition: The Rise of the Moral Mother," *Feminist Studies* 4 (1978): 101–26, and Bloch, "The Gendered Meanings of Virtue in Revolutionary America," *Signs* 13 (1987): 37–58.

[3] For a cogent critique of the concept of "separate spheres" both as a descriptive metaphor for gender relations among nineteenth-century Americans and as a historiographical construct employed by twentieth-century historians, see Linda K. Kerber, "Separate Spheres, Female Worlds, Woman's Place: The Rhetoric of Women's History," *JAH* 75 (1988): 9–39.

[4] Catherine Clinton, "Equally Their Due: The Education of the Planter Daughter in the Early Republic," *JER* 2 (1982): 39–60; Donald G. Mathews, *Religion in the Old South* (Chicago, 1977), pp. 119–20.

[5] John B. Boles, *The Great Revival, 1787–1805* (Lexington, Ky., 1972), esp. chaps. 1–2, 4–6; Mathews, *Religion in the Old South,* pp. 46–52, 129–31; Jan Lewis, *The Pursuit of Happiness: Family and Values in Jefferson's Virginia* (Cambridge, 1983), pp. 51–68;

260 Richard Rankin, *Ambivalent Churchmen and Evangelical Churchwomen: The Religion of the Episcopal Elite in North Carolina, 1800–1860* (Columbia, S.C., 1993), pp. 28–66.

[6] Mathews, *Religion in the Old South*, pp. xvi–xviii, 11–20; Boles, *Great Revival*, chap. 3; Rhys Isaac, *The Transformation of Virginia, 1740–1790* (Chapel Hill, N.C., 1982), pp. 167–70, 262–64.

[7] Sylvia R. Frey, *Water from the Rock: Black Resistance in a Revolutionary Age* (Princeton, N.J., 1991), chap. 8; Mathews, *Religion in the Old South*, pp. 51–52, 66–80, 85–86, 136–84; Boles, *Great Revival*, chap. 11; Mechal Sobel, *The World They Made Together: Black and White Values in Eighteenth-Century Virginia* (Princeton, N. J., 1987), chap. 15; Rachel N. Klein, *Unification of a Slave State: The Rise of the Planter Class in the South Carolina Backcountry, 1760–1808* (Chapel Hill, N.C., 1990), pp. 272–94; Richard R. Beeman, *The Evolution of the South Backcountry: A Case Study of Lunenberg County, Virginia, 1746–1832* (Philadelphia, 1984), 198–200; Anne C. Loveland, *Southern Evangelicals and the Social Order, 1800–1860* (Baton Rouge, La., 1980), pp. 24–26, 72, 186–218; Jean E. Friedman, *The Enclosed Garden: Women and Community in the Evangelical South, 1830–1900* (Chapel Hill, N.C., 1985), 9–15.

Stephanie McCurry argues that southern evangelicals upheld the authority of white men from the very beginning. See her *Masters of Small Worlds: Yeoman Households, Gender Relations, and the Political Culture of the Antebellum South Carolina Low Country* (New York, 1995), pp. 138–47. For a suggestive account of the "defeminization" of New England's Baptist churches during this period, see Susan Juster, *Disorderly Women: Sexual Politics and Evangelicalism in Revolutionary New England* (Ithaca, N.Y., 1994), chap. 4.

[8] Lewis, *Pursuit of Happiness*, pp. 48–54, 219–23; Jane Turner Censer, *North Carolina Planters and Their Children, 1800–1860* (Baton Rouge, La., 1984), pp. 5–6; Klein, *Unification of a Slave State*, pp. 276–82, 293–302.

For an extreme case of one great planter who responded to the revolutionary challenge by becoming a Baptist mystic and freeing some 500 slaves, see Shomer S. Zwelling, "Robert Carter's Journey: From Colonial Patriarch to New Nation Mystic," *American Quarterly* 68 (1986): 613–36.

[9] Elmer T. Clark et al., eds., *The Journal and Letters of Francis Asbury, 1775–1816*, 3 vols. (Nashville, Tenn., 1958), 1:488, 532, 643, 2:41, 263, 285, 721; Anne Newport Royall to Matt, 30 Apr. 1821, 8 June 1822, in *Letters from Alabama, 1817–1822*, ed. Lucille Griffith (University, Ala., 1969), pp. 205–8, 249; Mathews, *Religion in the Old South*, pp. 47–48, 102–3.

A contemporary Scottish visitor to Charleston also described Charleston's men as impious but praised the city's women for their religious "practise and principles" (Raymond A. Mohl, ed., " 'The Grand Fabric of Republicanism': A Scotsman Describes South Carolina, 1810–1811," *SCHM* 71 [1970]: 183).

[10] Clark et al., eds., *Journal and Letters of Francis Asbury*, 1:643, 2:263; William Spencer Diary, 1789–90, VHS; Mathews, *Religion in the Old South*, pp. 102–3.

[11] Joanna Bowen Gillespie, " 'Clear Leadings of Providence': Pious Memoirs

and the Problems of Self-Realization for Women in the Early Nineteenth Century," *JER* 5 (1985): 197–221; Cynthia A. Kierner, "Woman's Piety within Patriarchy: The Religious Life of Martha Hancock Wheat of Bedford County," *VMHB* 100 (1992): 79–98; Juster, *Disorderly Women,* pp. 68–69, 197–208.

¹² Ann Isabella Cleland Kinloch Commonplace Book [ca. 1794], 27 July 1794, SCHS; C. W. Andres, *Memoir of Anne R. Page* (Philadelphia, 1844), pp. 8–17; David Ramsay, *Memoirs of the Life of Martha Laurens Ramsay* (Philadelphia, 1811), p. 211; Joanna Bowen Gillespie, "1795: Martha Laurens Ramsay's Dark Night of the Soul," *WMQ,* 3d ser., 48 (1991): 80–91; "Female Piety," *Southern Literary Register* 1 (1820): 321–22; John Holt Rice, *A Sermon to Young Women* (Richmond, Va., 1819), p. 17.

¹³ Lucy Thornton to Sarah Jacquelin Rootes Cobb, 22 Mar., 15 Dec. 1812, 3 Nov. 1813, 21 Mar., 9 Apr. 1816, Jackson and Prince Family Papers, SHC, UNC-CH.

¹⁴ Mathews, *Religion in the Old South,* pp. 107–8; Klein, *Unification of a Slave State,* pp. 293–300; Loveland, *Southern Evangelicals and the Social Order,* pp. 132–33, Mc-Curry, *Masters of Small Worlds,* pp. 134–36. On the courts' reluctance to punish men who physically abused wives, see Victoria E. Bynum, *Unruly Women: The Politics of Social and Sexual Control in the Old South* (Chapel Hill, N.C., 1992), pp. 70–72, 77.

¹⁵ "A Vision of Female Excellence," *Monthly Review and Literary Miscellany of the United States* 7 (1807): 201–10; *Wilmington Gazette,* 23 May 1809; *Literary Magazine and American Register* 6 (1806): 203; *Sunday Visitant,* 17 Jan. 1818; "Miss More's Essays," in *The Lady's Pocket Library* (Philadelphia, 1792), p. 65; "Female Piety," *Southern Literary Register* 1 (1820): 321–22. On More's popularity among southern women readers, see Catherine Clinton, *The Plantation Mistress: Woman's World in the Old South* (New York, 1982), pp. 125–26; Elizabeth Fox-Genovese, *Within the Plantation Household: Black and White Women of the Old South* (Chapel Hill, N.C., 1988), p. 270; Rice, *Sermon to Young Women,* p. 3; Virginia [Randolph] Cary, *Letters on the Female Character, Addressed to a Young Lady on the Death of Her Mother* (Richmond, Va., 1828), pp. 141–42.

¹⁶ John Bennett, *Letters to a Young Lady, on a Variety of Useful and Interesting Subjects . . . to which is Prefixed Strictures on Female Education,* 2 vols. (Philadelphia, 1793), 2:7–16, 97; "Miss More's Essays," in *Lady's Pocket Library,* pp. 11–13. See also Thomas Gisbourne, *An Inquiry into the Duties of the Female Sex* (London, 1797), pp. 285–95.

¹⁷ "Fashionable Amusements: Fashionable Amusements are Expensive," *Monthly Visitant, or Something Old* 1 (1816): 169–73; "Description of a Party of Pleasure," *Southern Literary Register* 1 (1820): 141; "Of Innocent Amusements," *Christian Monitor* 2 (1817): 378–80; "The Race Week," *Charleston Observer,* 2 Mar. 1833. See also Loveland, *Southern Evangelicals and the Social Order,* pp. 97–102.

¹⁸ Alexander Macauley, "Journal," *WMQ,* 1st ser., 11 (1902–3): 182–83; Isaac Weld, Jr., *Travels through the States of North America, and the Provinces of Upper and Lower Canada, during the Years 1795, 1796, and 1797* (London, 1797), p. 82; Mohl, ed.,

" 'Grand Fabric of Republicanism,' " p. 182. See also the discussion in Bertram Wyatt-Brown, *Southern Honor: Ethics and Behavior in the Old South* (New York, 1982), pp. 90–98, 331–39. Significantly, Wyatt-Brown asserts the continuing importance of sociability among men as part of a masculine ideal of honor.

Some southern elites sought to perpetuate the older, more expansive type of hospitality. See, for instance, Alice DeLancey Izard to Margaret Izard Manigault, 31 Mar. 1811, Manigault Family Papers, SCHS. Cornelia Randolph, granddaughter of Thomas Jefferson, regretted his old-fashioned predilection for inviting strangers to dine with them daily. See Cornelia Randolph to Virginia Randolph, 8 Sept. 1819, Nicholas P. Trist Papers, SHC, UNC-CH.

[19] *Virginia Herald and Fredericksburg Advertiser,* 6 Sept. 1792; Julia Cherry Spruill, *Women's Life and Work in the Southern Colonies* (Chapel Hill, N.C., 1938), p. 107; Steven M. Stowe, *Intimacy and Power in the Old South: Ritual in the Lives of the Planters* (Baltimore, 1987), p. 56; Jane Pease and William H. Pease, *Ladies, Women, and Wenches: Choice and Constraint in Antebellum Charleston and Boston* (Chapel Hill, N.C., 1990), p. 15. See also Frances Trollope, *Domestic Manners of the Americans,* ed. Donald Smalley (1832; Gloucester, Mass., 1974), pp. 156, 299.

[20] Laura B. Rootes to Martha J. Cobb, 3 Dec. 1812, Jackson and Prince Family Papers, SHC, UNC-CH; Harriet Randolph to Jane Hollins Randolph, 10 Jan. [1822], Edgehill-Randolph Papers, UVa; Cornelia Randolph to Virginia Randolph, 14 Dec. 1817, and Cornelia Randolph to Jane Carr Randolph, 28 Jan. 1818, Nicholas P. Trist Papers, SHC, UNC-CH; Rachel Mordecai to Samuel Mordecai, 24 Mar. 1811; Rachel Mordecai to Ellen Mordecai, 4 Dec. 1814; and Ellen Mordecai to Samuel Mordecai, 11 Oct. 1818, all in Mordecai Family Papers, SHC, UNC-CH. The Mordecai sisters visited relatives in both Raleigh and Richmond.

[21] Eleanor Parke Custis Lewis to Elizabeth Bordley Gibson, 1 Mar. 1815, 4 July 1817, 19 Mar. 1832, in Patricia Brady, ed., *George Washington's Beautiful Nelly: The Letters of Eleanor Parke Custis Lewis to Elizabeth Bordley Gibson, 1794–1851* (Columbia, S.C., 1991), pp. 78, 82, 200; Rachel Mordecai Lazarus to Maria Edgeworth, 20 Dec. 1823, 13 Apr. 1828, in Edgar E. MacDonald, ed., *The Education of the Heart: The Correspondence of Rachel Mordecai Lazarus and Maria Edgeworth* (Chapel Hill, N.C., 1977), pp. 44, 168; Ann Blaws Barraud Cocke to Ann Blaws Barraud, 16 Apr. [1807], John Hartwell Cocke Papers, UVa. On the affectionate domestic life of Nancy Cocke and her husband, John, see Lewis, *Pursuit of Happiness,* pp. 82–89, 202–3.

One visitor to Virginia believed that the "planters' ladies" in that state "mixed with no society." See John Bernard, *Retrospectives of America, 1797–1811* (New York, 1887), pp. 149–50. By contrast, an analysis of northern etiquette books finds that after 1820 northern writers assumed that "women would have active and public social lives" and that they promoted "no great sex-differentiation" in social behavior. See Christina Dallett Hemphill, "Manners for Americans: Interaction Ritual and the Social Order" (Ph.D. diss., Brandeis University, 1988), pp. 507–8, 526.

[22] Bennett, *Letters to a Young Lady*, 2:25–28; Gisbourne, *Inquiry into the Duties of the Female Sex*, pp. 37–91; "Columbian Observer, No. 8: Encomium on Modern Manners," *American Museum* 9 (1791): 196.

[23] "On Education," [Charleston] *Columbian Herald*, 19 Aug. 1785; "Art of Dressing and Dancing," *Southern Evangelical Intelligencer*, 21 June 1819.

[24] "Female Learning," *Literary Magazine and American Register* 1 (1804): 245–46; "The Spirit of Female Conversations," ibid. 2 (1804): 187–90; "Equality of the Sexes," *Monthly Magazine and Literary Journal* 2 (1813): 312.

[25] Bennett, *Letters to a Young Lady*, 2:75–78; Gisbourne, *Inquiry into the Duties of the Female Sex*, pp. 37–91; "On the Education of Females," *Charleston Spectator and Ladies Literary Portfolio* 1 (1806): 70–71.

[26] "On the Education of Females," *Charleston Spectator and Ladies Literary Portfolio* 1 (1806): 70–71; Bennett, *Letters to a Young Lady*, 2:75–78. David Ramsay praised his wife, Martha, for teaching their daughters at home. See Ramsay, *Memoirs of the Life of Martha Laurens Ramsay*, p. 31.

[27] [Maria] Edgeworth, *Letters for Literary Ladies* (Georgetown, D.C., 1810), esp. pp. 28–44; Hannah More, *Strictures on the Modern System of Female Education*, in *The Works of Hannah More* (New York, 1838), esp. pp. 363–69, 385–91; James M. Garnett, *Lectures on Female Education: Comprising the First and Second Series of a Course Delivered to Mrs. Garnett's Pupils, at Elm-Wood, Essex County, Virginia*, 3d ed. (Richmond, Va., 1825), pp. 74–76, 79, 255; *Richmond Enquirer*, 17 Sept. 1805; *Raleigh Register*, 7 May 1807; "On the Female Sex," *Raleigh Register*, 18 Dec. 1804; "Female Literature," *Raleigh Register*, 15 May 1819; "Influence of the Female Sex on the Enjoyments of Social Life," *Charleston Spectator and Ladies Literary Repository* 1 (1806): 159; Rice, *Sermon to Young Women*, pp. 6–7.

Such sentiments also justified the founding of southern women's colleges in the antebellum era. See Christie Anne Farnham, *The Education of the Southern Belle: Higher Education and Student Socialization in the Antebellum South* (New York, 1994), esp. pp. 2–3, 77–79.

[28] *Columbia* (S.C.) *Gazette*, 20 June 1794. For contemporary schools offering comparable curricula, see *Virginia Gazette and American Advertiser*, 1 Oct. 1785; *Wilmington Centinel and General Advertiser*, 30 July 1788; *Virginia Herald and Fredericksburg Advertiser*, 8 May 1795.

[29] Raleigh Academy Paper, NCDAH; *Raleigh Register*, 21 Jan. 1805, 24 Jan., 16 June 1811.

[30] *Raleigh Register*, 14 Jan. 1805, 24 Jan. 1811; [Richmond] *Virginia Argus*, 19 Feb. 1808; *Richmond Enquirer*, 19 Apr. 1808, 22 Oct. 1813, 4 Jan., 25 Jan. 1817.

[31] Lucy Leinbach Wenhold, "The Salem Boarding School between 1802 and 1822," *NCHR* 27 (1950): 32–45; *Raleigh Register*, 24 July 1818; Mary Moore Stanford to Ann Moore, 4 Aug. 1805, Richard Stanford Papers, SHC, UNC-CH; William Polk to Mary Brown Polk, 25 July 1823, Polk, Badger, and McGehee Family Papers,

SHC, UNC-CH. For a comparable but somewhat older Moravian academy in Bethlehem, Pa., see Mary Beth Norton, *Liberty's Daughters: The Revolutionary Experience of American Women, 1750–1800* (Boston, 1980), pp. 283–87.

[32] Garnett, *Lectures on Female Education*, pp. 79–80, 94, 218; *Richmond Enquirer,* 9 Jan. 1813, 14 May, 27 Aug. 1819. The study of Latin probably was not widespread among planters' daughters, but see Clinton, *Plantation Mistress*, pp. 132, 270–71n, for several young women who received a classical education.

[33] Stowe, *Intimacy and Power in the Old South*, pp. 59–67; Jacob Mordecai to Rachel Mordecai, 10 Jan. 1797, Mordecai Family Papers, SHC, UNC-CH; Rachel Mordecai Lazarus to Maria Edgeworth, 25 July 1830, in MacDonald, ed., *Education of the Heart*, p. 198; Anne H. Nicholas to Judith C. Applewhaite, 5 Oct. 1807, and Eliza King to Louisa Maxwell, 12 Jan. 1803, John Hartwell Cocke Papers, UVa; William Polk to Mary Polk, 28 May 1822, Polk, Badger, and McGehee Family Papers, SHC, UNC-CH; Lucy Johnston Ambler to Sally Steptoe Massie, 7 Oct. 1823, in "Letters from Mrs. Lucy Ambler to Mrs. Sally Ambler," *VMHB* 23 (1915): 191.

[34] Thomas Jefferson to Martha Jefferson Randolph, 28 Mar. 1787, 2 Feb. 1791, in Edward M. Betts and James Adam Bear, eds., *The Family Letters of Thomas Jefferson* (Columbia, Mo., 1966), pp. 35, 71; Hore Browse Trist to Mary Brown Trist, [ca. 1802], Nicholas P. Trist Papers, SHC, UNC-CH; Peter Lyons to Lucy Hopkins, 8 Sept. 1805, Peter Lyons Papers, SHC, UNC-CH. See also Thomas E. Buckley, S.J., ed., "The Duties of a Wife: Bishop James Madison to His Daughter, 1811," *VMHB* 9 (1983): 102.

[35] Judith Randolph to Mary Randolph Harrison, 23 Feb. 1800, Harrison Family Papers, VHS; Sarah Spotswood to Mary Goode Spotswood, 3 Dec. [ca. 1800], Spotswood Family Papers, VHS; "The Journal of Elizabeth Ruffin, 1827," in Michael O'Brien, ed., *An Evening When Alone: Four Journals of Single Women in the South, 1827–67* (Charlottesville, Va., 1993), p. 61; Hetty Carr to Dabney S. Carr, 19 Apr. [1817], Carr-Cary Papers, UVa; Eliza Williams Haywood to Jane Williams, 21 Jan. 1808; Jane Williams to Eliza Williams Haywood, 16 May 1808; and Rebecca Williams Moore to Eliza Williams Haywood, 20 Oct. 1811, all in Ernest Haywood Collection, SHC, UNC-CH. See also the discussion of men's and women's plantation work in Stowe, *Intimacy and Power in the Old South*, p. 127.

[36] Mary Pocahontas Campbell to Susannah Hubard, 23 Dec. 1815, Hubard Family Papers, SHC, UNC-CH; Rebecca Tayloe Beverley to Robert Beverley, 2 Aug. 1817, Beverley Family Papers, VHS; "Journal of Elizabeth Ruffin, 1827," pp. 57–58, 62–63; Sarah Alexander to A. L. Alexander, 25 July 1828, Alexander-Hillhouse Papers, SHC-UNC-CH.

[37] Anne Cary Randolph Bankhead to Thomas Jefferson, 26 Nov. 1808, in Betts and Bear, eds., *Family Letters of Thomas Jefferson*, p. 366; Maria Campbell to David Campbell, 4 June 1825, Campbell Family Papers, DU; Eleanor Parke Custis Lewis to Elizabeth Bordley Gibson, 21 June 1826, in Brady, ed., *George Washington's Beautiful Nelly*, p. 179; William K. Bottorff and Roy C. Flannagan, eds., "The Diary of

Frances Baylor Hill of 'Hillsborough,' King and Queen County, Virginia, (1797),"
Early American Literature Newsletter 2 (Winter 1967): 6–53; Rachel Mordecai Lazarus
to Maria Edgeworth, 3 Nov. 1828, in MacDonald, ed., *Education of the Heart*, p. 178.

[38] John Gregory, *A Father's Legacy to His Daughters* (Philadelphia, 1775), pp.
51–52; Bennett, *Letters to a Young Lady*, 1:102–4; Thomas Jefferson to Martha Jefferson, 28 Mar. 1787, in Betts and Bear, eds., *Family Letters of Thomas Jefferson*, p. 35;
Raleigh Register, 7 May 1807; Eleanor Parke Custis Lewis to Elizabeth Bordley Gibson, 7 Oct. 1825, 14 Oct. 1851, in Brady, ed., *George Washington's Beautiful Nelly*, pp.
167, 263; Bottoroff and Flannagan, eds., "Diary of Frances Baylor Hill," passim. See
also Fox-Genovese, *Within the Plantation Household*, pp. 120–28.

[39] *Raleigh Register*, 22 Dec. 1808, 20 Nov. 1818, 31 Dec. 1819; [Columbia] *South
Carolina Gazette and Columbian Advertiser*, 13 Jan. 1813; *Richmond Enquirer*, 27 Sept.
1808, 27 Sept. 1815, 6 Jan. 1818, 26 Jan. 1819; *Camden* (S.C.) *Gazette*, 2 Apr. 1817.

[40] On parental misgivings, see Censer, *North Carolina Planters and Their Children*,
pp. 56–58; Clinton, *Plantation Mistress*, p. 136.

[41] *Richmond Enquirer*, 5 Sept. 1809, 22 Oct. 1813, 21 Dec. 1818; [Charleston] *City
Gazette and Daily Advertiser*, 4 Jan. 1820.

[42] *Richmond Enquirer*, 17 Sept. 1805. The use of familial rhetoric to describe academic environments continued through the antebellum era. See Steven M. Stowe,
"The Not-So-Cloistered Academy: Elite Women's Education and Family Feeling in
the Old South," in Walter J. Fraser, Jr., et al., eds., *The Web of Southern Social Relations: Women, Family, and Education* (Athens, Ga., 1985), pp. 92–94.

[43] *Raleigh Register*, 18 Aug. 1809; Stanley L. Falk, "The Warrenton Female Academy of Jacob Mordecai, 1804–1818," *NCHR* 35 (1958): 285–88. Rachel was the
daughter of Jacob Mordecai and his first wife, Judith Myers.

[44] *Richmond Enquirer*, 19 Sept. 1806; *Raleigh Register*, 22 Dec. 1808; [Charleston]
City Gazette and Daily Advertiser, 4 Jan. 1820.

[45] L. Minerva Turnbull, "Private Schools in Norfolk, 1800–1860," *WMQ*, 2d ser.,
11 (1931): 299–301; Margaret Meagher, *History of Education in Richmond* (Richmond,
Va., 1939), pp. 35–58; Charles L. Coon, *North Carolina Schools and Academies,
1790–1840: A Documentary History* (Raleigh, N.C., 1915); *Pendleton* (S.C.) *Messenger*, 6
Jan., 17 Feb. 1819; Mathews, *Religion in the Old South*, pp. 119–20; Sally G.
McMillen, *Southern Women: Black and White in the Old South* (Arlington Heights, Ill.,
1992), pp. 77–81.

The number of academies in Virginia, North Carolina, and South Carolina increased more than tenfold in the half-century after 1800. By 1850, these three states
had a total of roughly 800 academies, perhaps one-third of which educated girls and
young women. See Edgar W. Knight, *The Academy Movement in the South* (Chapel Hill,
N.C., 1919), esp. pp. 23–24.

[46] John Davis, *Travels of Four Years and a Half in the United States of America; During
1798, 1799, 1800, 1801, and 1802* (London, 1803), pp. 361–71; *Richmond Enquirer*, 8
Jan., 17 Dec. 1807; [Richmond] *Virginia Argus*, 6 Dec. 1799; [Columbia] *South Car-*

olina Gazette and Columbian Advertiser, 31 Jan. 1807; Orville Vernon Burton, *In My Father's House Are Many Mansions: Family and Community in Edgefield, South Carolina* (Chapel Hill, N.C., 1985), pp. 81–82.

⁴⁷ Meagher, *History of Education in Richmond,* pp. 43, 59; Raleigh Academy Paper, NCDAH.

⁴⁸ Rebecca Tayloe Beverley to Robert Beverley, 10 Oct. 1816, 26 Apr. 1817, Beverley Family Papers, VHS; Jane Bradshaw Beverley to Robert Beverley, 3 Mar. 1817, 29 May 1818, 14 Apr. 1821, and [1821], ibid.

⁴⁹ Louisa Lenoir to Elizabeth [?], 1819, Louisa Lenoir Letterbook, Lenoir Family Papers, SHC, UNC-CH; Louisa Lenoir to her mother, 1819, ibid.; Caroline Mordecai, "On the close of the year 1809," Mordecai School Papers, SHC, UNC-CH. See also Rachel Mordecai to Samuel Mordecai, 8 Dec. 1811, Mordecai Family Papers, SHC, UNC-CH; Clinton, *Plantation Mistress,* p. 136; Farnham, *Education of the Southern Belle,* chaps. 6–7. The classic discussion of the significance of such relationships, albeit in northern settings, is Carroll Smith-Rosenberg, "The Female World of Love and Ritual: Relations between Women in Nineteenth-Century America," *Signs* 1 (1975): 1–29.

⁵⁰ Rachel Mordecai to Samuel Mordecai, 1 Jan. 1809, 3 Apr., 3 July 1811, Mordecai Family Papers, SHC, UNC-CH; Rachel Mordecai to Ellen Mordecai, 2 Nov. 1817, ibid.; Falk, "Warrenton Female Academy," pp. 281–86; Thomas R. Rootes to Laura B. Rootes, 20 June 1813, 30 June 1814, 21 Jan., 9 Dec. 1815, Jackson and Prince Family Papers, SHC, UNC-CH.

⁵¹ *Raleigh Register,* 12 Nov. 1819.

⁵² G[ervase] Markham, *The English House-Wife, contain[in]g The inward and outward Vertues which ought to be in a Compleat Woman,* 8th ed. (London, 1675), pp. 1–2; Bennett, *Letters to a Young Lady,* 2:95–96; "Panegyric on the Marriage State," *Columbian Magazine* 1 (1786): 74; Gisbourne, *Inquiry into the Duties of the Female Sex,* pp. 1–8; "Miss More's Essays," in *Lady's Pocket Library,* pp. 5–83; "Parallel of the Sexes," *Monthly Magazine and Literary Journal* 1 (1812): 54.

On the tendency, even in ancient times, to differentiate the sexes and their places in society, see the discussion in Kerber, "Woman's Spheres," pp. 18–19.

⁵³ Fox-Genovese, *Within the Plantation Household,* pp. 61–66, 78–80; McCurry, *Masters of Small Worlds,* pp. viii, 72–85; Clinton, *Plantation Mistress,* pp. 5–12. On the gender ideals of the northern middle class, see, for instance, Nancy F. Cott, *The Bonds of Womanhood: 'Woman's Sphere' in New England, 1780–1835* (New Haven, Conn., 1977), pp. 55–62; Mary P. Ryan, *Cradle of the Middle Class: The Family in Oneida County, New York, 1790–1865* (Cambridge, 1981), esp. pp. 61–65, 146–55, 186–91; Stuart M. Blumin, *The Emergence of the Middle Class: Social Experience in the American City, 1760–1900* (Cambridge, 1989), esp. pp. 179–88.

⁵⁴ For a classic summary of the northern domestic ideal, see Barbara Welter, "The Cult of True Womanhood," *American Quarterly* 18 (1966): 151–74. Nor did the

rhetoric of separate spheres reflect the actual division of labor in many northern households, especially in rural areas. See Nancy Grey Osterud, *Bonds of Community: The Lives of Farm Women in Nineteenth-Century New York* (Ithaca, N.Y., 1991), esp. pp. 1–15; Joan M. Jensen, *Loosening the Bonds: Mid-Atlantic Farm Women, 1750–1850* (New Haven, Conn., 1986), pp. 36–38, 46–48; Ryan, *Cradle of the Middle Class*, pp. 198–218.

55 "Advice to a Young Wife," *Richmond Enquirer,* 19 Sept. 1817; "On the Female Sex," ibid., 18 Dec. 1804; *Charleston Spectator and Ladies Literary Portfolio* 1 (1806): 67. The first quotation, which appeared initially in the colonial press, was an early criticism of sociability that was more attuned to the discourse of the postrevolutionary era (*South Carolina Gazette,* 14 May 1753).

56 "On Love," *South Carolina Weekly Museum* 2 (1797): 229; "Matrimony," *Southern Literary Register* 1 (1820): 241; "Timon; or The Comforts of Marriage," *Raleigh Register,* 17 Mar. 1806; "Old Bachelors," *Camden* (S.C.) *Gazette,* 26 May 1817.

57 See, for instance, "On Matrimony," [Charleston] *Columbian Herald,* 4 Jan. 1785; "Marriage Ceremonies of different Countries compared," *Columbian Magazine* 1(1787): 497; "Has He a Fortune?" *American Museum* 10 (1791): 284; "The Essayist, No. II: Thoughts on Old Maids," *Lady's Magazine* 1 (1792): 60–62; "On Love," *South Carolina Weekly Museum* 2 (1797): 229; "A Short Sermon on Marriage," *Baltimore Weekly Magazine* 1 (1801): 249–50; Gisbourne, *Inquiry into the Duties of the Female Sex,* pp. 235–38; "Matrimony," *Southern Literary Register* 1 (1820): 241; Buckley, ed., "Duties of a Wife," p. 104; Lawrence Stone, *The Family, Sex, and Marriage in England, 1500–1800* (New York, 1977), esp. pp. 270–93; Lewis, *Pursuit of Happiness,* pp. 188–205; Censer, *North Carolina Planters and Their Children,* pp. 65–68, 72–74, 78–80. For a rare prerevolutionary public denunciation of mercenary matches as "downright Prostitution," see *North Carolina Gazette,* 6 Mar. 1752.

58 John Coalter's poems [1790–91], Brown, Coalter, Tucker Papers, CWM; Maria Rind to John Coalter, 3 May, 28 June 1791, ibid.; William Gaston to Eliza Worthington, 30 June, 11 Aug. 1816, Gaston Family Papers, SHC, UNC-CH; Eliza Custis to David Warden, 1 July 1814, quoted in Lewis, *Pursuit of Happiness,* p. 196; Rebecca Tayloe Beverley to Robert Beverley, 8 Mar. 1819, Beverley Family Papers, VHS.

59 "The Maiden's Choice," [Charleston] *Columbian Herald,* 14 Mar. 1785; "The Wedding-Ring," *American Museum* 6 (1789): 87; John Blair to [Mary Blair Braxton Burwell], 3 Oct. 1780, Blair, Banister, Braxton, Horner, Whiting Papers, CWM; M[argaret] D[avenport] to F. Currie, 2 June [1792], Brown, Coalter, Tucker Papers, CWM; Eliza Parke Custis to Elizabeth Bordley, 7 Feb. [1796], in Brady, ed., *George Washington's Beautiful Nelly,* p. 25; [Lucinda Lee Orr], *Journal of a Young Lady of Virginia, 1782,* ed. Emily V. Mason (Baltimore, 1871), p. 28; Lee Virginia Chambers-Schiller, *Liberty, a Better Husband: Single Women in America, the Generations of 1780–1840* (New Haven, Conn., 1984), esp. pp. 14–15.

⁶⁰ "On the Condition of Women," *Richmond Enquirer,* 18 Aug. 1804; "The Maid's Soliloquy," *Camden* (S.C.) *Gazette,* 22 Aug. 1816; "Journal of Elizabeth Ruffin, 1827," p. 67.

⁶¹ [Orr], *Journal of a Young Lady,* p. 28; M[argaret] D[avenport] to F. Currie, 25 May [1794], Brown, Coalter, Tucker Papers, CWM; Eliza Mitchell Waring to Harriet Hyrne Baker, [1785], 28 Apr. 1785, Baker-Grimké Papers, SCHS; Mary E. C. Randolph to Virginia Randolph, 5 Feb. 1820, Nicholas P. Trist Papers, SHC, UNC-CH. See also the discussion in Melinda S. Buza, " 'Pledges of Our Love': Friendship, Love, and Matrimony among the Virginia Gentry, 1800–1825," in Edward L. Ayers and John C. Willis, eds., *The Edge of the South: Life in Nineteenth-Century Virginia* (Charlottesville, Va., 1991), pp. 17–19.

⁶² Maria Rind Coalter to Frances Tucker, [Dec. 1791], Brown, Coalter, Tucker Papers, CWM; Sarah Robinson Rootes Cobb to Laura B. Rootes, 29 Oct. 1812, Jackson and Prince Family Papers, SHC, UNC-CH; Ann Blaws Barraud Cocke to Philip and Ann Blaws Barraud, 1 May 1803, and Ann Blaws Barraud to Ann Blaws Barraud Cocke, [May 1803], John Hartwell Cocke Papers, UVa; Eliza Scott to Margaret Christian Scott Peyton, 12 Dec. 1800, Peyton Family Papers, VHS. For similar sentiments, see also Hariott Lucas Huger to Charles Cotesworth Pinckney, Jr., 10 Aug. 1808, Huger Family Papers, USC; Lucy Johnston Ambler to Sally Steptoe Massie, 18 Apr. 1823, in "Letters from Mrs. Lucy Ambler," p. 189.

⁶³ John Haywood to Eliza Williams Haywood, 26 June 1798, 9 Mar. 1799, 24 Oct., 7 Dec. 1801, Ernest Haywood Collection, SHC, UNC-CH; Jane Williams to Eliza Williams Haywood, 16 Aug., 5 Nov. 1798, 28 May 1799, 16 May 1808, 25 Aug. 1816, ibid.; Eliza Williams Haywood to Jane Williams, 18 Mar. 1802, ibid.; Rebecca Williams Moore to Jane Williams, 20 Sept., 30 Sept. 1812, ibid.

⁶⁴ Jack P. Greene, ed., *The Diary of Landon Carter of Sabine Hall, 1752–1758,* 2 vols. (Charlottesville, Va., 1965), 2:830, 849; McMillen, *Southern Women,* pp. 42–45. On married women's property laws, see also Norma Basch, "Equity vs. Equality: Emerging Concepts of Women's Political Status in Jacksonian America," *JER* 3 (1983): 297–318, and Suzanne D. Lebsock, "Radical Reconstruction and the Property Rights of Southern Women," *JSH* 43 (1977): 196–207.

⁶⁵ Bequests of Elizabeth B. Elliott, 5 Feb. 1768, 4 Jan. 1769, Baker-Grimké Papers, SCHS; Will of Sarah Baugh, 15 June 1792, Short Family Papers, VHS; Will of Elizabeth Anderson, 7 July 1791, Anderson Family Papers, VHS; Will of Ann Murray, 9 Sept. 1797, Nash Family Papers, VHS; Will of Jane Hunter Charlton, 21 Feb. 1801, Robinson Family Papers, VHS; Suzanne Lebsock, *The Free Women of Petersburg: Status and Culture in a Southern Town, 1784–1860* (New York, 1985), chap. 5.

⁶⁶ Thomas Jefferson to Martha Jefferson Randolph, 4 Apr. 1790, in Betts and Bear, eds., *Family Letters of Thomas Jefferson,* p. 51; Anne Cary Randolph to St. George Tucker, 23 Sept. 1788, Tucker-Coleman Papers, CWM; Martha Jefferson Randolph to Nicholas P. Trist, [Sept. 1818], Nicholas P. Trist Papers, SHC, UNC-CH;

Sarah Hillhouse Gilbert to A. L. Alexander, 15 Mar. 1822, Alexander-Hillhouse Papers, SHC, UNC-CH.

[67] Eleanor Parke Custis Lewis to Elizabeth Bordley, 4 Nov. 1799, in Brady, ed., *George Washington's Beautiful Nelly*, pp. 61–62; Martha Jefferson Randolph to Thomas Jefferson, 31 Mar. 1797, in Betts and Bear, eds., *Family Letters of Thomas Jefferson*, p. 143; Martha Jefferson Randolph to Virginia Randolph, 14 Nov. 1814, 23 Apr. 1819, Nicholas P. Trist Papers, SHC, UNC-CH; Ann Barraud to Ann Blaws Barraud, 18 Oct. 1801, John Hartwell Cocke Papers, UVa; Sarah Tayloe Washington, notes, 1811–26, Louise Anderson Patten Papers, VHS; Jane Williams to Eliza Williams Haywood, 11 Dec. 1811, Ernest Haywood Collection, SHC, UNC-CH; Martha Laurens Ramsay to David Ramsay, Jr., 14 May 1810, in Ramsay, *Memoirs of the Life of Martha Laurens Ramsay*, p. 282.

For more extensive evidence of love and companionship in marriage and women's joy in motherhood during this period, see, for instance, Lewis, *Pursuit of Happiness*, chap. 5; Censer, *North Carolina Planters and Their Children*, pp. 34–41, 96–97; Sally G. McMillen, *Motherhood in the Old South: Pregnancy, Childbirth, and Infant Rearing* (Baton Rouge, La., 1990), pp. 119–22, 169–70, 187; Buza, " 'Pledges of Our Love,' " pp. 20–30.

[68] [Charleston] *Columbian Herald*, 14 Nov. 1785.

[69] Cott, *Bonds of Womanhood*, pp. 60–74; Jeanne Boydston, *Home and Work: Housework, Wages, and the Ideology of Labor in the Early Republic* (New York, 1990), chap. 7.

[70] The nature of the antebellum southern economy remains hotly contested. Scholars such as Robert W. Fogel and Stanley L. Engerman, James Oakes, and Laurence Shore stress the modernity of southern planters in their attempts to maximize profits. Others, most notably Eugene D. Genovese and Elizabeth Fox-Genovese, emphasize the premodern paternalistic relationship between master and slave, a characterization that is less persuasive for the relations between planters and poor whites during this period. See Genovese, *The Political Economy of Slavery: Studies in the Economy and Society of the Slave South* (New York, 1965), pp. 13–36; Fox-Genovese, *Within the Plantation Household*, esp. pp. 53–66; Fogel and Engerman, *Time on the Cross: The Economics of American Negro Slavery* (Boston, 1974), pp. 406, 467–78; Oakes, *The Ruling Race: A History of American Slaveholders* (New York, 1982), esp. pp. xi–xiii, 127–30; Shore, *Southern Capitalists: The Ideological Leadership of an Elite, 1832–1885* (Chapel Hill, N.C., 1986), chap. 1.

[71] *Wilmington Centinel and General Advertiser*, 3 Sept. 1788; "The Happy Man," *North Carolina Gazette*, 15 Nov. 1794; "Happy Fire-Side," *Raleigh Register*, 11 June 1804; "Home," *Raleigh Register*, 3 Mar. 1806; "Wife and Home," *Raleigh Register*, 21 Feb. 1817; "The Wife," *Georgetown* [S.C.] *Gazette*, 7 May 1824.

[72] Hore Browse Trist to Mary Brown Trist, 2 Sept. 1802, Nicholas P. Trist Papers, SHC, UNC-CH; John Marshall to Polly Ambler Marshall, 11 July 1797, 12 Mar. 1826, in "Letters from John Marshall to His Wife," *WMQ*, 2d ser., 3 (1923):

75–76, 87; John Haywood to Eliza Williams Haywood, 21 Jan. 1820, Ernest Haywood Collection, SHC, UNC-CH; Wilson J. Cary to Virginia Randolph Cary, 16 Jan. 1822, Carr-Cary Papers, UVa. See also Karen Lystra, *Searching the Heart: Women, Men, and Romantic Love in Nineteenth-Century America* (New York, 1989), p. 195.

Orville Burton found that the white inhabitants of antebellum Edgefield, S.C., "glorified home and family," but he quotes eight men and one homesick schoolgirl to support this observation (Burton, *In My Father's House*, pp. 104–5).

[73] Harriott Pinckney Horry journal, 1793–94, SCHS; Elizabeth Preston Madison to John Preston, 14 Dec. 1794, Preston Family Papers, VHS; Rachel Mordecai Lazarus to Maria Edgeworth, 18 July 1833, in MacDonald, ed., *Education of the Heart*, p. 248; Jane Cary Randolph to Mary Randolph Harrrison, 1813, Harrison Family Papers, VHS; Frances Tucker Coalter to John Coalter, 6 Oct. 1802, [1808], and Frances Tucker Coalter to Mrs. Davenport, [1808], Brown, Coalter, Tucker Papers, CWM; Sarah Alexander to A. L. Alexander, 30 Mar. 1825, Alexander-Hillhouse Papers, SHC, UNC-CH. On the increasing popularity of spas, especially among women, see Perceval Renier, *The Springs of Virginia: Life, Love, and Death at the Waters, 1775–1900* (Chapel Hill, N.C., 1941), chap. 3; Clinton, *Plantation Mistress*, pp. 148–50.

[74] Willie Lee Rose, "The Domestication of Domestic Slavery," in William W. Freehling, ed., *Slavery and Freedom* (New York, 1982), pp. 18–36; Philip Morgan, "Three Planters and Their Slaves: Perspectives on Slavery in Virginia, South Carolina, and Jamaica, 1750–1790," in Winthrop D. Jordan and Sheila L. Skemp, eds., *Race and Family in the Colonial South* (Jackson, Miss., 1987), pp. 39–40; Mathews, *Religion in the Old South*, chap. 4; Fox-Genovese, *Within the Plantation Household*, pp. 128–45; Clinton, *Plantation Mistress*, pp. 21–23, 27–29.

[75] White women in the mid-eighteenth-century Chesapeake appear to have married in their early twenties. Impressionistic evidence suggests that white southern women were more likely to marry in their teens after 1800, though both Jane Turner Censer and Catherine Clinton found that twenty was the median age of brides among their respective samples of antebellum elites. See Allan Kulikoff, *Tobacco and Slaves: The Development of Southern Cultures in the Chesapeake, 1680–1800* (Chapel Hill, N.C., 1986), pp. 57–61; Daniel Blake Smith, *Inside the Great House: Planter Family Life in Eighteenth-Century Chesapeake Society* (Ithaca, N.Y., 1980), p. 128; Censer, *North Carolina Planters and Their Children*, pp. 91–94; Clinton, *Plantation Mistress*, pp. 60, 233; Burton, *In My Father's House*, pp. 118, 120; Wyatt-Brown, *Southern Honor*, pp. 203–4; Anne Firor Scott, *The Southern Lady: From Pedestal to Politics, 1830–1930* (Chicago, 1970), pp. 23–26.

[76] Thomas Jefferson to Mary Jefferson Eppes, 7 Jan. 1798, in Betts and Bear, eds., *Family Letters of Thomas Jefferson*, p. 152; Thomas Jefferson to Martha Jefferson Randolph, 5 Jan. 1808, ibid., 319–20; Rice, *Sermon to Young Women*, p. 10; Buckley, ed., "Duties of a Wife," p. 104; Mary Randolph, *The Virginia House-Wife* (1824; Co-

lumbia, S.C., 1984), pp. ix–xi; [Maria Elizabeth Rundell], *A New System of Domestic Cookery, Formed upon Principles of Economy and Adapted to the Use of Private Families* (Philadelphia, 1807), pp. i–iii, and *The American Domestic Cookery, Formed on Principles of Economy, for the Use of Private Families* (Baltimore, 1819), pp. 9–12.

Rundell was English, but her books went through at least thirty-seven American editions, "effectively replacing all eighteenth-century cookbooks" in the South and elsewhere. See Karen Hess, Introduction to Randolph, *Virginia House-Wife*, p. xx.

[77] Martha Jefferson Randolph to Thomas Jefferson, 16 Jan. 1791, in Betts and Bear, eds., *Family Letters of Thomas Jefferson*, p. 68; Ann Blaws Barraud Cocke to John Hartwell Cocke, 14 May [1805?], John Hartwell Cocke Papers, UVa.

[78] Richard L. Bushman and Claudia L. Bushman, "The Early History of Cleanliness in America," *JAH* 74 (1988): 1214–25; "On Cleanliness," *Raleigh Register,* 27 Jan. 1801; Buckley, ed., "Duties of a Wife," p. 104; *Southern Literary Register* 1 (1820): 179. One South Carolinian, however, ridiculed women who cleaned obsessively, suggesting that excessive cleaning was "a general inconvenience to business and health." See "On Cleaning," *South Carolina Weekly Magazine* 2 (1797): 329–30.

[79] Diary of Ann Isabella Cleland Kinloch, 1799, SCHS.

[80] On sewing and knitting, see Bottoroff and Flannagan, eds., "Diary of Frances Baylor Hill," passim; Lucy Johnston Ambler to Sally Steptoe Massie, 3 Aug. 1823, in "Letters from Mrs. Lucy Ambler," pp. 188–89; Mary Burnet Brown Claiborne to Herbert Augustine Claiborne, 6 May 1804, Claiborne Family Papers, VHS; Ann Blaws Barraud Cocke to Philip and Ann Blaws Barraud, 2 Mar. 1803, John Hartwell Cocke Papers, UVa; A[nne] C[ary] B[ankhead] to [Martha Jefferson Randolph], 2 Feb. 1810, and Cornelia Randolph to Virginia Randolph, 7 Nov. 1814, Nicholas P. Trist Papers, SHC, UNC-CH; Fox-Genovese, *Within the Plantation Household*, pp. 120–28.

Catherine Clinton argues persuasively that plantation mistresses worked hard within their households, but her assertion that such women were the "slaves of slaves" is an obvious overstatement. See Clinton, *Plantation Mistress*, pp. 16–35, for a suggestive overview of the domestic chores performed by elite rural women.

[81] "Domestic Economy," *Raleigh Register,* 4 June 1819; Lucy Johnston Ambler to Sally Steptoe Massie, 18 Apr. 1823, in "Letters from Mrs. Lucy Ambler," pp. 190–91; Peggy Nicholas to Jane Hollins Randolph, [1819], Edgehill-Randolph Papers, UVa; John Hartwell Cocke to Ann Blaws Barraud Cocke, 13 Jan. 1804, John Hartwell Cocke Papers, UVa; Mrs. F. A. Stevenson to Sarah Woodville, 8 Feb. 1795, William Samuel Slack Collection, SHC, UNC-CH.

[82] [Anne Ritson], *A Poetical Picture of America, Being Observations Made during a residence of Several Years at Alexandria, and Norfolk, in Virginia* (London, 1809), pp. 105–8, 163; John Coalter to Margaret Davenport Coalter, 29 Mar. 1795, Brown, Coalter, Tucker Papers, CWM. On soapmaking and candlemaking, see also Frances Tucker Coalter to John Coalter, 9 Mar. 1804, Brown, Coalter, Tucker Papers, CWM; Peggy

Nicholas to Margaret Nicholas, 28 Dec. 1821, Edgehill-Randolph Papers, UVa; Virginia Campbell to Catherine Campbell, 18 Mar. 1832, Campbell Family Papers, DU.

[83] *Sixth Census . . . of the Inhabitants of the United States of America* (Washington, D.C., 1841), pp. 206, 220; *Statistics of the United States of America, . . . as Collected and Returned by . . . the Sixth Census* (Washington, D.C., 1841), pp. 232, 244.

See also W[ilson] J. Cary to Virginia Randolph Cary, [December 1821], Carr-Cary Papers, UVa; Eleanor Hall Douglas to Mary Hall, 15 Feb. 1819, 8 Jan. 1820 [ca. 1821], Eleanor Hall Douglas Papers, DU; Jane Cary Randolph to Mary Harrison, 11 Nov. 1813, Harrison Family Papers, VHS; Ann Blaws Barruad Cocke to Ann Blaws Barraud, 20 Oct. 1811, John Hartwell Cocke Papers, UVa; Hariott Lucas Huger to Mary E. Huger, Huger Family Papers, USC; Frances S. Scott to Elizabeth Whiting, 22 Feb. [ca. 1810], Blair, Banister, Braxton, Horner, Whiting Papers, CWM; Alice DeLancey Izard to Ralph Izard, 8 Jan., 16 Feb. 1795, Ralph Izard Papers, USC; Indenture between Edward and Sarah Coleman and Mary Murfey, 1787, Holladay Family Papers, VHS; "Home Manufactures in Virginia in 1791," *WMQ*, 2d ser., 2 (1922): 139–48.

[84] Slave accounts of Peggy Nicholas, 12 Jan.–30 Sept. 1821, Edgehill-Randolph Papers, UVa.

[85] McCurry, *Masters of Small Worlds*, pp. 72–78; Henry Izard to Margaret Izard Manigault, 26 Apr. 1813, Manigault Family Papers, USC; Cornelia Randolph to Virginia Randolph, 1 Dec. 1820, Nicholas P. Trist Papers, SHC, UNC-CH.

[86] McMillen, *Motherhood in the Old South*, pp. 31–33, 107; Censer, *North Carolina Planters and Their Children*, pp. 24–25; McCurry, *Masters of Small Worlds*, pp. 59–60. For a different view, see Jan Lewis and Kenneth A. Lockridge, " 'Sally Has Been Sick': Pregnancy and Family Limitation among Virginia Gentry Women, 1780–1830," *Journal of Social History* 22 (1988): 5–19.

[87] Colonial southerners solicited wetnurses in their local papers, a practice that was uncommon by 1800. See, for instance, *South Carolina Gazette* 24 Mar. 1759, 23 Feb. 1760, 14 Sept. 1762, 17 Mar., 10 Dec. 1764, 7 Jan., 25 May, 19 Oct. 1765, 14 July 1766, 23 Mar., 2 Nov. 1767, 2 Mar. 1769, 10 May 1770, 7 May, 6 Aug. 1772, 31 Jan., 20 June, 17 Oct. 1774, 20 Feb., 10 Apr. 1775; *South Carolina Gazette and Country Journal,* 2 May 1769, 24 Apr. 1770, 23 June 1772; *Virginia Gazette,* (Purdie and Dixon), 25 Feb. 1773; *Virginia Gazette* (Dixon and Hunter), 23 Dec. 1775; *Virginia Gazette* (Purdie), 18 Apr. 1777.

Philip Fithian believed that wealthy Virginians often employed black wetnurses, a practice Eliza Lucas Pinckney also found common in colonial South Carolina. See Harriott Horry Ravenel, *Eliza Pinckney* (New York, 1896), pp. 151–52; Hunter Dickinson Farish, ed., *Journal and Letters of Philip Vickers Fithian, 1773–1774: A Plantation Tutor of the Old Dominion* (Williamsburg, Va., 1943), p. 39. Lewis and Lockridge suggest that some colonial women relied on breast-feeding to limit fertility ("Sally Has Been Sick," pp. 9–10).

[88] Hugh Smith, *Letters to Married Women, on the Nursing and Management of Children* (Philadelphia, 1792), pp. vii–x, 50–55; Gisbourne, *Inquiry into the Duties of the Female Sex*, p. 363; [Elisha Cullen] Dick, *Doctor Dick's Instructions for the Nursing and Management of Lying-In Women: with Some Remarks Concerning the Treatment of New-Born Infants* (Alexandria, Va., 1798), p. 15; *The London Practice of Midwifery; To which are added, Instructions for the Treatment of Lying-In Women, and the Principal Diseases of Children* (New York, 1820), pp. 267–68; Ramsay, *Memoirs of the Life of Martha Laurens Ramsay*, p. 29; "A tribute of Sensibility from Frances, to Georgiana Christiana, on seeing her Suckle her Child," *Wilmington Centinel and General Advertiser*, 10 Sept. 1788; "Addressed to the Ladies, on Maternal Duty," *American Museum* 8 (1790): app. 1, p. 34; "A Picture of Cunnubial Felicity," *South Carolina Weekly Magazine* 2 (1797): 727; "A Mother's Address to the Infant at Her Bosom," *Raleigh Register*, 16 June 1816.

Although practice did not necessarily reflect prescription, nineteenth-century women were far more likely than their predecessors to discuss both the joys and difficulties of breast-feeding in their private writing. For evidence of widespread breast-feeding, see McMillen, *Motherhood in the Old South*, chap. 5; Censer, *North Carolina Planters and Their Children*, pp. 34–36; Lewis and Lockridge, "Sally Has Been Sick," pp. 9–10.

[89] Diary of Ann Isabella Cleland Kinloch, 1799, SCHS; Caroline Eliza Burgwin Clitherall Journals, 5:52–53, SHC, UNC-CH.

[90] Mary Dandridge Spotswood Campbell to John Spotswood, ca. 1790, Spotswood Family Papers, VHS; List of Negroes . . . according to the division [of the estate of Mary Dandridge Spotswood Campbell], ca. 1795, ibid.; Eliza Williams Haywood to Jane Williams, 20 Dec. 1803, Ernest Haywood Collection, SHC, UNC-CH; Judith Randolph to Frances Tucker Coalter, 1804, Brown, Coalter, Tucker Papers, CWM; Will of Susanna Harrison Hoxton, 24 Mar. 1808, Reid W. Leigh Papers, VHS; Lebsock, *Free Women of Petersburg*, pp. 137–38.

For a survey of white women's frequent complaints about their slave domestics, see Scott, *Southern Lady*, pp. 46–54.

[91] Eliza Williams Haywood to Jane Williams, 20 Dec. 1803, Ernest Haywood Collection, SHC, UNC-CH; M. Elizabeth Randolph Eppes to Jane Hollins Randolph, 18 June 1824, Edgehill-Randolph Papers, UVa.

[92] Martha Jefferson Randolph to Thomas Jefferson, 12 July 1803, in Betts and Bear, eds., *Family Letters of Thomas Jefferson*, p. 247; A[nne] H. Nicholas to Ann Blaws Barraud Cocke, 10 Sept. 1804, John Hartwell Cocke Papers, UVa; Eliza Williams Haywood to Jane Williams, 20 Jan. 1813, Ernest Haywood Collection, SHC, UNC-CH; M[ary] H[arrison] to Virginia Randolph Cary, 15 Mar. 1818, Carr-Cary Papers, UVa. On medical care generally, see McMillen, *Motherhood in the Old South*, chap. 6.

[93] Lucy Armistead to Maria Carter Armistead, 10 Feb. 1788, Armistead-Cocke Papers, CWM; Hetty Carr to Dabney S. Carr, 21 Dec. [1817], Carr-Cary Papers, UVa.

[94] Anne H. Nicholas to Judith C. Applewhaite, 5 Oct. 1807, John Hartwell Cocke Papers, UVa; Eleanor Parke Custis Lewis to Elizabeth Bordley Gibson, 1 Mar. 1815, 7 Oct. 1825, 5 Dec. 1833, in Brady, ed., *George Washington's Beautiful Nelly*, pp. 78, 167, 212.

[95] Martha Jefferson Randolph to Virginia Randolph, 24 Sept. 1817, Nicholas P. Trist Papers, SHC, UNC-CH; Mary Burnet Browne Claiborne to Herbert Augustine Claiborne, [1804], Claiborne Family Papers, VHS. Guests arrived frequently at Monticello. See Merrill D. Peterson, ed., *Visitors to Monticello* (New York, 1989), pp. 3–4.

[96] Lucy Thornton to Martha Robinson Rootes, 15 Nov. 1799, Jackson and Prince Family Papers, SHC, UNC-CH; Judith Randolph to Mary Randolph Harrison, 5 June 1794, 17 Sept. 1796, 23 Feb., 25 Oct. 1800, 24 Nov. 1805, Harrison Family Papers, VHS; Judith Randolph to St. George Tucker, 5 Nov. 1797, Tucker-Coleman Papers, CWM; Judith Randolph to Frances Tucker Coalter, 8 Dec. 1805, Brown, Coalter, Tucker Papers, CWM; Ann Cleve Armistead to Jane Armistead, 6 Feb. 1793, Armistead-Cocke Papers, CWM. See also the discussion in Lewis, *Pursuit of Happiness*, pp. 224–28.

[97] Laurel Thatcher Ulrich, " 'A Friendly Neighbor': Social Dimensions of Work in Northern Colonial New England," *Feminist Studies* 6 (1980): 392–405; Norton, *Liberty's Daughters*, pp. 17–20; Jensen, *Loosening the Bonds*, pp. 36–37, 44–45; Osterud, *Bonds of Community*, chap. 8; [Ritson], *Poetical Picture of America*, p. 150; Mrs. F. A. Stevenson to Sarah Woodville, 8 Feb. 1795, William Samuel Slack Collection, SHC, UNC-CH; Alice DeLancey Izard to Margaret Izard Manigault, 1 June 1813, Ralph Izard Papers, USC.

When Harriet Martineau visited the United States in the 1830s, she also found that husbands, rather than wives, "usually charge themselves with the business of marketing." See Martineau, *Society in America*, ed. Seymour Martin Lipset (Gloucester, Mass., 1968), p. 302.

6. Women's Spheres

[1] *Richmond Enquirer*, 2 May 1820.

[2] *Memorial Home for Girls, Formerly Female Humane Society, 1805–1925* (Richmond, Va., 1925), pp. 7–8, 27–31. Some northern obituaries also ignored women's public activities during this period. See Joanna Bowen Gillespie, " 'Clear Leadings of Providence': Pious Memoirs and the Problems of Self-Realization for Women in the Early Nineteenth Century," *JER* 5 (1985): 216.

[3] The pertinent texts are M[ary] Randolph, *The Virginia House-Wife: Method is the Soul of Management* (Washington, D.C., 1824 and subsequent editions), and Virginia [Randolph] Cary, *Letters on the Female Character, Addressed to a Young Lady on the Death of Her Mother* (Richmond, Va., 1828), both of which are discussed in detail below.

[4] Elizabeth Fox-Genovese is the most forceful proponent of the view that south-

ern paternalism and proslavery ideology prevented women from entering and influ-encing public life. See her *Within the Plantation Household: Black and White Women of the Old South* (Chapel Hill, N.C., 1988), esp. pp. 29–30, 38–45, 70–81. In fact, some southern women participated in public activities and debates, though they rarely questioned — and most often supported — slavery and white supremacy (ibid., chap. 5; Drew Gilpin Faust, *A Sacred Circle: The Dilemma of the Intellectual in the Old South, 1840–1860* [Baltimore, 1977], pp. 115–16, 183n).

[5] For a different view, which stresses women's lack of moral authority at home, as well as in the schools and churches, see Stephanie McCurry, *Masters of Small Worlds: Yeoman Households, Gender Relations, and the Political Culture of the Antebellum South Carolina Low Country* (New York, 1995), pp. 185–90. On women's lack of for-mal authority in the churches, see also Jean E. Friedman, *The Enclosed Garden: Women and Community in the Evangelical South, 1830–1900* (Chapel Hill, N.C., 1985), pp. 6–20.

Frederick A. Bode has discovered some tantalizing instances in which women voted in Baptist congregations. See his "A Common Sphere: White Evangelicals and Gender in Antebellum Georgia," *GHQ* 79 (1995): 783–84, 800.

[6] On the glorification of motherhood, see Sally G. McMillen, *Motherhood in the Old South: Pregnancy, Childbirth, and Infant Rearing* (Baton Rouge, La., 1990), pp. 3, 170.

[7] "The Mother," *Raleigh Register,* 25 Feb. 1820; "On Maternal Piety," *Charleston Observer,* 26 Apr. 1828; "On the Right Use of Female Influence," *Charleston Gospel Messenger* 4 (1827): 340; "Advice to Christian Mothers . . . ," *Christian Index* 4 (1831): 140–41. Other evangelical writers recognized mothers' special religious influence, while stressing the common responsibility of both parents for their children's spiri-tual upbringing. See Bode, "Common Sphere," 777, 788–89.

[8] John Holt Rice, *A Sermon to Young Women* (Richmond, Va., 1819), p. 13; "Lec-tures of Father Paul," *Raleigh Register,* 10 Oct. 1817; "Female Influence," *Christian Index* 6 (1832): 324.

[9] "On Female Influence," *Columbian Star, and Christian Index* 1 (1829): 67.

[10] C. W. Andrews, *Memoir of Mrs. Anne R. Page* (Philadelphia, 1844), pp. 18, 30, 47–48, 72–80; Mary Moore Stanford to Richard Moore, 25 Jan. 1804, and Mary Moore Stanford to Grizey Moore, 4 June 1804, Richard Stanford Papers, SHC, UNC-CH; Armand John DeRosset to Catherine Fullerton DeRosset, 10 May 1818, DeRosset Family Papers, SHC, UNC-CH; Sarah Hillhouse Gilbert to A. L. Alexan-der, 8 Apr. 1822, and A. L. Alexander to Sarah Alexander, 2 Mar. 1826, Alexander-Hillhouse Papers, SHC, UNC-CH.

[11] *Christian Index* 6 (1832): 311; Frederick A. Bode, "The Formation of Evangel-ical Communities in Middle Georgia: Twiggs County, 1820–1861," *JSH* 60 (1994): 772–23. The median age of conversion for men dropped sharply after 1840, suggest-ing that evangelical parents encouraged piety in both their sons and daughters.

¹² David Ramsay, *Memoirs of the Life of Martha Laurens Ramsay* (Philadelphia, 1811), pp. 31–32, 34; Caroline Eliza Burgwin Clitherall Journals, 5:52–53, SHC, UNC-CH.

¹³ Eliza Williams Haywood to George Washington Haywood, 30 Jan. 1817, Ernest Haywood Collection, SHC, UNC-CH; John Haywood to Thomas B. Haywood, 4 Nov. 1819, ibid.; Anna Maria Deans Garretson to Jonah Garretson, 27 Mar. 1823, Anna Maria Deans Garretson Letters, SHC, UNC-CH; Martha Laurens Ramsay to David Ramsay, Jr., 7 June 1810, in Ramsay, *Memoirs of Martha Laurens Ramsay*, pp. 280–81; Caroline Eliza Burgwin Clitherall Journals, 6:3, SHC, UNC-CH.

¹⁴ Minutes of the Trail Creek [Georgia] Sunday School Society, 1819, pp. 5, 7–13, Jackson and Prince Family Papers, SHC, UNC-CH; "Report of the South Carolina Sunday School Union," *Charleston Observer*, 19 July 1828, 3 July 1830; "Sunday Schools," *Charleston Observer*, 7 Aug. 1830. Statistics collected by the American Sunday School Union, which excluded Episcopalian and Methodist schools, show that the South had 456 schools affiliated with other Protestant denominations. With 105 schools, 1,270 teachers, and 8,264 scholars, Virginia led the region. North Carolina had 61 Sunday schools; South Carolina had 29.

On women's prominence in the northern Sunday school movement, see Anne M. Boylan, "Evangelical Womanhood in the Nineteenth Century: The Role of Women in Sunday Schools," *Feminist Studies* 4 (1978): 62–80; and Boylan, *Sunday School: The History of an American Institution* (New Haven, Conn., 1988), pp. 114–26.

¹⁵ *Christian Monitor* 2 (1817): 372–73; "Sunday Schools," *Raleigh Register*, 24 May 1816; "Sunday School," *Pendleton Messenger*, 4 July 1820; "Report of the South Carolina Sunday School Union," *Charleston Observer*, 19 July 1828, 3 July 1830; "The Sunday School Cause," *Charleston Observer*, 15 June 1833; Richard Rankin, *Ambivalent Churchmen and Evangelical Churchwomen: The Religion of the Episcopal Elite in North Carolina, 1800–1860* (Columbia, S.C., 1993), p. 89; Guion Griffis Johnson, *Antebellum North Carolina: A Social History* (Chapel Hill, N.C., 1937), pp. 419–22.

¹⁶ *Southern Evangelical Intelligencer*, 23 Dec. 1820; Anna Maria Deans Garretson to Isaac Garretson, 29 Feb. [ca. 1820], Anna Maria Deans Garretson Letters, SHC, UNC-CH; Caroline Eliza Burgwin Clitherall Journals, 6:68, SHC, UNC-CH; Orville Vernon Burton, *In My Father's House Are Many Mansions: Family and Community in Edgefield, South Carolina* (Chapel Hill, N.C., 1985), p. 132; Cynthia A. Kierner, "Woman's Piety within Patriarchy: The Religious Life of Martha Wheat of Bedford County," *VMHB* 100 (1992): 96–97.

¹⁷ "On the Right Use of Female Influence," *Charleston Gospel Messenger* 4 (1827): 340; "I Love the Sunday School," ibid. 9 (1832): 147–48; *Southern Evangelical Intelligencer*, 23 Dec. 1820; "What One Lady Can Do," *Christian Index* 8 (1833): 43.

For a subtly different view, see Cary, *Letters on the Female Character*, pp. 71–72, who provides a flattering portrayal of a modest and deferential Sunday school teacher and a telling critique of her more aggressive — and less effective — competitor.

[18] "Eliza's Letters, No. II," *Southern Intelligencer,* 11 May 1822.

[19] "The Sunday School Cause," *Charleston Observer,* 15 June 1833.

[20] Dickson D. Bruce, Jr., *And They All Sang Hallelujah: Plain-Folk Camp-Meeting Religion, 1800–1845* (Knoxville, Tenn., 1974), pp. 76, 86–87; Anne C. Loveland, *Southern Evangelicals and the Social Order, 1800–1860* (Baton Rouge, La., 1980), pp. 77–79. Jean E. Friedman stresses women's powerlessness in the churches, but she does not examine their extracongregational activities (*Enclosed Garden,* pp. 11–18).

[21] Joe L. Kincheloe, Jr., "Transcending Role Restrictions: Women at Camp Meetings and Political Rallies," *Tennessee Historical Quarterly* 40 (1981): 160–63; Loveland, *Southern Evangelicals and the Social Order,* pp. 72–75; Donald G. Mathews, *Religion in the Old South* (Chicago, 1977), pp. 105–6; McCurry, *Masters of Small Worlds,* pp. 149–50.

[22] "Six Days' Meeting at the Baptist Church, High Hills of Santee, S.C.," *Christian Index* 5 (1831): 284; Bode, "Common Sphere," pp. 802–3; Kierner, "Woman's Piety within Patriarchy," pp. 92–93; Kincheloe, "Transcending Role Restrictions," pp. 165–67.

[23] "Eliza's Letters, No. 1," *Southern Intelligencer,* 4 May 1822.

[24] John Dunn to John Woodville, 13 Aug. 1825, William Samuel Slack Collection, SHC, UNC-CH; John Randolph to Betsy Coalter, 25 Dec. 1828, quoted in Catherine Clinton, *The Plantation Mistress: Women's World in the Old South* (New York, 1982), p. 161.

[25] These important distinctions are drawn most clearly in Nancy A. Hewitt, *Women's Activism and Social Change: Rochester, New York, 1822–1872* (Ithaca, N.Y., 1984), and Anne M. Boylan, "Women in Groups: An Analysis of Women's Benevolent Groups in New York and Boston, 1797–1840," *JAH* 71 (1984): 497–523. Victoria E. Bynum found evidence of a more moderate antislavery movement in piedmont North Carolina, where women participated in the short-lived North Carolina Manumission Society, which disbanded by 1835 (*Unruly Women: The Politics of Social and Sexual Control on the Old South* [Chapel Hill, N.C., 1992], pp. 54–55).

For different views of the public activities of antebellum southern women, see McCurry, *Masters of Small Worlds,* pp. 188–90, and Gail S. Murray, "Charity within the Bounds of Race and Class: Female Benevolence in the Old South," *SCHM* 96 (1995): 56–57. McCurry minimizes both the numbers and diversity of women's organizations, while Murray largely ignores evangelicalism and accordingly concludes that the women of the region "never moved into advocacy or reform activities."

[26] "The Ladies Friends, No. III: Thoughts on Benevolence," *Lady's Magazine* 1 (1792): 225; G. J. Barker-Benfield, *The Culture of Sensibility: Sex and Society in Eighteenth-Century Britain* (Chicago, 1992), pp. 228–29.

[27] John Bennett, *Letters to a Young Lady, on a Variety of Useful and Interesting Sub-*

jects . . . to which is Prefixed Strictures on Female Education, 2 vols. (Philadelphia, 1793), 1:65–66; John Gregory, *A Father's Legacy to His Daughters* (1765; Philadelphia, 1775), pp. 20–21; [Maria Eliza Rundell], *A New System of Domestic Cookery, Formed upon Principles of Economy and Adapted to the Use of Private Familes* (Philadelphia, 1807), pp. iv, xii, and [Rundell], *The American Domestic Cookery, formed on Principles of Economy, for the Use of Private Families* (Baltimore, 1819), pp. 13, 236–40; Thomas E. Buckley, S.J., ed., "The Duties of a Wife: Bishop James Madison to His Daughter, 1811," *VMHB* 91 (1983): 104; "Female Influence," *Southern Baptist and General Intelligencer,* 9 Oct. 1835.

On the southern evangelical concept of benevolence, which could apply to men as well as women, see Loveland, *Southern Evangelicals and the Social Order,* pp. 161–62, 167–71, and Bode, "Common Sphere," p. 795.

[28] *Richmond Enquirer,* 26 Feb. 1818, 26 Sept. 1820.

[29] Suzanne Lebsock, *"A Share of Honour": Virginia Women, 1600–1945* (Richmond, Va., 1984), p. 61; Patricia C. Click, *The Spirit of the Times: Amusements in Nineteenth-Century Baltimore, Norfolk, and Richmond* (Charlottesville, Va., 1989), pp. 73–74; Margaret Simons Middleton, "A Sketch of the Ladies' Benevolent Society, Founded 1813," in *Yearbook, 1941: City of Charleston, South Carolina* (Charleston, S.C., 1942), pp. 215–16; Johnson, *Antebellum North Carolina,* p. 163.

[30] Constitution of the Charleston Ladies' Benevolent Society, 1813, in Middleton, "Sketch of the Ladies' Benevolent Society," p. 217; Annual Reports of the Board of Managers, 1824–26, ibid., pp. 224–32; *The Ladies' Benevolent Society, Charleston, South Carolina: Centennial Pamphlet* (Columbia, S.C., 1913), pp. 6, 13–14.

[31] Annual Report of the Board of Managers, Dec. 1825, in Middleton, "Sketch of the Ladies' Benevolent Society," p. 229. Several board reports, as well as a subsequent constitution, make it clear that Charleston's benevolent women did not seek to aid poor men whom they deemed physically able to work. See ibid., pp. 224–26, and *Ladies' Benevolent Society,* pp. 6, 11, 13, 38.

[32] Suzanne Lebsock, *The Free Women of Petersburg: Status and Culture in a Southern Town, 1784–1860* (New York, 1984), pp. 196–211; *Memorial Home for Girls, Formerly Female Humane Society, 1905–1925* (Richmond, Va., 1925), pp. 53–54; Barbara L. Bellows, *Benevolence among Slaveholders: Assisting the Poor in Charleston, 1670–1860* (Baton Rouge, La., 1993), p. 72; *Charleston City Gazette,* 22 Sept. 1814; "The Ladies' Society Charity School," *Southern Evangelical Intelligencer,* 21 June 1819; "Annual Report of the Board of Managers of the Ladies' Benevolent Society," *Southern Evangelical Intelligencer,* 8 Oct. 1820, pp. 244, 246.

[33] *Memorial Home for Girls,* pp. 27–31, 53; *Southern Evangelical Intelligencer,* 4 Sept. 1819; Annual Report of the Board of Managers of the Ladies' Benevolent Society, 15 Sept. 1824, in Middleton, "Sketch of the Ladies' Benevolent Society," p. 226.

[34] See, for instance, Hetty Barnwell Heyward to Mary Barnwell, 18 Sept. 1817, Heyward and Ferguson Family Papers, SHC, UNC-CH. On women's developing business skills, see Lebsock, *Free Women of Petersburg,* pp. 201–25, and Lori D.

Ginzberg, *Women and the Work of Benevolence: Morality, Politics, and Class in the Nineteenth-Century United States* (New Haven, Conn., 1990), pp. 48–53.

[35] Elmer T. Clark et al., eds., *The Journal and Letters of Francis Asbury, 1775–1816*, 3 vols. (Nashville, Tenn., 1958), 2:428; Lebsock, *"A Share of Honour,"* p. 61; *Memorial Home for Girls*, p. 8; "Annual Report of the Board of Managers of the Ladies' Benevolent Society," *Southern Evangelical Intelligencer*, 8 Oct. 1820; "Report of the Female Bible Society of Charleston," *Charleston Observer*, 14 Apr. 1827; Bellows, *Benevolence among Slaveholders*, pp. 40–41.

[36] Click, *Spirit of the Times*, pp. 74–77; Lebsock, *Free Women of Petersburg*, p. 216; Loveland, *Southern Evangelicals and the Social Order*, pp. 167–68; "The Female Bible Society of Charleston," *Southern Evangelical Intelligencer*, 26 June 1819; *Columbian Star, and Christian Index* 2 (1830): 36; Christine Stansell, *City of Women: Sex and Class in New York, 1789–1860* (New York, 1986), pp. 30–36; Hewitt, *Women's Activism and Social Change*, pp. 40–41.

[37] Rankin, *Ambivalent Churchmen and Evangelical Churchwomen*, pp. 47, 139; *Camden Gazette*, 22 Nov. 1817.

[38] *Southern Evangelical Intelligencer*, 1 Jan. 1820.

[39] Ibid., 23 Oct. 1819.

[40] "Eliza's Letters, No. VII," *Southern Intelligencer*, 6 July 1822.

[41] *Raleigh Register*, 27 Mar. 1818. On rural missionary societies, many of which also left scant evidence of their existence, see Fannie E. S. Heck, *In Royal Service: The Mission Work of Southern Baptist Women* (Richmond, Va., 1913), pp. 53–54, 63.

[42] Jane Williams to Eliza Williams Haywood, 13 Oct. 1816; Ann Eliza Gales to Eliza Williams Haywood, 5 Sept. 1817; [?] to Eliza Williams Haywood, 24 Nov. 1818; Abner [?] to Eliza Williams Haywood, 29 Mar. 1819; Rebecca E. Goodwin to Eliza Williams Haywood, 20 Sept. 1820; List of tracts sent by the Religious Tract Society of Philad[elphi]a to the Female Religious Tract Society of Raleigh, 25 Oct. 1825, all in Ernest Haywood Collection, SHC, UNC-CH.

[43] "The Female Bible Society of Charleston," *Southern Evangelical Intelligencer*, 26 June 1819.

[44] *Richmond Enquirer*, 14 Apr. 1818, 12 Mar. 1819. Men, especially those who wrote for the secular press, rarely acknowledged the activities of women's independent associations, though they often praised those of the women's auxiliaries, which had more contact with men's groups and were more deferential toward male authority. On this point, see also Lebsock, *Free Women of Petersburg*, p. 230. For a rare public acknowledgment in the secular press of women's autonomous benevolent activities, see "To the Baltimore Female Humane Society," *Baltimore Weekly Magazine* 1 (1801): 186.

The Charleston Female Bible Society donated a substantial sum to its male counterpart on at least one occasion. See Richard Furman to Mrs. Palmer, 9 Jan. 1818, Richard Furman Papers, Furman University (microfilm).

[45] *Southern Evangelical Intelligencer*, 10 July, 4 Sept. 1819, 8 Apr. 1820; *Columbian*

280 Star, and *Christian Index* 2 (1830): 36; "North Carolina Advancing," *Christian Index* 4
(1831): 371; Bellows, *Benevolence among Slaveholders,* pp. 25–26, 40–42; Johnson, *Antebellum North Carolina,* p. 424. See also "The Female Mite Societies of South Carolina," manuscript, 1950, USC.

⁴⁶ *Southern Evangelical Intelligencer,* 10 July 1819, 10 June 1820; "Charleston
Protestant Episcopal Female Domestic Missionary Society," *Charleston Gospel Messenger* 6 (1829): 273–74. Charleston women did, however, encourage sailors to come
to the special boardinghouses they ran to promote morality and temperance. See
"Annual Report of the Female Seaman's Friend Society," *Charleston Observer,* 14 Apr.
1827, 16 Apr. 1831, 13 Apr. 1833; Bellows, *Benevolence among Slaveholders,* pp. 115–17.

⁴⁷ Loveland, *Southern Evangelicals and the Social Order,* chap. 8; Mathews, *Religion
in the Old South,* chap. 4; Eugene D. Genovese, *Roll, Jordan, Roll: The World the Slaves
Made* (New York, 1972), pp. 50–53, 186–90.

⁴⁸ Johnson, *Antebellum North Carolina,* pp. 410–16, 425; Heck, *In Royal Service,*
pp. 28, 35–36, 362, 372–73; *Charleston Observer,* 27 May 1837. Fifteen of these sixteen
were Baptists; the other was a Presbyterian. On 24 Apr. 1835, the *Charleston Observer*
described another southern Presbyterian, Eleanor MacComber, as a "Missionary
destined for Burmah," but it is unclear whether she ever went there.

⁴⁹ "The Female Bible Society of Charleston," *Southern Evangelical Intelligencer,* 26
June 1819; "Report of the Congregational and Presbyterian Female Association, for
assisting in the Education of Pious Youth for the Gospel Ministry," *Charleston Observer,* 30 June 1827; "Annual Report of the Board of Managers of the Ladies'
Benevolent Society," *Southern Evangelical Intelligencer,* 8 Oct. 1820; Annual Report of
the Board of Managers of the Ladies' Benevolent Society, 15 Sept. 1824, in Middleton, "Sketch of the Ladies' Benevolent Society," p. 225.

⁵⁰ Rebecca E. Goodwin to Eliza Williams Haywood, 20 Sept. 1820, Ernest Haywood Collection, SHC, UNC-CH; Sarah Polk to Mary Brown Polk, 12 Apr. 1824,
Polk, Badger, and McGehee Family Papers, SHC, UNC-CH.

⁵¹ "Eliza's Letters," *Southern Intelligencer,* 4, 11, 18 May, 1 June, 6, 13 July 1822.

⁵² Rice, *Sermon to Young Women,* p. 14; William Polk to Mary Brown Polk, 10 Apr.
1824, Polk, Badger, and McGehee Family Papers, SHC, UNC-CH; "Report of the Female Domestic Missionary Society of Charleston," *Charleston Observer,* 8 Mar. 1828;
Richard Furman to Mrs. Palmer, 9 Jan. 1818, Richard Furman Papers, Furman University (microfilm). On women's fairs, which were common after 1830, see Lebsock,
Free Women of Petersburg, pp. 211, 218–20, and *Charleston Observer,* 2 Mar. 1833.

⁵³ Richard Rankin argues that North Carolina's Episcopal church embraced the
emotional style that appealed to women in order to win back female parishioners
from the more aggressively reformist evangelical congregations. The Episcopal
church also promoted church-affiliated women's associations to replace the evangelical groups, which it regarded as subversive. See Rankin, *Ambivalent Churchmen and
Evangelical Churchwomen,* esp. pp. xi–xii, 52–73, 139–40.

⁵⁴ "Female Influence," *Charleston Observer,* 2 Feb. 1833; Bertram Wyatt-Brown,

Southern Honor: Ethics and Behavior in the Old South (New York, 1982), pp. 278–79;
Loveland, *Southern Evangelicals and the Social Order,* pp. 130–41.

⁵⁵ Loveland, *Southern Evangelicals and the Social Order,* pp. 130–33; Click, *Spirit of the Times,* pp. 77–81; Bellows, *Benevolence among Slaveholders,* p. 115; Johnson, *Antebellum North Carolina,* p. 169.

⁵⁶ Ian R. Tyrell, "Women and Temperance in Antebellum America, 1830–1860," *Civil War History* 28 (1982): 131. Northern church-affiliated temperance groups also appear to have marginalized women members. See Barbara Leslie Epstein, *The Politics of Domesticity: Women, Evangelism, and Temperance in Nineteenth-Century America* (Middletown, Conn., 1981), p. 92.

⁵⁷ "Prince William Temperance Society," *Columbian Star* 1 (1829): 179–80; "Constitution of the Rocky Creek, Ga., Temperance Society," ibid., p. 196; "Temperance," *Columbian Star, and Christian Index* 2 (1830): 195.

⁵⁸ "Prince William Temperance Society," *Columbian Star* 1 (1829): 179–80; "Constitution of the Rocky Creek, Ga., Temperance Society," ibid., p. 196; "Temperance," *Columbian Star, and Christian Index* 2 (1830): 195.

⁵⁹ Loveland, *Southern Evangelicals and the Social Order,* pp. 141–46, 193–206. In her study of piedmont North Carolina, Victoria Bynum found that the 1850s were the pivotal decade in the emergence of hostility to the temperance movement in that region of middling farmers (*Unruly Women,* pp. 54–55).

For an excellent exploration of the linkages between temperance, abolitionist, and feminist activities among northern women after 1840, see Tyrell, "Women and Temperance," pp. 128–52.

⁶⁰ Stephanie McCurry, "The Two Faces of Republicanism: Gender and Proslavery Politics in Antebellum South Carolina," *JAH* 78 (1992): 1249–58; Eugene D. Genovese and Elizabeth Fox-Genovese, "The Religious Ideals of Southern Slave Society," *GHQ* 70 (1986): 7–9, 15–16; Eugene D. Genovese, " 'Our Family, White and Black': Family and Household in the Southern Slaveholders' World," in Carol Bleser, ed., *In Joy and in Sorrow: Women, Family, and Marriage in the Victorian South* (New York, 1991), pp. 69–75.

⁶¹ Quoted in Johnson, *Antebellum North Carolina,* p. 456. Although neither Johnson nor the Reverend James Thomas, whom she quoted, connected the decline of the evangelical temperance movement to the rise of the American Anti-Slavery Society, the coincidence cannot have been accidental. On the Daughters of Temperance, see Bynum, *Unruly Women,* p. 54.

⁶² Lebsock, *Free Women of Petersburg,* p. 229; Click, *Spirit of the Times,* pp. 80–81; Loveland, *Southern Evangelicals and the Social Order,* pp. 149–50; Burton, *In My Father's House,* p. 78; Daniel J. Whitener, Jr., *Prohibition in North Carolina, 1715–1945* (Chapel Hill, N.C., 1945), p. 31; Ruth M. Alexander, " 'We Are Engaged as a Band of Sisters': Class and Domesticity in the Washingtonian Temperance Movement, 1840–1850," *JAH* 75 (1988): 771, 777–78, 780; Tyrell, "Women and Temperance," pp. 136–37.

Members of the governing class also enacted legislation to promote sobriety among African Americans. See Richard C. Wade, *Slavery in the Cities: The South, 1820–1860* (New York, 1964), pp. 153–55; William H. Pease and Jane H. Pease, *The Web of Progress: Private Values and Public Styles in Boston and Charleston, 1828–1843* (New York, 1985), p. 165.

⁶³ Genovese, *Roll, Jordan, Roll*, pp. 70–75; Fox-Genovese, *Within the Plantation Household*, pp. 29–45, 232–35; Clinton, *Plantation Mistress*, pp. 6, 87–89, 204–10.

⁶⁴ Lebsock, *Free Women of Petersburg*, pp. 228–31; Bynum, *Unruly Women*, pp. 52–56. Barbara Bellows similarly suggests that the public influence of Charleston's women's groups declined during this period, but she attributes their downfall to the depression of 1840 and the increasing prevalence of unsympathetic attitudes toward the needy (*Benevolence among Slaveholders*, pp. 166–67).

⁶⁵ Pease and Pease, *Web of Progress*, p. 149; Bode, "Common Sphere," pp. 781–82.

⁶⁶ The classic overview of this stereotype is Anne Firor Scott, *The Southern Lady: From Pedestal to Politics, 1830–1930* (Chicago, 1970), chap. 1.

⁶⁷ W. G. Stanard, "Randolph Family," *WMQ*, 1st ser., 8 (1899–1900): 119–20; Sterling P. Anderson, Jr., " 'Queen Molly' and *The Virginia Housewife*," *Virginia Cavalcade* 20 (1971): 29–35; Margaret Husted, "Mary Randolph's *The Virginia Housewife*: America's First Regional Cookbook," *Virginia Cavalcade* 30 (1980): 76–78; "Randolph, Mary" in Edward T. James et al., eds., *Notable American Women, 1607–1950: A Biographical Dictionary*, 3 vols. (Cambridge, Mass., 1971), 3:117–18.

⁶⁸ Fairfax Harrison, *The Virginia Carys: An Essay in Genealogy* (New York, 1919), pp. 112–13; Jan Lewis, *The Pursuit of Happiness: Family and Values in Jefferson's Virginia* (Cambridge, 1983), pp. 193–94; Virginia Randolph Cary, *Christian Parent's Assistant, or Tales, for the Moral and Religious Instruction of Youth* (Richmond, Va., 1829); [Virginia Randolph Cary], *Ruth Churchill; or, The True Protestant: A Tale for the Times* (New York, 1851).

⁶⁹ Mary Randolph, *The Virginia House-Wife; or, Methodical Cook* (1824; Baltimore, 1839), pp. ix–x. The Preface was reprinted in subsequent editions, which listed the book's author as "Mrs. Mary Randolph." This edition and all subsequent antebellum ones are virtually identical to that published in 1828, the last year of Randolph's life. See Mary Randolph, *The Virginia House-Wife*, ed. Karen Hess (Columbia, S.C., 1984), p. 228.

⁷⁰ Randolph, *Virginia House-Wife* (1839 ed.), pp. ix–xii. On Beecher, see Kathryn Kish Sklar, *Catharine Beecher: A Study in American Domesticity* (New Haven, Conn., 1973), esp. chap. 11.

⁷¹ Randolph, *Virginia House-Wife* (1839 ed.), pp. xi–xii, 19, 51–52, 133, 178–80.

⁷² Ibid., p. xi.

⁷³ See her obituary in the [Washington] *National Intelligencer*, 24 Jan. 1828, and the *Richmond Enquirer*, 29 Jan. 1828.

⁷⁴ See, for instance, the letters exchanged by the following couples: John and

Frances Tucker Coalter, [1804], 4, 9, 15, 25, 26 Apr., 1 May, 10, 16, 29 Sept., 13 Nov. 1809, Brown, Coalter, Tucker Papers, CWM; Richard and Mary Moore Stanford, 25 Jan. 1804, 8 Mar. 1808, Richard Stanford Papers, SHC, UNC-CH, and 8 Nov. 1812, 4 Dec. 1815, Richard Stanford Papers, NCDAH; Isaac and Anna Maria Deans Garretson, 10 May 1817, 20 Apr. 1822, 24 Jan. 1824, Anna Maria Deans Garretson Letters, SHC, UNC-CH.

[75] Sarah Alexander to A. L. Alexander, 25 Jan. 1824, Hillhouse-Alexander Papers, SHC, UNC-CH; Caroline Eliza Burgwin Clitherall Journals, 6:13, SHC, UNC-CH. For a slaveholding woman who took in long-term boarders, see H[etty] C[arr] to [Dabney S. Carr], 15 Feb. [1818], and H[etty] C[arr] to Maria Carr, 6 Apr. [1818], Carr-Cary Papers, UVa.

Some scholars portray antebellum southern marriages as more "companionate" than patriarchal. See, for instance, Jane Turner Censer, *North Carolina Planters and Their Children, 1800–1860* (Baton Rouge, La., 1984), esp. pp. 72–74, 150–54; Lewis, *Pursuit of Happiness*, pp. 188–204; Bode, "Common Sphere," 775–81.

[76] Randolph, *Virginia House-Wife*, ed. Hess, p. 228. Southern agricultural writers promoted a "farmwife ideal" that in many ways resembled Randolph's ideal of domesticity. See D. Harland Hagler, "The Ideal Woman in the Antebellum South: Lady or Farmwife?" *JSH* 46 (1980): 405–18.

[77] Mary Jane [?] to Virginia Cary, 12 Dec. 1818, Nicholas P. Trist Papers, SHC, UNC-CH.

[78] Cary, *Letters on the Female Character*, esp. pp. v–vi, 23, 43–45, 49–50.

[79] Ibid., p. 20; Fox-Genovese, *Within the Plantation Household*, pp. 195–200; Rankin, *Ambivalent Churchmen and Evangelical Churchwomen*, pp. 72–87.

[80] Cary, *Letters on the Female Character*, pp. vi, 44–45.

[81] Ibid., pp. 22–24, 104–5.

[82] Ibid., pp. v–vii, 22, 149.

[83] Ibid., pp. 24, 50, 76, 143–44; Cary, *Christian Parent's Assistant*, pp. iii–iv, xiii, xvi.

[84] Cary, *Letters on the Female Character*, pp. 134–35, 172–78.

[85] Mitchell Snay, *Gospel of Disunion: Religion and Separatism in the Antebellum South* (Cambridge, 1993), chaps. 2–3.

Conclusion: Patriarchy and Its Limits

[1] Louisa S. McCord, "Enfranchisement of Women" and "Woman and Her Needs," in her *Political and Social Essays*, ed. Richard C. Lounsbury (Charlottesville, Va., 1995), pp. 105–55. See also the discussion of McCord's life and writing in Elizabeth Fox-Genovese, *Within the Plantation Household: Black and White Women of the Old South* (Chapel Hill, N.C., 1988), pp. 243–89.

[2] Gerda Lerner, *The Creation of Patriarchy* (New York, 1988), p. 239.

[3] Willie Lee Rose, "The Domestication of Domestic Slavery," in William W. Freehling, ed., *Slavery and Freedom* (New York, 1982), pp. 18–29.

⁴ Linda K. Kerber, *Women of the Republic: Intellect and Ideology in Revolutionary America* (Chapel Hill, N.C., 1980), pp. 85–99; Joan R. Gundersen, "Independence, Citizenship, and the American Revolution," *Signs* 13 (1987): 59–77; Gordon S. Wood, *Radicalism of the American Revolution* (New York, 1992), pp. 187–89; Joyce Appleby, *Liberalism and Republicanism in the Historical Imagination* (Cambridge, Mass., 1992), pp. 29–30.

For a perceptive analysis of the interplay between republican and liberal ideals in revolutionary America, see James T. Kloppenberg, "The Virtues of Liberalism: Christianity, Republicanism, and Ethics in Early American Political Discourse," *JAH* 74 (1987): 9–33.

⁵ On the real or rhetorical dichotomy between men's politics and women's religious and benevolent works in many northern communities, see the discussion in Paula Baker, "The Domestication of Politics: Women and American Political Society, 1780–1920," *AHR* 89 (1984): 628–31, as well as Christine Stansell, *City of Women: Sex and Class in New York, 1789–1860* (New York, 1986), chap. 4, and Lori D. Ginzberg, *Women and the Work of Benevolence: Morality, Politics, and Class in the Nineteenth-Century United States* (New Haven, Conn., 1990), esp. pp. 32–37. On the potentially liberating consequences of sexual separatism among northern women, see Nancy F. Cott, *The Bonds of Womanhood: "Woman's Sphere" in New England, 1780–1835* (New Haven, Conn., 1977), pp. 194–98, 201–6, and Estelle Freedman, "Separatism as Strategy: Female Institution Building and American Feminism, 1870–1930," *Feminist Studies* 5 (1979): 512–29.

Suzanne Lebsock suggests that a similar division of public labor obtained in antebellum Petersburg until the 1850s (*Free Women of Petersburg: Status and Culture in a Southern Town, 1784–1860* [New York, 1984], chap. 7). Other historians of the Old South, by contrast, contend that men and women often participated together in southern religious and benevolent efforts, and some suggest that men impeded the development of women's autonomous public activities. See, for instance, Barbara L. Bellows, *Benevolence among Slaveholders: Assisting the Poor in Charleston, 1670–1860* (Baton Rouge, La., 1993), pp. 44–45; Jean E. Friedman, *The Enclosed Garden: Women and Community in the Evangelical South, 1830–1900* (Chapel Hill, N.C., 1985), pp. 6–20; Anne C. Loveland, *Southern Evangelicals and the Social Order, 1800–1860* (Baton Rouge, La., 1980), pp. 162–74; Richard Rankin, *Ambivalent Churchmen and Evangelical Churchwomen: The Religion of the Episcopal Elite in North Carolina, 1800–1860* (Columbia, S.C., 1993), pp. 100–102, 124–45.

⁶ Fox-Genovese, *Within the Plantation Household*, pp. 37–70, 334–38; Stephanie McCurry, *Masters of Small Worlds: Yeoman Households, Gender Relations, and the Political Culture of the South Carolina Low Country* (New York, 1995), pp. 215–25; Drew Gilpin Faust, ed., *The Ideology of Slavery: Proslavery Thought in the Antebellum South, 1830–1860* (Baton Rouge, La., 1981), pp. 2–6.

⁷ D. Harland Hagler, "The Ideal Woman in the Antebellum South: Lady or

Farmwife?" *JSH* 46 (1980): 14-17; Victoria E. Bynum, *Unruly Women: The Politics of Social and Sexual Control in the Old South* (Chapel Hill, N.C., 1992), pp. 48–49.

[8] "Economy in a Family," *Southern Watchman and General Intelligencer,* 28 Apr. 1837, p. 68; Daniel R. Hundley, *Social Relations in Our Southern States,* ed. William J. Cooper, Jr. (Baton Rouge, La., 1979), p. 73.

[9] Margaret Simons Middleton, "A Sketch of the Ladies Benevolent Society, Founded 1813," in *Yearbook, 1941: City of Charleston, South Carolina* (Charleston, S.C., 1942), pp. 215–39; *Memorial Home for Girls, Formerly Female Humane Society, 1805–1925* (Richmond, Va., 1925); Frederick A. Bode, "A Common Sphere: White Evangelicals and Gender in Antebellum Georgia," *GHQ* 79 (1995): 781, 783, 791.

[10] Elizabeth R. Varon, "Tippecanoe and the Ladies, Too: White Women and Party Politics in Antebellum Virginia," *JAH* 82 (1995): 494–521. For one woman's continued interest in political affairs and her willingness to disagree — at least privately — with the politics of her husband, see Carol Bleser, "The Perrys of Greenville: A Nineteenth-Century Marriage," in Walter J. Fraser, Jr., et al., eds., *The Web of Southern Social Relations: Women, Family, and Education* (Athens, Ga., 1985), pp. 79–84.

Index

6/00

GAYLORD S